Falling from grace

Manchester University Press

For one who never did and one who never will.

Joan Laura Gertrude Bothwell-Botton (née Brace)
1925–2004
&
Madeleine Dee Pineau
(born 17 September 2005)

Falling from grace

Reversal of fortune and the English nobility, 1075–1455

J.S. BOTHWELL

Manchester University Press

Manchester and New York

Distributed exclusively in the USA by Palgrave

Published by Manchester University Press
Oxford Road, Manchester M13 9NR, UK
and Room 400, 175 Fifth Avenue, New York, NY 10010, USA
www.manchesteruniversitypress.co.uk

Distributed exclusively in the USA by
Palgrave, 175 Fifth Avenue, New York,
NY 10010, USA

Distributed exclusively in Canada by
UBC Press, University of British Columbia, 2029 West Mall,
Vancouver, BC, Canada V6T 1Z2

British Library Cataloguing-in-Publication Data
A catalogue record for this book is available from the British Library

Library of Congress Cataloging-in-Publication Data applied for

ISBN   978 0 7190 75216   *hardback*

First published 2008

17 16 15 14 13 12 11 10 09 08   10 9 8 7 6 5 4 3 2 1

Typeset in 10.5/13pt Jenson
by Graphicraft Limited, Hong Kong
Printed in Great Britain
by Biddles Ltd, King's Lynn

With domineering hand she moves the turning wheel,
Like currents in a treacherous bay swept to and fro:
Her ruthless will has just deposed once fearful kings
While trustless still, from low she lifts her conquered head;
No cries of misery she hears, no tears she heeds,
But steely hearted laughs at groans her deeds have wrung.
Such is the game she plays, and so she tests her strength;
Of mighty power she makes parade when one short hour
Sees happiness from utter desolation grow.

> (Boethius, *The Consolation of Philosophy*,
> early 6th century)

The world is like a chery fayre,
Ofte chaungeþ all his þynges.
Riche, pore, foul, & fayre,
Popes, prelates, & lordynges,
Alle are dedly, and so ben kynges.
Or deþ lede 3ow in his les,
Arraye by-time 3oure rekenynges,
And trete wiþ god to gete 3ow pes.

> (*What Profits a Kingdom* (1401), in R.H. Robbins, ed.
> *Historical Poems of the XIVth and XVth Centuries*)

Contents

Illustrations

Acknowledgements

Many thanks to the Social Sciences and Humanities Research Council of Canada, the British Academy and the University of Leicester for providing the funding for this project. In terms of libraries, archives and museums, the staffs of the National Archives (Kew), the British Library, the Bodleian Library, the British Museum, Rochester Cathedral Library, University of Glasgow Special Collections, University of Leicester Special Collections, Birmingham City Archives and the Bibliothèque Nationale de France have all given considerable help with the collation of material for this book.

John Langdon, Chris Given-Wilson, Mark Ormrod, Tony Goodman, Michael Bennett, Andrew Ayton and Michael Prestwich have all offered valuable support at various stages of the writing of this book, and the anonymous referees of both the initial proposal and the final manuscript are to be thanked for being so thorough, as are Alison Welsby, Emma Brennan, Monica Kendall and all the production staff at Manchester University Press. And, as ever, my family are to be thanked: my brother, Mark, for all his support and assistance through the years, my friends Tracey and Keith Pineau – and Peter, Pat, Adam and, of course, Eliza Riedi, my partner, for putting up with me dragging my laptop everywhere I went. Finally, this book is dedicated to two people, my mother Joan and my goddaughter Maddie, who I never met but who will always have one thing in common – neither have ever, or will ever, fall from grace.

J.S.B.
Leicester

Abbreviations

Full references to be found in the Bibliography. Unless otherwise noted, all manuscript references are from The National Archives, Kew, London.

AHR	*American Historical Review*
ANS	*Anglo-Norman Studies*
ASC	*Anglo-Saxon Chronicle*
BIHR	see HR
BJRL	*Bulletin of the John Rylands Library*
BL	British Library
CCharR	*Calendar of Charter Rolls*
CCR	*Calendar of Close Rolls*
CFR	*Calendar of Fine Rolls*
CIM	*Calendar of Inquisitions Miscellaneous*
CIPM	*Calendar of Inquisitions Post Mortem*
CP	*The Complete Peerage*
CPR	*Calendar of Patent Rolls*
DNB	*Oxford Dictionary of National Biography*
EcHR	*Economic History Review*
ECR	*An English Chronicle of the Reigns of Richard II, Henry IV, Henry V, and Henry VI, Written before the Year 1471* J.S. Davies, ed. (London, 1856)
EHD	*English Historical Documents*
EHR	*English Historical Review*
HJ	*The Historical Journal*
HR	*Historical Research* (formerly BIHR – *Bulletin of the Institute of Historical Research*)
HSJ	*Haskins Society Journal*
JBS	*Journal of British Studies*
JMH	*Journal of Medieval History*
MP	*Medieval Prosopography*
NH	*Northern History*

NMS	*Nottingham Mediaeval Studies*
Rot. Litt. Claus.	*Rotuli Litterarum Clausarum* T. Duffus Hardy, ed. (London, 1833)
RP	*Rotuli Parliamentorum*
SR	*Statutes of the Realm*
TRHS	*Transactions of the Royal Historical Society*
VCH	*Victoria County History*
YAJ	*Yorkshire Archaeological Journal*

Chronology

Introduction:
the medieval English nobility
and the wheel of fortune

1 BL Royal 18 D. II, f. 30v: John Lydgate, *Troy Book*, wheel of fortune;
England, c. 1455–62.

Fortune is like a turning wheel. One moment she suddenly lifts a man up, the next throws him down; and conversely she raises the man who is prostrate and trodden in the dust more generously than he could have hoped.[1]

Fortune, modernity and medieval foundations

An integral part of understanding how medieval man perceived success and failure – and the vast spectrum of experience in between – the substantive presence of the rotating 'wheel of fortune' is now dated to the period after the Norman Conquest.[2] However, though increasingly popular in the twelfth, thirteenth and fourteenth centuries in western Europe as a whole, the more general idea of a personification of 'fortune' and the existence of a 'wheel' goes much further back, at least as far as Greco-Roman civilisation. Unsurprisingly then, given its long history, the relationship between the two major components of the image has changed over time.[3] By the high Middle Ages,[4] fortune herself is no longer represented as on the wheel, but is the force that makes the wheel move, and it is Man who must suffer the consequences. Fortune is an active agent, turning the wheel at her own speed, raising people up – and bringing them down. This image lived not just in the minds of medieval writers, but also of balladeers, bishops and artists entrusted with decorating the walls of cathedrals and churches. To some modern commentators, such as Alexander Murray, the wheel represents the attempt to rationalise the many changes and disruptions that had taken place since the fall of the Roman Empire, the last period when there was seen to be real security of life, and lifestyle. For others such as Charles Radding, chance is the more prevalent ingredient, and historical events and processes less fundamental, in the evolving image of fortune: 'the meaning of the Wheel of Fortune is thus quite general: that everyone in human society is subject to the whims of Fortune, that not all of the world's gifts or the world's tragedies are deserved'.[5] Whichever view one takes, throughout the later Middle Ages there was a considerable amount of interest in the turning of fortune's wheel, an interest which remains alive to this day. And this is true not only in a wide variety of modern academic research ranging from textual analysis of Layamon's *Brut* to connections between wall murals in Rochester Cathedral and the fortunes of the local gentry families (see Fig. 2).[6] This interest also thrives in mainstream culture, with the rise and fall of business and media magnates, footballers, actors and pop stars gracing the front pages of glossy magazines and tabloids, as well as the editorial and media analysis sections of the broadsheets. Taken as entertainment, 'light' news, or serious cultural critique, the fate of those in the limelight of their chosen vocations, especially those who have risen from relatively humble beginnings, continues to dominate the popular imagination.

2 Rochester Cathedral: wheel of fortune wall painting; England, thirteenth century.

Indeed, intimately connected with fortune's wheel in the minds of medieval people – artists, patrons and audience – were the careers and fates of those on the top rungs of society. 'Nobility' itself was often seen as a 'gift' of fortune,[7] and very rarely were those depicted on the wheel neither royal nor noble[8] – even King Arthur ended up contemplating the wheel from time to time (see Fig. 3). Nothing so interested the general populace, then as now, as to watch an individual fall, especially from great heights. This usually ill-meant curiosity in the declining providence of one's social superiors, a form of class-based *schadenfreude*, not only influenced much of the artistic expression of the period – even the precursor to the Romantic 'Et in Arcadia Ego' theme, as seen in funereal monuments and the Three Living/Three Dead motifs of many post-Black Death wall paintings, was basically saying to those wealthy enough to appreciate it 'now you are prospering, but wait a few years and you may not be'[9] – it also inspired contemporary writers and chroniclers, a

3 BL Additional 10294, f. 89: *La Mort le Roi Artus*, King Arthur's vision
of fortune's wheel; France, c. 1316.

crucial source for understanding the thoughts and biases of the medieval world. Poets in particular had a great deal to say about the fall of the great, as this anonymous writer's words of warning to nobles everywhere upon the arrest in 1450 of William de la Pole, duke of Suffolk, show:

> Be ware, al men, of that blame,
> And namly ye of grete fame,
> Spirituall and temperall, be ware of this,
> Or els hit will not be well, I-wis.
> God saue þe kyng, and god forbede
> Þat he suche apes any mo fede.
> And of þe perille that may be-fall
> Be ware, dukes, erles and barons alle.[10]

A couple of generations earlier, the eldest of a company of ladies in *The Knight's Tale* took a similar line about well-bred women caught up in worldly events, a common fate for many female relatives, as we will see:

> Upon us wrecched wommen lat thou falle,
> For, certes, lord, ther is noon of us alle
> That she ne hath been a duchesse or a queene.
> Now be we caytyves [miserable wretches], as it is wel seene,
> Thanked be Fortune and hire false wheel,
> That noon estaat assureth to be weel.[11]

Moreover, rarely does a medieval chronicler, monastic or secular, pass up the chance to comment on an individual fallen from position, and usually with a considerable amount of venom. When the author of the *Vita Edwardi Secundi* considers the reasons why Piers Gaveston was heading for a fall in the early years of the fourteenth century, he does not limit himself to a discussion of the politics or personalities of the period, but takes an enthusiastically, and vehemently, moralistic view of the whole of Piers's existence:

> and Piers remained a man of big ideas, haughty and puffed-up. I fear that his pride will bring about his ruin and headlong fall; for it is written, the heart is exalted before destruction. He who dwells on high and looks down upon the lowly hates pride above all things. This it was that hurled Lucifer, an angel of wonderful brightness, down to the depths; this likewise cast queen Vashti from the throne of her kingdom; nor is it surprising if he in his pride should be acceptable to neither God nor man.[12]

Late in the next reign, when Thomas Walsingham wrote of the overthrow and banishment of Edward III's mistress, Alice Perrers, during the Good Parliament of 1376, though his own interests were also at stake (she had a land dispute with his abbey of St Albans over the manor of Oxhey Walround in Hertfordshire),[13] he nonetheless speaks of her with an often unwarranted degree of spleen, constantly referring to her as a 'harlot' and her actions as 'shameless', 'licentious' and 'lascivious'.[14] Fortune taking up, and then abandoning, individuals, the great and especially – as we will often see – the newly so, is a much tastier subject for literature and art, as for talk by the fireside, than when she is always their best friend.

Favour, patronage and life inside the court

In the light of the king's countenance *is* life; and his favour *is* as a cloud of the latter rain. (Proverbs 16:15, italics in original)

Royal favour was the passport to prosperity, a key which unlocked doors, an insurance against adversity, the *sine qua non* of baronial peace of mind.[15]

And it is the fortunes of the English nobility which lie at the heart of this work – fortunes which were often most dramatically, though by no means solely, determined by the policies, interests, and whims, of kings or those governing in their name. However, to examine the impact which royal disfavour could have on the life of a medieval noble, one must first have some understanding of how important royal or governmental support, both material and psychological, was for a nobleman's interests and behaviour. Materially, as is well known, medieval nobles benefited from grants of estates, offices, annuities, substantial moveable gifts and token, yet significant, gestures from the hand of the king. Throughout the Middle Ages an increasing variety of resources was used in order to show favour to such individuals, from the traditional – rights over lands in the king's possession or under his control, money from the treasury and moveable gifts – to the innovative, including payments off customs, confiscated lands, alien priories and, in some cases by the mid-fourteenth century, taxation.[16] Moreover, reputation and rank also arose from this sense of being favoured, as well as more directly as a result of the king's gifts. Indeed, royal grace was not only the basis of the material position of a favourite, it also decided whether, and how far, one was 'inside' or 'outside' the royal court and therefore the 'golden circle' – a psychological as much as material factor which could have considerable impact upon his lifestyle and actions. Without this mental advantage over the rest of society, especially those close in wealth though not yet in status, it would often be quite difficult to differentiate oneself from the rank and file in the kingdom. The Furnivalles and Cauntelos were both established peerage families during Edward III's reign, but they rarely received favour from the king of any sort[17]

– and so were often closer in political positioning and clout to county gentry families than to peers of the realm.

However, though the immediate result of royal or royally inspired grace, these were not its only effects. First, such favour helped position individuals whereby they could create or defend their own retinues, granting out properties, annuities and offices. It is notable that the ability to develop, enhance and/or protect affinities, or even spheres of influence, was itself to a large degree dependent upon royal favour.[18] If a noble was not given sufficient rights or offices in his area of interest, he would find it very difficult to sustain an affinity: something of which the Courtenay earls of Devon would become well aware in the fourteenth and fifteenth centuries.[19] It was, in other words, rare to find a generous noble who had not been the recipient of large amounts of royal patronage at one time or another.[20] Psychologically, such favour also put nobles in the larger social milieu, and mindset, of the patron: not only would a medieval noble give for his own security, but also as imitating a more general pattern of giving which influenced all with access to expendable wealth or power, large or small, secular or religious, mercantile or noble. Moreover, over the past few decades, the focus of academic research has shifted from patronage and largesse as being simply a political issue between kings, nobles and gentry, to the matter of what nobles did with that extra bounty, both for themselves and for others – and with this shift, yet more questions arise. Would many noblewomen have been such a force in the artistic world, were it not ultimately for the king's patronage to their husbands, which in turn freed up wealth for them?[21] Would Robert and William of Mortain have been able to indulge in religious patronage in both Normandy and England had it not been for the favour, or at least passive goodwill, of William the Conqueror, William Rufus and, for a while, Henry I?[22] Would nobles and other landowners in general really have felt secure enough to concern themselves with academic education, either for their own children or for others?[23] Would substantial religious endowments or provision for alms and other forms of charity, beyond what was necessary to ensure one's place in heaven, have even been a consideration?[24] Thus not only did royal patronage help the noble get much needed material wealth – in the form of lands, chattels or finance – and influence his success in social climbing, land deals, court cases and other venues for potential personal aggrandisement, but such favour also tended to ripple outwards to other sectors of society. Without these conduits, there was little way the king could effectively redistribute the wealth that had come into his hands: to make the royal bounty effective, the monarch had to give not only to those in power, but also to those who knew where further material assistance was needed. Favour, then, could not only make or break a noble's position in the royal court, and in the larger social and political hierarchy, but also affect the king's ability to patronise efficiently and effectively those lower down the social order, and especially those in the provinces. Royal patronage was, in other words, a crucial factor in the life of any king or aristocrat, and in medieval society in general, one which was ignored at peril.[25]

Kings generally realised this crucial facet of medieval political life, and used their position and power accordingly. Obviously, patronage had always been a key part of monarchical power, overlapping with, but usually considered more pointed and personalised than, the ever-present feudal and quasifeudal bonds which dominated economic and social interaction well into our period. The king's largesse took giving one step further than traditional ideas of feudalism, with the relationship not only being connected with exchange of lands, rents and rights for services, loyalty and fealty, but involving the use of such wealth in exchange for less tangible, but more crucial, individualised adherence and often tactically arranged support. The Book of Proverbs, a quotation from which started this section, gives at least an idea as to how the religiously minded medieval man might have viewed royal favour.[26] Though the passage is without reference to the dark side of such favouritism, an aspect which was all too real to medieval man (as we will see), it still emphasises the crucial position of favour in the life of the king's subjects. Part of the definition of an exemplary king throughout the medieval period was one who was a good donor, who was able to give gifts to his followers. The importance of this relationship surfaced early on in battle accounts, as in the eulogy of the 'Malden Poet' on the death of the thegn Offa:

> yet he had accomplished what he promised to his lord,
> as he vowed formerly to his treasure-giver
> that they must both ride back to their dwelling,
> safe into the homestead, or die amongst the Vikings,
> perish with wounds on the field of slaughter.
> He lay near a lord as a thegn should.[27]

Conversely, the guilt bestowed by the poet upon the followers of Beowulf as they stood over the body of their betrayed patron and leader is understated but profound:

> There they found him lifeless on the sand,
> the soft bed where he slept, who often before had given them rings;
> that good man's days on earth were ended.[28]

Even in the late medieval period, when representative assemblies and legislation throughout Europe had begun to limit the king's power and actions in a number of ways, it was still recognised that it was both a right and a duty, not to mention in his interests, for the monarch to distribute favour and largesse. According to Christine de Pisan:

The good prince who loves the universal good more than his own should be liberal, a very necessary quality from which he will profit triply; first it is for the good of his soul (if he is discreet), secondly, for the praise and honour of his reputation; thirdly, he will attract the hearts of his own subjects to himself as well as those of strangers.[29]

Sir John Fortescue struck a similar note in his treatise on the governance of fifteenth-century England when speaking of a king's poverty: 'But we must hold it to be undoubted, that no realm may prosper, nor be worshipful, under a poor king.'[30] Though councils and commissions might be set up to help arrange and distribute patronage (as in the Ordinances of 1311 and during Henry IV's reign), and the sources of patronage themselves questioned, along with the characters of the recipients, for the medieval period at least it was almost always accepted as a key royal duty to exercise this right.[31]

Historiography, source use and purpose

However, as generous as medieval kings or those acting in their name could be,[32] if they believed themselves to be betrayed, let down, or otherwise outwitted by a noble, then they had both an institutional and a moral right to rescind that same favour – and, if the situation was serious enough, to take more aggressive steps. This could come through executive action by the king, council or parliament, by noble pressure, or even the general populace taking matters into their own hands, but ultimately it represented, for whatever reason, the start of an individual's fall from political, social and often economic position. That said, though there are books on crime, including treason and rebellion in the Middle Ages,[33] and articles on forfeitures and attainders in various reigns,[34] there is nothing which traces political, social and economic downfalls of the most privileged in society over the span of the later Middle Ages as a whole. We now have several long-range studies examining how individuals rose,[35] which show the importance of performance at court, royal favour and use of patronage for the career of a noble. But we have few case studies, let alone more general examinations, of how individuals, and especially nobles, fell, and almost nothing about their time in exile and how some managed to redeem themselves afterwards. Yet the history of the later Middle Ages is, in many ways, often a history of declines, or at least slips and slides, especially from the highest levels, when leadership and power structures were in a state of rapid transition, and when the individual, as well as the group, not only had an eye for the main chance, but also for when that chance had come to an end. Not to acknowledge this is to ignore one of the main characteristics of the age.[36] This book, then, aims to rectify this omission, and also hopes to shed new, albeit refracted, light on the monarchy, nobility and medieval society as a whole by examining how and why it shunned its previously most favoured, what they did while ostracised or outcast, and in what ways they, or their families, could sometimes regain position and prominence.

The sources looked at for this book are many and varied: aside from a wide selection of very useful recent research in the form of monographs, surveys and articles without which the following could never have been written, government and church records, chronicles, treatises, laws, literature, philosophy and various types of artistic expression have all been used to unearth the mentality and reality behind falls from grace of individuals, and groups. There are, of course, obvious problems with such primary sources, including, most importantly for this work, record survival and bias. Concerning the former, one will find from time to time that cases are returned to, because they are the *fullest* cases we have of falls from grace, rather than using other, less complete examples, to make a possibly less convincing point. In defence of this, aside from being one of the more general pitfalls of medieval studies, especially over a long timeframe, this book is not meant to be a quantitative study, but instead an attempt to enter into the experiences of both perpetrators and victims of falls from grace. So, while it is important that sufficient evidence is put forth to back up points, it is equally important that a clear understanding of the motivations and mental processes of our players is also evident. If for that, we have to return to a few of the juicier cases every now and again, so be it. Secondly, there are the biases within the sources, perhaps the more important of the two issues, especially when looking at such highly charged events as falls from grace. Just as now, 'slanted' reporting almost always comes into play to one degree or another, whether because the one doing the reporting has a stake in the issue or, at the other end of the spectrum, simply for the sake of telling a good story. Nonetheless, even though the impact of these prejudices has to be kept in mind, such biases themselves allow us a good insight not just into the minds of the reporters, but also their audience. Considering that the outside view, as much as internal perception, of a fall from grace is almost always a crucial part of the reality of that fall, especially when examining its beginning, its larger impact, and how it has survived to come down to us, it is often just as important as the chain of events or issue which the document under consideration purports to discuss. Even the chronicles, despite their biases and unreliable nature at times, are not only an essential source for the substance and run of events of the Middle Ages – especially before the rise of a relatively coherent, unbroken stream of governmental documents in the early thirteenth century – they also, and equally importantly, help to lay bare the attitude of medieval man, his ambitions and his pettinesses, which in turn is fundamental for understanding the 'reality' of the wheel of fortune in medieval life. In other words, a large part of the fall of individuals, then and now, starts in the minds of others (as well as one's own), rather than in any more physical manifestation of declines in favour, and to ignore this is to overlook the foundation from which much of the later 'action' derives.

If this book has a starting point, then, it is from another quotation of the Book of Proverbs:

> The king's favour *is* toward a wise servant: but his wrath is *against* him that causeth shame. (Proverbs 14:35)

and the impact it had on the subject of that anger. But it is not just about the loss of the king's favour to a noble, but also their loss of favour with the larger world, whether it be from those holding the reins of monarchy, the greater political community, or even the general populace: all could cause falls from position, though in the final analysis the cause of their disgrace did usually come under the aegis of royal rights. Falling from grace, then, in this work at least, means not just falling from the king or regime's favourable disposition, whatever the route, but also from those in various other sectors of society. It is, in other words, a study of how medieval aristocrats as individuals faired when their fortunes were in decline for various reasons – loss of royal favour, legal transgression, rebellion, civil war, etc. – how they reacted to the situation, and how others reacted to them. And, if the subject of this book seems large, both in its chronological sweep and in the number and variety of individuals and estates dealt with, it is unashamedly so. The spectrum running from 'Inside' to 'Outside' court/acceptable political society is coherent enough a concept throughout the later Middle Ages that we can examine the reasoning for demises, and their impact, over a period of several centuries;[37] from the Earls' Revolt of 1075, the first major post-Conquest era revolt involving members of the titled nobility, to the beginning of the Wars of the Roses in 1455 – when forfeiture, a key component of 'falls from grace', would come to be at its most defined and most powerful with the Acts of Attainder, both the high point and, as a result, something of an end point, for such developments.[38] A clear rationale for this broader view is that only by stepping back from such a topic can we really understand the changes in the nature of downfall, exile and redemption in the medieval world, both to those involved and to those looking on. Finally, the process of exclusion and reintegration which lies at the heart of this book has its – though often unwritten – rules, rules which developed over time, and only by examining these may we also begin to interpret realities of aristocratic 'deviancy' and its many repercussions, for polity and populace, during the English Middle Ages.

Notes

1 *The Ecclesiastical History of Orderic Vitalis* M. Chibnall, ed. and trans. (Oxford, 1968–80), vi, 242.

2 A. Murray, *Reason and Society in the Middle Ages* (Oxford, 1978), pp. 98–101; E. Mason, 'Magnates, Curiales and the Wheel of Fortune', *Battle Conference II* (Woodbridge, 1980), 118–19.

3 Though perhaps with some earlier manifestations than previously thought. See Radding's discussion of Fortune being 'off' the wheel in the work of the sixth-century writer Boethius. C. Radding, 'Fortune and her Wheel: The Meaning of a Medieval Symbol', *Mediaevistik* 5 (1992), 127–9; also see the quotation from Boethius at the beginning of this book. For pushing the imagery of the wheel even further back, see J. Barry, *Art, Culture and the Semiotics of Meaning: Culture's Changing Signs of Life in Poetry, Drama, Painting and Sculpture* (New York, 1999), pp. 33–4.

4 Due to the long-range nature of this study, and for the sake of brevity, throughout this work 'high Middle Ages', and variants thereon, have been used to designate the later eleventh, twelfth and first half of the thirteenth century, whereas 'later Middle Ages', and variants thereon, have been used to designate the period between this point and the late fifteenth century.

5 Radding, 'Fortune and her Wheel', 133.

6 C. Weinberg, 'Victor and Victim: A View of the Anglo-Saxon Past in Layamon's *Brut*', in D. Scragg and C. Weinberg, eds. *Literary Appropriations of the Anglo-Saxons from the Thirteenth to the Twentieth Century* (Cambridge, 2000), 22–38; A.E. Bell, 'The Revolving Fortunes of the Knights of Rochester', *MP* 16 (1995), 69–109.

7 Murray, *Reason and Society*, p. 99.

8 For comparison, see *British Library Image Database* (www.imagesonline.bl.uk/ britishlibrary).

9 C. Platt, *King Death* (London, 1996), pp. 150–64; for a recent discussion of the plague's impact on the visual arts, see P.G. Lindley, 'The Black Death and English Art: A Debate and Some Assumptions', in W.M. Ormrod and P.G. Lindley, eds. *The Black Death in England* (Stamford, 1996), 125–46.

10 R.H. Robbins, ed. *Historical Poems of the XIVth and XVth Centuries* (New York, 1959), p. 187 ll. 23–30.

11 *The Riverside Chaucer* L.D. Benson, ed. 3rd edn (Oxford, 1988), p. 38 ll. 921–6.

12 *Vita Edwardi Secundi* N. Denholm-Young, ed. and trans. (London, 1957), p. 16.

13 T. Walsingham, *Gesta Abbatum Monasterii S. Albani* H.T. Riley, ed. (London, 1869), iii, 228–30.

14 T. Walsingham, *The St Albans Chronicle: The Chronica Maiora of Thomas Walsingham I, 1376–1394* J. Taylor, W.R. Childs and L. Watkiss, ed. and trans. (Oxford, 2003), pp. 45, 47, 987, 991.

15 W.L. Warren, *Henry II* (London, 1973), p. 388.

16 For examples, see J.A. Green, *The Government of England under Henry I* (Cambridge, 1986); S.L. Waugh, *The Lordship of England: Royal Wardships and*

Marriages in English Society and Politics (Princeton, 1988); J.S. Bothwell, *Edward III and the English Peerage: Royal Patronage, Social Mobility and Political Control in Fourteenth Century England* (Woodbridge, 2004).

17 Bothwell, *English Peerage*, p. 146.

18 For the later Middle Ages, see J.G. Bellamy, *Bastard Feudalism and the Law* (Portland, 1989), pp. 102–22.

19 M. Cherry, 'The Courtenay Earls of Devon: The Formation and Disintegration of a Late Medieval Aristocratic Affinity', *Southern History* 1 (1979), 90–7.

20 E.g. M. Bennett, *Community, Class and Careerism: Cheshire and Lancashire in the Age of Sir Gawain and the Green Knight* (Cambridge, 2002), Chapter 10.

21 For a detailed discussion of women and art, see L.L. Gee, *Women, Art and Patronage from Henry III to Edward III 1216–1377* (Woodbridge, 2002).

22 See B. Goulding, 'The Religious Patronage of Robert and William of Mortain', in R. Gameson and H. Leyser, eds. *Belief and Culture in the Early Middle Ages* (Oxford, 2001), 211–30.

23 For education and the nobility, see N. Orme, *English Schools in the Middle Ages* (London, 1973), pp. 29–36, 202–3; also N. Orme, *From Childhood to Chivalry: The Education of the English Kings and Aristocracy 1066–1536* (London, 1984).

24 E.g. M. Hicks, 'Chantries, Obits and Almshouses: The Hungerford Foundations, 1325–1478', in C.M. Barron and C. Harper-Bill, eds. *The Church in Pre-Reformation Society* (Woodbridge, 1985), 123–42.

25 Despite recent questioning of the importance of patronage. See E. Powell, *Kingship, Law and Society: Criminal Justice in the Reign of Henry V* (Oxford, 1989), pp. 5–6; E. Powell, 'After "After McFarlane": The Poverty of Patronage and the Case for Constitutional History', in D.J. Clayton, R.G. Davies and P. McNiven, eds. *Trade, Devotion and Governance* (Stroud, 1994), 1–16; C. Carpenter, 'Political and Constitutional History: Before and After McFarlane', in R.H. Britnell and A.J. Pollard, eds. *The McFarlane Legacy: Studies in Late Medieval Politics and Society* (Stroud, 1995), 175–206.

26 The Book of Proverbs is verbose about favour: Proverbs 11:27, 12:2, 13:15, 16:15.

27 *The Battle of Malden AD 991* D. Scragg, ed. and trans. (Oxford, 1991), p. 31 v. 289–94.

28 *Beowulf* K. Crossley-Holland, ed. and trans. (Oxford, 1999), pp. 100–1 v. 3032–5.

29 C. de Pisan, *The Book of the Body Politic* K. Langdon Forhan, ed. and trans. (Cambridge, 1994), p. 26.

30 J. Fortescue, *On the Laws and Governance of England* S. Lockwood, ed. and trans. (Cambridge, 2002), p. 93.

31 For instances of criticisms and attempted controls on royal patronage, see the Ordinances of 1311, the reaction to Edward III's endowments, and Henry IV's parliaments. M. Prestwich, 'The Ordinances of 1311 and the Politics of the Early Fourteenth Century', in J. Taylor and W.R. Childs, eds. *Politics and Crisis in Fourteenth-Century England* (Gloucester, 1990), 10; Bothwell, *English Peerage*, pp. 127–31; A.L. Brown, 'The Commons and the Council in the Reign of Henry IV', *EHR* 79 (1964), 10, 14–15, 18–19.

32 Again, to prevent undue repetition, and unless otherwise indicated, throughout this book royal or monarchical will and power will be shorthand for either the king himself or those holding the reins of power. Monarchical government is monarchical government throughout this period, whoever held the reins – no one, even in the lower orders, wanted to get rid of the king, as most famously witnessed in the rebel demands during the Peasants' Revolt.

33 E.g. J.G. Bellamy, *The Law of Treason in England in the Later Middle Ages* (Cambridge, 1970); C. Valente, *The Theory and Practice of Revolt in Medieval England* (Aldershot, 2003).

34 E.g. M.V. Clarke, 'Forfeitures and Treason in 1388', in M.V. Clarke, *Fourteenth Century Studies* L.S. Sutherland et al., eds. (Oxford, 1968), 115–45; C. Ross, 'Forfeiture for Treason in the Reign of Richard II', *EHR* 71 (1956), 560–75; J.R. Lander, 'Attainder and Forfeiture, 1453 to 1509', *HJ* 4 (1961), 119–51; M. Hicks, 'Attainder, Resumption and Coercion, 1461–1529', *Parliamentary History* 3 (1984), 15–31.

35 E.g. R.V. Turner, *Men Raised from the Dust: Administrative Service and Upward Mobility in Angevin England* (Philadelphia, 1988); Green, *Government of England*; Bothwell, *English Peerage*.

36 For a general discussion of upward mobility in this period, see F.R. du Boulay, *An Age of Ambition: English Society in the Late Middle Ages* (London, 1970), Chapter 4.

37 According to Horrox, there were 'real continuities of purpose and attitude'. R. Horrox, 'Caterpillars of the Commonwealth? Courtiers in Late Medieval England', in R.E. Archer and S. Walker, eds. *Rulers and Ruled in Late Medieval England* (London, 1995), 2; for more general concepts of 'court' in this period, also see M. Vale, *The Princely Court: Medieval Courts and Culture in Northwest Europe* (Oxford, 2003), Chapter 1.

38 The Yorkist and Lancastrian attainders have already been thoroughly studied by Bellamy, Lander and Hicks, among others.

I

Black books:
many roads to perdition

4 BL Royal 14 E. IV, f. 10: Jean de Wavrin, *Chronique d'Angleterre*, Richard II
holding a court after his coronation; S. Netherlands (Bruges),
late fifteenth century.

I do know however that the court is not time; but temporal it is, changeable and various, space-bound and wandering, never continuing in one state. When I leave it, I know it perfectly: when I come back to it I find nothing or but little of what I left there: I am become a stranger to it, and it to me.[1]

You have often heard the proverb which says: he who acts falsely towards his rightful lord or does any wrong which causes him annoyance can be sure of getting his merited punishment.[2]

Both as event and environment the royal court was a lively place, *the* place to be for members, and would-be members, of the medieval political establishment. It was where patronage was arranged, connections made, knowledge obtained, marriages set up and careers publicised. Any noble with ambitions could ill afford to ignore the court, and had to show up there at least semi-regularly during his career. To fail to do so was to risk at best marginalisation and at worst complete loss of position – it was, after all, the focus of all the most important information in the realm, and without this knowledge one could not know how anyone else fared, let alone oneself. However, it was also a dangerous, uncertain world, full of the instabilities of individuals vying for position and power, where the wrong actions, words or friends could precipitate the early demise of a career, family or even a life. Rumours and half-truths were spread and exaggerated, confrontations, as well as recon-ciliations, brought about – it was, in other words, the venue for the most important individuals, the most important ideas and the most important projects of the kingdom to gain or lose attention and status.[3]

Royal disfavour

When discussing falls from grace, one must first consider the psychological background, one steeped in the Judeo-Christian themes of Original Sin and the Exile from the Garden: 'So he drove out the man; and he placed at the east of the garden of Eden Cherubims, and a flaming sword which turned every way' (Genesis 3:24). This theme of sin, downfall, and sometimes exile and redemption, appears frequently in the Scriptures, from Cain to the Prodigal Son, as well as in saints' lives and patristic texts[4] – possibly most well known being Augustine's attempts to overcome his lusts and desires and lead a life of spiritual grace as chronicled in the first part of his *Confessions*.[5] It is unsur-prising, then, that early English writers also took up the theme. Gildas, and using him, Bede, argued that the decline of post-Roman Britain and the increas-ing incursions by Angles, Saxons and Jutes were basically the result of the wickedness of its people[6] – a line Alcuin would also adopt as a reason for the Viking raids on Britain.[7] Later medieval chroniclers had a similar tradition of putting a righteous gloss on the punishment of those out of favour, one often connected more with the morality of the fallen than the seriousness of the transgression. We have already seen the *Vita's* assessment of the whole of Piers Gaveston's existence in the last chapter, and we also have the Waverley Annalist's report, most likely based on the lost *Winchester Annals*,[8] of the capture and incarceration of Robert Curthose after losing to Henry I at Tinchebrai in 1106: though the punishment was clearly the consequence of an attempt to take England from his brother, Henry I, according to this source Robert's fall was more importantly a result of God exchanging 'vice for vice', especially Robert's neglect of Jerusalem after taking part in capturing it, preferring to pursue 'quiet and sloth' in his duchy of Normandy.[9] Thus it was the Lord, acting through Henry, who set Robert the appropriate punishment of perpetual idleness through eternal imprisonment – an act sanctioned by the appearance of a comet in the Heavens. Later on, and on a much grander level, the physical demise of a large section of society through a series of plagues starting in 1348 was mainly blamed by chroniclers and other commentators on the immorality of individuals living at the time. From a contemporary poem we hear 'how England mourns, drenched in tears / The people, stained by sin, quake with grief / Plague is killing men and beasts / Why? Because vices rule unchallenged here'[10] – vices, it has to be said, also to be linked with the Peasants' Revolt of 1381 in the popular mind.[11] And, according to the chroniclers at least, it was not sin alone which caused men to fall – it also often caused them to be great in the first place, but a greatness that could cause considerable suffering for others:

> The Lord spoke of this [the prosperity of men with great names] when He declared to David, His king, in these words: 'I have made thee a great name, like unto the name of the great ones that are on the earth.' Whereas he possessed his prosperity with happiness, our contemporaries possess it with unhappiness, for in these times no one achieves a great name except by the greatest of crimes.[12]

The sins of the individual could not only cause his own torment, but also that of many around him: a theme evident, if not overemphasised, throughout contemporary comment of the later Middle Ages.[13]

Indeed, though there were exceptions,[14] most transgressions resulting in falls from grace tended to be serious in both cause and, as we will see later on, execution in medieval England. First of all, there were cases of royal favourites getting on the wrong side of the established nobility and gentry, for which the latter would often press for their demotion and/or degradation – and, if they were feeling so inclined, execution and loss of estate. Though in the later eleventh and twelfth centuries the 'old' nobility were not normally so aggressive about the make-up of the king's court – mainly because they still

lacked the requisite mixture of coherence and confidence needed to challenge the
king's personal preferences – by the thirteenth century the situation had begun
to change. In particular, the problems which established nobles had with
favourites of both John and Henry III would make their way either implicitly
or explicitly into the baronial reforms of the Magna Carta (1215), the Paper
Constitution (1244), the Provisions of Oxford (1258) and the Provisions of
Westminster (1259). In these instances, the issue was foreign favourites – either
those of John's court noted in Magna Carta (clause 50), or the Poitevins and
Savoyards of Henry III's reign. In the later medieval period, however, the foci
of baronial criticism were usually home grown, noble, but often also newly
promoted or at least newly empowered. Several quite well-known cases from
the fourteenth and fifteenth centuries emphasise this point, all of which will
be returned to again at a later stage but are useful to briefly introduce here.
First, in the early 1320s, lords holding lands on the south Welsh marches became
infuriated by the encroachments of the Despensers into their sphere of
influence, in part a delayed effect of the marriage of the younger Despenser
to the eldest Clare coheiress in 1306.[15] Edward II was more than willing to
back his new favourites in their ambitions, but local landowners were not nearly
as keen, and petitioned the king not to 'introduce a new law, contrary to
customs used and approved from time out of mind'. Even so, the younger
Despenser continued to press his interests in the area, and apparently began
referring to the allegations of the Marcher coalition blocking him as 'treason'.[16]
This state of affairs, and the more general avarice and arrogance of the
Despensers since before the start of the decade,[17] pushed the barons to work
furiously to bring about their first downfall in 1321.[18] Similarly, in Richard II's
reign, the established nobility, as well as the Commons, ran into conflict with
some of the king's most problematic favourites (most notably Robert de Vere,
Michael de la Pole and Simon Burley), as seen in the Wonderful Parliament
of 1386 and complaints concerning royal patronage, access to the king and more
general issues of curial corruption[19] – and despite Richard's famous riposte
that he would not 'dismiss the humblest of his kitchen staff from his post at
their behest'.[20] And, in the mid-fifteenth century, William de la Pole, duke
of Suffolk, though remaining popular with Henry VI, suffered a change in
noble, gentry and even more general public opinion towards him – first made
clear in a Commons petition backed by the Lords but continually publicised
by rumours and bills put up throughout London. This was in part for his
policy towards France, but also because of his purge of baronial critics from
the king's council, his treatment of the duke of Gloucester and his often
blatantly corrupt practices.[21] Even Edward III's generally popular promotions
did not escape the rancour of their more blue-blooded compatriots, as in the
Earl Warenne's famous, and very pointed, comment concerning the apparently

offensive presence of some of Edward's 'new men' in the parliamentary chamber in place of other, more established, nobles during the 1341 session.[22] Nothing irritated certain members of the establishment more, then as now, than to see others usurping their position, or becoming too powerful, however able they may have been.

Even without the further provocation of individuals such as Piers Gaveston making up rude names for baronial critics (e.g. the earl of Warwick, the 'Black Dog of the Arden'; the earl of Lincoln, 'burstbelly'),[23] noble opinion could, then, when powerful or incensed enough, cause serious problems for royal favourites. But establishment pressure on those it perceived as parvenus or to have risen above their station was not the only reason for a decline in fortunes. Often, the situation was reversed: pressure on the king by new favourites for the removal of members of an older guard. There are, again, cases of this throughout the Middle Ages as we will see (e.g. Piers Gaveston's attitude towards Edward I's established nobility at the start of his son's reign; the influence on an elderly Edward III by a group of courtiers in the 1370s), but a good instance worth introducing in some detail to start with is the destabilisation and eventual overthrow of Henry III's justiciar Hubert de Burgh by Peter des Roches, bishop of Winchester and his nephew, Peter de Rivallis, in the early 1230s.[24] De Burgh was a long-time royalist, having served King John, and later a leading member of the young Henry's minority government; des Roches was his main curial rival, again from the time of John,[25] an individual against whom, in 1221, de Burgh was said to have been at odds with enough to 'engineer' a charge of treason.[26] Throughout the 1220s, though not overly popular with the kingdom as a whole, de Burgh held his own against the uncle and nephew team. With the return of des Roches from Crusade in 1231, however, and the appointment of de Rivallis as treasurer of the King's Chamber and keeper of the Small Seal, the mood towards de Burgh shifted. Increasingly isolated from the bulk of the nobility by the duo's machinations, de Burgh also began to be blamed for not having dealt with Prince Llewellyn and the Welsh, as well as a more general lack of royal funds.[27] Despite attempts to shore up his position, by late July 1232 des Roches and de Rivallis had enough accumulated influence with the king to ensure de Burgh was ousted from the justiciarship, all royal castles and other estates confiscated, a demand made for an audit of all his accounts, and a miscellany of other charges which sealed his fate.[28] As the final insult, apparently influenced by the growing ferocity of the attack on de Burgh, Henry III himself was said to have accused his justiciar of having taken from the treasury a precious stone which had the power whereby its wearer could not be defeated in battle.[29] Kings too, it would seem, were not immune to the scent of blood whipped up by their courtiers, however loyal the previous service.

Similar plottings by newly favoured or newly empowered nobles can also be found in actions by the duke of Suffolk against the duke of Gloucester in the 1440s alluded to previously, which ultimately helped lead to the latter's downfall in 1447;[30] and, on an even larger and bloodier scale, the revenge of the Despensers on the Contrariants after Boroughbridge, especially those who had given them grief in South Wales in the early 1320s.[31] In many ways, then, the de Burgh example is just part of the nature of medieval court politics, and though its outcome was potentially deadly, it was still one of the accepted hazards of high-level political life. Arguably more serious than problems with courtiers or the establishment was a breach of faith with monarchy and country. To backbite within the court was one thing, to betray the king, kingdom and arguably English society as a whole was very much another. One of the most notable early cases of noble (albeit by a lesser noble) 'treason' in our period was that of Thomas de Turberville during the mid-1290s.[32] Turberville, one of Edward I's household knights, had been captured and imprisoned in France, during which time he was brought into a plot against the English monarch. According to the *Chronica Buriensis*, it was agreed with the French king, Philip the Fair, that Turberville would be allowed to escape if he would 'raise all England, Ireland, Scotland and Wales in war at one and the same time, so that while the king of England was engaged on all sides the French army could put ashore at whatever English port it chose without any difficulty or resistance'.[33] Though the plan was overly ambitious, when back in England Turberville did attempt to pass on much crucial information, including a report on the state of the defences of the Isle of Wight and the Welsh situation to the Provost of Paris[34] – for which, as we will see, he was granted a supremely gruesome and painful death, all for the sake of his freedom from a French royal prison and 100 pounds' worth of land.[35] Those north of the Border were also likely accomplices for treacherous activities. This time, supposedly for the good of the king and the 'profit of the realm', a deal between the Contrariants and the Scots was well advanced by the time it was uncovered in the early 1320s, as this letter from various nobles to James, Lord Douglas, indicates:

> Know that the conference that has been between us is now in train for performance, because the earl of Her[eford], Sir Roger Dammory, Sir Hugh Daudele, Sir Bartholomew de Badelesmere, Sir Roger de Clifford, Sir John Giffard, Sir Henry Tyeys, Sir Thomas Mauduyt, Sir John de Wylyngton, and I and all the others are come to Pountfreyt, and they are ready to make surety to you that if you complete the matters spoken of in the conference, to wit to come to our aid and go with us in England and Wales, we on the other hand pray you to assign us day and place where we can meet you and complete the matters faithfully, and live and die with us in our quarrel, and we pray you to cause us to have safe-conduct for 30 horsemen to come into your parts.[36]

Such betrayals, however, could be taken very personally by the king, especially when he had shown great – and often publicly proclaimed – faith in
an individual. A little later in the decade, Andrew de Harcla, the victor of
Boroughbridge in 1322, was, within the year of his triumph, charged with
treasonous association with the Scots.[37] Prior to this, Edward II had gone to
considerable lengths to praise and reward Harcla for his crucial service: most
importantly, making him earl of Carlisle (a new title) and endowing him with
1000 marks' worth of land, the first such direct linkage in English history.[38]
Unsurprisingly, then, the king was livid when Harcla's betrayal, again
encouraged by Lord Douglas, was uncovered. According to the *Brut*, the judge
sentenced the treacherous noble as follows:

> Sir Andrew, the king . . . did unto you much honour, and made you earl of Carlisle,
> and thou, as a traitor to thy lord the king, leddest his people of this country,
> that should have helped him at the battle of Byland, . . . away by the country
> of Copeland, and through the earldom of Lancaster, wherefore our lord the king
> was discomfited . . . by the Scots through thy treason and falseness; and if
> though hadst come betimes, he had had the mastery. And all that treason thou
> didst for the great sum of gold and silver, that though tookest of James
> Douglas, a Scot, the king's enemy. And our lord the king's will is that the order
> of knighthood, by which thou undertookest all thine honour and worship upon
> thy body, be all brought unto nought, and thy state undone, so that other knights
> of lower degree may after thee beware.[39]

In other words, one of the best ways to incense a king and bring about one
own's quick, and often painful, demise was not only to betray the monarch's
sacred trust – his realm – but to do so after the king had been foolish enough
to show great favour, especially in such a visible manner. After all, the prefer-
ential treatment of an ultimately treacherous noble was as much a condemnation of the king's judgement as any contemporary comment, however caustic,
and few of the king's most important subjects would have missed the point.

However, even more of a threat to the king or ruling regime was when the
nobility were found plotting among themselves against the monarch's person
or his government: if medieval society was perceived to be a living organism,
each part in a generally beneficial relationship with the others, such acts were
seen as cancerous, to be cut out wherever possible, and as quickly as possible.
Internal dissension and rebellion were so much of a commonplace in the
medieval period, evidence of which will be seen throughout this book, that
there is little reason for giving anything but the briefest of mentions at present. From the rebellions of Waltheof and the earls under William I, through
the 1215–17 and 1264–5 rebels, to the revolts in the early years of the reign
of Henry IV and beyond, insurrection was a clear, direct way not only to make
one's point of view known, but also to fall out of favour with the king and/or

the government of the realm. In the case of Thomas, earl of Lancaster, the leading rebel of Edward II's reign, the *Lanercost* chronicler thought that such treachery was the breaking point for any idea of merciful treatment:

> Howbeit, other adequate cause was brought forward and alleged, to wit, that he had borne arms against the King of England in his own realm; but those who best knew the king's mind declared that the earl never would have been summarily beheaded without the advice of parliament, nor so badly treated, had not that other cause prevailed, but that he would have been imprisoned for life or sent into exile.[40]

Somewhat less common but even more serious, the cause of downfall could be a nearer and clearer threat to the monarchy in the shape of royal family infighting, potentially one of the most destructive forms of aristocratic restiveness and striking at the heart of the medieval polity. Blood against blood was not a good recipe for the kingdom's, let alone dynastic, stability, and few kings prospered who forgot this. Politically astute monarchs, it must be said, usually made provision for their immediate families first and foremost, mainly through grants of lands or marriages – Henry I in his later years, Edward I and Edward III all realised that well-propertied, contented children, especially male ones, made for a stable realm,[41] at least in their own lifetimes. However, not all monarchs had the disposition, or were positioned well enough, to do as such – or, if arrangements were made, the offspring were too greedy to make the settlement work. One of the earliest post-Conquest cases of revolt within the immediate royal family was that by Robert Curthose against his brother Henry I, mentioned at the start of this section, over the right to the English throne, which ultimately led, through Tinchebrai, to Robert's downfall and permanent imprisonment.[42] That said, both Robert and Henry themselves had earlier revolted against William the Conqueror's eldest son, William Rufus, for similar reasons and faced similar punishments.[43] But perhaps the most famous case of royals battling one another is that of Henry II, his wife and his sons, mainly over the division of lands and power within the Angevin Empire. On the two decades through which Henry's family quarrelled, Gerald of Wales mused:

> O ye gods, if these illustrious brothers had been united by the ties of fraternal love, and had regarded their father with filial affection, if they had been bound together by the twofold cords of good-will and of nature, how great, how inestimable, how splendid and incomparable in the present age, would have been the glory of the father, and the triumphs of the sons? . . . To what a magnitude, and height, and strength the tree would have grown, if the branches had been naturally knit together, and had drawn their sap from the roots, is manifest from the premature decay and heavy fall of what was so precious. For as branches

lopped from the stem of a tree cannot reunite, so the tree stripped of its boughs, a treasonable outrage, is shorn both of its dignity and gracefulness.[44]

Gesta Regis Henrici Secundi referred to these incessant family troubles between Henry, Henry the Young King, Richard, John and, often at the back of it all, his wife Eleanor of Aquitaine, as being in fulfilment of a prophecy of Merlin[45] – giving the idea, at least, that not all kings were destined to fall out with their families through earthly forces alone. Notably, however, as the medieval period continued, the immediate royal family (i.e. the king, his wife and their offspring) was usually less interested in actively rebelling against the monarch – Prince Edward did so briefly against Henry III during the Barons' Wars of 1264–5, and Queen Isabella put her son in place of her husband in 1327. But whether because of greater provision for those within the royal family mentioned above, the more general fear of an increasingly unified, coherent, 'non-royal' nobility, or even more structured views on the royal succession, by the fourteenth century, when rebellions took place, never were they instigated or led by children, or even siblings for that matter, of reigning monarchs.[46]

Nonetheless, over the same period, falls from grace did become more and more connected with the unpopularity of a disgraced, deposed or dead monarch than with the actions or popularity of the ill-fated individuals themselves. Throughout the eleventh and twelfth centuries, aside from the period of the Anarchy, when kings got into trouble, or when they died, very rarely was there a sharp, violent reaction against those who had been closest to them. Favourites such as Henry I's 'men raised from the dust' and Richard I's courtiers may have lost their positioning after the demise of their monarch, but rarely were they targeted specifically with serious and/or bloody recriminations because of their previous status as favourites – though, of course, they would be attacked for other reasons throughout reigns, as we will see. However, by the later Middle Ages, perhaps in part resulting from the growing distinction between court and anti-court parties due at least in part to developing ideas of set baronial interests, as well as the generally more volatile political environment, the indisposition, change or fall of a monarch had increasingly dire consequences for his supporters. The Despensers and the earl of Arundel, while hated in their own right by many in England, ended up losing power because of Isabella's invasion of 1326, which itself, as has often been pointed out, was primarily the result of mismanagement of the monarchy by Edward II.[47] Similarly, the appeals of 1388 were primarily concerned with Richard II's actions as king rather than simply the sins of his favourites: though de la Pole, de Vere and Burley were problematic in their own right, in his extreme favouritism towards them, as well as his use of all three as supports for his own power, Richard II undoubtedly can be seen as the real cause of their downfall.[48] And when in turn, the 'Duketti' of 1397 fell in 1399, it was mainly because of Richard II's second and final fall from power:[49] by the later Middle Ages, falling from grace, in other words, was often inextricably bound up with the fate of a monarch as it had rarely been in the high medieval period. That said, it was not simply the indisposition of a monarch that could set in train such downfalls, but also the fall of a regime. When Isabella's minority government fell in 1330, not only was Mortimer beheaded, but also many henchmen – including John Maltravers, Simon Bereford and Thomas Gourney – were ordered arrested and had their lands taken into royal custody.[50] Even senility or other mental incapacity, as in the case of Edward III and Henry VI, could lead to falls from grace, as in the Good Parliament: Alice Perrers, William Latimer and Richard Lyons, it could be argued, might have stayed in their positions much longer if Edward III had still been able to defend them – the fact that their condemnations were reversed within the year, mainly through the efforts of Edward's fourth son, John of Gaunt, says as much.[51]

At times kings or those holding the reins of power could even precipitate ends of careers by pre-emptive action, as when Henry II had his suspected enemies arrested in 1183 – those who had taken part in the previous rebellions of his sons, including the earls of Gloucester and Leicester – though none of this, according to the *Gesta Regis Henrici Secundi* at least, lessened the fury of the remaining rebels on the countryside.[52] More successfully, Edward II's moves against Andrew de Harcla in early 1323, once he had proof that not only was Harcla dealing with the Scots, but also that 'shots across the bow' would not work, were meant to see off a potential Anglo-Scottish invasion/revolt.[53] Or, an individual's fate itself might also be the result of a carefully laid plan by the king or those acting in his name. The classic case is the trap believed to have been laid by the Minority regime in order to capture Edmund, earl of Kent, Edward II's half-brother, in 1330. Though Kent was initially greatly favoured by Mortimer and Isabella, he later took part in the 1328–9 Bedford rebellion and, while later reconciled with the Minority regime, was in effective political opposition by the end of the decade.[54] As a result, and apparently through the machinations of Mortimer, Kent was led to believe that Edward II was still alive, held captive in Corfe Castle. Going to his rescue, Kent was caught in the act, with sealed letters revealing his treason on him.[55] But not all such acts were so immediate. Retributive moves like this could be delayed until a more appropriate time for the monarch, especially if he was unsure of his position when the offending acts had taken place. It has been argued, though not without much debate,[56] that Richard II himself bided his time for almost a decade before seeking revenge for the injustices of the Lords Appellant in 1388: if true, a clear instance, again, of a demise being in essence precipitated by a king, and involving a considerable amount of forethought. Whatever the case, those in power were often not adverse to making the first move against political enemies, especially if they considered the time was right.

Hints and indicators

And when the said Thomas Norton came to the Kinges presence The kinge estraunged his loke from him And he perceivid that and departid from the Courte to Braynesforde And all the Courte hath him in suche lothnes that no Creature accompanyed nor made him anny chere.[57]

Looking back several centuries, while it is fairly clear when an individual's fall from grace ends (death, dismemberment, disinheritance and sometimes redemption), it is not always easy to identify the point at which it begins. The earliest indications can be easily missed or misinterpreted. The lack of a summons to a royal council could as easily indicate the slip-up of a chancery clerk as a mark of a king's or ruling regime's disfavour.[58] However, in a society bound by status and tradition, in which rank and the persistence of memory were inextricably intertwined, often as not such omissions meant something. The lack of attendance at the Anglo-Norman royal court, for example, could either indicate or initiate trouble: according to Green, 'from the lord's point of view, it was both dangerous to attend and dangerous not to do so'.[59] If one was lucky, any royal wrath could be pre-empted by the attitude of those around the king – as when in 1252, according to Matthew Paris at least, Henry III confronted Simon de Montfort over various misdeeds mainly connected with the governance of Gascony:

When the earl [Simon de Montfort] had offered enough evidence of his blame-lessness, and the other side had been refuted and silenced, still the king spoke against him, but when he saw that Earl Richard and all the rest backed Earl Simon, since they were ruled by discretion, he did not dare to put the royal strict-ness in force against him, provoked as he was.[60]

However, in this case, continued discussion between Henry and de Montfort again pushed matters to crisis, especially with the dredging up of old wrongs and broken agreements, and 'the king, who could scarcely restrain his anger, would have ordered him to be arrested there and then, had he not been assured that such a move would not in any way have been allowed by the magnates'.[61]

Royal or governmental allies were often asked, or looked for, ways to turn a rebellious noble's actions back to the path of righteousness, or at least one that would avoid serious dispute or bloodshed. Pressure for a man to con-form and follow the official line often came on the king's behalf from leading churchmen, who had not only political and social standing, but also often wielded the strongest of both ecclesiastical and moral influences. When Roger, earl of Hereford, began to associate with disruptive elements in the mid-1070s, Archbishop Lanfranc tried to talk some sense into him.[62] At first, this simply took the form of a strong, yet friendly, reminder of the duty of subjects to their king, especially with respect to the loss of castles to the king's enemies.[63] This entreaty went unnoticed, so another letter, sharper in tone, was sent to the errant noble:

> I grieve more than I can say at the unwelcome news I hear of you. It would not be right that a son of earl William – a man whose sagacity and loyalty to his lord and all his friends is renowned in many lands – should be called faithless and be exposed to the slur of perjury or of any kind of deceit. On the contrary, the son of such a great man should follow his father's example and be for others a pattern of integrity and loyalty in all respects. I therefore beg you, as a son whom I cherish and the dearest of friends, for the sake of God and your own good name, if you are guilty of such conduct to return to your senses; and if you are not, to demonstrate this by the clearest possible evidence.[64]

As we will later see, the earl of Hereford would fail to heed even this pointed advice, and would come to suffer the consequences. Or, the king could try to bring an individual back into the fold himself, especially if that individual was also previously his friend. Henry II, of course, had tried to do this with Thomas Becket in the months before the meeting at Clarendon and, at the other end of our period, Henry V originally made overtures through his advisors to the Lollard, and friend of the king, Sir John Oldcastle. Encouraging him to mend his ways, this Henry's efforts proved to have little effect on the hardened heretic: 'but when, at length, this man of sedition could not be turned from his obstinate and damnable belief by either coaxing or intimidation or, indeed, by any means of persuasion, the king ordered him to be smitten with the sword, first the spiritual, then the temporal – him whom neither soft words nor harsh threats could wean from those udders from which he had sucked his most impious notions'.[65]

When such attempts to divert problematic behaviour by a noble failed to work, then, the king could subtly, or not so subtly, indicate his state of mind. Not to be invited to the king's Christmas or Easter feast could be as clear a sign of decline in favour as the deliberate stopping of an individual summons to parliament – likewise, nobles were expected to show up with New Year's gifts for the king,[66] and not to be in a position to do so could further hurt their curial standing. According to one recent commentator, 'In the world of the court, if you wanted to get on you did what your lord wanted doing',[67] but how could you do that if you were not there? Moreover, an individual could also be shut out from royal councils, summons to parliaments and even more general presence around the court. Charter witness evidence, if used carefully, can tell us much about who was in favour, and who was not, at various times, even as early as the Anglo-Norman period. As Hollister points out in his discussion of Robert Malet, a major East Anglian, and indeed, national landowner of varying fortunes, the 'attestation statistics accurately reflect the ups and downs of his career under the first three Norman kings'.[68] Later on, one can see how quickly Roger D'Amory, William Montagu and Hugh Audley, three key members of Edward II's 1316–19 court party, disappeared from witness lists after the king found it no longer politic to keep them around.[69] The quantity and quality of grants from the king could be a similar, if more pointed, indicator of lack of support: royal patronage could be limited, or even stopped, when one was out of favour with the king or ruling regime. Staying with the case of Hugh Audley, when Edward III made the 1337 earldom promotions, though he gave the majority of them a considerable amount of patronage, to Audley, who was due the earldom of Gloucester by right of his wife, he gave very little – while also often continuing to keep him off the charter witness lists.[70] Part of this may well have been Hugh's age, which was well above the other 1337 earls, not making him much of a boon companion for the young Edward III, and part the already considerable size of his wife's inheritance; but part was also probably down to the memory of Hugh's disloyalty to his father, Edward II, in the early 1320s. Indeed, despite his modern reputation for mercy and fairness,[71] Edward III was not always a king keen to forgive past wrongs. Later in the reign, another of the 1337 earls, William Clinton, was mainly absent from the patronage of the 1340s and 1350s, including the fulfilment of annuities, as well as, more noticeably, from membership in the newly founded Order of the Garter – perhaps in connection with his part in the opposition to Edward III in the crisis of 1340–1.[72] Other indicators of disfavour were more forthright. The fact that King John was unwilling to help the earl of Salisbury defend royal grants lately given to him pushed Salisbury onto the side of Prince Louis when he invaded in 1216: according to Holden, Salisbury recognised the 'chill of royal suspicion and favour', and simply acted accordingly.[73] Similarly, Richard, earl of Pembroke, the Earl Marshal, could be fairly certain that he was seriously outside the favour of Henry III, and that the king suspected him of false dealings, when the latter ordered, on 18 July 1233, the bailiffs of south-coast ports to search the earl's messengers, Brother Richard Runcevalle and William Malet, one of Richard's knights, for correspondence harmful to the royal interests when they returned from abroad.[74] Finally, some events can be seen with hindsight as having more significance than they probably had at the time. During the funeral of Richard II's beloved Anne in 1394, the king attacked the earl of Arundel with the baton of one of his attendants, causing him to fall bloodied to the floor.[75] Though the king's reasons were ostensibly that the earl was late to the proceedings, and then had the nerve to ask for licence to withdraw owing to certain urgent causes,[76] the virulence of his reaction is possibly also an indication that the king had not forgotten Arundel's part in the events of 1388, as would become even more evident during the events of 1397. The earl ended up in the Tower for his impropriety, having to make a surety of £40,000 for his freedom.[77]

And the closer the noble was to the king, the more pointed could be his exclusion. Returning to Henry III's somewhat dramatic early dealings with Simon de Montfort, word of premarital relations with the king's sister (at least according to Matthew Paris: see below) – though in fact more than likely instead presumptuous credit arrangements by de Montfort[78] – caused Henry to vent his anger. So it was, in August 1239, when a number of noble-women gathered in London to accompany the queen to a monastery for her purification after the birth of her son, the future Edward I:

> When Simon de Montfort, earl of Leicester, arrived with his wife, the king called him an excommunicate, and prohibited him and his wife, whom he had sordidly and secretly dishonoured before the marriage had been contracted, to be present at the festivities; and, after many admonishments from him, the earl and his wife withdrew in confusion, and returned by water to their quarters, at the palace of the late lord bishop of Winchester, which the king had generously lent the earl. The king, however, immediately ordered them to be forcibly turned out. And though they returned with tears and pitiful begging for pardon, they did not calm the king's annoyance . . . [Diatribe by the king accusing him of seducing his sister] . . . The earl was humiliated by these words, and in the evening embarked on the Thames into a little boat with his wife, who was pregnant, and a small retinue, and hastily going down to the sea coast immediately crossed the straits.[79]

Though Paris appears to have got the cause of the outburst wrong, it still gives the sense of severe and/or rapid chill in relations which could happen when a noble crossed the king. With such shifts in favour being common-place, many nobles were as a result very sensitive to deteriorations in their relationship with the king or ruling oligarchy, and were ready to act accordingly in defence of their interests. In early July 1232, just before his ultimate disgrace, Hubert de Burgh was getting clear indications that all was not well and so had enrolled in the Charter Rolls an official statement making clear that if the king ever invalidated gifts, charters or confirmations made to him and his wife, de Burgh would 'take care to impede that purpose and do all in his power to preserve the said charters inviolate'.[80] In this case, de Burgh was not far wrong, as within a few weeks he had lost the justiciarship, though it had previously been granted to him for life.[81] And, even if still apparently favoured by the ruling regime with no indications of a change in royal policy imminent, recent events taught how quickly times could change and how nobles should thus be forearmed. When Thomas, earl of Norfolk, was given 1000 marks of land from the Despenser estates in 1327, it is unsurprising, considering recent history, that the grant ended with an increasingly common clause by the later Middle Ages 'binding the king and his heirs to compensate the earl or his heirs for any of the foregoing that may be recovered by judgement of the king's court; with reversion to the king and his heirs'[82] – a clause which not only helped protect Thomas's gains from other landowners but also from changing whims of kings, as well as the fallout from changing regimes.

Capture and arrest

> There were, as Miss Clark has pointed out, two conflicting tendencies – the desire to find means of judging great men for crimes beyond the normal law; and the insistence that such means must be clothed in due legal form.[83]

Once an individual had definitely fallen from favour, the next thing was, if he was not already, to get him into royal custody. This, however, was rarely as straightforward as it sounds. Not only did noble retinues grow in importance if not in size in the later Middle Ages,[84] making the capture of a disgraced individual potentially an issue of military, as well as administrative, force, but simply catching a man in the far-flung reaches of the kingdom, or beyond, before the development of a national, professionalised, non-partisan police force could also be quite difficult – after all, the 'law' in a locality was often as not the disgraced noble himself, or one of his followers or allies. On a slightly different note, there was also the issue of the manhandling and arrest of a noble in public, especially considering the growing importance of physical manifestations of social identity, whether robes of ermine or coats of arms, ownership of the local manor or a fine destrier.[85] To treat roughly those wearing such heavily symbolic dress in front of all and sundry before they had even been judged could not only encourage the more active members of the local population to support one side or the other in an arrest, and cause even more law and order issues as a result, it could also lessen respect towards local nobles and gentry, as well as erode the more general, and ever essential, environment of deference. At least in part to counteract these dangers, throughout our period there were a couple of 'softening-up' processes which often took place before the use of force by the royal government was resorted to. First, to remove power from the accused and put him in a situation where he had to give himself up and/or accept the king's judgement, there was the suspension or removal of offices, as we have already seen with de Burgh in

1232 and as when Edward II stripped Andrew de Harcla of his offices in the north prior to his arrest in February 1323;[86] or, at a less serious level, when Walter de Manny lost his post as the sergeant of the Marshalsea in the mid-1350s as a result of his unlicensed marriage to one of the Norfolk coheiresses.[87] Next, there were usually attempts to get recalcitrant nobles to surrender themselves, a cheaper and often less disruptive option than hunting them down. In 1398, Richard II's government ordered the sheriff of Bedford and Buckingham, among others, to announce in public various places that the duke of Norfolk was to appear, under pain of forfeiture of life and limb, in person before the king in fifteen days' time to face treasonous charges made by the duke of Hereford.[88] The obverse of this document shows that the sheriff had the writ read out in towns throughout his jurisdiction, including Woburn Chapel, Stony Stratford, Aylesbury, Buckingham, Newport Pagnell, Bedford, Olney, Wycombe and Leighton. In the next reign, Henry IV had publicly proclaimed by, among others, the sheriff of London and Middlesex, that if the rebels Henry Percy, earl of Northumberland, and Thomas Lord Bardolf came in of their own accord within the allotted time, they would be given the king's security and be allowed to state their case in front of the king alone. If they did not, they would be considered convicted of the crimes of which they were accused.[89]

Arrest warrants, commissions and similar devices were usually issued, if not at the same time, then quickly after such methods had failed. For instance, immediately after Boroughbridge, the adherents of Thomas, earl of Lancaster, and other Contrariants were ordered to be arrested wherever they might be[90] – though some would, as we will see, remain abroad and continue to cause problems in the English countryside throughout the mid-1320s.[91] Likewise, soon after Radcot Bridge in 1387, an order went out to various sheriffs and even John of Gaunt, listed as 'King of Castile', to arrest Robert de Vere, Michael de la Pole and Robert Tresilian and detain their goods, wherever they shall be found.[92] And, in the mid-1450s a bill was quickly arranged in parliament to apprehend and imprison the earl of Devon and Lord Bonville for carrying on a private feud in the south-west.[93] Speed, then, was of the essence in such cases, lest the wanted man cause further trouble for the king's government in his efforts not to get caught. Sometimes, depending on the crime's seriousness and the unwillingness of the individual involved to surrender himself, further measures might be necessary, especially if it was thought that the accused might or had taken flight either to remote parts of the kingdom, or to mainland Europe. In September 1233, sheriffs, constables and bailiffs were ordered to aid Amaury de Saint Amand, the king's steward, in capturing Richard Siward, Warin Basset and Philip Basset, allies of the earl of Pembroke and defenders of the cause of Hubert de Burgh,[94] and to raise 'the hue and cry in all parts through which they pass'.[95] Similarly, in 1323 Edward II ordered the mayor and sheriff of London to raise the hue and cry against the Contrariant Roger Mortimer, recently escaped from the Tower of London.[96] However, in this case, though the Londoners did their best to find Mortimer, sending out horsemen into the countryside around the city, the accused made good his escape to the Continent. Nonetheless, if earlier processes had failed to work to a sufficient degree, these more public methods, however potentially detrimental to ideas of hierarchy and deference, were often resorted to in order to get a problematic noble under royal control.

Indeed, once it had been decided that an individual should be arrested, it was also made very plain that his friends should not try to help him – after all, noble or not, he had now given up all legal right to aid from his friends and supporters, and if the latter were permitted to continue to assist him, it could clearly have larger social as well as political ramifications. In the case of Mortimer, the king's government threatened immediate forfeiture for any who should aid and abet him;[97] earlier, in the decade after Evesham, orders went out to find out and capture people aiding and abetting Amaury, son of Simon de Montfort, also reminding the king's subjects that they should in future not assist him in any way.[98] Some individuals did not heed such advice, however, and went on regardless, believing that their first loyalty was to their lord or friend rather than the king or his government. If such help *was a fait accompli*, but the situation appeared to be turning, the abettors involved would often be wise to seek a pardon as soon as possible. During the early part of Edward III's independent rule, a number of men, including members of the peerage and higher gentry, had to obtain pardons for harbouring the exile John Maltravers during a secret visit to England, an individual under an arrest warrant for various crimes, including those connected with the death of Edward II.[99] That said, it was usually best to keep as distant as possible from unsuccessful troublemakers, especially considering the often wide fallout of their activities, deliberate or otherwise. Many of the forfeitures of the 1320s were initially quite indiscriminate, and a number of people holding properties of, or supposedly connected with, the forfeitees had to petition to get their lands back, as did Aymer Despenser, William de Bentham, Robert Gille and Henry de Keu from the forfeited estate of the Contrariant John de Giffard.[100] Finally, though usually fairly effective, not all accused subjects obeyed royal warrants and/or came in quietly or less quietly, and instead tried to test the royal administration's resolve in a most public manner, even in the face of force or military threat noted above. When Henry V ordered Archbishop Arundel to act against John Oldcastle on charges of heresy, instead of complying, Oldcastle shut himself up in Cooling Castle, refusing to have anything to do with the archbishop – or anyone else for that matter.[101] Oldcastle was a very brave man to ignore the orders of his king so openly and directly, and would later pay an exceedingly high price for his wilfulness.

High medieval justice: by royal will and by battle

After the individual was in royal custody, though also *in absentia*, there was then the issue of justice. In terms of procedure itself, in the eleventh, twelfth and thirteenth centuries, the chance of judicial or semi-judicial trials for downfallen nobles tended to be limited, dependent more on political pressures, attendance at court and the interests of the king than any set procedures, let alone rights the nobility might have had. We do have some limited evidence of noble trials from the Anglo-Norman and Angevin periods – though how formal, let alone impartial or representative, these were is altogether another issue. Despite his 'lack of military action, his confession, apparent contrition, and the support of Archbishop Lanfranc',[102] Waltheof, earl of Huntingdon, after many delays, was brought to trial in Westminster at Christmas time for the rebellion of 1075, with his wife, also William's niece, acting as one of the witnesses – and the king himself already regarding Waltheof as 'deeply implicated' in the plot.[103] In the next reign, the bishop of Durham, one of the conspirators of the 1088 revolt, also faced judicial proceedings, though they were said to have lasted only one 'winter's day'.[104] Somewhat more significantly, in 1102 Robert de Bellême, earl of Shrewsbury and one of the main rebels of Henry I's early reign, was summoned to Henry's court to answer forty-five charges committed 'in deed or word' against the king and Robert Curthose, commanding him 'to answer publicly to each one'.[105] Later, in 1112 Shrewsbury was tried in the King's Court at Bonneville on charges of acting wrongfully against his lord, not coming to the King's Court though summoned three times and not having made any returns to the exchequer relating to offices held in Argentan and other lands on the Continent.[106] Both these instances connected with Shrewsbury, then, do show that the king's side had to offer some detailed rationale for its actions, if nothing else. However, for most of the high Middle Ages, there is only limited evidence of noble trials based on any clear ideas of rules of law, equity or even set procedure, most rather tending to be relatively closed, curial and arbitrary affairs on the part of the monarchy, however long the accusation list might become. Even when a somewhat wider consensus was looked for in this period, it was often quickly ignored if it did not agree with the king's wishes. In 1205, when William Marshal, usually a strong supporter of the Angevin regime, quarrelled with King John over William's unwillingness to fight against the king of France, also his feudal lord, the king accused him of treason and called his barons to back him up on the accusation; however, the men present refused to pass judgement, so John instead used the more dubious authority of the presumably overawed knights bachelor around him.[107] That said, the appeal by William Marshal to common interest with the barons present during this confrontation does also foreshadow, along with trial in parliament, some of the rationale behind the development of trial by peers in the next century:[108]

> Sirs, look at me, for, by my faith, I am this day an example for all of you. You hear what the king says and what he proposes to do to me; that, and more also, will he do to every one of you, if he can get the upper hand.[109]

Nonetheless, perhaps because of the potentially dangerous and destabilising nature of high medieval conflicts, in the cases of the Anarchy, Henry the Young King's rebellion of 1173–4 and the Barons' Wars of 1215 and 1265, as well as many problematic cases in between, formal public trial and punishment were not commonly used as the main way to pass judgement on disgraced or down-fallen nobles.

Rather, until the fourteenth century, for the nobility at least, summary royal authority and/or trial effectively by outcome of various forms of force tended to be the norm. Moreover, despite the shift from judgement by ordeal to trial by jury during these centuries,[110] the authority for both processes still notably came ultimately from God. Whether because the Lord, or through him the king, was felt to be the only authority capable of judging the nobility, or that such judgements were the most incontestable at a time when the nobility were beginning to flex their muscles, for much of the high Middle Ages these two types of justice played off each other as a way to deal with erring nobles. Concerning the early use of summary royal authority, when King Stephen and the earl of Chester were at last brought face to face to negotiate during the Anarchy, the issue did not turn out quite as the earl would have wished:

> So, when the king at last, though unwillingly, had acquiesced in good advice to this effect they at once gathered together and approached the earl, who had no such suspicions, and promised that the king would be very ready and eager to help him in any emergencies that ill fortune had produced, if he had his agreement on the points already mentioned. But when the earl at once answered that he had not come to court for this purpose, had not even been given any notice of the matter or deliberated over it with his advisers, both sides began to use haughty and contentious language, one party crying out that the earl was devising a crafty and treasonable plot against the king, while he, embarrassed and shamefaced, since he was conscious of his treachery, first denied it and then changed the subject; upon this they suddenly laid hands on him, delivered him to the king's guards, chained him, and put him in prison.[111]

Similarly, William de Braose's demise, along with the ill-treatment of his family, came mainly through the ill-will of John,[112] and though in the next reign de Burgh's downfall was helped along by des Roches and de Rivallis, it still ended up being Henry III who let it continue unabated.[113] In Edward I's reign, Thomas de Turberville, introduced a bit earlier in this chapter, also suffered a quite highhanded process for dealing with the French. Turberville was brought to London, and there 'were found upon him both letters addressed to him by the French king, and copies of letters sent by him to the French king, instruments of his treason which proved his deeds clearer than light'.[114] In this case, then, though some form of evidence was presented to back up the king's judgement – showing the way to the future – and the judgement pronounced by a chief justice of the King's Bench, nonetheless ultimate authority still lay more with Edward I as an individual rather than any wider agency.[115] Sometimes, such 'evidence' to fuel the king's arbitrary exercise of power could come from the confessions of the supposed perpetrators themselves, as when in a very late example of such behaviour, the earl of Kent and others appealed the duke of Gloucester in 1397, and, being in Calais, he offered his 'confession' to Sir William Rickhill – though famously, if genuine, under considerable duress and probably facing death at the time.[116] Nonetheless, though considered highly irregular by critics at the time, this case would point more to the tenor, if not the execution, of summary justice in the form of attainder in the fifteenth century than to the exercise of the king's will of the twelfth and thirteenth centuries noted above.[117]

Indeed, instead of a definite continuity between high medieval royal judgements against disgraced nobles and later parliamentary – or otherwise semi-representative, though also sometimes summary – legal procedures, a clearer link between the two periods lies in the issue of trial by battle – that is, the judgement of God concerning the outcome of physical conflict, whether by armies or individuals. In its broadest sense, as we have seen and will see, in the period 1075–1455 many members of the higher nobility who fell from grace with either king or ruling elite ended up falling in battle, from Tinchebrai through Evesham to Shrewsbury and beyond. If, in other words, perceived transgressions against the establishment and the backbiting and ostracism that often came with them marked the early scenes of a play, then battle was often the final act, with the climax in the action seen to be decided by God. Whether the earl of Leicester's ultimate defeat in battle near Bury during the rebellion of 1173–4,[118] the rout of the earl of Northumberland's forces at Bramham Moor in 1408,[119] or any number of other such 'judgements by God' (to the medieval mind at least), while man might be the agency of victory on the battlefield, God was the prime mover. As the author of the *Vita Edwardi Secundi* noted, the royalist victory at Boroughbridge against superior forces was 'a marvellous thing and one indeed brought about by God's will and aid, that so scanty a company should in a moment overcome so many knights'.[120]

God was also much in evidence in Froissart's description of the Appellant victory at Radcot Bridge against the royal favourites in 1387: 'Then they [the scouts] rode back to the Duke of Gloucester and told him: "Sir, God and the river are on your side today" . . . The Duke answered: "God be with us then. We have some share in those arms, my brother and I. Let's ride forward in the name of God and St George." '[121] The Lord passed judgement and settled the outcome of battles, so the reasoning went: tactics, strategy and military prowess had helped decide the issue, but as these too were also ultimately in the gift of God, any military victory in the Middle Ages was, in the final analysis, the result of divine providence. The psychological importance of religious preparations before battles had long emphasised this connection in the popular mind,[122] and both Edward I and Edward III took such ideas one step further by asking their people as a whole to pray for the success of English troops on campaign.[123] But it was Shakespeare's Henry V who prob-ably put the public face of victory after trial by battle, and its connection with divine will, best just after the battle of Agincourt in 1415: 'And be it death proclaimed through our host / To boast of this, or take that praise from God / Which is his only.'[124]

Somewhat less obviously when it came to downfall by force, there was also the continuity in trial by single combat over the course of our period – the outcome of which was again attributed to divine judgement. In particular, by the high Middle Ages the ultimate transgression against those in power, treason, was intimately connected with trial by individual battle, especially since, as 'both parties, accuser and accused, would often be members of the military aristocracy, it is psychologically quite understandable that the issue would be resolved by battle'.[125] After the rebellion of 1095, William Rufus held his Christmas court at Windsor and there, Geoffrey Barnard, probably the king's champion, accused William of Eu of treason, and defeated him in trial by combat.[126] Seventy-odd years later, in the early 1160s, as a result of leaving the field of battle at Counsylth in 1157, Robert de Montfort accused Henry of Essex, an up-and-coming member of Henry II's nobility, of treason, over-came him in judicial combat and left him for dead on the field – though in this case the defeated man was then collected by monks of the monastery at Reading, later to take the habit himself.[127] And, in Edward I's reign, William de Vescy challenged the Lord of Offaly to battle after the latter accused him of treacherous words 'against our lord and his estate' including those imputing the king's bravery and honour, especially in the run-up to Evesham – though in this case, Offaly failed to show up and Vescy claimed judgement by default and through, though more importantly for the future, parliament.[128] Unsurprisingly, then, considering its continued if select popularity, by the later Middle Ages there had arisen a series of treatises regulating trial by battle and its aftermath, especially though not solely in connection with the developing Court of Chivalry.[129] For treason specifically, the vanquished of the battle 'was disarmed in the lists and drawn behind a horse in the charge of the Marshal to the place of execution, where he was beheaded or hanged'[130] – though, as we will see in the next chapter, there were variations on such practices for a condemned man. Nonetheless, by Richard II's reign, disputes with considerable political resonance could potentially be decided in light of such rules, as in the famous case of the earl of Nottingham's accusation against the earl of Derby in 1398 (see Fig. 5):

> Lord Derby, I maintain that you thought and spoke what you ought not to have done against your natural lord and master, the King of England, in saying that he is unworthy of ruling land or kingdom, since without forms of justice or consultation with his men, he unsettles his realm and with no shadow of justification drives out from it the gallant men who would help him to protect and uphold it: wherefore I offer you my gage and am ready to prove by my body against yours that you are false, miscreant and a traitor.[131]

Trial by battle, in other words, unlike other 'trials by ordeal' in the later Middle Ages, continued if somewhat sporadically throughout most of our period, especially in connection with justice towards those out of favour with the king or establishment for what was perceived to be treasonous activity.[132] Whether because it lay the onus of judgement ultimately on God, or whether because it was simply the preferred method of deciding issues for members of the noble military elite, in some instances at least the sword and the lance still took the place of more rational, logical means of deciding the fate of rebellious or unpopular nobles.

Later medieval justice: parliamentary, peerage and summary

For the most part, however, by the fourteenth century, there was an increasing attempt 'to devise a peaceful and "legal" procedure for dealing with political disputes',[133] something conceivably meant to reproduce in both tone and tenor for the nobility the revolution in trial and sentencing going on for the lesser of the king's subjects (especially the end of the ordeal and the rise of the jury) from the royal courts down to local tribunals. Moreover, with the legal end of ideas of 'legitimate' baronial resistance as a result of Edward I's extension of treasonous activity to cover acts of armed rebellion,[134] another lawful venue for some form of political expression in moments of high crisis from all sides, as well as of course a way to pass judgement against nobles, needed to be developed as quickly as possible. Increasingly, then, in the middle

5 BL Harley 4380, f. 141: *Froissart's Chronicles*, the Earl Marshal challenges
the earl of Derby to a duel; S. Netherlands (Bruges), 1470–5.

of our period we have the rise of the 'state' trial of nobles and gentry in parliament, a development which had precedents in the trials of David ap Gruffyd in 1283 and Nicholas Segrave in 1305.[135] Notably for Prince David's treatment, Edward I set an example by 'calling a "general parliament" which included elected representatives of shires and boroughs to Shrewsbury, to decide on the punishment'.[136] And some form of trial by peers in this broadest of senses, or at least others than the king and his immediate councillors, continued to develop, becoming something of a norm for disgraced nobles by the end of our period[137] – though, of course, usually leaving the king or those controlling the crown with the final say. Indeed, whether because of the growing power of both parliament and the nobility or the need to justify increasingly harsh, often capital, judgements over the remainder of our period, justice by royal authority alone, or by ordeal and various forms of combat, was gradually complemented, and at least partially superseded, by trial by wider representative councils and/or parliament. For instance, in July 1321, the baronial grievances were aired in parliament at Westminster and judgement and punishment handed down: condemnation, banishment and disinheritance of both Despensers, all of which was protected by a clause that 'the judgement, confirmed by such weight of authority, should never be reversed'.[138] Even the record and process of judgement against Thomas, earl of Lancaster, in the next year,[139] so one-sided and already decided in most ways – it has been referred to as a 'show trial'[140] – was nonetheless in front of a semi-representative council of his peers, including the earls of Kent, Warenne, Richmond, Pembroke, Arundel, Athol and Angus, with only Warenne and Arundel clearly against Lancaster.[141]

However, it must be emphasised that even in the early fourteenth century few such processes could be argued to be a trial in the modern sense; rather they were statements of sentence in, and for, the public arena:[142] a process which opened up such justice to a wider audience, though still not giving the accused or his would-be supporters the right officially to influence proceedings. According to Vernon Harcourt, both Roger Mortimers (of Chirk and Wigmore), as well as Bartholomew de Badlesmere and Henry Tyes, all went through a similar process to the earl of Lancaster after Boroughbridge (though in these cases notably not still in front of peers of the realm), namely

> A writ was issued to certain persons enjoining them to visit the prisoner and pass judgement upon him according to the tenor of a document scheduled to the writ; [containing] . . . the formula that his crimes are notorious and the king records the fact; thereupon the commissioners thus appointed visited the prisoner and read aloud to him the words of the schedule. That was all. In the four cases mentioned none was tried, none of the commissioners appointed was a peer of the realm.[143]

It was, in other words, the sentencing itself and the publicity for the outcome, more than the exercise of justice, that was the main point of these 'trials'. And it was not just royally sponsored record keeping or publicity (parliamentary rolls, royal proclamations, letters patent, etc.) that spread the word of the dangers of crossing the king: as Plucknett notes, 'medieval chroniclers often give detailed accounts of state trials which evidently were supplied from official quarters; the sentence on the Despensers was so widely circulated that most manuscript collections of statutes contain it'.[144] Despenser the younger's sentence reads as follows in the letter books of the Monastery of Christ Church, Canterbury:

> Thus Hugh as you have been proved to be a traitor, therefore all the good men of the realm, both great and small, both rich and poor, and by common assent, condemn you Hugh, so that as you have been found guilty as a thief therefore you shall be hanged; and as you have been found guilty as a traitor therefore you shall be drawn and quartered, and your quarters dispersed through the kingdom; and as you were outlawed, by our Lord the King and by general consent, and have come back to the Court, therefore you shall be beheaded; and because at all times you have been disloyal and a fomenter of strife between our Lord the King and our most noble Lady the Queen and others of the realm therefore you shall be disembowelled, and after that your bowels shall be burned. Confess yourself a traitor and a renegade! and so go to meet your doom, Traitor, Evildoer and Convicted![145]

Though at points problematic in its transmission,[146] it is also fairly clear that most of the material in the passage was coming at some stage from the official record. Gatherings of this sort, then, especially in the 1320s, were more a venue for declaring and publicising as widely as possible sentences of guilt and setting out punishment than for trying to get to the truth of allegations – unsurprising considering the nature of the times. Lancaster's 'trial' and other 'trials' of Edward II's reign, increasingly representative as they were, were still mainly a case of record (especially royal), statement of notoriety and sentencing.[147]

However, fairly quickly thereafter, there began a relatively quiet but important shift in the nature of justice for members of the peerage, one which would have important ramifications for centuries to come for both the legal position of the individual noble and, more generally, the social distance of the nobility as a whole from the lower orders. Most notably, the *Modus Tenendi Parliamentum* (early 1320s) suggests rules concerning the conduct of justice between the king and peers, and within the peerage, including the set-up of a parliamentary committee to deal with difficult cases[148] – perhaps as an antidote to what was actually going on in the kingdom during the tract's composition. In practice as well, some trials of nobles began to have a distinctly 'modern' feel about them, especially in the recognition by the prosecution of the need for some form of set judicial process acknowledged by all. Indications that change was afoot came as early as 1327, when it was recorded in front of king and council in parliament that the judgements against John Mowbray, executed in 1322, should be reversed, because Mowbray was adjudged to death without any form of judgement by peers, in defence of which not only was Magna Carta clause 39 cited, but also the fact that the kingdom was officially at peace at the time of the judgement.[149] A year later, in 1328, Henry de Harcla, the nephew and heir of the executed earl of Carlisle, petitioned king and council that he be allowed to inherit his uncle's lands, as the forfeiture had not been done by an inquisition of peers.[150] Even the increasing use of evidence, including alibi, started to give proceedings against disgraced nobles a different, arguably more modern, air. When Thomas Berkeley was brought before the Lords in 1330 concerning the death of Edward II, he pleaded that he was ill and not in Berkeley Castle at the time of the supposed murder of the king, of which he had heard nothing – which helped convince the jury (another relatively recent innovation for noble trials) to find him not guilty.[151] In other words, clear ideas about how and when peers of the realm were to be tried for the most serious of crimes had now begun to crystallise in the minds of lawyers, government officials and parliament as a whole, ideas which were to influence the next phase of the treatment of disgraced nobles.

But more important than even this, the growing representativeness, and public nature, of the bodies involved and the increasing number of responsibilities that they undertook in the decision-making process as a whole – a role first prominent during the proceedings against Edward II in 1327, but now also being used against the nobility themselves – also helped change the nature of 'state' trials. One of the most important, and well publicised, of such noble trials of the later Middle Ages was that of Roger Mortimer, earl of March, after the Nottingham coup of 1330. According to the Rolls of Parliament, the proceedings were in front of the 'earls, barons and peers of the realm on behalf of the king',[152] during which Edward III made the accusations against Mortimer and his accomplices an issue of common complaint and common judgement (at least officially), though also made it clear that he thought Mortimer guilty – as did the commonalty by 'notoriety'. Notably, according to Le Baker, Mortimer was not allowed to appear before them or argue his case[153] – perhaps, if nothing else, because it would quickly show the holes in the nascent justice system for nobles discussed above; instead, those assembled quickly found him guilty as charged and sentenced him to execution three days later. Such a 'process', however tainted in modern eyes, was not only another important development of a way of judging the kingdom's most powerful, it was also crucial for Edward III if he did not want to be accused of the same 'arbitrary rule' of his father and the Minority regime. Moreover, though bringing such trials firmly into the public consciousness, and making parliament responsible for part of the judgement, Mortimer's is also notable as the last great case where 'notoriety' was used to secure a conviction (though notably, the crime was already not being recorded on the 'king's record' in this case – the problems with this procedure having been emphatically pointed out by Henry of Lancaster in 1327 when arguing against his brother's conviction in 1322 by such means).[154] This, and the ultimate reversal of Mortimer's conviction in 1354 in parliament, according to Plucknett, 'established the rule that arraignment and hence an opportunity for defence were essential to a valid trial', as well as the importance of nobles being tried by their peers.[155]

Indeed, such adjustments and refinements in the late 1320s and early 1330s may well have helped the nobility push their point for trial by peers during the 1340–1 crisis, versions of an idea which can be dated back to Magna Carta, clause 39, if not to pre-Conquest Normandy.[156] A council made up of lay and ecclesiastical peers in the parliament of April 1341 made clear reference back to the wording of this clause:

> The peers of the land are advised that all the peers of the land, officers or otherwise, either by reason of their office or of the things relating to their office, or for any other cause, ought not to be brought into judgement, nor lose their temporalities, lands, tenements, goods or chattels: nor be arrested, imprisoned, outlawed or condemned, and ought not to respond or be judged, except in full parliament, and before the peers where the king takes part. Saving to our lord the king the laws rightly used by due process, and saving the suit of the party.[157]

Excited by the demands of Archbishop Stratford for the right of trial by peers in the face of royal accusations of maladministration of the kingdom during Edward III's absence on the Continent, the judgement, and right, though saving Stratford's skin and reinforcing the position of the king's critics within the parliamentary peerage, was annulled in 1343 when Edward regained control of the political situation.[158] Even so, the concept would survive, and be reinforced by both future appeals to the right, as by William Latimer in 1376,[159] and the statutory definition of the privileges of peers in 1388, which stated that any important cases concerning the peers of the land would only be tried in parliament 'and not by the civil law, nor the common law of the land, [which is] practised in other, lower courts of the realm'[160] – in other words, not by laws most clearly open to influence by the royal will. Even when Henry V was away from parliament, and faced with a conspiracy on the eve of going to France, he himself felt it necessary by this time to convene some sort of peerage council in order to judge the accused. The chronicler John Capgrave, alive at the time of the Southampton Plot (1415) of the earl of Cambridge,

Henry Scrope and Thomas Grey, showed that the proceedings, which came across as quite summary, were still not based on the king's authority alone, but 'condempned be her peres'.[161] Trial by peers was seen as enough of a right by 1450 for the duke of Suffolk to offer to forego it, along with 'submitting himself to the king's "rule and governaunce"', in exchange for a five-year exile rather than a grimmer fate.[162] The premise behind trial by peers further survived throughout the fifteenth century and into the modern period, even coming in theory to include noblewomen by the 1440s.[163] Thus, whether as a safety valve for the noble desire for justice theoretically free from influence by the king, or as a more general statement of the nobility's position at the top of the social hierarchy, trial by peers would remain a popular concept with the highest echelon of society for centuries to come.

But it was not just the developing idea of trial by one's social equals which helped delineate the position of the disgraced noble in our period; there was also, of course, the Statute of Treasons of 1352 and its subsequent reissues and precedental references:

> When a Man doth compass or imagine the Death of our Lord the King, or of our Lady his [Queen] or of their eldest Son and Heir; or if a Man do violate the King's [Companion], or the King's eldest Daughter unmarried, or the Wife of the King's eldest Son and Heir; or if a Man do levy war against our Lord the King in his Realm, or be adherent to the King's Enemies in his Realm, giving to them Aid and Comfort in the Realm or elsewhere, and thereof be [probably] attainted of open Deed by [the People] of their Condition . . . ; And if a Man slea the Chancellor, Treasurer, or the King's Justices of one Bench or the other, Justices in Eyre, or Justices of Assize, and all other Justices assigned to hear and determine, being in their Places, doing their Offices: And it is to be understood, that in the Cases above rehearsed, [that] ought to be judged Treason which extends to our Lord the King, and his Royal Majesty.[164]

Overall, this statute was attempting to set limits to, and consequently shrink, the claims the first three Edwards had made for treasonous activity, and as such would also play its part in the judgements of nobles, both by their peers and by more general royal agency. In particular the treasons' statutes identified what were the most serious transgressions against the king or those holding the crown's power, and as such not only clarified the reasons for any subsequent falls, but also limited the charges of treachery to defined breaches against those holding royal power, rather than any more vague or amorphous accusations. Nonetheless, as we will see, treason legislation in various guises continued to be widely used, adjusted and abused by kings or those acting in their name throughout the later Middle Ages. Most notably, aside from those nobles charged with treason in Richard II's reign through either baronial or royal pressure, discussed below, as well as those who rebelled against

Henry IV in the first half of his reign, both English and Welsh, this statute was used as precedent for the accusations against the Southampton plotters,[165] arguably some of the most dangerous men to the peace of the kingdom. Finally, to close the noose still further around overly problematic nobles, another issue treason legislation came to deal with in the later medieval period was spoken words or writings, and more generally 'plotting', all of which could now also be indictable as high treason: known of as 'constructive treason', and despite some debate among modern historians, it would help cause the downfall of over a dozen men between 1402 and 1461.[166] All this, then, gave more structure to, as well as limitation on, the reasons for (and the ways in which) noblemen accused of the highest crimes were removed from position and power.

Because of these changes to the authority, procedure, definition and delineation of crimes, official falls from grace by nobles in the reigns of Richard II and Henrys IV and V took place for the most part in parliament, though influenced by the will of the king or ruling elite. However, the rise of impeachment by common petition in parliament, more than likely spurred on by this growth of parliamentary justice for nobles, was also crucial to this development. First effectively used in a parliamentary context in 1376 against Edward III's courtiers, but a 'private' legal process dating back to at least the early part of the fourteenth century, impeachment basically meant accusation of crimes and transgressions in parliament by the commonality of the realm rather than by any one member or group of members, which was then brought before the lords for judgement.[167] In other words, not only did this in theory protect any accuser (and their allies and supporters) from later recriminations, but in an era of increasing public awareness if not public pressure, it also showed the all-important fact that any such act was being done on the part of the members of parliament and, by extension, the kingdom as a whole. In the Good Parliament of 1376, when William Latimer and Richard Lyons were impeached, it was by the commonality of the realm,[168] and a similar process was used against Michael de la Pole in 1386.[169] This, however, was a premature heyday for the process of impeachment, its development being halted by the reply of the judges to Richard II's questions concerning royal rights in 1387. Rather, following on from, and for a time replacing, impeachment, there developed the idea of 'appeals' in parliament for treason. Originally used for theft and burglary, this common law process was 'essentially an oral accusation of crime made by someone closely affected'.[170] Adopted for use in parliament in 1387–8 by the 'Appellants' (the duke of Gloucester and the earls of Arundel, Derby, Nottingham and Warwick), in 1397 *against* the Appellants by Richard II's supporters, and more tentatively, in 1397–8,[171] appeals initially provided those in power with a very powerful tool to deal with enemies, either royally backed or otherwise.[172] According to one recent commentator on the issue of appeals, 'in seeking for a lawful method with which to assail the most hated of the royal supporters, and deprived of "impeachment" by the judges' replies to the king at Shrewsbury and Nottingham, the Appellants did not fashion a new weapon but more rightly refurbished an old one'.[173] Thus, for its first brief phase of use, impeachment (and following on from it, appeal – though as noted above this would later be turned against the royal critics in 1397, and would be outlawed by statute in 1399)[174] was for the most part 'quite independent of the Crown, which had no part in the proceedings'.[175] In other words, for a short time towards the end of the fourteenth century, both impeachment and appeal could be used by the Commons (and, in the case of appeal, by the Lords), or by the Commons under royal influence, but the crown was not able to directly use the procedure. Though their importance should not be overplayed,[176] both processes nonetheless showed how individuals could fall through the ill-will of the larger political community as well as that of the monarch.

Finally, by this point, when normal, 'public', due legal procedure was not employed against the nobility, such as when Richard II used the prerogative Court of Chivalry against his enemies, it was noticed and, in 1399, condemned.[177] However, Richard, never one to let justice to his nobles get in the way of his ideas of royal supremacy, not only failed to react to this criticism, but also continued to spur on the development of attainder, a procedure which was to bring together royal and parliamentary power. The last stage in the story of the judicial downfall of nobles lies in the rise of this device – in essence a case of summary judgement, usually the behest of the king though also increasingly through the venue of parliament, and with one of the consequences being that heirs were unable to either inherit or transmit estate rights. According to some, attainders acted in place of impeachment (and presumably appeal in both forms, as a baronial critique and as a royal tool) during the Wars of the Roses.[178] That said, similar actions were also around previously, with some historians dating attainder's origins much further back, at least to the Treason Statute of 1352, if not the statements of record and notoriety of Edward II's reign.[179] More crucial than its legal genesis, however, this procedure had its main political foundations in the wider rearticulation of the royal prerogative in Richard II's reign in the court, the arts and in monarchical theory. Most importantly, though not widely circulated at the time of composition (between 1272 and 1285), a tract entitled the *Prerogativa Regis*, giving a semi-official overview of the royal rights of forfeiture and wardship, was resurrected by Richard II (and later Henry VII) as a justification for fundamental royal rights.[180] Based on this, according to Walker, 'A still more thoroughgoing application of the concerns of the *Prerogativa* occurred in the king's treason legislation in 1398, with its "reversion to Bracton's view of forfeiture as total deprivation of the traitor and his family".'[181] Even the bishop of Exeter's parliamentary sermon on Ezekiel 37:22 'One king shall be king to them all' in the previous September pushed the importance of the royal prerogative, and the dangers of ignoring it.[182] Hence the environment was right, in the royal court at least, for the evolution of attainting as a major political tool. Attainders are discussed again later in this book when the issue of forfeiture is examined,[183] but its importance for the present lies in the fact that, with the development of attainder, royal legalised summary process had now begun to be exercised in parliament, thereby also giving it the authority of public knowledge. Though versions of it were most notably used against the Percies in 1404 for levying war against the king, and again posthumously against the duke of Suffolk in 1450,[184] attainder was most famously and frequently witnessed at the end of our period in the downfalls of the Wars of the Roses, including those of three dukes, one marquis, nine earls, one viscount and eleven barons.[185] Nevertheless, as we have already seen, attainder's fundamental development lies well within our period, and would come to represent the ultimate expression of the potential summary power of the late medieval executive – as exercised by either the king himself or those controlling the throne. Finally, to complicate matters still further when it came to legal processes against falling nobles, by the mid-fifteenth century not only did the venue and authorisation tend to be parliamentary whatever the procedure, but there naturally also developed a certain degree of theoretical tension between the idea of attainder and versions of trial by peers[186] – between, in other words, summary and representative justice for disgraced nobles – a tension which would not be resolved during the remainder of the Middle Ages. It shows the tenacity of this tension that both processes would long outlast our period, and only be taken off the law books in 1870 and 1948 respectively – despite continuing to have the potential to be mutually contradictory over the outcome of any case concerning the nobility.

In sum, the reasons for disgrace were many and varied: however moralistically contemporary chroniclers might view adverse changes of fortune for members of the nobility, in reality they could be the result of the disfavour of the monarch or established nobility, or the criticisms and backbiting of royal intimates – either by members of the royal family, or by favourites. Whatever the reason, for substantial falls from favour to take place, the breaches did tend to be serious throughout our period: treason, perceived betrayal, civil wars, dynastic struggles and, increasingly, the indisposition and/or fall of a king. And not only did the indicators of being out in the cold become more formalised with the growth of record keeping (charter witness lists, parliamentary summons etc.), and various forms of political and social organisations from which one could be excluded more developed (e.g. peerage, Order of the Garter, rather than just more nebulous ideas of court and grace), we have also seen the growth in the use of trial for suspect or disgraced nobles. Though trial by battle – either single joust or, literally, on the battlefield – remained a way throughout our period to decide the fate of those out of favour with the king or ruling regime, there also needed to be a way which did not presuppose demonstrations of military might – after all, the situation was not always right or appropriate for armed force. From judgement by God – either through trial by combat or, lest we forget, by king through an early version of summary justice – we have the gradual development of a more formal, if still somewhat arbitrary, trial and sentencing system for those nobles who fell from grace. This system, though far from uniform and still rather dependent upon the noble and the crime in question, moved the power of judgement over the downfallen noble from the king and his immediate band of supporters alone to a larger forum. That said, trial in parliament or, more particularly, trial by peers and later trial by impeachment and the process of appeal, as prevalent as it would become for disgraced nobles, would also force the king/those in power to find ways to retain control over the trial of the most extraordinary or important of crimes, or those over which they needed to have a clear and decisive say. Hence we not only have the honing and adapting of treason laws after 1352 and the hijacking of the 'appeal' by Richard II in the final years of his reign in dealing with his enemies from the 1386–8 crisis, but also the development of summary justice by attainder, a handy tool for both king and those in power, as well as a good counterbalance to the aforementioned semi-representative judicial processes arising mainly through pressure from those outside the monarchy.

Notes

1 W. Map, *De Nugis Curialium* M.R. James, ed. and trans. (Oxford, 1983), p. 3.

2 J. Fantosme, *Chronicle* R.C. Johnston, ed. and trans. (Oxford, 1981), p. 65.

3 One of the best studies of court and favour, and the spectrum between 'in' and 'out', is still J.C. Holt, *The Northerners: A Study in the Reign of King John* (Oxford, 1961), Chapter 12.

4 For a detailed discussion, see B. Murdoch, *Adam's Grace: Fall and Redemption in Medieval Literature* (Woodbridge, 2000).

5 Augustine, *Confessions* R.S. Pine-Coffin, ed. and trans. (Harmondsworth, 1979), Books 2–8.

6 Gildas, *The Ruin of Britain and Other Works* M. Winterbottom, ed. and trans. (London, 1978), pp. 18–27; Bede, *The Ecclesiastical History of the English People* L. Sherley-Price, ed. and trans. (Harmondsworth, 1990), pp. 61–2.

7 *Alcuin of York: His Life and Letters* S. Allot, ed. and trans. (York, 1987), pp. 36–41.

8   A. Gransden, *Historical Writing in England* (New York and London, 1974–82), i, 333.

9   *Annales Monastici* H.R. Luard, ed. (London, 1864–9), ii, 212.

10 R. Horrox, ed. and trans. *The Black Death* (Manchester, 1994), p. 126.

11 For example, 'Warnyng to be Ware', in R.B. Dobson, ed. *The Peasants' Revolt of 1381* 2nd edn (London, 1983), 357–8.

12 Henry of Huntingdon, *The History of the English People: 1000–1154* D. Greenway, ed. and trans. (Oxford, 2002), p. 104.

13 For examples, see pp. 116, 149–50.

14 E.g. the confiscation of Stephen Segrave's estate for failure to do military service (*CCR 1307–13*, 35), or Irish lands seized from Walter Manny and the earl of Pembroke for similar reasons (*CPR 1370–4*, 89–90).

15 N. Fryde, *The Tyranny and Fall of Edward II 1321–1326* (Cambridge, 1979), pp. 42–9; J.C. Davies, 'The Despenser War in Glamorgan', *TRHS* 3rd Ser. 9 (1915), 21–64.

16 *Vita Edwardi Secundi*, pp. 108–9.

17 J.R. Maddicott, *Thomas of Lancaster* (Oxford, 1970), pp. 261–3.

18 B. Wilkinson, 'The Sherburn Indenture and the Attack on the Despensers, 1321', *EHR* 63 (1948), 1–28; G.L. Haskins, 'The Doncaster Petition, 1321', *EHR* 53 (1938), 478–85; Maddicott, *Thomas of Lancaster*, pp. 279–80; M. Prestwich, 'The Charges Against the Despensers, 1321', *BIHR* 58 (1985), 95–100.

19 See N. Saul, *Richard II* (New Haven and London, 1997), pp. 157–65.

20 *Knighton's Chronicle 1337–1396* G.H. Martin, ed. and trans. (Oxford, 1995), p. 355.

21 R.A. Griffiths, *The Reign of King Henry VI* (Stroud, 1998), pp. 676–86; J. Watts, 'Pole, William de la, First Duke of Suffolk (1396–1450)', *DNB* (Oxford, 2004).

22 *Chroniques de London* G.J. Aungier, ed. (London, 1844), p. 90.

23 J.S. Hamilton, *Piers Gaveston, Earl of Cornwall 1307–1312* (Detroit, 1988), p. 75; *Vita Edwardi Secundi*, pp. 8, 25.

24 Somewhat ironically, de Burgh himself was viewed as a 'new man' by Wendover and Paris. F.J. West, 'Burgh, Hubert de, Earl of Kent (*c.* 1170–1243)', *DNB* (Oxford, 2004); for de Burgh, also see N. Vincent, *Peter Des Roches: An Alien in English Politics 1205–1238* (Cambridge, 1996), Chapter 8.

25 F.A. Cazel, 'Intertwined Careers: Hubert de Burgh and Peter des Roches', *HSJ* 1 (1989), 173–81.

26 D. Carpenter, 'The Fall of Hubert de Burgh', *JBS* 19 (1980), 2.

27 Carpenter, 'Hubert de Burgh', 4–10.

28 *Roger de Wendover Liber Qui Dicitur Flores Historiarum* H.G. Hewlett, ed. (London, 1887), iii, 31–4.

29 *Roger de Wendover Flores*, iii, 33.

30 Watts, 'Pole, William de la', *DNB* (2004).

31 Fryde, *Tyranny*, pp. 108ff.

32 M. Prestwich, 'Turberville, Sir Thomas de (d. 1295)', *DNB* (Oxford, 2004). For the treason debate, see Chapter 3.

33 *Chronica Buriensis 1212–1301* A. Gransden, ed. and trans. (London, 1964), p. 128.

34 J.G. Edwards, 'The Treason of Thomas Turberville', in R.W. Hunt, W.A. Paintin and R.W. Southern, eds. *Studies in Medieval History* (Oxford, 1948), 296–309.

35 *Annales Monastici*, iii, 399.

36 CCR *1318–23*, 525, 526.

37 H. Summerson, 'Harclay, Andrew, Earl of Carlisle (*c.* 1270–1323)', *DNB* (Oxford, 2004).

38 J.E. Powell and K. Wallis, *The House of Lords in the Middle Ages* (London, 1968), p. 296.

39 The *Brut*, as in M.H. Keen, 'Treason Trials Under the Law of Arms', *TRHS* 5th Ser. 12 (1962), 89.

40 *The Chronicle of Lanercost 1272–1346* H.E. Maxwell, ed. and trans. (Glasgow, 1913), p. 234.

41 C.W. Hollister, *Henry I* (New Haven and London, 2001), pp. 335–9; K.B. McFarlane, *The Nobility of Later Medieval England* (Oxford, 1973), pp. 252–3; W.M. Ormrod, 'Edward III and his Family', *JBS* 26 (1987), 398–442.

42 For Robert's later years, see C.W. David, *Robert Curthose, Duke of Normandy* (Cambridge, Mass., 1920), pp. 177–89.

43 F. Barlow, *William Rufus* (Berkeley, 1983), Chapter 6.

44 *Historical Works of Giraldus Cambrensis* T. Forester, ed. and trans.; revised by T. Wright (London, 1887), p. 164.

45 *Gesta Regis Henrici Secundi Benedicti Abbatis* W. Stubbs ed. (London, 1965), i, 42–3.

46 See also Conclusion.

47 For Edward II's fall, see Fryde, *Tyranny*, Chapters 13 and 14; C. Valente, 'The Deposition and Abdication of Edward II', *EHR* 113 (1998), 852–81.

48 For detailed discussion, see A. Goodman, *The Loyal Conspiracy: The Lords Appellant Under Richard II* (London, 1971); G.L. Harriss, *Shaping the Realm: England 1360–1461* (Oxford, 2005), pp. 451–68.

49 For background, see Saul, *Richard II*, Chapter 16.

50 See C. Shenton, 'Edward III and the Coup of 1330', in J.S. Bothwell, ed. *The Age of Edward III* (Woodbridge, 2001), 13–35.

51 See G.A. Holmes, *The Good Parliament* (Oxford, 1975), Chapter 6.

52 *Gesta Regis Henrici Secundi*, i, 294.

53 Summerson, 'Harclay, Andrew', *DNB* (2004).

54 At least going from witness lists. S.L. Waugh, 'Edmund, First Earl of Kent (1301–1330)', *DNB* (Oxford, 2004).

55 Fryde, *Tyranny*, pp. 224–5; *Chronicle of Lanercost*, pp. 264–6.

56 See R.A.K. Mott, 'Richard II and the Crisis of July, 1397', in I. Wood and G.A. Loud, eds. *Church and Chronicle in the Middle Ages* (London, 1991), 165–77.

57 *The Great Red Book of Bristol* E.W.W. Veale, ed. (Bristol, 1953), IV, 71.

58 For problems with government records, see M.T. Clanchy, *From Memory to Written Record* 2nd edn (Oxford, 1993), p. 183.

59 J.A. Green, *The Aristocracy of Norman England* (Cambridge, 1997), p. 256.

60 M. Paris, *Chronica Majora* H.R. Luard, ed. (London, 1964), v, 289–90.

61 Paris, *Chronica Majora*, v, 290.

62 Though Lanfranc was also in charge of the kingdom while William I was in Normandy. D.C. Douglas, *William the Conqueror* (London, 1964), p. 232.

63 *The Letters of Lanfranc, Archbishop of Canterbury* H. Clover and M. Gibson, ed. and trans. (Oxford, 1979), pp. 119–21.

64 *Letters of Lanfranc*, pp. 120–1; see also CP vi, 449–50 footnote i.

65 *Gesta Henrici Quinci* F. Taylor and J.S. Roskell, ed. and trans. (Oxford, 1975), p. 5; C.T. Allmand, *Henry V* (Berkeley, 1992), pp. 295–6.

66 J.A.R. Pimlott, *The Englishman's Christmas: A Social History* (Hassocks, Sussex, 1978), p. 29.

67 Horrox, 'Caterpillars', 6.

68 Hollister, *Henry I*, p. 503; for similar use of charter witness material, see R. Heiser, 'The Royal *Familiares* of King Richard I', *MP* 10 (1989), 30–5.

69 J.S. Hamilton, 'Charter Witness Lists for the Reign of Edward II', in N. Saul, ed. *Fourteenth Century England I* (Woodbridge, 2000), 14–15.

70 C. Given-Wilson, *The English Nobility in the Late Middle Ages: The Fourteenth Century Political Community* (London, 1987), pp. 35–42; C. Given-Wilson, 'Royal Charter Witness Lists, 1327–99', *MP* 12 (1991), 64, 66.

71 E.g. A. Tuck, *Crown and Nobility 1272–1461* (London, 1985), pp. 103–5; W.M. Ormrod, *The Reign of Edward III: Crown and Political Society in England 1327–1377* (New Haven and London, 1990), p. 59.

72 Ormrod, *Edward III*, p. 105; for lack of annuity fulfilment and other grants, see J.S. Bothwell, 'Royal Endowment of Peerage Creations in the Reign of Edward III' (University of St Andrews PhD, 1996), appendices 2–5.

73 B.W. Holden, 'The Balance of Patronage: King John and the Earl of Salisbury', *HSJ* 8 (1996), 89.

74 *Royal and Other Historical Letters Illustrative of the Reign of Henry III* W.W. Shirley, ed. (London, 1862), i, 417.

75 C. Given-Wilson, 'Fitzalan, Richard (III), Fourth Earl of Arundel and Ninth Earl of Surrey (1346–1397)', *DNB* (Oxford, 2004).

76 Johannis de Trokelowe et Henrici de Blaneforde, *Chronica et Annales* H.T. Riley, ed. (London, 1866), p. 424.

77 Given-Wilson, 'Fitzalan, Richard (III)', *DNB* (2004).

78 J.R. Maddicott, *Simon de Montfort* (Cambridge, 1997), pp. 23–6; Carpenter paints Henry as initially pushing for the marriage, rushing 'through the wedding in secret in his own private chapel in Westminster palace'. D. Carpenter, *The Reign of Henry III* (London, 1996), pp. 202–3.

79 Paris, *Chronica Majora*, iii, 566–7.

80 *CCharR* 1226–57, 164–5.

81 Carpenter, 'Hubert de Burgh', 10.

82 *CCharR* 1327–41, 3–4.

83 A. Rogers, 'Parliamentary Appeals of Treason in the Reign of Richard II', *American Journal of Legal History* 8 (1964), 95.

84 For a discussion concerning household size, see C.M. Woolgar, *The Great Household in Late Medieval England* (New Haven and London, 1999), pp. 9–15.

85 See D. Crouch, *The Image of Aristocracy* (London, 1992), pp. 247–51; K. Mertes, *The English Noble Household 1250–1600: Good Governance and Political Rule*

(Oxford, 1988), pp. 102–4; for the potential impact of abusing nobles in public, see pp. 68–9.

86 Summerson, 'Harclay, Andrew', *DNB* (2004).

87 In de Manny's case, the king showed his particular pique by granting the office to the royal cook. *CPR 1354–8*, 147, 325; *CCR 1354–60*, 119–20.

88 C255/3/7/1; for similar announcements C255/3/7/2–22; for the earl of Arundel's various crimes C255/3/7/22–39.

89 C255/3/8/17: clear evidence on the obverse of this and similar writs that this was done. Similar warrants for proclamations for Richard II's reign: C255/3/7/2–38.

90 C255/16/1/11A.

91 See pp. 151–3.

92 *CCR 1385–9*, 478–9.

93 C49/30/14 33 Henry VI; *RP* v, 332.

94 F.M. Powicke, *King Henry III and the Lord Edward: The Community of the Realm in the Thirteenth Century* (Oxford, 1947), pp. 128–9.

95 *CPR 1232–47*, 26.

96 C255/16/1/12.

97 C255/16/1/12.

98 C255/3/1.

99 Including Edmund Bereford, Thomas and Maurice Berkeley, William Montagu and the abbot of Malmesbury. *CPR 1334–8*, 88, 89, 111.

100 SC8/5/221; SC8/91/4502; SC8/112/5580; SC8/119/5943; as well as those Giffard held lands of, such as the bishop of Worcester (SC8/150/7482), and those holding lands of Giffard's allies (e.g. SC8/136/6768).

101 Allmand, *Henry V*, p. 295.

102 C. Tyerman, *Who's Who in Early Medieval England* (London, 1996), p. 20. For Lanfranc's involvement, see pp. 26, 131.

103 *CP* vi, 639; C.P. Lewis, 'Waltheof, Earl of Northumbria (*c.* 1050–1076)', *DNB* (Oxford, 2004).

104 Barlow, *William Rufus*, p. 85.

105 *Ecclesiastical History of Orderic Vitalis*, vi, 21; C.W. Hollister, 'The Campaign of 1102 against Robert of Bellême', in C. Harper-Bill, C.J. Holdsworth and J.L. Nelson, eds. *Studies in Medieval History Presented to R. Allen Brown* (Woodbridge, 1989), 193–202.

106 *Ecclesiastical History of Orderic Vitalis*, vi, 179; Hollister, *Henry I*, pp. 226–7.

107 See Powell and Wallis, *House of Lords*, pp. 118–19.

108 See pp. 41–2.

109 From Powell and Wallis, *House of Lords*, p. 118.

110 J.H. Langbein, *Torture and the Law of Proof* (Chicago, 1977), p. 9; J.H. Baker, *An Introduction to English Legal History* 4th edn (London, 2002), pp. 72–6.

111 *Gesta Stephani* K.R. Potter, ed. and trans. (Oxford, 1976), p. 197.

112 R.V. Turner, *King John* (London, 1994), pp. 197–8, 220–1.

113 Vincent, *Peter Des Roches*, pp. 311–20.

114 Florence of Worcester, *Monachi Chronicon ex Chronicis* B. Thorpe, ed. (New York, 1964), ii, 278–9.

115 The speed at which Turberville was tried also indicates a lack of council and deliberation. According to Prestwich he was arrested on 24 September, and was tried 'promptly' on 8 October. Prestwich, 'Turberville, Thomas de', *DNB* (2004).

116 Saul, *Richard II*, p. 379.

117 See below, pp. 44–5, 103.

118 D. Crouch, 'Breteuil, Robert de, Third Earl of Leicester (*c.* 1130–1190)', *DNB* (Oxford, 2004).

119 J.M.W. Bean, 'Percy, Henry, First Earl of Northumberland (1341–1408)', *DNB* (Oxford, 2004).

120 *Vita Edwardi Secundi*, p. 125.

121 J. Froissart, *Chronicles* G. Brereton, ed. and trans. (Harmondsworth, 1978), pp. 323–4.

122 On this, see D.S. Bachrach, *Religion and the Conduct of War c. 300–c. 1215* (Woodbridge, 2003), pp. 43–62, 152–64.

123 Though often as much for propaganda as for religious purposes. D.W. Burton, 'Requests for Prayers and Royal Propaganda under Edward I', in P.R. Coss and S.D. Lloyd, eds. *Thirteenth Century England III* (Woodbridge, 1991), 25–35; A.K. McHardy, 'Some Reflections on Edward III's Use of Propaganda', in Bothwell, ed. *Age of Edward III*, 171–92.

124 *Henry V*, Act iv, Scene viii; on the importance of post-combat rites in an earlier period, see Bachrach, *Conduct of War*, pp. 41–3.

125 R. Bartlett, *Trial by Fire and Water: The Medieval Judicial Ordeal* (Oxford, 1986), p. 106.

126 The next example initially from Bartlett, *Trial by Fire*, p. 107.

127 E. Amt, 'Essex, Henry of (*d.* after 1163)', *DNB* (Oxford, 2004).

128 Though he still lost the Irish justiciarship probably as a result. Also see CP xii: 2, pp. 281–2; on this case also see M. Prestwich, *Edward I* (New Haven and London, 1997), p. 353.

129 G.D. Squibb, *The High Court of Chivalry: A Study of Civil Law in England* (Oxford, 1997), pp. 22–4; for the late thirteenth-century legal compilation known as 'Britton' on the procedure surrounding trial by battle in detail, see *Britton* F.M. Nichols, ed. and trans. (Washington, 1901), pp. 88–91.

130 Squibb, *Court of Chivalry*, p. 23.

131 Froissart, *Chronicles*, p. 436.

132 Bartlett, *Trial by Fire*, pp. 106–8.

133 G.A. Holmes, 'Judgement on the Younger Despenser, 1326', *EHR* 70 (1955), 261.

134 W.M. Ormrod, *Political Life in Medieval England 1300–1450* (Basingstoke, 1995), p. 76.

135 G.L. Harriss, 'The Formation of Parliament, 1272–1377', in R.G. Davies and J.H. Denton, eds. *The English Parliament in the Middle Ages* (Manchester, 1999), 44.

136 A. Harding, *The Law Courts of Medieval England* (London, 1973), p. 82.

137 L.W. Vernon Harcourt, *His Grace the Steward and Trial of Peers* (London, 1907), pp. 335ff.; for 'trial by peers' itself, see also below.

138 *Vita Edwardi Secundi*, p. 114; also SR i, 181–4; for another account of 1321, see N. Pronay and J. Taylor, eds. and trans. *Parliamentary Texts of the Later Middle Ages* (Oxford, 1980), pp. 155–73.

139 Trokelowe, *Chronica*, pp. 112–24.

140 J.R. Maddicott, 'Thomas of Lancaster, Second Earl of Lancaster, Second Earl of Leicester, and Earl of Lincoln (*c.* 1278–1322)', *DNB* (Oxford, 2004).

141 Though as Maddicott points out, the real deciding factors were the king and the Despensers. Maddicott, *Thomas of Lancaster*, p. 312.

142 T.F.T. Plucknett, *Studies in English Legal History* (London, 1983), pp. 542–3; e.g. John Giffard's trial: R.F. Butler, 'Last of the Brimpsfield Giffards and the Rising of 1321–2', *Transactions of the Bristol and Gloucestershire Archaeological Society* 76 (1958 for 1957), 88ff.

143 Vernon Harcourt, *Trial of Peers*, p. 299; also J.N. Langston, 'The Giffards of Brimpsfield', *Transactions of the Bristol and Gloucestershire Archaeological Society* 65 (1946–7), 126, who includes John Giffard of Brimpsfield in similar treatment.

144 Plucknett, *Legal History*, pp. 542–3.

145 *Literae Cantuarienses* J. Brigstocke Sheppard, ed. (London, 1889), iii, 413.

146 J. Taylor, 'The Judgment on Hugh Despenser, the Younger', *Medievalia et Humanistica* 12 (1958), 72.

147 Bellamy, *Treason*, p. 51.

148 Pronay and Taylor, eds. *Parliamentary Texts*, p. 87.

149 SC8/196/9788 (with aid of PROCAT). Also, according to the document, Edward II had never ridden out with banners unfurled, indicating a state of war, and so the justice of the realm was still open to all.

150 SC8/50/2500; CIM 1307–49, 265–6.

151 RP ii, 57; though there are a series of questions about Berkeley's alibi (Plucknett, *Legal History*, p. 546); also see W.J. Smith, 'The Rise of the Berkeleys: An Account of the Berkeleys of Berkeley Castle 1243–1361', *Transactions of the Bristol and Gloucestershire Archaeological Society* 70 (1952 for 1951), 77.

152 RP ii, 52–3.

153 *Chronicon Galfridi le Baker de Swynbroke* E.M. Thompson, ed. (Oxford, 1889), p. 47.

154 Plucknett, *Legal History*, pp. 549–52.

155 Plucknett, *Legal History*, p. 552.

156 Magna Carta, clause 39; C.R. Lovell, 'The Trial of Peers in Great Britain', *AHR* 55 (1949–50), 69–70; more generally, see A.L. Brown, *The Governance of Late Medieval England 1272–1461* (London, 1989), p. 180 footnote. In France in the first half of the fourteenth century there were also noises being made about 'trial by peers', though as Cuttler points out, 'the hallowed process of trial by peers thus never really existed in a pure form in later medieval France', the king always having a substantial part in the proceedings. S.H. Cuttler, *The Law of Treason and Treason Trials in Later Medieval France* (Cambridge, 2003), p. 114.

157 *RP* ii, 127. Magna Carta, clause 39 (all Magna Carta clause translations from British Library website): 'No free man shall be seized or imprisoned, or stripped of his rights or possessions, or outlawed or exiled, or deprived of his standing in any other way, nor will we proceed with force against him, or send others to do so, except by the lawful judgment of his equals or by the law of the land.'

158 Ormrod, *Edward III*, pp. 14–17.

159 T.F. Tout, *Chapters in the Administrative History of Mediaeval England: the Wardrobe, the Chamber and the Small Seals* (Manchester, 1928), iii, 301.

160 *RP* iii, 244.

161 J. Capgrave, *The Chronicle of England* F.C. Hingeston, ed. (London, 1858), p. 309; also see Allmand, *Henry V*, pp. 76–7.

162 Watts, 'Pole, William de la', *DNB* (2004).

163 *RP* v, 56.

164 *SR* i, 319–20; extensions of the treason laws: E.C. Lodge and G.A. Thornton, eds. *English Constitutional Documents 1307–1485* (Cambridge, 1935), pp. 23, 26–7; on the 1352 statute, see Bellamy, *Treason*, Chapter 4.

165 Allmand, *Henry V*, p. 329.

166 R.B. Manning, 'The Origins of the Doctrine of Sedition', *Albion* 12 (1980), 103–4; most recently on treason by word, see E.K. Harris, 'Censoring Disobedient Subjects: Narratives of Treason and Royal Authority in Fifteenth-Century England', in D. Biggs, S.D. Michalove and C. Reeves, eds. *Reputation and Representation in Fifteenth-Century Europe* (Leiden, 2004), 213–20.

167 See Plucknett, *Legal History*, pp. 153–64; T.F.T. Plucknett, *A Concise History of the Common Law* 5th edn (Boston, 1956), p. 204.

168 For the Good Parliament impeachments, see Holmes, *Good Parliament*, Chapter 5.

169 Plucknett, *Legal History*, pp. 165–7; J.S. Roskell, *The Impeachment of Michael de la Pole, Earl of Suffolk* (Manchester, 1984).

170 Baker, *Legal History*, p. 503.

171 Rogers, 'Parliamentary Appeals', 95.

172 Plucknett, *Legal History*, pp. 145–6.

173 J.G. Bellamy, 'Appeal and Impeachment in the Good Parliament', *BIHR* 39 (1966), 45.

174 Rogers, 'Parliamentary Appeals', 96.

175 Plucknett, *Common Law*, p. 204.

176 For impeachment, see A. Musson and W.M. Ormrod, *The Evolution of English Justice: Law, Politics and Society in the Fourteenth Century* (Basingstoke, 1999), pp. 27–8.

177 Ormrod, *Political Life*, p. 76.

178 Potter, H. *Potter's Historical Introduction to English Law and its Institutions* 4th edn (London, 1958), pp. 180–1.

179 Ross, 'Forfeiture for Treason', 574–5; Bellamy, *Treason*, Chapter 7; or possibly further back, into Edward II's reign. Vernon Harcourt, *Trial of Peers*, pp. 388–9 footnote 3. For the relationship between impeachments, appeals and attainders, see Plucknett, *Legal History*, pp. 145–58.

180 *Prerogativa Regis* S.E. Thorne, ed. (New Haven, 1949), p. xl; F.W. Maitland, 'The Praerogativa Regis', *EHR* 6 (1891), 67–72; S. Walker, 'Richard II's Views on Kingship', in Archer and Walker, eds. *Rulers and Ruled*, 54–5; Prestwich, *Edward I*, p. 269.
181 Walker, 'Richard II's Views', 55.
182 J. Scattergood, 'Social and Political Issues in Chaucer: An Approach to *Lak of Stedfastnesse*', in J. Scattergood, *Reading the Past: Essays on Medieval and Renaissance Literature* (Dublin, 1996), 197–8; more generally on literature and Richard II's ideas of kingship, see L. Staley, *Languages of Power in the Age of Richard II* (Philadelphia, 2005), esp. Chapters 2 and 3.
183 See Chapter 3. Both impeachment and attainder were seen by Plucknett as being part of the developing monopoly of parliament over state trials. Plucknett, *Legal History*, p. 553.
184 Bellamy, *Treason*, pp. 185–8.
185 For Henry VI, Edward IV and Richard III's reigns. This group of nobles also included eleven royals. J.R. Lander, *Crown and Nobility 1450–1509* (Montreal, 1976), Appendix C.
186 See Vernon Harcourt, *Trial of Peers*, pp. 388–99.

At His Majesty's pleasure:
punishment, execution
and degradation of wayward nobles

Be ye afraid of the sword: for wrath *bringeth* the punishments of the sword, that
ye may know *there is* a judgment. (Job 19:29 italic in original)

For the medieval nobility, royal punishment for criminal or otherwise unacceptable behaviour tended to be punitive (and in some cases, retributive), preven-
tative in so far as an imprisoned or executed person could no longer cause
problems for the king's government (and so in turn could also serve as a deter-
rent for the future) and rehabilitative in no discernible manner whatsoever.[1]
The main point was to show royal disapproval or anger with an individual's
conduct, and to stop him or her from doing it again. Once judgement of whatever variety, and through whatever means, had been passed, however, there
was a wide spectrum of options open to the monarch and his government,
ranging from fines to hanging and beheading. All have their histories, and
procedures, as we will see in this chapter; but whatever the options available,
some indication that royal power was being exercised, even just in the form
of relatively minor monetary exaction, was crucial. Not only was it part of
the monarch's duty (or those in power) to act as lawgiver and judge, but also,
if the king wished royal power to be preserved if not enhanced, either he
or his government had to be perceived to be exercising it, especially against
problematic nobles. Even the most incompetent and/or insensitive of kings
realised this and tried to act accordingly. As the king must be judge, so too
ultimately must he be enforcer and jailor.

Fines and agreement to bonds

That said, the payment of a monetary fine, large or small, was often the
first level of punishment for a disgraced individual for most of our period.
Financial penalties for ignoring the wishes of the king or his government have
a continual history in England from at least the time of King Ine, mainly handed

down directly by the monarch or his council in the case of the realm's nobility. Fines instead of other sorts of punishment were common in the Anglo-
Saxon period, wergilds (along with *wite* (fines paid to royal authority), and
the more general term *bot* for compensation) being the most well known.[2]
Financial recompense on a sliding scale for personal injury paid to the victim
or his family, the wergild dealt with crimes against everyone from the king
to the lowest serf: for instance, the life of an ordinary freeman in seventh-
century Wessex had a wergild of 200 shillings, while a nobleman had one of
1200 shillings.[3] The monarch himself, of course, always had by far the highest wergild, whatever the law code; according to one historian, it was of such
a value 'as to act as safeguard to his life in the face of possible assassination'.[4]
Consequently, later Anglo-Saxon administrators found such fining for
breaches against the king and his family could also be helpful for the royal
treasury, rather than just the enforcement of justice, and began to act accordingly, restating and strengthening rights to fine when and where necessary.[5]
Nevertheless, once Norman influence began to take hold, though remaining
important, fines were initially superseded by other forms of penalty, at least
when serious transgressions by the upper nobility were involved. Monetary
exactions, though often associated with lesser crimes,[6] were not usually the
primary form of punishment for erring nobles during the later eleventh and
twelfth centuries; if anything, imprisonment, loss of lands and goods, mutilation and, though only on the odd occasion in this period, execution, took
precedence. When the 1075 rebels were brought to justice, we have little
evidence of fines, only physical punishment and property seizure; similarly,
those individuals connected with Robert Curthose and the problems of
the early years of Henry I's reign tended to be punished physically and with
estate confiscation rather than fines *per se*. Even during the Anarchy and the
rebellions of Henry's sons, there was infrequent use of fines against nobles –
perhaps, in part, as a result of the breakdown of central authority though
also more than likely because the situation turned violent quickly enough to
preclude monetary exaction by the government.[7]

   This, however, began to change in the early thirteenth century, at least in
part because of the growing ability of the royal administration to record fines
as much as the determination of the king's government to exact them. As Magna
Carta was later to try to rectify,[8] nobles and knights in particular often paid
inordinately large sums for the sake of soothing the king's anger throughout
John's reign: for instance, Thomas de St Valery offered to pay 1000 marks
for the king's goodwill in 1209, probably the result of his in-law relationship
with the disgraced baron William de Braose.[9] Likewise, a number of the 1215–17
barons who made their peace with royal authority, often did so through the
use of fines, as when Roger de Leyburn was taken prisoner at Rochester Castle

in 1215, paying a fine of 250 marks to regain his freedom.[10] After John's death and the Peace of Kingston (1217), a series of generally quite large fines and ransoms were imposed or reimposed upon the remaining rebels – including those for the son of the earl of Norfolk and sixteen prisoners held by Peter de Mauley in Corfe Castle.[11] And though for many decades Henry III had little call to use such monetary exactions against his most important subjects, once faced with the continued revolt of a large section of the defeated nobility after Evesham (1265) against a policy of total forfeiture, the attitude of the royal government went through a sea change.[12] According to the clauses of the *Dictum of Kenilworth*, there was to be a stepped series of fines dependent on the wealth of the rebel involved, his part in the revolt and, to a degree at least, how much the royal administration wanted his lands.[13] By the later thirteenth century the royal government was expecting most penalties of imprisonment – for all but the most serious of crimes – eventually to be commuted to a fine.[14] As in the *Dictum* itself, future fining would now often be dependent as much on the prisoner's economic and social status as the crime involved, the higher amounts being paid off in instalments at the exchequer, sometimes making up a significant portion of the annual royal income. For example, after Boroughbridge (1322), John de Botetourt, a fairly important member of the parliamentary peerage, was fined £1000, and Bewes de Knovill, a knight never individually summoned to parliament, was forced to pay a 1000 mark fine[15] – showing their different levels in the social hierarchy, as well as their culpability, at the time. However, not all fining of nobles was connected with high crimes: such exactions could be more for insubordinate, rather than treasonous, activities. In 1250, Walter de Clifford, a Marcher baron, suffered a financial penalty for abusing a royal messenger, forcing him to eat the letters which he had delivered, complete with wax seal.[16] For this, Clifford 'did not dare to stand trial' but submitted to royal mercy, punished by imprisonment and 'all the money he had or could have, namely one thousand marks' – though he was allowed to return home after entering into a financial bond for this amount. Many fines were indeed sureties to ensure future good behaviour, rather than meaning to be fulfilled immediately, if ever. Henry VII famously was said to have used financial bonds to control his peerage,[17] but there were also many earlier cases, perhaps some of the most important being connected with those individuals involved in the events of the 1320s[18] – for instance, thousands of pounds in bonds which William Montagu and Hugh Audley had been forced to undertake under pressure from the Despensers and the king's government.[19]

Whatever the reason, such fines could often be for substantial amounts, especially by the later Middle Ages, enough to curtail expenditure and limit the ability of an individual to sustain the lifestyle of a member of the nobility, an all-important issue.[20] And, though rarely enough to ruin a family, there was the odd, very telling, exception – most notably, the Ferrers earl of Derby's fine as set out by the *Dictum of Kenilworth*. Indeed, in part the result of the escape of Prince Edward from Robert's custody during the Barons' Wars, but also going back to conflicting claims over the lordship of Peveril, the growing animosity between Ferrers and the heir to the throne was to colour Ferrers's treatment in the postwar settlement.[21] Consequently, his fine was one of the highest of the *Dictum*, so high as to be unpayable by the earl or his family, and the estate itself ended up going to Henry III's younger son, Edmund – despite many later attempts by Ferrers and his descendants to get it back.[22] As fining at so unpayable a level was undoubtedly deliberate, it shows how such penalties were not always meant simply as a harsh or less harsh slap on the wrist, and instead aimed at permanently harming the noble in question. Taking away large amounts of money, though not as ultimately important as lands or lives, was still a good way to hit a noble where it hurt, limit his ability to act 'as a noble' and remind him that fortune could be lost as well as won.

Physical punishment and execution

> For two centuries after the Conquest, the frank, open rebellions of the great folk were treated with a clemency which, when we look back to it through intervening ages of blood, seems wonderful.[23]

Following on from monetary penalties, though often connected with them, was the issue of bodily punishment for nobles.[24] Execution had been used as the ultimate penalty for treason, murder and other serious crimes in the later Anglo-Saxon period – connected most likely with the revival of the Roman concept of *majestas* to deal with the most serious crimes against royal authority:[25]

> There were two distinct offenses against *majestas* – *perduellio*, or levying war against the Roman people, giving aid and comfort to their enemies, or inciting mutiny in their armies, and *laesa majestas*, which was much broader and included every act by which the public authority was resisted or usurped, or which denigrated from or showed disrespect to the authority of the state, or the state's personification, the emperor.[26]

These – as well as other crimes often deemed too serious for punishment by confiscation, fines or use of the wergild alone – helped to give a legal basis for prosecution of the most serious cases.[27] For instance, fighting in the king's household meant not only forfeiture of all possessions, but also possibly one's life as well: as the king's institutional importance and wergild, as that of his family, was much higher than members of the nobility, any crimes connected

with him, or which infringed his rights, had more severe, long-lasting penalties attached to them.[28] By the time of Alfred (871–99), execution was
the most serious of a fairly standard set of punishments for infringements
on royal rights,[29] including plotting against the king's life, violation of the
king's burgh, and forcible entry into the king's residence.[30] After the Norman
Conquest, however, the attitude towards capital punishment appears to have
shifted. Though the clause of the so-called 'Laws of William the Conqueror'
abolishing the death penalty may have had no official status – the authentic-
ity of the laws as a unified set of regal enactments is open to question[31] –
nonetheless such punishment quickly went into decline for members of the
nobility after 1066. Some historians have gone so far as to argue that the Norman
Conquest itself ultimately helped usher in a new, more merciful treatment of
rebellious nobles by monarchs.[32] Whatever the case, faced with the attempted
rebellion in 1075 of the earls of Hereford, Norfolk, Huntingdon and their
followers, the last serious rebellion by Anglo-Saxon nobles during his reign,
William I ordered the execution only of the latter.[33] Throughout the rest of
his reign, though William plundered rebel estates, especially after 1075, he
generally avoided taking the lives of members of the nobility.[34] And this trend
continued into his sons' reigns and beyond. William II and Henry I, though
not particularly merciful kings in other ways, only infrequently used capital
punishment against nobles who had gone against their wishes. As Strickland
notes, aside from executions while on campaign, the hanging of William of
Eu's steward, William de Alderie, in William Rufus's reign stands in 'virtual
isolation', and even this may have been connected with a plot against the king's
life[35] – unsurprisingly, if this *was* the case, Alderie was also hanged on the
gallows' cross.[36] Thereafter almost no English nobles suffered staged executions, not even during the 1215–17 war or in 1264–5: until Edward II's reign,
nobles (especially of the higher nobility) were imprisoned, and later on in this
period fined, but they were rarely killed as a judicial punishment.[37]

However, there was also another form of physical penalty – corporal punishment, sometimes to the point of loss of life, but not with that as its object
– which was used at times in the Anglo-Norman period, in part perhaps to
help substitute for the more serious financial punishments of the Anglo-Saxon
period. Indeed, the disappearance of Anglo-Saxon wergild and similar penalties with 'marvellous suddenness' in the century after the Conquest,[38] and
the delay of the revival of a robust system of fining until the early thirteenth
century, left the way open for an early flourishing of legalised mutilation. In
fact, in the early high Middle Ages at least, for more serious crimes there can
be said to have developed a system of punitive ranking, albeit loose and changeable, between those transgressions that meant mutilation and/or imprisonment (the latter to be discussed in Chapter 4) and those, though increasingly

rarely for the high Middle Ages at least, which meant execution. Be that as it may, bodily mutilation was initially considered, as Glanvill notes, a form of leniency – as opposed to capital penalties for treason – because the 'punishment of the guilty involves only loss of limbs',[39] as well as still allowing the individual some chance to save his soul. And though the associated replacement of execution by mutilation in the Laws of William the Conqueror can be seen as a little too neat,[40] mutilation did thereafter offer Anglo-Norman kings dire, though not intentionally fatal, ways of punishing rebellious nobles. Sometimes the threat of such punishment was enough. In 1095, William Rufus was said to have gained control of Robert Mowbray's castle of Bamburgh by threatening to put out his eyes unless the castle, held by his wife and steward, was surrendered.[41] The castle unsurprisingly was given up and its steward became an informant on those who had been unfaithful to the king. Nevertheless, the threat could also be acted upon. In one of the most high-profile trials of the reign, Rufus ordered that the above-mentioned William of Eu, having lost a trial by battle with the king's champion, was to be 'deprived of his eyes and his virility' (notably a physical form of the later attainder, cutting out any idea of direct inheritance) – while, aside from his steward, the rest of the nobles involved in the treason plot were only to be confined.[42] However, it is really Henry I's reign that was connected with mutilation,[43] a practice further emphasised in the *Leges Henrici Primi*, a collection of materials which date back to the Anglo-Saxon period, but also showing where Henry's beliefs in punishment at least partly arose.[44] Blinding in particular was used as a form of penalty less serious than execution but greater than imprisonment or any other bodily mutilation, especially during the later Anglo-Norman period. After the subduing of Brionne in Normandy in c. 1124, Henry had the man who had been its castellan blinded,[45] as he did 'his kinsman', the earl of Moretuil.[46] Earlier in his reign this king had William, count of Mortain, blinded while a prisoner in the Tower for breaking his homage.[47] Blinding, as castration, left it difficult for a man to function in a feudal society, a society needing not only heirs but also service in return for property. When it came to 'public' opinion on the matter, though, the tone was accepting: as Hollister notes, 'mutilations under Henry I seem to have been generally condoned and often applauded as appropriate to the customs of war and the sacred duties of the peacekeeping king'.[48] That said, after Henry I's reign, mutilation, as execution, went into decline[49] – disappearance of the wergild or no, this was not seen as the way to punish transgressions by a noble.

The cause of this softening of approach by kings towards those who had fallen out of favour with them – using imprisonment, exile and, later on, a revitalised system of fining, in place of bodily penalties – is far from clear, though many factors probably came into play. There were, of course, relatively obvious reasons for William I's initial lenient treatment: mainly the difficulty, and potential inadvisability, of trying to enforce his punishments against all his numerous enemies in post-Conquest England, but also the fact that he had fought under a papal banner, as would John, putting him under certain restrictions, especially concerning the use of capital punishment.[50] Part of the continued leniency thereafter, however, may also be linked with the onset of the Anarchy: bringing about not only problems with enforcement but perhaps also a desire by the participants not to add torture and execution to the list of dangers for either side (much as the use of chemical weapons was informally avoided during World War II). Part also, doubtless, was to do with the growing security of the nobility with respect to their landed estates, a security which Henry II reinforced, though at least in part inadvertently, by the development of such procedures as *Novel Disseisin* and *Mort D'Ancestor*, and which would make even the most forthright king hesitate before moving towards mutilation and execution as a way of dealing with landowners.[51] More generally, by the time of Magna Carta, the growing power of nobility over-all, and the imprudence of making recriminations too harsh when dealing with this group, doubtless also came into play, as well, of course, the visible weakness of some of the kings of the period, most notably Stephen, John and Henry III: even Richard's continual absence from the kingdom, and Henry II's often still precarious position after the Anarchy, made it inad-visable to sentence nobles to irreversible punishments. And a final part of the growing leniency towards rebel nobles in the high Middle Ages may also, when it came to bodily punishment at least, have been connected with the development of *diffidatio* – the right to rebel against the king when all other means failed[52] – a right which would make monarchs all the more cautious when it came to the legality of the execution of such opponents. Though Gillingham sees the merciful treatment of nobles as coming first, followed on by the *diffidatio* (which he dated back to at least the late 1130s),[53] either way each would have played off the other, and no doubt helped to develop a more lenient, responsive situation. Some medieval commentators and modern historians can even talk of medieval 'theories' of resistance, and the idea that the nobility had both a right and a duty to oppose an unjust king, by violence if necessary, was fairly common currency throughout the period.[54]

Whatever the reason, or more likely, mixture of reasons, for this high medieval leniency, in the later thirteenth century the treatment of those who had seriously fallen from grace, along with other types of troublemaker, went through another, more legally defined and structured sea change, one which would in the end prompt a return to an even more violent treatment of the king's enemies. Again, as with the shift from violence to leniency in the high

Middle Ages, why this change happened at this point is open to question. Some view the issue within quite narrow parameters:

> The modern debate over the increasing harshness with which opposition was treated centres round whether the changes occurred because of a new definition of treason under the influence of Roman law, or whether changing political circumstances simply allowed the exaction of the full penalties which had always been potentially there.[55]

But though the issues voiced here are important, this is clearly too restricted and polarised a view to ever give a full sense of the causes of the change. Rather, a number or mixture of other reasons, again, have and should be put forth for so momentous a shift: the brutalising impact of the Barons' Wars of 1264–5 on royal/noble relations; the crisis of law and order in England starting in the later thirteenth century;[56] the need to counteract the growing power of both the nobility, and later the parliamentary peerage, when it started to become clear that a more measured approach might not work; and the increasing contact with the more violent 'Celtic' political worlds, especially with Edward I's renewal of claims of overlordship of the whole of the British Isles.[57] Likewise, there was, of course, the broadening concept of medieval treason, including the increasing irrelevance of the above-mentioned idea of *diffidatio*, as a result of Edward I's legislation.[58] More broadly, Continental factors may also have played a part, including the increasingly permanent perception of the loss of Normandy and the growing lack of need for caution and clemency lest revenge be taken on the other side of the Channel, as well as the weakening power of the Roman Church over national politics (especially concerning execution), most clearly seen after the Babylonian Captivity and the Great Schism, but also possibly dating back to *Clericis Laicos* (1296) and the fall of the Templars. Even the increasing use of the image of the 'body of a tortured God nailed to a cross' for guild and municipal occasions could have had an impact upon more general ideas of the unity and sanctity of the human body.[59] But whatever the cause or, again more likely, causes, the most serious of breaches between those in power and problematic nobles was now being punished with execution, and often execution in the most brutal manner possible.[60]

The theoretical underpinnings for such a policy of execution were already well established by the time they came to be again acted upon. Early on, the *Leges Henrici Primi*, looking back well before Henry I's reign, were quite articulate on those crimes warranting the harshest of penalties, especially those connected with betraying one's lord, whether immediate feudal superior or king:

> If anyone kills his lord, then if in his guilt he is seized, he shall in no manner redeem himself but shall be condemned to scalping or disembowelling or to human

punishment which in the end is so harsh that while enduring the dreadful agonies of his tortures and the miseries of his vile manner of death he may appear to have yielded up his wretched life before in fact he has won an end to his sufferings, and so that he may declare, if it were possible, that he had found more mercy in hell than had been shown to him on earth.[61]

The mid-thirteenth-century jurist Bracton argued for similar punishment for like crimes,[62] and even Thomas Aquinas pushed for the necessity of capital punishment in certain instances, though noted that it only should be exercised by princes, 'who by virtue of their public authority are responsible for the common good'.[63] Nevertheless, from the later thirteenth century, this extreme treatment for the most serious of crimes became fact as well as theory. Not only was execution of rebel nobles to be frequently performed, but it was increasingly connected with bodily mutilation, both of the living and the dead, as it had never been in the high Middle Ages. The Celtic neighbours of England were the first to face the brutality of the change, though they themselves already practised such punishments with a fair degree of regularity.[64] Nonetheless, the execution of Prince David in 1283 is generally accepted to have been a turning point for the English in this regard as in others, with his drawing, hanging, disembowelling (his intestines were also burnt, according to the *Flores Historiarum*)[65] and decapitation.[66] It was this execution, and that of William Wallace in 1305, which marked a milestone in the developing harshness of punishment for serious crimes or transgressions committed by nobles, gentry and others. According again to the *Flores*:

> Wilielmus Waleis, a man without pity, a robber given to godlessness, arson and murder, more toughened in brutality than Herod, more raging in insanity than Nero . . . was condemned to a most cruel but justly deserved death; first, he was drawn through the streets of London by the tails of horses, until he reached a gibbet of remarkable height, especially prepared for him; there he was suspended by a halter; but taken down while yet alive, he was mutilated, his bowels torn out and burned in a fire.[67]

As one modern commentator has it, 'As he had committed many crimes, so he suffered in numerous ways.'[68] The execution of the traitor Thomas de Turberville in the previous decade also emphasised this new brutality: he was the first Englishman of the upper classes, albeit at the lower end, to be so treated in recorded memory. Turberville, after being found guilty of treasonous dealings with the French discussed in the last chapter, was, on the eve of St Denis in 1295, torn apart by horses, and his head sent to be affixed onto the walls of the Tower of London.[69] Extreme torment ending in death, in other words, was no longer simply for the 'lesser peoples' of Britain: it was now thought fit for transgressions by the English upper classes.

This brutalisation of the treatment of disgraced nobles quickly moved upwards and towards the centre by the first quarter of the fourteenth century;[70] in part more than likely owing to the reasons stated above, but also, it has been argued, connected with the 'extremely personal and embittered nature of political controversy in the reign of Edward II'.[71] One of the first marks of this shift was, somewhat oddly, the execution of Gaveston on Blacklow Hill near Warwick in 1312 by the critics of Edward II, which nevertheless seems to have set the precedent for Edward's own treatment of the Contrariants ten years later.[72] Nonetheless, Gaveston's was a relatively tame execution compared to that which would come later, one executioner running him through with a sword and the other cutting of his head.[73] Thereafter, perhaps simply giving like-for-like in terms of the execution itself, after the battle of Boroughbridge in 1322 Edward II had little compunction about ordering the execution of a number of noble rebels[74] – though notably in a much more physically abusive and public manner. For example, Warin de Lisle was captured, declared a traitor and dragged by horses to Pontefract and hanged, as were Lord Clifford and Lord Mowbray at York.[75] Hanging in these instances was a great insult, usually performed on common thieves: higher nobles generally tended to be beheaded, kneeling or standing, either erect or head bowed, some blindfolded with arms bound around their back.[76] Initially, when Thomas, earl of Lancaster, the main thorn in Edward II's side, was captured during Boroughbridge and taken to his own castle 'sitting on a despicable ass, clothed only in a shabby tunic',[77] he *did* face an ignoble death:

> and there, in revenge for the death of Piers de Gaveston (whom the earl had caused to be beheaded), and at the instance of the earl's rivals (especially of Hugh Despenser the younger), without holding a parliament or taking the advice of the majority, caused sentence to be pronounced that he should be drawn, hanged and beheaded.[78]

Nevertheless, while some nobles were hanged after the 1321–2 rising as the greater insult, in other cases those ordering the execution relented to a degree, primarily either in the name of mercy or in an attempt to preserve the mystery of nobility in the midst of a 'blue' bloodbath. Lancaster himself, indeed, was only beheaded despite the above pronouncement:

> But, forasmuch as he was the queen's uncle and the son of the king's uncle, the first two penalties were commuted, so that he was neither drawn nor hanged, only beheaded in like manner as this same Earl Thomas caused Piers de Gaveston to be beheaded.[79]

According to the illumination on the Luttrell Psalter, he faced this 'noble' execution unblindfolded but kneeling at prayer, the executioner using a sword and laying one hand on Thomas's head (see Fig. 6).[80]

6 BL Additional 42130, f. 56: Luttrell Psalter, Thomas, earl of Lancaster
kneels before the executioner; England (East Anglia), c. 1325–35.

Similarly, around the same time, one of his allies, John Giffard, was ordered
to be hanged, drawn and quartered: however, according to one source, when
a tomb connected with the Giffard family was opened in 1853 for some
repairs, 'A stone coffin was found . . . and a skeleton nearly perfect, with the
skull placed on one side of the body, as though the body had been decapitated.'[81] Blood and rank, in other words, might at times win out in even the

most serious of cases. Such favour, however, was generally not evident in the 1320s, though it would be by the end of the century.

Whatever the fate of individual nobles in this period, overall, as J.R.S. Phillips points out, 'It is quite clear that something of a deeply unpleasant nature was developing within English political society, starting early in the reign of Edward II and reaching an extended and bloody climax between 1322 and 1330.'[82] The brutality of later executions rarely again reached these heights – in particular, far fewer nobles were drawn, or more importantly eviscerated while living, in the next tempestuous period of royal/noble relations, that of Richard II and Henry IV – or even for that matter the remaining Lancastrian kings in the Middle Ages. Most notably, both the Appellants themselves and Henry IV were careful how they treated their enemies in 1386–8 and 1399–1400, the first such spate of noble executions since the 1320s, and, aside from the irregular case of John Oldcastle, hanged and burnt for heresy, by the fifteenth century when executions did take place most treasonous or otherwise seriously problematic nobles simply tended to be beheaded.[83] When drawing (though more rarely again evisceration) *was* used in the late Middle Ages, it usually was the result of personal offence to the king, as with the treatment of Henry Lord Scrope, one of the 1415 Southampton plotters. According to the *Gesta Henrici Quinti*, 'And Henry, lord Scrope, the more culpable an enemy because the more intimate a friend, having on account of the infamy of his offence been drawn through the middle of the town to the place of execution, was there decapitated.'[84] Perhaps the development of increasingly honed and public legal instruments for such transgressions – especially attainder, but also sharper rules concerning the forfeiture of entailed and enfeoffed-to-use property – made the physical punishments less necessary as a way to make a point to the public; perhaps, as will be discussed a bit later, the events of the Peasants' Revolt made those in power now hesitate to abuse to excess their compatriots, however hated, within sight of the lower orders. Whatever the case, though in Richard II's reign the earl of Arundel still had to have the special grace of the king to be beheaded rather than hanged, drawn and quartered,[85] by this time the practice of excessive abuse and torment before death was far less common than it had been a couple of generations earlier. Finally not everyone was comfortable with the fierce treatment of fallen nobles, even at the height of such brutality. In 1330, when Edmund, the earl of Kent, was beheaded outside the gates of Winchester Castle, he had to stand there from prime to vespers, as no one was willing to behead him – until someone from the Marshelsea was at long last sent out to dispatch him.[86]

But execution, as indicated, was not just for punishment or political/ personal revenge, it was also for the sake of justice being seen to be done: an important issue, especially in times of monarchical instability or political unrest.

Before the printing press, as Cohen rightly notes, governmental power was often displayed in a visual, theatrical form: 'solemn royal or urban processions, festivals, and, most commonly, the public execution of criminals'.[87] Again, according to Binski, 'just as royal bodily division dramatized the process of salvation, public execution dramatized the reaffirmation of temporal power'.[88] The fact that Thomas de Turberville was taken to judgement surrounded by 'six tormentors dressed as devils', as we will see in greater detail below, though punitive and religious in tone,[89] was also a part of the spectacle and pageant of royal power,[90] especially when showing its control over the nobility. Though not as pointed, the last hours of the ill-fated earl of Arundel in 1397 have a similar feel:

> the erl was lad fro the place of his jugement, and his handis bounde behynde him, thorough the cite of Londoun unto the Tourhille, and there his hed was smyte of. And vj of the lordis that sat on his jugement, riden with him with greete strengthe of men of armes and archiers to se the execucion done aftir thair jugement, for thay dradde that the erl sholde haue be rescued be thaym of Londoun.[91]

In part a necessary security measure, this show of military strength was also a clear manifestation of renewed royal control over the political community of the realm. Further along these lines, Edward II, for the sake of subduing the followers of disgraced nobles, is said to have 'adopted the novel expedient of despatching his victims for execution to the areas where they held lordship',[92] a sure way of hammering home the strength of royal power. According to the *Lanercost Chronicle*, after Boroughbridge in 1322, Bartholomew de Badlesmere, Henry Tyes and other nobles were executed in their own districts 'for their greater disgrace',[93] as well as to let the locals know in a very graphic manner that their old allegiances were no more. During the revolution of 1326, Hugh Despenser the younger was taken to Hereford, the nearest large town to the site of his aggressive territorial aggrandisement in the early 1320s,[94] tried and condemned to death for treason, the event being made as public as possible: 'First, he was dragged on a hurdle, to the sound of horns and trumpets, through all the streets of Hereford, until he reached the main square of the town, where the people had gathered. There he was bound to a long ladder, so that everyone could see him. A bonfire had been lit in the square.'[95] (See Fig. 7.) Executions, by this time at least, were for public instruction and edification as much as the punishment for crimes committed, a far cry from the more 'private', and usually less violent and dramatic, downfalls of the high Middle Ages.

However, the point of such spectacles was not just to educate the general populace of the dangers of getting on the wrong side of the king or those

7 Bibliothèque Nationale de France FR 2643, f. 11: Jean Froissart, *Chroniques*, the execution of Hugh Despenser the younger; Belgium, later fifteenth century.

controlling the throne. Public humiliation was also an important aspect,[96] especially when the noble could be shown at his worst in front of his social inferiors and, accordingly, more completely disempowered. Returning to the end of Thomas de Turberville in 1295:

> He came from the Tower, mounted on a poor hack, in a coat of ray, and shod with white shoes, his head being covered with a hood, and his feet tied beneath the horse's belly, and his hands tied before him: and around him were riding six torturers attired in the form of the devil, one of whom held his rein, and the hangman his halter, for the horse which bore him had them both upon it: and in such manner was he led from the Tower through London to Westminster, and was condemned on the dais in the Great Hall there; and Sir Roger Brabazun pronounced judgement upon him, that he should be drawn and hanged.[97]

The Despensers, and Wallace, as we have seen, also faced such humiliation before their deaths: others, such as the earl of Warwick in 1397, thought it better to humiliate themselves to avoid execution. When faced with his sentence, 'like a wretched old woman, he began to weep and sob and wail, declaring that he had indeed, like a traitor, done everything that was alleged in the appeal; and he placed himself entirely at the king's mercy . . . [and] kept on begging for mercy from the king'.[98] Either way, humiliation of one sort or another was often a foregone conclusion. There were, however, dangers in such treatment of nobles for all involved: it was perhaps little coincidence that two of the most important general revolts of the later Middle Ages, the Peasants' Revolt of 1381 and Jack Cade's Rebellion of 1450, came soon after the severe public criticism and abuse of members of the higher echelons of society, if only in parliament – but reports of which had gradually trickled out both to the chroniclers and to the writers and singers of more popular verse.[99] Publicly abusing members of the nobility, whether by deed or word, could then be a double-edged sword, especially when the abuse could be said to be laying bare the whole mystique, and in many cases rationale, of the upper echelons of the social hierarchy to the public gaze. Indeed, outside these two events, the only executions of nobles by the common people in our period – that of the rebels against Henry IV, John Montagu, earl of Salisbury, Thomas Holland, earl of Kent, and Ralph Lord Lumley, by the people of Cirencester – were soon after the deposition of Richard II and the Epiphany Rising of 1400, and despite the efforts of the king's officers to take control of the situation.[100]

Of course, not all noble victims were willing to submit to such abuse in their last hours. One of the most vicious treatments of a disgraced noble was that visited on Andrew de Harcla, earl of Carlisle. In February 1323, suspected of treasonous dealings with the Scots, Harcla was tried in Knaresborough, found guilty and condemned to execution in the most brutal and degrading manner. The rancour spewed at him by the sentencing judge, presumably at the instance of the king, we have already seen evidence of in the last chapter – but this did not mean that Harcla was willing to demean himself in front of his peers or his lessers in order to mitigate his sentence. According to *Lanercost*:

> And so, with most steadfast countenance and bold spirit, as it seems to the bystanders, he went to suffer all these pains, and, while being drawn through the town, he gazed upon the heavens, with hands clasped and held aloft and likewise his eyes directed on high. Then under the gallows, whole in body, strong and fiery in spirit and powerful in speech, he explained to all men the purpose he had in making the aforesaid convention with the Scots, and so yielded himself to undergo the aforesaid punishment.[101]

When facing his end, the earl was reported to have said: 'Ye have divided my carcase according to your pleasure, and I commend my soul to God.' And, if going a bit out of our subject to problematic churchmen, according to the poem *On the Death of Archbishop Scrope* (1405): 'When he was brought vnto the hyll, he held hym both mylde and styll; he toke his deth with full gode wyll'; he was even said to have forgiven his executioner, and asked for five axe-strokes for the five wounds the Lord had suffered for man.[102] Despite the obvious seriousness of the situation, a few nobles could even joke, and face death with a degree of bravery unknown to some of their compatriots. According to Capgrave, at the earl of Arundel's execution in 1397: 'Whan he cam to the place there he schuld deye he chaunged no chere, but took the swerd fro him that schuld smyte, and felt if it were scharp, and seyde, "It is scharp inow; do thi ded. I forgive the my death." '[103] Oldcastle's death in 1417, as both a heretic and perceived traitor, was similarly defiant, claiming that even if Peter and Paul were present, he would not wish to confess to them.[104] Further, though Oldcastle was ordered to be hanged and 'burnt while hanging there', according to one source at least he vowed – tongue presumably firmly in his soon to be singed cheek – that he would win out in the end, with an idea that on the third day he would rise from the ashes, and asked Lord Erpingham, if this did happen, to pardon his followers.[105]

There were also other less formal methods of dispatch for problematic nobles. Most famously, if a bit out of our period, there was George, duke of Clarence, found guilty of treason in February 1478 and said to have been executed by drowning in a butt of malmsey wine.[106] This, of course, was political murder rather than execution, though the basic reasoning, and the outcome, were similar – to get rid of someone out of favour with those in power. There were, however, other types of execution which also seem to have had the, albeit unrecorded, sanction of the king. When the duke of Gloucester was forcibly taken to Calais in the late 1390s, he found himself the victim of judicial murder. According to Froissart:

> Just at the hour when the tables were laid for dinner in the castle of Calais and he was about to wash his hands, four men rushed out from a room and, twisting a towel round his neck, pulled so hard on the two ends that he staggered to the floor. There they finished strangling him, closed his eyes and carried him, now dead, to a bed on which they undressed his body. They placed him between two sheets, put a pillow under his head and covered him with fur mantles. Leaving the room, they went back into the hall, ready primed with their story, and said this: that the Duke had had an apoplectic fit while he was washing his hands and had been carried to his bed with great difficulty. This version was given out in the castle and the town. Some believed it, but others not.[107]

And, at the very end of our period, comes another unofficial execution. Though this time coming from the nobility supposedly acting in the kingdom's interests, or at least the interests of themselves, the end of the duke of Suffolk was nasty and bloody, however private in execution. In 1450, after a series of attacks in parliament over treasonous activity and corruption, Suffolk, having been saved by Henry VI from execution, was instead sentenced to five years' exile. On his way into banishment, however, he was unceremoniously beheaded when his ship was boarded by men from the *Nicholas de la Tour*. His death was supposedly foretold by his astrologer,[108] and according to the Paston Letters:

> And some sey he was arreyned yn the sheppe on here maner upon the appechementes and fond gylty, etc.

Also he asked the name of the sheppe, and whanne he knew it, he remembred Stacy that seid, if he myght eschape the daunger of the Towr, he should be saffe; and thanne his herte faylyd hym, for he thowghte he was desseyvyd, and yn the syght of all his men he was drawn ought out of the grete shippe yn to the bote; and there was an exe, and a stoke, and oon of the lewdeste of the shippe badde hym ley down his hedde, and he should be fair ferd wyth, and dye on a swerd; and toke a rusty swerd, and smotte of his hedde withyn halfe a doseyn strokes, and toke awey his gown of russet, and his dobelette of velvet mayled, and leyde his body on the sonds of Dover; and some sey his hedde was sette oon a pole by it, and hes men sette on the londe be grette circumstaunce and preye.[109]

Notably, such 'political murders', however covert and rare, were very much a creature of the later Middle Ages, as were public humiliations and executions. For the high medieval period at least, if one treated individuals with noble or royal blood as such, especially initially in secret, and if such treatment then got out, one risked the loss of one's crown – as King John found with Arthur of Brittany and the wife and son of William de Braose, both of whom he was accused of causing the deaths of, in the most horrific of manners,[110] and which would form an important part of the background to the accusations against him in 1215.

Disposal of the body

One shall ride the high gallows and upon his death hang until his soul's treasury, his bloody bone-framed body, disintegrates. There the raven black of plumage will pluck out the sight from his head and shred the soulless corpse – and he cannot fend off with his hands the loathsome bird of prey from its evil intent. His life is fled and, deprived of his senses, beyond hope of survival, he suffers his lot, pallid upon the beam, enveloped in the mist of death. His name is damned. (*The Fortunes of Men*)[111]

As has become obvious, by the early fourteenth century, not only was execution more prevalent in England, but also abuse and mutilation – though not of those expected to live, as in the Anglo-Norman period, but those expected to die, if they were not corpses already. And it was not just the body that suffered torment, the soul also faced punishment being, in theory at least, not allowed the sacraments before death nor Christian burial afterwards.[112] Indeed, the treatment of the deceased was going through some major changes in this period, bodily partition in connection with royal and noble burials in particular becoming increasingly popular, probably because it allowed the person involved to be remembered in a greater number of places. Unsurprisingly, then, considering religious teachings about the sanctity of the body, such division was also increasingly controversial, with the Church condemning corpse division for whatever reason[113] – it was one thing for Christ symbolically to offer up his body and blood at the Last Supper, it was very much another for medieval men to do so in reality, and especially in order to make either personal or political points. Nonetheless, by the middle of our period corpse partition was also a common form of posthumous punishment for the disgraced and their relatives, both as a visible abuse of the individual, and as a way to publicise his end in a number of places at once – especially, as we will see, on London Bridge and the 'four corners of the kingdom'.

That said, it must first be pointed out that not all bodies were equal: in cases of rebellions by the king's immediate family or kin, or those (once) closely connected with the royal family, if there was a body to be disposed of, it was usually done in a fitting manner. In the case of Robert Curthose, the passage of time between transgression by the noble and his death also probably helped make for a humane burial. After twenty-eight years' captivity in Devizes, and then Cardiff, Castle, the ever-problematic Curthose succumbed to old age in 1134: on the orders of Henry I, his body was buried in Gloucester Abbey, and a light set to burn before the altar for the sake of his wayward brother's soul.[114] Somewhat more surprisingly, after Evesham, the final disposal of Simon de Montfort's body was in the end a subdued, even humane, affair. Initially, just after the battle, Henry III's brother-in-law's corpse was brutally treated. According to the *Waverley Annals*: 'Lord Simon de Montfort, his head cut off, his body dismembered, and, horrible to relate, his private parts removed, suffered glorious martyrdom, so we believe, for the peace of the land and the restoration of the realm and the Mother Church';[115] thereafter, his head and privates being then sent to the wife of one of his enemies.[116] However, in the end, 'through licence of the lord king, the bodies of Simon de Montfort, his son Henry and Hugh Despenser were buried in the abbey church at Evesham before the lowest step in front of the high altar'.[117] Leader of the rebels or not, de Montfort was also the king's brother-in-law and, lest Henry III be seen to denigrate the status of the royal family (albeit an extended one), he was due, and needed, a certain degree of respect in death, if not in life. However, though common decency, religious sensibility and respect for rank and royal blood could all mitigate harsh treatment of the corpse, there could also be other reasons for ensuring a proper burial. After the rebellion of 1075, Earl Waltheof was summarily beheaded outside Winchester, his severed head supposedly finishing the *paternoster* he had begun before the axe fell:[118] if such stories were believed, or at least the impact of them feared by the authorities, it is unsurprising that his body was allowed to be properly buried in the end.[119] Conversely, sometimes already respectful burials, especially of the late fourteenth century, had to be adjusted for similar reasons. In 1397, after his decapitation, to which he went 'no more shrinking or changing colour than as if he were going to a banquet', the earl of Arundel's body was 'buried atte ffrere Austynes, in Londoun'.[120] However, thereafter stories started to develop that Arundel's head and torso had been inexplicably brought back together just after his execution, causing crowds to come to his burial place,[121] and threatening to cause the development of a cult of political sainthood as had surrounded the burial place of Thomas of Lancaster, his great-uncle.[122] As a result of these reports, the king ordered his most import-ant nobles, including the duke of Lancaster and the earls of Rutland, Kent, Northumberland and Nottingham, to hold a vigil at Arundel's tomb at night to check the validity of the story, and then arranged that the earl's body be disinterred, and reburied in an unmarked grave.[123]

Thus, despite what they had done in life, for some men there was a chance of a proper Christian burial.[124] By 1332, even Roger Mortimer's wife was allowed to bury her estranged husband, perhaps at Wigmore, though initially the Friars Minor, who had control of the body, refused to give it up.[125] Moreover, if one were a rebel against the king's government, rather than the king, and that king was still in power, sooner or later a decent interment would also take place. Edward II looked to the care of his favourite, Piers Gaveston, in death as in life, whatever the possible political recriminations might be. In November 1314, the sheriff of Oxford and Berkshire was ordered to pay the king's clerk, Thomas de London, 'his expenses for himself and companions about the custody of the body of the late earl of Cornwall at the friars preachers, Oxford';[126] and similarly, in December 1315, there was an 'order to cause twenty-three tuns of wine to be bought and provided and taken to Langele for the expenses of the burial there of Peter de Gaveston'.[127] Likewise, in 1395, when his power was beginning to revive, Richard II arranged for the body of his downfallen (though by the Appellants' efforts, not his) favourite, Robert de Vere, to be moved from Lovain, where he died in exile, to Colne Abbey (Essex), and properly interred: the body itself, according to one source, was in an open cypress casket at the funeral, and the king touched de Vere's face before he was buried, 'publicly showing to Robert, when dead, the affection which he had shown him previously, while alive'.[128] In the next century, the ill-fated duke of Suffolk, despite being beheaded in an open boat and reportedly having his body thrown upon Dover Beach, ended up being buried at the family manor of Wingfield, Suffolk, probably in June 1450[129] – presumably with the goodwill of the king. Even Humphrey de Bohun, the earl of Hereford, an on again/off again friend of Edward II and one of the highest ranking of the Contrariants, was given a proper burial after Boroughbridge in 1322: though notably, for convenience sake, in the vicinity of the battle (at the Friar Preachers in York) rather than where he had indicated in his will, namely at Walden (Essex), alongside his wife Elizabeth.[130]

However, those not lucky enough to be closely related to, or connected with, the king, even as an enemy, faced a different fate, and were as likely as not, in the later Middle Ages at least, to have parts of their bodies sent to various important towns and cities of the kingdom. According to Binski, such acts of division and dispersal of the body marked 'an inversion of royal largesse in the interests of disempowerment',[131] in other words, a blatant sign of downfall in an increasingly visual age. In the high Middle Ages, on the rare occasion when execution did happen, simpler, though still callous, treatment of the body after death was most common for disgraced or downfallen individuals. Before its belated interment noted above, Earl Waltheof's beheaded body was hastily buried, apparently without ceremony, at the place of his execution by William I's servants;[132] likewise, it seems highly unlikely that there was a proper burial for Braose's wife and son, initially at least, left to starve to death by John in Corfe Castle.[133] That said, handling of the body of condemned individuals after death went through something of a 'textual' revolution, again, in the later thirteenth century, and at least in part, going from the reasons for the connected executions, owing to the gradual development of laws for treason – though perhaps again also due to changes in burial practices noted above, the growing influence of the harsher Celtic practices that Edward I and his administrators came in contact with because of his claim to the overlordship of the whole of the British Isles;[134] and even, though more arguably, a reflection of the developing idea of a division of king and crown starting in the mid-thirteenth century in the treatment of the noble,[135] namely between the fate of the individual noble and the dignity of nobility. Whatever the case, the disgraced noble's body had now become a canvas for political statement. In England, according to Bynum, 'chronicle accounts make it clear that dismemberment was reserved for the most repulsive crimes and that the populace was expected to be able to interpret the nature of the offense from the precise way in which the criminal's body was cut apart and the pieces displayed'.[136] The body, in other words, was now being abused not just before death or during the death sentence, but also afterwards, and in each abusive act, points were being made. One of the most famous early cases, notably initially all of Welsh or Scottish origin, of this more symbolic treatment of the body was that of Prince Llewellyn in 1282. After his death:

> his head was brought to the king in North Wales, who immediately dispatched it to his army stationed in Anglesey; and after the people of Anglesey had had their fill of the spectacle, he ordered it to be immediately sent to London. On the morrow of St Thomas the Apostle, the Londoners went out to meet it with trumpets and cornets, and conducted it through all the streets of the city, with a spectacular noise. After this, they fixed it up firmly upon their pillory for the remainder of the day; and towards evening of that day it was carried to the

Tower of London, and stuck on a high pole. As for the prince's body, cut and mutilated, it was interred in the Cistercian abbey of Cunheir.[137]

Less than a year later, according to Carr, Prince David 'for his treason . . . was dragged by horses to the place of execution; then, for the killing of Fulk Trigold during the attack on Hawarden, he was hanged and cut down alive, and for his blasphemy in going to war at Passiontide he was eviscerated and his intestines were burned. Finally, because he had planned the death of the king in various parts of the kingdom, his body was quartered.'[138] Notably, this particular execution was also a novel act not because it was the first hanging, drawing and quartering, which had been done before though at a lower social level, but because it was the first time that this act was connected with an 'English State Trial'.[139] David's head was thereafter placed on London Bridge, and his quarters sent to Shrewsbury, Lincoln, Bristol (where his two sons were imprisoned) and Winchester.[140] Two decades later, William Wallace's head was cut off and put on London Bridge, his body divided into four, and the quarters sent to four parts of Scotland: 'Behold the end of the merciless man, who himself perishes without mercy.'[141] Such treatment was gradually adopted for English traitors as well, with Turberville's head sent to the Tower for exhibit on its walls.[142] It was ordered that

> he should hang so long as anything should be left whole of him; and he was drawn on a fresh ox-hide from Westminster to the Conduit of London, and then back to the gallows; and there is he hung by a chain of iron, and will hang, so long as anything of him may remain.[143]

With such gruesome precedent, then, it is unsurprising that few blinked an eye when the Contrariant Lord Mowbray's body was left on display, hanging in chains, until 1325, when it was buried in a Dominican friary in York.[144]

Le Baker tells a similar story for Hugh Despenser the elder upon his capture by the queen's forces at Bristol in late 1326. Though he was executed there instead of Winchester, the honorific centre of his earldom, his death was nonetheless very instructive for the local populace. The queen ordered that he suffer the harshest torture possible: bound, with legs and arms stretched, he was disembowelled and his intestines burnt, and his body was drawn by horses and 'suspended on a fork like any common thief'.[145] To show the people of Winchester that Hugh had been demoted, his head was put on display in the town towards the end of 1326,[146] 'where you were earl against law and reason'.[147] His son's body faced similar desecration:

> When he had been bound, his member and his testicles were first cut off, because he was a heretic and a sodomite, even, so it was said, with the King; and it was allegedly on his suggestion that the King had driven away the Queen. When his

private parts had been cut off, they were thrown into the fire to burn; then his heart was ripped from his body and thrown into the fire, because he was false-hearted and a traitor, who by his treacherous advice and encouragement had led the King to bring disgrace and misfortune upon his realm and to behead the greatest lords of England, by whom the kingdom ought to have been upheld and defended.[148]

According to the *French Chronicle of London*, Despenser the younger's severed head was then 'carried, with the sound of trumpets, through Chepe, to London Bridge; and there the head was fixed':[149] the rest of his body was sent to 'four cities in England'.[150] The treatment of the Despensers' bodies was therefore a pointed and bloody message to the citizens of the kingdom, and especially those who wished to test the new regime's resolve. Four years later, in 1330, when the earl of March was drawn to his death like a common felon and hanged at Tyburn, and quartered, his body was deliberately left on the gallows for two days and nights.[151] Sometimes such bodies could be left for years before they were buried, another poignant warning for future would-be rebels. Some cases have already been noted above, as that of Mowbray in 1322, though this treatment could go to extremes. After his execution on Harraby Hill, Carlisle, Andrew de Harcla's head was put on London Bridge, while his quarters were displayed in Newcastle, Bristol, Shrewsbury and London – only to be given a proper Christian burial in 1328, five years after his execution.[152] And, though the actual process of execution became somewhat less painful after Edward II and early Edward III's reign, the treatment of the corpse was no less gruesome – again, in the main, for the sake of hammering home the extreme dangers of going against the king. Though Richard II usually avoided such treatment of corpses, Henrys IV and V returned to it with a vengeance, as witness the ends of Hotspur (Henry Percy), the earl of Worcester, duke of Norfolk and Henry le Scrope,[153] all of whose bodies were treated in a particularly ignoble manner. Hotspur faced further degrading, if not grotesque, treatment after rumours of him still being alive began to circulate, with Henry IV as a result having his body dug up and displayed between two millstones in Shrewsbury marketplace.[154] Indeed, this generally brutal treatment of corpses by Henrys IV and V was especially true when a rebel died in battle, it being not uncommon for remains to then be used as a bloody warning to others thinking about rebellion. For instance, in 1408 Thomas Bardolf, a player in the earl of Northumberland's revolt, was defeated at Bramham Moor, dying a few hours later of his wounds. His remains were quartered, with his head being placed on one of the gates of Lincoln, though these were later given to his widow for burial.[155]

Finally, degradation from rank, rather than of the body, could come before or after execution. Either way, it was a serious affair, by act and by ceremony, and one that was to become increasingly important as the centuries progressed and the social hierarchy and the trappings of class became more developed and nuanced.[156] In the case of Andrew de Harcla in 1323, degradation came just before the execution: 'condemning him first to be degraded and stripped of the dignity of earldom by being deprived of the sword given him by the king, and in like manner of knightly rank by striking off from his heels the gilded spurs'.[157] The *Brut* had the sword, with which he was made an earl, broken over his head, and he was made to remove his tabard and hood, fur coats and girdle; and then the judge said to him: 'Andrew . . . now art thou no knight, but a knave; and for thy treason the king's will is that thou be hanged and drawn.'[158] He was hanged first, and then his body decapitated, the hanging of course being an indication of his loss of dignity (and the 'low' nature of his crime), as well as the standard punishment for felonies.[159] Likewise, when the earl of Arundel faced trial in 1397, while the Counter-appellants came in 'red silk robes banded with white silk and powdered with letters of gold', Arundel was brought in attired in a robe with a scarlet hood: 'Then John, duke of Lancaster and steward of England, who had been appointed to undertake this task, formally told Lord Nevill, "Remove his belt and his hood", which was done.'[160] And any heraldry, an increasingly important physical manifestation of social status, was also forfeit at such times,[161] and baronial liveries put up to ridicule, as faced the Contrariants and their retainers in 1322.[162] When, four years later, Hugh Despenser the elder was taken, he was drawn through Bristol 'in his coat of arms (so that those arms should never again be borne in England), and afterwards hanged and then beheaded'.[163] Mutilation of the corpse and degradation from status merged into one at times in the minds of the chroniclers. During Hugh Despenser the younger's execution, according to Thomas Walsingham's version of events:

> Moreover, he was drawn in a sleeveless tunic with his own embroidered arms, on which was legibly written the good words of the Psalms, 'What glory in malevolence' unto the verse 'I also as an olive': concerning which it is thus written:
>
> > 'Rope with wood, to you, miserable man, sword and fire,
> > From Hugh, axe, horse, all grace was absent'
>
> 'Rope' since he was drawn; 'wood' since he was hung, 'sword', since he was decapitated; 'fire' since he was disembowelled, and viscera burnt; 'axe' since he was quartered; 'horse' surely since he was dragged.[164]

There could even be a macabre hierarchy to executions, as when in 1300, the earl of Athol's head was placed above that of William Wallace and Simon Frazer on London Bridge, 'because he was akin to the King'.[165] Thus, both body and identity of a downfallen noble were no longer simply something to abuse; they were now a canvas for those in power to show the rest of the nobility, as well as society as a whole, what happened when one crossed the ever more visible line between favour and disgrace.

Being at His Majesty's pleasure meant being open to a spectrum of fates throughout the period, though there were some substantive changes over the course of the Middle Ages as a whole in the treatment of downfallen nobles. In the high Middle Ages, Anglo-Saxon punishments of wergild and execution were replaced in the first instance by a tendency to move towards mutilation and/or imprisonment rather than execution (though mutilation itself would also go into limbo after Henry I's reign), and in the early thirteenth century by an increasingly complex series of fines. However, after a relatively lenient period for most of the later twelfth and thirteenth centuries, punishments again turned bloody. Though many seeds were sown well before, this change occurred mainly during Edward I's reign – whether, among other reasons, as a result of increasing contact with the more violent Celtic worlds and his claims to overlordship over them, the lack of Normandy as a place of refuge for nobles or as a cause of concern for kings, fear of mass baronial revolt as his father had seen or, of course, the developing ideas of treason and the seriousness with which they were treated. Nonetheless, first Celtic rebels, then lower members of the nobility, faced psychological and bodily torment and execution in a manner rarely before seen at the highest social levels. By Edward II's reign, a mixture of public humiliation, drawing, hanging, eviscerating, quartering, beheading and other horrors was a common fate to face disgraced nobles, a fate which would continue into the first years of Edward III's reign. In many ways, though, this was the high point of such treatment. Though there were many executions thereafter in the fourteenth and fifteenth centuries, torment and excessive abuse before death seem to have become somewhat less popular with those in power. Perhaps it was felt that the 1320s had gone beyond the pale in this regard, and, in terms of public shame, death and dismemberment of disgraced individuals were now seen to be enough. Perhaps it was thought, after the rising of 1381 and the treatment of members of the upper orders by the peasantry, that excessively humiliating nobles in public, whatever their crimes, was not such a good idea. On this point, even the usually level-headed author of the *Vita Edwardi Secundi*, perhaps catching the mood of those who backed the hierarchy the most, laments after Boroughbridge: 'O calamity! To see men lately dressed in purple and fine linen now attired in rags, bound and imprisoned in chains!'[166] Nevertheless, executions went on, often in place of the fining and/or imprisonment of the high Middle Ages, and would continue over the course of the later Middle Ages. Consequently, there *was* more and more opportunity to use the corpse of the executed in any number of ways.

In the fourteenth and fifteenth centuries, indeed, the bodies of downfallen nobles quickly became the medium for increasingly nuanced symbolism, with the use of heads, and quarters, and other parts of the body – though the closer to the king one was, even if one had then revolted, the quicker one would ultimately get a Christian burial. Even while the downfallen lived, there was an increasingly elaborate way of degrading him from both public respect and social rank – as can be seen most vividly with the degradations of Thomas de Turberville in 1295, Andrew de Harcla in 1323 and the Despensers in 1326. Overall, then, punishment of whatever sort was not meant to reform the disgraced noble in the Middle Ages (though his example was often used to educate his peers, as well as the greater populace, of the dangers of going against the king's wishes): it was a method either to get him out of the way or to punish him for bad conduct. That said, as the later Middle Ages continued, it cannot be denied that more and more nobles tended to meet not only bloody, but also increasingly pointed, ends, often in a very instructive manner. A large part of this, of course, was to do with the nature of politics and society of the time, and the long-term fallout from Edward I's policies in particular. But part, as we will see in the next chapter, played off other factors, especially the decline in feudalism and the changing nature of land law, both of which would have a substantial impact on the amount of land coming back to the king, and in turn the way nobles and their families would be treated in the future.

Notes

1 See also H.R.T. Summerson, 'Attitudes to Capital Punishment in England, 1200–1350', in M. Prestwich, R. Britnell and R. Frame, eds. *Thirteenth Century England VIII* (Woodbridge, 2001), 125.

2 W.A. Chaney, *The Cult of Kingship in Anglo-Saxon England* (Manchester, 1970), p. 222.

3 H.R. Loyn, *The Governance of Anglo-Saxon England 500–1087* (London, 1984), p. 45.

4 A. Reynolds, *Later Anglo-Saxon England: Life and Landscape* (Stroud, 1999), p. 59.

5 See P. Stafford, *Unification and Conquest: A Political and Social History of England in the Tenth and Eleventh Centuries* (London, 1989), p. 141.

6 Both Bartlett and Strickland mention fining, but give it less emphasis than other sorts of punishment for problematic nobles. R. Bartlett, *England under the Norman and Angevin Kings 1075–1225* (Oxford, 2000), p. 187; M. Strickland, *War and Chivalry: The Conduct and Perception of War in England and Normandy 1066–1217* (Cambridge, 1996), pp. 240–7.

7 See Warren, *Henry II*, p. 140; though lower down the social scale, Henry was not overly hesitant in exacting monetary fines. See Warren, *Henry II*, p. 387; though Keefe tends to play the role of monetary exaction in Henry II's reign down.

T.K. Keefe, *Feudal Assessments and the Political Community under Henry II and His Sons* (Berkeley, 1983), Chapter 5.

8 'Earls and barons shall be fined only by their equals, and in proportion to the gravity of their offence.' Clause 21, Magna Carta.

9 Turner, *King John*, p. 220.

10 See *CP* vii, 630; see also discussion of pardons in Chapter 5.

11 D. Carpenter, *The Minority of Henry III* (London, 1990), p. 46; according to Carpenter, however, these amounts were nowhere near what John would have exacted from them if he had still been alive. Carpenter, *Minority of Henry III*, pp. 46–7.

12 See *SR* i, 12–18; C.H. Knowles, 'The Resettlement of England after the Barons' War, 1264–7', *TRHS* 5th Ser. 32 (1982), 25–41.

13 See also pp. 97–8; for an example of harsh treatment, see Ferrers, pp. 57–8.

14 J.G. Bellamy, *Crime and Public Order in the Later Middle Ages* (London, 1973), pp. 190–1.

15 *CP* ii, 233; *CFR 1319–27*, 154.

16 Paris, *Chronica Majora*, v, 95.

17 Lander, *Crown and Nobility*, pp. 267–300. Though more recently questioned. T.B. Pugh, 'Henry VII and the English Nobility', in G.W. Bernard, ed. *The Tudor Nobility* (Manchester, 1992), 57–65.

18 For list of recognisances transferred, see E163/4/29.

19 E208/2/88(bundle 3); *CCR 1333–7*, 96; E159/106/24.

20 On expenditure and lifestyle, see Mertes, *Noble Household*, p. 103.

21 J.R. Maddicott, 'Ferrers, Robert de, Sixth Earl of Derby (*c.* 1239–1279)', *DNB* (Oxford, 2004).

22 For the Ferrers family's attempts to retrieve lands, or at least some form of redress, see McFarlane, *Nobility*, pp. 254–6; *Select Cases in the Court of King's Bench under Edward I* G.O. Sayles, ed. and trans. (London, 1936), i, 20–1; M. Bateson and J. Denton, 'Usury and Comital Disinheritance: The Case of Ferrers versus Lancaster, St Paul's, London, 1301', *Journal of Ecclesiastical History* 43 (1992), 60–96.

23 F. Pollock and F.W. Maitland, *The History of English Law before the Time of Edward I* 2nd edn (Cambridge, 1968), ii, 506.

24 Imprisonment will be dealt with in Chapter 4.

25 See also pp. 88–9.

26 A.H. Forbes, '*Laesa Majestas* and the Security Legislation of Edward III: The Statutes of Treasons, Provisors and Praemunire', *Studies in Medieval Culture* 4 (1974), 359.

27 Or for individuals unable to pay the, usually large, fine involved. J. Hudson, *The Formation of the English Common Law* (Harlow, 1996), pp. 77–8.

28 See Loyn, *Governance of Anglo-Saxon England*, pp. 46–7.

29 See below and Chapter 3.

30 *EHD c. 500–1042* D. Whitelock, ed. and trans. (London, 1996), pp. 409ff.

31 Hudson, *Common Law*, p. 78; for the laws see *EHD 1042–1189* D.C. Douglas and G.W. Greenaway, ed. and trans. (Oxford, 1953), pp. 399–400.

32 E.g. J. Gillingham, 'Killing and Mutilating Political Enemies in the British Isles from the Late Twelfth to the Early Fourteenth Century: A Comparative Study', in B. Smith, ed. *Britain and Ireland 900–1300: Insular Responses to Medieval European Change* (Cambridge, 1999), 114ff.

33 A. Williams, *The English and the Norman Conquest* (Woodbridge, 1997), Chapter 3.

34 See J. Gillingham, '1066 and the Introduction of Chivalry into England', in G. Garnett and J. Hudson, eds. *Law and Government in Medieval England and Normandy* (Cambridge, 1994), 40–1.

35 Strickland, *War and Chivalry*, pp. 241–2.

36 ASC M.J. Swanton, ed. and trans. (London, 1996) (1095E); Barlow, *William Rufus*, pp. 357–8.

37 D. Carpenter, 'From King John to the First English Duke: 1215–1337', in R. Smith and J.S. Moore, eds. *The House of Lords: A Thousand Years of British Tradition* (London, 1994), 29; also see L. Van Eickels, 'Gendered Violence: Castration and Blinding as Punishment for Treason in Normandy and Anglo-Norman England', *Gender and History* 16 (2004), 595. Also see Gillingham, 'Chivalry', 44–5, 49–50; though Gillingham also notes some exceptions in wartime.

38 Pollock and Maitland, *English Law*, ii, 458; though it has been dated to Henry I's reign at the latest. Hudson, *Common Law*, p. 81.

39 *The Treatise on the Laws and Customs of the Realm of England Commonly called Glanvill* G.D.G. Hall, ed. and trans. (Edinburgh, 1965), pp. 176–7. Though reference to castration as leniency 'immediately raises the question of irony'. Van Eickels, 'Castration and Blinding', 590. Little connection should be made between these penalties and torture, which was usually used to exact confessions before judgement, and which tended to be a Continental practice. According to Peters, after 1166, 'torture did not have a place in the law of England'. E. Peters, *Torture* (Oxford, 1985), p. 59.

40 *EHD 1042–1189*, p. 400, clause 10.

41 ASC (1095E).

42 *The Annals of Roger de Hoveden* H.T. Riley, ed. and trans. (London, 1853), i, 185; for Eu, also see *Ranulfi de Diceto Decani Lundoniensis Opera Historica* W. Stubbs ed. (London, 1876), i, 220; Barlow, *William Rufus*, p. 357.

43 C.W. Hollister, 'Royal Acts of Mutilation: The Case Against Henry I', *Albion* 10 (1978), 330.

44 *Leges Henrici Primi* L.J. Downer, ed. and trans. (Oxford, 1972), pp. 5, 249.

45 *The Gesta Normannorum Ducum of William of Jumièges, Orderic Vitalis, and Robert of Torigni* E.M.C. van Houts, ed. and trans. (Oxford, 1992–2001), ii, 237.

46 *Annals of Roger de Hoveden*, i, 225.

47 Hollister, 'Mutilation', 337; though some doubt has been cast on the blinding. Hollister, *Henry I*, p. 205 footnote 4.

48 Hollister, 'Mutilation', 338–9.

49 Carpenter, 'King John to the First English Duke', 29; Van Eickels, 'Castration and Blinding', 595.

50 The Church, of course, 'would not condone "judgements of blood"' of its own, and had a more general tendency to find 'penance for sin than punishment for crime'. Warren, *Henry II*, p. 464.

51 See also pp. 92–4.

52 Which was in effect taken away by Edward I's legislation, which made going with an army into the field against the king a treasonable offence. See Bellamy, *Treason*, Chapter 3.

53 Gillingham, 'Chivalry', 48–9.

54 Most recently, Valente, *Revolt*, pp. 18–32.

55 W. Childs, 'Resistance and Treason in the *Vita Edwardi Secundi*', in M. Prestwich, R.H. Britnell and R. Frame, eds. *Thirteenth Century England VI* (Woodbridge, 1997), 180.

56 R. Kaeuper, *War, Justice and Public Order: England and France in the Later Middle Ages* (Oxford, 1988), pp. 174–6.

57 Though there are problems with this. See Gillingham, 'Killing and Mutilating Political Enemies', 133.

58 See also p. 61.

59 For Christ's body and such occasions, see K. Royer, 'The Body in Parts: Reading the Execution Ritual in Late Medieval England', *Historical Reflections* 29 (2003), 326.

60 For an overview, and Carpenter's argument for the importance of the loss of Normandy, see Carpenter, 'King John to the First English Duke', 30–5; also see Gillingham, 'Killing and Mutilating Political Enemies', 114–34. For further discussion, see pp. 63ff., 101, 117.

61 *Leges Henrici Primi*, p. 233.

62 H. Bracton, *On the Laws and Customs of England* S.E. Thorne, ed. and trans. (Cambridge, Mass., 1968), ii, 335.

63 Thomas Aquinas as cited in Summerson, 'Capital Punishment', 123.

64 Gillingham, 'Killing and Mutilating Political Enemies', 114–34.

65 *Flores Historiarum* H.R. Luard, ed. (London, 1890), iii, 58. I am using drawing/drawn in the sense of dragging/dragged throughout: however, when the word shows up in quotations, if it is before hanging it usually means to be dragged, if after hanging it usually means to be eviscerated (*OED*).

66 H. Bateson, 'The Ancient Penalty of High Treason', *Notes and Queries* 167 (1934), 442.

67 *Flores Historiarum*, iii, 123–4; on the chronicle, see Gransden, *Historical Writing*, i, 378 footnote 171.

68 R.C. Finucane, 'Sacred Corpse, Profane Carrion: Social Ideals and Death Rituals in the Later Middle Ages', in J. Whaley, ed. *Mirrors of Mortality: Studies in the Social History of Death* (London, 1981), 51.

69 Florence of Worcester, *Chronicon*, ii, 279; also see *Annales Monastici*, iii, 399.

70 For the more general brutalisation of political society, see J.R.S. Phillips, 'Simon de Montfort (1265), the Earl of Manchester (1644), and Other Stories: Violence and Politics in Thirteenth and Early Fourteenth Century England', in R.W. Kaeuper, ed. *Violence in Medieval Society* (Woodbridge, 2000), 79–89.

71 Phillips, 'Simon de Montfort', 88.

72 Carpenter, 'King John to the First English Duke', 29–30; for this change, see also Pollock and Maitland, *English Law*, ii, 460–2.

73 P. Chaplais, *Piers Gaveston: Edward II's Adoptive Brother* (Oxford, 1994), p. 88.

74 Fryde, *Tyranny*, pp. 60–2.

75 *Chronica Monastario de Melsa* E.A. Bond, ed. (London, 1868), ii, 343; *Flores Historiarum*, iii, 207.

76 E.g. from Daniell's discussion of Lancaster's beheading. C. Daniell, *Death and Burial in Medieval England 1066–1550* (London, 1997), p. 80; according to Daniell, 'those who were beheaded as a legal punishment usually knelt with no support' (Daniell, *Death and Burial*, p. 80), perhaps allowing the condemned a bit of dignity at the very end.

77 CP vii, 395 footnote h.

78 *Chronicle of Lanercost*, p. 234.

79 *Chronicle of Lanercost*, p. 234.

80 Daniell, *Death and Burial*, p. 80.

81 See Butler, 'Brimpsfield Giffards', 94–5.

82 Phillips, 'Simon de Montfort', 86.

83 Also see Royer, 'Body in Parts', 336.

84 *Gesta Henrici Quinci*, p. 19.

85 *Eulogium Historiarum sive Temporis* F.S. Haydon, ed. (London, 1858–63), iii, 375.

86 *The Anonimalle Chronicle 1307–1334* W.R. Childs and J. Taylor, ed. and trans. (Leeds, 1991), pp. 142–3.

87 E. Cohen, 'Symbols of Culpability and the Universal Language of Justice: The Ritual of Public Executions in Late Medieval Europe', *History of European Ideas* 11 (1989), 407. Though it has also been argued that by the late thirteenth century it was the 'theatricality, not the brutality, that was new'. Royer, 'Body in Parts', 323.

88 P. Binski, *Medieval Death: Ritual and Representation* (Ithaca, 1996), p. 66.

89 For the latter, see *Leges Henrici Primi* on execution: 'For in the case of every extravagance of human wickedness the comforting alleviations of a healing legal remedy have been made available, except in the case of betrayal of one's lord and blasphemy against the Holy Ghost (that is, impenitence of heart), which, according to the word of the Lord, shall not be forgiven to anyone, either in this world or in the world to come.' *Leges Henrici Primi*, p. 233.

90 Though the procession of members of the lower orders to the gallows was somewhat less flamboyant in tone. Summerson, 'Capital Punishment', 132.

91 ECR, p. 10.

92 Fryde, *Tyranny*, p. 61.

93 *Chronicle of Lanercost*, p. 237.

94 See Chapter 1, p.

95 *Chronique de Jean le Bel* J. Viard and E. Déprez, ed. (Paris, 1904–5), i, 27–8.

96 W.R.J. Barron, 'The Penalties for Treason in Medieval Life and Literature', *JMH* 7 (1981), 190; Royer, 'Body in Parts', 330; similar points made for medieval

and early modern continental Europe. See F. Egmond, 'Execution, Dissection, Pain and Infamy – A Morphological Investigation', 105–6 and E. Cohen, 'The Expression of Pain in the Later Middle Ages: Deliverance, Acceptance and Infamy', 214, both in F. Egmond and R. Zwijnenberg, eds. *Bodily Extremities: Preoccupations with the Human Body in Early Modern European Culture* (Aldershot, 2003). Whether individuals such as Turberville and Mortimer were drawn to execution on an oxhide for the sake of humiliation, or to keep them alive longer, is open to debate. See Summerson, 'Capital Punishment', 124 footnote 6.

97 *The French Chronicle of London A.D. 1259–A.D. 1343* H.T. Riley, ed. and trans. (London, 1863), p. 295.

98 *The Chronicle of Adam of Usk 1377–1421* C. Given-Wilson, ed. and trans. (Oxford, 1997), p. 35.

99 For examples, see Dobson, ed. *Peasants' Revolt*, part I and pp. 336–42.

100 A. Dunn, *The Politics of Magnate Power in England and Wales 1389–1413* (Oxford, 2003), pp. 81–2.

101 *Chronicle of Lanercost*, p. 245. Though he might not have been all that calm in mind judging by the number of confessions made to his parish priest and various friars. H.R.T. Summerson, *Medieval Carlisle: The City and the Borders from the Late Eleventh to the Mid Sixteenth Century* (Kendal, 1993), i, 255.

102 From J. Scattergood, *Politics and Poetry in the Fifteenth Century* (London, 1971), p. 120.

103 Capgrave, *Chronicle*, p. 265; see also M. Bennett, *Richard II and the Revolution of 1399* (Stroud, 1999), p. 103.

104 J. Capgrave, *Liber de Illustribus Henricis* F.C. Hingeston, ed. (London, 1858), i, 122–3.

105 T. Walsingham, *Historia Anglicana* H.T. Riley, ed. (London, 1863–4), ii, 328.

106 A belief still held. C. Ross, *Edward IV* (New Haven and London, 1997), p. 243.

107 Froissart, *Chronicles*, p. 431; for a slightly different take on Gloucester's death, see T. Walsingham, *Ypodiigma Neustiae* H.T. Riley, ed. (London, 1876), p. 378.

108 According to one chronicle, Suffolk had asked an 'astronomer' what his end would be, and was told to beware of the 'Tour'. However, this was not the Tower of London, which his friends promptly moved him out of when they heard this, but the *Nicholas de la Tour*, whose men boarded his ship on the way to France. ECR, p. 69.

109 *The Paston Letters* J. Gairdner, ed. (Gloucester, 1986), ii, 146–7; also see R. Virgoe, 'The Death of William de la Pole, Duke of Suffolk', BJRL 47 (1965), 489–502.

110 Turner, *King John*, pp. 220–1; M. Jones, 'Arthur, Duke of Brittany (1187–1203)', DNB (Oxford, 2004).

111 S.A.J. Bradley, ed. and trans. *Anglo-Saxon Poetry* (London, 1995), p. 342.

112 Hudson, *Common Law*, p. 78.

113 C.W. Bynum, *The Resurrection of the Body in Western Christianity, 200–1336* (New York, 1995), pp. 323–4; more generally, E.A.R. Brown, 'Death and the Human Body in the Later Middle Ages: The Legislation of Boniface VIII on the Division of the Corpse', *Viator* 12 (1981), 221–70; K. Park, 'The Life of the Corpse:

Division and Dissection in Late Medieval Europe', *Journal of the History of Medicine and the Allied Sciences* 50 (1995), 111–32.

114 *Ecclesiastical History of Orderic Vitalis*, vi, 379–81, 413.

115 *Annales Monastici*, ii, 365. See also p. 188.

116 *The Chronicle of William de Rishanger* J. Halliwell, ed. (London, 1840), p. xxxii.

117 *Waverley Annals* in *Annales Monastici*, ii, 365.

118 As in Lewis, 'Waltheof, Earl of Northumbria', *DNB* (2004).

119 Florence of Worcester, *Chronicon*, ii, 12; also *Ranulfi de Diceto Opera*, i, 209.

120 Given-Wilson, 'Fitzalan, Richard (III)', *DNB* (2004); ECR, p. 10.

121 P. Morgan, 'Henry IV and the Shadow of Richard II', in R.E. Archer, ed. *Crown, Government and People in the Fifteenth Century* (Stroud, 1995), 3–4. Notably, there were similar stories concerning Waltheof's body. Lewis, 'Waltheof, earl of Northumbria', *DNB* (2004).

122 See also pp. 191–3.

123 Given-Wilson, 'Fitzalan, Richard (III)', *DNB* (2004). See also p. 192.

124 Finucane, 'Sacred Corpse, Profane Carrion', 51; Summerson sees this as usually happening eventually. Summerson, 'Capital Punishment', 131.

125 SC8/61/3027; on Mortimer's burial, also see *Adae Murimuth Continuatio Chronicarum: Robertus de Avesbury De Gestis Mirabilibus Regis Edwardi Tertii Avesbury* E.M. Thompson, ed. (London, 1889), p. 62; though some debate over where his body ended up and how it ended up there. See CP viii, 441 footnote g.

126 CCR 1313–18, 125.

127 CCR 1313–18, 139; notably it took Edward II two and a half years to bury Gaveston at King's Langley, though this delay may also have been connected with his earlier excommunication. Chaplais, *Gaveston*, pp. 110–11.

128 *The Chronica Maiora of Thomas Walsingham 1376–1422* D. Preest and J.G. Clark, ed. and trans. (Woodbridge, 2005), p. 295.

129 CP xii: 1, p. 447; Watts, 'Pole, William de la', *DNB* (2004).

130 CP vi, 470.

131 Binski, *Medieval Death*, p. 66.

132 Florence of Worcester, *Chronicon*, ii, 12; also see *Ranulfi de Diceto Opera*, i, 209.

133 Or at Windsor. Most recently on Braose, see R.V. Turner, 'Briouze, William (III) de (d. 1211)', *DNB* (Oxford, 2004).

134 See p. 62.

135 On the distinction between king and crown, see M. Prestwich, *Plantagenet England 1225–1360* (Oxford, 2005), pp. 34ff.

136 Bynum, *Resurrection*, p. 324.

137 Florence of Worcester, *Chronicon*, ii, 227.

138 A.D. Carr, ' "The Last and Weakest of His Line": Dafydd ap Gruffydd, the Last Prince of Wales', *Welsh History Review* 19 (1999), 393.

139 Carr, 'Last and Weakest', 393.

140 *Annales Cambriae* J. Williams, ed. (London, 1860), p. 107. Carr has Northampton, Chester, Winchester and York receiving his quarters, with the latter two fighting over his right shoulder. Carr, 'Last and Weakest', 393.

141 *Flores Historiarum*, iii, 123–4.

142 Florence of Worcester, *Chronicon*, ii, 279.

143 *French Chronicle of London*, p. 295.

144 R.E. Archer, 'Mowbray, John (I), Second Lord Mowbray (1286–1322)', *DNB* (Oxford, 2004).

145 *Chronicon Galfridi le Baker*, pp. 24–5.

146 *Chronica Monastario de Melsa*, ii, 352.

147 Stubbs as in J.S. Hamilton, 'Despenser, Hugh, the Elder, Earl of Winchester (1261–1326)', *DNB* (Oxford, 2004).

148 *Chronique de Jean le Bel*, i, 28.

149 *French Chronicle of London*, p. 266; *Adae Murimuth Continuatio Chronicarum*, p. 283.

150 *Chronicle of Lanercost*, p. 254.

151 R.R. Davies, 'Mortimer, Roger (V), First Earl of March (1287–1330)', *DNB* (Oxford, 2004).

152 Summerson, 'Harclay, Andrew', *DNB* (2004); in the next year, according to another contemporary chronicle, parts of Harcla were sent to Carlisle and Newcastle, as well as London, Bristol and Dover. *Chronicle of Lanercost*, p. 245.

153 See entries in CP.

154 S. Walker, 'Percy, Sir Henry (1364–1403)', *DNB* (Oxford, 2004).

155 CP i, 420; H. Summerson, 'Bardolf, Thomas, Fifth Baron Bardolf (1369–1408)', *DNB* (Oxford, 2004).

156 On noble trappings, see Crouch, *Image of Aristocracy*, part II.

157 *Chronicle of Lanercost*, p. 245.

158 The *Brut* as in Keen, 'Treason Trials', 89.

159 Harding, *Law Courts*, p. 57. Along with the lack of any 'reputing' (declaration of an individual as the king's enemy) or outlawry of Harcla, Bellamy notes that 'the degradation of the prisoner was an undoubted novelty', more than likely resulting from the affront to the king's feelings. Bellamy, *Treason*, p. 52.

160 C. Given-Wilson, ed. and trans. *Chronicles of the Revolution* (Manchester, 1993), p. 58.

161 Harding, *Law Courts*, p. 104.

162 F. Lachaud, 'Liveries of Robes in England, *c.* 1200–1330', *EHR* iii (1996), 297.

163 *Chronicle of Lanercost*, p. 252.

164 Walsingham, *Historia*, i, 185.

165 *Chronicle of Lanercost*, p. 179.

166 *Vita Edwardi Secundi*, pp. 124–5; for the balanced view of the author of the *Vita*, see also *Vita Edwardi Secundi* W.R. Childs, ed. and trans. (Oxford, 2005), pp. xxxi–xxxii.

3

The harder they come:
estate seizure in
the later Middle Ages

The herrere degre, þe more wys;
Þe gretter worschip, þe noblere fame;
Þe herrere degre, þe more nys;
Þe gretter foly, þe more blame.
After foly, folweþ þe shame;
Repreued of frendis, and scorned of fo,
After þy ded, ressayue þy name.
Eche man be war, er hym be wo.[1]

But it was not just the body that suffered when an individual fell from
political grace in the medieval period, it was also his economic position, and
potentially those of his descendants. Some of this has already been discussed
in the section on financial penalties in the last chapter, but loss of money was
only a small part of the process, and very rarely did a fine completely eradic-
ate an individual's previous position.[2] Rather it was the state of one's landed
presence which was usually the crucial aspect – with his estate confiscated,
in other words, an individual's position within a feudal, property-based society quickly became very tenuous. Throughout the later Middle Ages, the
importance of the royal right of forfeiture, used either by the king or by those
presuming to act in his name, was increasingly evident in two main ways: its
impact on the forfeitee's lifestyle, and on those of his heirs. For the forfeitee
himself, the loss of lands, offices and chattels could not but severely impede
any desire to keep up with his compatriots, especially when one also considered the income lost from the same forfeited estates.[3] Though rarely were such
great men permanently laid low, loss on this scale was bound to weaken one
of the main ways in which a noble showed his social and economic superi-
ority to the rest of society. And it was not just the individual who suffered
when his property was confiscated, but also his line – just as his blood could
be attainted, so could his family be disinherited, not to mention socially
ostracised. Disinheritance of this sort could effectively end the importance of

a family for years to come, often not allowing it to re-emerge into courtly life until property and possessions were either returned or amassed anew. Though to us perhaps a minor consideration compared to loss of life, lifestyle and status, to the medieval noble dispossession of heirs was an issue of the utmost seriousness, one which fed directly back into his own position in posterity. It was, in other words, something to be avoided at all costs.

Royal rights of confiscation in the high Middle Ages

The family land is very dear to every man,
provided that there in his own house he may enjoy
everything that is right and proper in constant prosperity.
                                                    (*The Rune Poem*[4])

As with bodily penalties (especially execution) discussed in the last chapter, Anglo-Saxon ideas about total forfeiture appear to have come about mainly as a result of the Germanic wergild's (and more generally *wite*'s and *bot*'s) inability to deal with the most dangerous of crimes – serious transgressions against the king or kingdom. It became increasingly obvious to kings and lawmakers alike that crimes contrary to the fundamental interests of the monarch, monarchy and public order were of a different rank, and could not simply be put on the same sliding scale of monetary penalties as other transgressions. Rather, to cover these most serious of lapses, as we have seen, the idea of crimes against the Roman concept of *majestas* (majesty or dignity of the sovereign or the state) came to be revived (especially in the form of *laesa majestas*: injury to such majesty/dignity), probably around the ninth century.[5] Initially meant to deal with plotting against the lives of the chief magistrates, transgressions against *majestas* were quickly expanded to include the most serious crimes against royal authority and the royal person. Take clause 4 of the Laws of Alfred: 'If anyone plots against the king's life, directly or by harbouring his exiles or his men, he is liable to forfeit his life and all that he owns,'[6] a theme reiterated in clause 30 of Æthelred's law code of 1008, and clause 57 of the Laws of Cnut.[7] These were the 'botless' crimes which no amount of money could compensate, more serious than any other form of crime to the realm, and therefore dealt with by complete loss of all one had, as well as often one's life[8] – in other words, the end of one's tenurial as well as physical existence. This concept of *majestas* (and especially *laesa majestas*), moreover, intermingled with the continued predominance of the Germanic idea of breaking faith with one's lord, whomever that may be, also then helped form the background for the associated 'legal extension of jurisdiction and its territorialization beyond the originally sacral presence of the king's person alone',[9] a crucial development which increased the impact of changing ideas of Anglo-Saxon forfeiture further still by widening its geographical limits.

It was these developments which apparently laid the foundation of the legally backed 'total forfeiture' of estates and possessions for treasonous activity, from which there was no way for the individual to redeem himself, save only through the king's mercy, oath 'adequate in number of oath-helpers, and perhaps in solemnity, to the wergild of the king', or possibly trial by ordeal.[10] Overall, laws of total property forfeiture of 'all that one has' became increasingly stringent and frequent in the late Anglo-Saxon period,[11] though versions of the penalty itself had been around at least since Ine for the crime of fighting in the king's household.[12] By the tenth and eleventh centuries, other serious crimes against the king (and also one's lord) were often being punished by such forfeiture, including theft, piracy, fornication, adultery, as well as the aforementioned defiance of royal authority and treachery.[13] And it was not just the Anglo-Saxon kings who engaged in such activity. Lawson tentatively suggests that some of the executions and forfeitures of Cnut's early reign 'followed a proper legal process, and showed Cnut using the charge of treachery to seize lands according to English precedent'.[14] Æthelred and Cnut were two of the more enthusiastic users of forfeiture in the pre-Conquest period – probably arising from the unstable nature of the first few decades of the eleventh century – though the Scandinavian monarch was ultimately more successful at it than his Anglo-Saxon predecessor.[15] However, whatever the method of confiscation, the point remained that certain crimes against the monarch or monarchy were too serious to be 'paid off' by the perpetrator. In committing such a crime, he had lost what rights he previously possessed, and whatever he might expect from the king was through the king's exercise of forgiveness than any strength of his own position. This remained a fundamental basis, or at the very least an ultimate ideal, throughout the Middle Ages: total forfeiture was just that – not a fine of money or possessions, which implied some retention of rights, but the complete abrogation of an individual's control over his possessions, moveable and immoveable, and often his life, which could only be regained at the king's mercy.[16]

And, if the early Normans borrowed many ideas from their Anglo-Saxon predecessors,[17] those about forfeiture seem to be among them – though at this point, as we will see, implementation was still more about making examples of rebels than about following any sort of developed policy. Nonetheless, the type of feudalism encouraged by William the Conqueror further aided the definition, if not the reality, of the punishment of the 'botless' crime by emphasising the king's ultimate rights over all levels of the Anglo-Norman tenurial structure. Combine this with the reinvigoration of Roman law (and therefore potentially not just the concept of *majestas*, but also *laesa majestas* and even *perduellio*) throughout Europe in the later eleventh and twelfth centuries – something while not said to directly have influenced England did have an impact through the number of English administrators and churchmen being trained on the Continent at this time[18] – and it is unsurprising the treatment faced by some of those who incurred the new dynasty's wrath. Initially, of course, whether a result of mercy or practicality, William the Conqueror was relatively lenient to those individuals who had not actively resisted the Normans, and allowed many of the Anglo-Saxons willing to submit to retain their lands and offices.[19] However, following a number of uprisings, especially in Exeter and the north, by the mid-1070s William had abandoned this policy in favour of a more aggressive approach to his conquered foes:[20] by 1075, according to Fleming, 'the majority of wealthy pre-Conquest landholders were already dispossessed, and their lands had long ago been given out to other men'.[21] The Conqueror himself, faced with the rebellion in 1075 of the Anglo-Saxon earls of Hereford, Norfolk and Huntingdon, took away the rebels' lands and titles and redistributed many of them among his followers – though as we have seen only Waltheof, earl of Huntingdon, was executed.[22] And though considerable provision was made for the latter's wife and daughter thereafter,[23] perhaps through some sense of delayed remorse for the earl's death,[24] in the next century, when Orderic Vitalis was asked by the monks of Crowland to come up with an epitaph for their patron-cum-saint, Waltheof, the main moral of his life story remained: 'Honoured in war, revered by all, he flourished / Yet knowing worldly wealth and fame are shadows.'[25] Faced with such revolts early in his reign due at least in part to overlenient policy, by the time of the 'Revolt of the Earls', William I had learned to hit hard when it came to material treatment of rebels against his authority.

This, if somewhat belated, harsh handling of Anglo-Saxon noble estates also spilled over at times into the treatment of the first Norman rebels. If nothing else, Norman kings from 1075 onwards now had clear recent precedent for using long-term or permanent confiscation when dealing with rebellious nobles. While William Rufus was relatively lenient towards those who had simply obeyed the duties of liege homage when going into revolt in 1088,[26] he was far harsher with the main instigators in the upper Anglo-Norman nobility. The leader, and particular loser, was Odo, once one of William the Conqueror's favourites, now forfeit of an estate worth some £3050 a year and spread over twenty-two counties;[27] though other main plotters such as William de St Calais, bishop of Durham, and Robert de Mowbray were also said to have been harshly treated in this regard as well, the former losing his fiefs and the latter perhaps sent into exile with him.[28] However, though the threat was there, and despite the statement in the *Anglo-Saxon Chronicle* that a number of 'French men' lost their estates and went into exile,[29] most of the noble rebels taking part in the events of 1088, as other liege vassals, were treated more leniently.[30] For some, the return to favour was apparently only partial: Robert of Mortain received a pardon and ended up dying on his estate in 1090, having withdrawn there after his ill-fated association with Odo; the Clares were under suspicion and never regained full favour with William Rufus.[31] Others were luckier: Roger Bigod and Geoffrey of Coutances were quickly restored to full favour, so quickly that they were able to take part in the trial of the bishop of Durham. Nonetheless, even if not always exercised, forfeiture to varying degrees for nobles was a real threat by the end of William's reign, and he was, indeed, to use it once more in the aftermath of the revolt of 1095, when William of Eu and Stephen of Aumale lost lucrative lordships, while Robert de Mowbray, rebelling yet again, forfeited the earldom of Northumberland, and Odo, count of Champagne, was disinherited.[32]

But, as noted by Southern, Hollister and Green, it was Henry I who really took this developing right over confiscated lands to its extreme, as he had with mutilation. This king, primarily resulting from the need to build up his power base among the nobility, took a firmer, if 'dispassionately political',[33] line with the estates of those who had risen against him.[34] Though some of the land Henry used to endow supporters came from substantial alienations of the royal demesne, other property was from estates of individuals who had displeased him, such as those who backed the duke of Normandy – for instance, Robert de Bellême and his brothers, William, count of Mortain, and Robert de Stuteville – as well as those who later backed Robert's son, William Clito.[35] Throughout the period, these and other forfeited estates – including those of Robert Montfort, Ralph Bainard, Roger of Poitou and the valuable Malet honour of Eye – were used either in part or in whole to raise or reward Henry's servants and favourites, usually under permanent terms: according to the chronicler Orderic Vitalis, 'so he [Henry I] pulled down many great men from positions of eminence for their presumption, and sentenced them to be disinherited for ever'.[36] In one case, Henry disinherited three nobles at once – Philip de Briouze, William Malet and William Bainard – at a Whitsun court at Windsor in 1110,[37] and two years later deprived the 'eorl of Evreux' and William Crispin of their estates and drove them out of Normandy.[38] As a consequence of this generally hard-line policy, Henry, helped by an increasingly efficient royal administration as well as the precedents of his father and elder brother, was one of the first kings to have such a well-managed selection of patronage at his disposal.[39] Most famously, this king used many of these estates to raise men 'from the dust' – including Geoffrey de Clinton and Ralph Basset, both individuals to be used to counterbalance existing noble power in central England – as part of a larger endowment programme which also included both legitimate and illegitimate members of the royal family as well as those of the established nobility.[40] Though after 1120, there were 'few if any permanent confiscations', this was mainly because Henry I's increasingly dominant position made it unnecessary,[41] rather than signalling any change in royal policy: in other words, vigorous use of royal powers early on, especially those connected with forfeiture, allowed him to spend his declining years in relative peace.

For the first three-quarters of a century after the Norman Conquest, then, there was, if initially somewhat sporadic, a harshening of royal policy of estate forfeiture towards those who had most displeased the king, especially after the misplaced leniencies towards the Anglo-Saxon rebels of the 1060s and early 1070s. However, thereafter, though both Stephen and Matilda tried to exercise the full spectrum of regal feudal rights over recalcitrant vassals, at times by use of land confiscation, the problem was almost always enforcement – examples of individuals who had forfeited ignoring confiscations and/or retaking lands arose throughout the Anarchy, including those of Baldwin Redvers, Simon de Senlis and even Robert of Gloucester, the bastard son of Henry I and the main supporter of Queen Matilda.[42] Thus, for the development of forfeiture at the highest levels at least, the Anarchy really was a period of chaos, with neither claimant's royal administration being able to take a firm, or at least sustainable, line towards land seizure. Unsurprising, then, was the clause in the charter of Henry II issued immediately after his coronation in 1154, that his subjects would hold the lands 'as freely and peaceably and fully in everything as King Henry, my grandfather, granted and conceded to them'[43] – in effect putting to nought all the forfeitures and regrants of the previous nineteen years. Rather, and in the long term more important than the Anarchy, at least in terms of kings' landed relations with their subjects, another mainly contrary development – that of secure inheritance – had continued apace. This development gradually muted the character of the king's right of forfeiture, and made Henry I's policy of long-term confiscation and regrant even more out of place by the later twelfth century. The increasing importance of security of tenure was first clearly documented – if rarely put into effect at the time – in Henry I's *Coronation Charter* (1100) where clauses were included promising, among other things, only 'lawful' reliefs on inheritance and allowing widows and other relatives the wardships of minors.[44] More important than the words of kings at coronations, however, was the fact that, over the course of the twelfth century, through the practice of sons receiving their fathers' lands over a series of generations, families also began to gain *de facto* rights over the descent of their estates. Through this process, as de Aragon has noted, inheritance had become relatively secure by the latter half of Henry I's reign, and most land repossessions that did happen, did indeed come primarily through political turmoil: specifically sixteen forfeitures from 1086 to 1113/14 and five from 1136 to 1154 – the first set mainly, as we have seen, a result of the battles between the surviving sons of William the Conqueror, and the second the result of the Anarchy.[45] In other words, even by the end of the Anarchy, inheritance and the passing of land from father to son was an increasingly fundamental part of feudal tenurial life, and both kings and landholders ignored this development at their peril.

Nonetheless, when such estates did forcibly revert to the crown, the question of how royal administrations treated forfeited lands was at times raised in this period. It was an issue for the twelfth-century writer commonly known as 'Glanvill', one of the key legal texts for the period – notably, in this case, the writer clearly dividing the issue of royal pardon from that of reseisin, making clear the immediate lord's rights connected with the case, and so even here again reinforcing the importance of such property rights in general in the period:

> If anyone has been duly outlawed and later restored to the peace by royal favour, neither he nor his heirs may on that account recover from their lord any inheritance which he had, except by grace and favour of the lord; for the lord king does not wish, when pardoning wrongdoing or outlawry, to infringe thereby the rights of others.[46]

Indeed, following on Henry II's settlement after the Anarchy, there was a determined effort by the king's government to sort out many of the disputes over forfeited land that had rumbled on over the last quarter-century; and, though mainly meant to be a restatement of royal rights, this also helped set landownership on a firmer basis. Moreover, the administration's continued concern with property regulation in the 1160s and 1170s, as witness the 'Writ of Right', *Novel Disseisin* and *Mort D'Ancestor*,[47] may further have tempered Henry's own reaction to those who aided his son, Henry the Young King, in rebellion in 1173–4, if in no other way than by giving royal officers clearer parameters within which to work. Of the nobles who took part in this rebellion, none were executed, and few lost their estates for any length of time. According to Warren, Henry II was 'content to make the peace on the basis of the *status quo ante bellum*' and, in the words of the official announcement:

> Our lord the king and all his liegemen and barons are to receive possession of all their lands and castles which they held fifteen days before his sons withdrew from him; and in like manner his liegemen and barons who withdrew from him and followed his sons are to receive possession of their lands which they held fifteen days before they withdrew from him.[48]

As noted, this was to include both those who had been connected with his sons' revolts, as well as other rebels, clearly indicating a fairly wide use of leniency. As a result of the peace treaty of September 1174, Robert de Breteuil, earl of Leicester, and his wife were released from custody,[49] and though his castles at Leicester and Groby were destroyed, and Mount Sorrel and Pacy-sur-Eure retained by the king, most of his estate returned by early 1177.[50] Another important player of 1173–4 who also regained his lands in fairly short order was Hugh Bigod, earl of Norfolk. In July 1174 Norfolk surrendered and did homage to the king, having to pay a 1000 mark fine for the trouble he had caused, though notably one of the few recorded for the period.[51] Nonetheless, as a consequence of being back in favour by 1175 or 1176, most of his lands were granted to his son, Roger, upon his death in 1177 – though again some strategically important castles such as Framlingham and Bungay were destroyed in the interim.[52] Finally, Hugh, earl of Chester, one of the key players in the revolt, had a similar, if somewhat more complex and drawn-out, experience: after being taken prisoner at the siege of Dol in the summer of 1174, and shunted back and forth between England and France, Hugh was 'deprived' of his earldom – though he was then admitted to the general peace later in that year, and by early 1177, as a result of the Council of Northampton, the earldom, as well as his lands on both sides of the Channel, were restored to him.[53]

Overall, then, along with little evidence during the 1173–4 rebellion that estates were granted out to others as patronage rather than, if actually seized, simply held in guardianship by the king's government, and the line was quite clear on the rebels and their lands: according to the contemporary tract the *Dialogus de Scaccario*, 'few of them lost their property, none their civil rights or life or limb';[54] or, as one modern commentator put it for the period as a whole, throughout his reign Henry II 'rejected confiscation as a penalty for political misbehaviour'.[55] Add this to the development of the King's Bench and Common Pleas, and the more general growth in record keeping in the kingdom as a whole during the last half of the twelfth century and the first half of the thirteenth,[56] and the situation was ripe for making control of land a more owner 'friendly' and transparent issue as the high Middle Ages continued. Indeed, even if one had dared to incur royal or governmental displeasure, this growth of the importance of record keeping – and more generally of criminal and civil litigation with an emphasis on property rights by both king and landowners – was bound to make the legal protection of estates more of an issue, and more one that any individual facing downfall would look to in order to protect not just himself, but his family's position within society. After all, if royal administrations were looking to enforce and exploit their rights to the fullest through the use of record keeping, then it was difficult to argue against the king's subjects using the same materials for defending their own positions – a use exemplified not only in the trawling of royal records by landowners and their lawyers intent on proving their point,[57] but also by landowners themselves paying to get their charters and deeds entered on the royal rolls. All this tended further to build up, as well as expand, the importance of both royal record keeping and litigation as the Middle Ages progressed – which in turn obviously made it increasingly difficult, initially anyway, for kings simply to 'grab back' lands permanently from those who had fallen from grace.

The individual's control over his property, then, for himself and, gradually, his heirs, was becoming more secure through the impact of time and practice. Even King John, well known for extracting and abusing hostages from nobles who had displeased him, as well as other tricks to gain as much wealth (cash or land) out of them as he could (extortionate reliefs, fines, etc.), only ever permanently dispossessed a handful of barons prior to the civil war of 1215–17, the most important being William de Braose, who raised the king's ire by accusing him of the murder of Prince Arthur.[58] Otherwise, though lesser individuals may have been targeted, the estates of nobles were not normally forfeited in full while England was at peace. Even when their lands *were* given to others, few of these pre-war grants were made with any degree of permanence; most, according to S.D. Church, being under limited terms (e.g. 'so long as the same man shall serve us well' or 'as long as it shall be pleasing to us'), and rarely in fee.[59] And this policy of relative leniency towards estates of disgraced rebels continued throughout the last, tumultuous, years of the reign and beyond. After the initial agreement between John and the barons at Runnymede, it is noticeable that, when the chancery writs went out concerning redressing of wrongs, including seizures of land, Warren notes few to whom entire estates needed to be given back.[60] Even the second, more active, phase of rebellion by the barons did not cause mass long-term forfeiture for most of those nobles involved, though the author of *The History of William the Marshal* notes that the rebels themselves did demand their 'liberties', and that both sides went to extremes.[61] Of the members of the higher nobility who lost their estates, most received back their lands either by John's death in late 1216 or within a year or so of Henry III's accession. Though some rebel landowners did lose parts or all of their estates, there was no set disinheritance policy[62] – despite the fact that the government was desperate for money in this period and, according to Turner, 'both magnates and local officials proved reluctant to fulfil their financial obligations to the royal government'.[63] The lands late of John Maltravers in Woodchester (Glos.) were given to Walo des Cotesne,[64] the lands of Hamo Peche in Corby (Lincs.) to Thomas Peverill,[65] and there were also wider grants of rebel lands in various counties[66] – most of which were granted for 'as long as it pleased the king' or similar terms, and almost all of which would be returned within a few years. Similarly, there were the cases of William de Cantelupe, who was granted the estate of Nicholas de Verdun, and Robert Camponia, given all the lands of William Basset in his bailiwick[67] – both of which would make substantial, if short-term, additions to their estates. And though, as Church notes, most properties returned to their original owners because of regime change rather than any foreseeable adjustment in policy on the part of John,[68] nevertheless, when the Minority government, which was still royalist and mainly staffed with administrators of John, came to power, it quickly looked to return the lands as a sound and relatively simple route to stability. As with 1173–4, there was a general acceptance that estates should be given back *status quo ante bellum*[69] – though notably, foreshadowing events in 1265, some still had ransoms to pay, while others had evidently come off the worse.[70]

Thus, as has recently been pointed out, 'during the Angevin period, the complete dispossession of aristocratic rebels seems to have been a rare occurrence',[71] a statement which holds true for most of Henry III's reign as well. Nonetheless, this favouring of effectively temporary confiscation over a more full-blooded use of the royal feudal right of forfeiture was briefly suspended after Simon de Montfort's defeat at Evesham in 1265. Pushed along by the greed of royal supporters eager to augment their estates, and undoubtedly also by the growing number of illicit confiscations which was turning the English countryside into a free-for-all, in the autumn of that year Henry III announced the confiscation of the lands of rebel barons and their redistribution among his supporters: Knowles reckons that the estates belonging to 254 rebels were granted to 71 royalists:[72] for instance, on 12 January 1266, the king granted to his son Edmund all the lands, held both directly and indirectly of the king, of both de Montfort and Nicholas de Segrave, to hold to him and his heirs.[73] Reseisins were also popular, especially the reversing of grants forced on the king by de Montfort, though also causing yet another group of potential claimants to develop. Four days after Evesham, in August 1265, the king made a perpetual grant of Garthorpe manor from the estate of one of the closest advisors of Simon de Montfort, also reversing any connected grants made in the king's name during his imprisonment by the rebels:

> August 8, 1265 (Worcester) Whereas during the king's stay in Gascony he granted to Robert Walerand by charter the manor of Garthorp, late of William de Gaugy, deceased, who held of the king in chief, and upon whose death the said manor escheated to the king, and whereas while the king was in the ward of Simon de Monte Forti, earl of Leicester, the said manor was granted to Peter de Monte Forti, which grant with all such grants the king wishes to revoke and annul; grant, in form of letters patent, of the king's free will, of the said manor to the said Robert, and his heirs, to hold by the service due therefrom.[74]

Initially at least, then, the terms were very harsh for the rebels and all connected with them, though the king's government clearly realised that there

might be further fallout as a result. On 25 October 1265, Warin de Bassing-
burn was granted for himself and his heirs lands and rights of Thomas de
Estlegh, Robert de Hardredeshull, Giles de Argentein and Walter de Coleville,
all of whom had been followers of de Montfort, with the protecting clause
over the grants: 'the said lands to be held by the said Warin, and his
heirs, from the chief lords of the fee by the services due therefrom, so that
the said lords shall lose nothing in wards, reliefs or other things by reason
of this gift; with special clause of warranty against the former owners'.[75]
In other words, not only was the king protecting the land grant against
future claims, he was also making sure that others, especially presumably those
who had remained loyal to him, did not lose out on the land grants either –
looking back to the general tenor of the clause from Glanville quoted earlier.[76]
Grants throughout the immediate aftermath had similar clauses covering
other lords' interests as well as those of the king[77] – evidently the king and
his administrators trying to disrupt the estates of other landowners, as well
as royal interests, as little as possible.

Unsurprisingly, this policy of rebel estate redistribution primarily for the
sake of his supporters and mainly with an air of permanency, however controlled, soon proved unworkable, and hundreds of dispossessed men, many
having played only limited parts in the Barons' Wars, now resorted to guer-
rilla tactics in order to get their estates back. Henry III's government, faced
with renewal of the civil war, was forced to arrange a modified version of the
Dictum of Kenilworth, allowing former rebels their lands back through a gra-
dated system of fines, the main point being 'the rejection of the policy of total
forfeiture in favour of redemption at fixed terms'.[78] The ranking of fines was
threefold: those who were to pay three times the yearly worth of their lands,
those to pay five and those to pay seven – though, according to Powicke, only
the Ferrers earl of Derby, Henry de Hastings (the commander of the garrison at Kenilworth Castle), and 'those who had mutilated the royal messenger' there were included in the latter.[79] The other two ranks of fines dealt
with, firstly, those who had fought during the war and its aftermath against
the king as willing participants (the largest group) and those who had
supported the rebels. Though the majority of grants and pardons in the Patent
Rolls do not mention the specific terms involved – for example, William
Marmion's and Nicholas Segrave's[80] – it appears from the Exchequer Lord
Treasurer's Remembrancer, Memoranda Rolls (E368) that the idea of a scale
of fines, as per the *Dictum*, was the one which was used.[81] However, since it
was clear that many individuals could not even pay these fines without access
to the income of their estates in the interim, a further compromise was reached
concerning the control of the properties involved. Ignoring the opposition of
royalists who had benefited from the confiscations, the king's government,

spurred on by the belated armed rebellion by Gilbert de Clare, accepted the idea of the quick reseisin of estates so that fines could be paid and the lands redeemed.[82] But despite such acts, the monarchy was by no means a complete loser in the final outcome for, as well as securing the administration large sums of money, the *Dictum* did help to reinforce royal power by holding substantial fines over the heads of a number of very important landowners – and though most were paid off, mitigated or forgiven by the end of the decade,[83] a few, such as Nicholas Segrave, who owed 2000 marks to Edmund of Lancaster for lands in Leicestershire, continued well into Edward I's reign.[84] Overall, however, medieval landholders now had a far clearer idea of what they believed went 'beyond the pale' when it came to confiscation of their estates by the government – even when it came to punishment for rebellion – and were more than willing to react forcibly if the king or those holding the reins of power ventured beyond its boundaries. For the disgraced or out-of-favour noble, then, this was a period of relative tenurial security, even in rebellion.

Shifting definitions of forfeiture

> If he is convicted he shall suffer the extreme penalty with torture, the loss of all his goods, and the perpetual disherison of his heirs, who are admitted neither to their paternal nor their maternal inheritance. For this crime is so serious that his heirs are hardly permitted their lives. If they are sometimes admitted to the succession it will be more as a matter of grace than of right. (Bracton, 'On the Crime of Lese-Majesty' (mid-thirteenth century))[85]

> And if the defendant be vanquished, let the judgement be this, that he be drawn and hanged, or put to such other painful death as we shall direct, and that all his movable goods be ours, and his heirs disinherited; and his children shall be incapable of ever holding land in our realm. (Britton, 'On the Outcome of Trial by Battle' (1290))[86]

In essence, then, the century or so between the end of the Anarchy and the aftermath of Evesham marked in practice a period of primarily temporary estate confiscations – and in the cases where this was ignored in favour of a more full-blooded, permanent and permanently regranted forfeiture policy, soon thereafter dissension, violence and, ultimately, grant reversal often ensued. However, this relatively – if somewhat unavoidably – 'soft' attitude towards material penalties for falling from grace was gradually replaced by an altogether more virulent, and controversial, approach to the royal right of forfeiture by the later Middle Ages. Part of this change, of course, was the result of the political history of the period – most notably, changes in the royal reaction to dissent. In particular, Edward I had seen what a lax hand had done to his father's authority, and was determined not to let it happen to his own. As with bodily penalties, to be able to outface potential rebellions in Scotland, Wales and Ireland, as well as to keep his barons in line at home, Edward felt the necessity to act more forcefully against the estates who went against him. It is unsurprising, then, that not only did this king bring out a series of enactments to enhance royal tenurial power in general, much as Henry II had done after the Anarchy, but also, as his great-grandfather had done (if quite a bit more effectively), he tried to hone the power and tone of existing legislation to make it once again more of a tool for a government trying to protect its rights rather than for subjects working to establish theirs.[87] *Quo Warranto* and the connected Hundred Rolls in particular reinforced the idea of the land law of the realm, and any resulting records, primarily being an instrument for the king, to be used in his interests, even if they would later be useful for landowners pushing to prove their points. At roughly the same time, however, new ideas concerning treason were also being worked out (whether or not under the influence of the revival of interest in Roman jurisprudence),[88] especially the refinements of Bracton in *Fleta* and *Britton*,[89] and though Edward I's lawyers still mainly defined treacherous activity as being against the king's person or those doing his work, they were now willing to think more widely about such crimes as well, with consequently more encompassing applications of forfeiture:

> he [Edward I] was prepared (where Scotland was involved) to accept it could be against the people of the realm. [Moreover] to the general notions of lese-majesty, he added the raising of war against the king (riding armed with banner unfurled), while plotting treasonous acts was taken as seriously as actually carrying them out.[90]

This was, in other words, a broadening of treachery legislation focusing more clearly on potential troublemakers and their estates – mainly, as it would turn out for future kings at least, those among the nobility – while also reviving in part the Roman concept of *perduellio*, reaffirming the idea of *laesa majestas*, and looking forward to the idea of 'constructive treason', and especially treason 'by words', of the fifteenth century.[91] Finally, when it came to the prosecution of such crimes, 'the legal procedure against offenders was not the usual indictment or appeal, but the idea of public repute "on the king's record" (at the word of the king and his advisers)',[92] again not only emphasising that the record was for the king's sake rather than his subjects, but that it was, theoretically at least, usually for acts well within the public consciousness. These developments, then, potentially made more far reaching the material, not to mention physical, penalties which could be exacted from those who fell too far from favour with the king.

However, two other developments were also contributory factors to the shift in the nature of the royal right of forfeiture, which helped move it by the fourteenth century towards the idea of longer-term disinheritance rather than temporary confiscation. Both were connected with changes in royal feudal overlordship in the later Middle Ages. First, until the later thirteenth century, there was the continual process of subinfeudation, the breaking down of knights' fees into smaller parcels for the sake of retainers, their retainers and so on. Though halted in practice (for the king at least) by writs starting in 1256, and by the statute *Quia Emptores* (1290) for both king and nobles, in many ways the damage had been done to the king's control over his feudal rights (wardship, marriage, escheat, delay in relief payment), it being increasingly difficult to enforce the royal prerogative over a fragmenting, and now in effect inheritance-based, system.[93] However, the main legislation brought about to control these problems, *Quia Emptores*, which allowed the feudal chain only to contract and no new tenancies to be created,[94] also made the monarch the prime loser from the legal or illegal evasion of a growing number of feudal incidents. This was true not only because the monarchy was increasingly put in the position of tenant-in-chief as a result (and therefore directly affected when it came to the decay or loss of such incidents), but also because, more generally, the king was, of course, 'always lord and never tenant',[95] and so continually at a disadvantage when such loss did take place, not being able to recoup that loss further up the chain. In the next century the rise of uses,[96] and to a lesser degree the further development and execution of entails, jointures and dower rights,[97] all had a further dampening (or at least delaying) impact on the number and value of wardships, marriages and reliefs, as well as escheats, coming in to the king, and made any land which did or could return by other means – including most notably for this discussion forfeiture – all the more important. Bean notes this development (especially as a result of the development of 'enfeoffments-to-use'), and the impact it would have upon royal feudal rights – though he argues that 'a real consciousness of the inroads that uses were making into the profits of feudal incidents could occur only when the Crown saw the need for action because it was attempting to exploit those revenues to the full and find its efforts impeded through the existence of uses', a need which he dates to the later fifteenth century.[98] That said, surely a more general awareness of the declining vitality, or at the very least mishandling, of royal feudal rights as a whole, rather than just in connection with uses, should be considerably backdated – especially as there were concerns forcefully voiced well before this point, concerns presumably not without cause. The complaints about wasting royal resources (including those for patronage) and structured demands for resumption of grants based on feudal rights starting as early as the Ordinances of 1311 and continuing throughout our period (e.g. 1340–1, 1376, 1400, 1407, etc.),[99] suggest that stress was being put on the lands and profits from feudal incidents returning to the king – at the same time, notably, that legal methods used to avoid them were becoming more prominent. The fact that, by the end of the fourteenth century, and despite considerable controversy at the time, uses and entails had all been included in forfeitures by traitors,[100] not only closed a significant legal loophole, but also helped the king's government to again, to a degree at least, exploit royal rights over confiscation of lands more fully.

And, in the same period that this weakening, and attempted retrenching, of the actuality of royal feudal rights over the king's resources was taking place, further enhanced by a more general shortage of suitable property for large-scale purchase by nobles by the fourteenth century,[101] and possibly even the longer-term if delayed impact of the loss of Normandy and associated patronage in 1204,[102] a third process was also active which placed any such available land at a premium – namely the development of an increasingly hereditary parliamentary peerage and the desire for monarchs to get their favourites and supporters secure within it.[103] The development of this institution, and especially the increasing connection of certain amounts of land with certain ranks with it (e.g. as noted in the *Modus Tenendi Parliamentum*),[104] meant that, by the second quarter of the fourteenth century, any royal supporters (especially those who had come up through the ranks) raised to either baronies or earldoms had often to be granted considerable, and increasingly set, amounts of lands. Apparently following on, or connected with, the ideas put forth in the *Modus Tenendi Parliamentum* of around the same time, the endowment of Harcla for the earldom of Carlisle in 1322 was the first substantive recognition by a ruling regime that a sufficient amount of land was necessary to sustain an individual within the peerage[105] – though it was quickly followed by Mortimer's effective endowment for the Earldom of March in 1328, and of course the many promotions into the peerage of Edward III's majority.[106] At roughly the same time, moreover, the impact of the more general political situation, in particular Edward II's problems and Edward III's insecurities, meant that the monarchy was under considerable pressure to show a new aggressiveness in its exploitation of other possible sources of lands to entrench their supporters in the landed community, whether their record warranted it, like Harcla and Edward III's 'new men', or not, like the Despensers. Indeed, the statute of 1327, noted as important by Bean,[107] was in essence the reaction by the major landowners in parliament, indicating that the king (Edward II, and conceivably Edward I also in this instance) had been trying to go too far in attempting to expand reasons for land confiscation, and that forfeiture for such a relatively minor matter as unlicensed alienation of land was simply unpardonable.[108] Therefore, in the same period when the amount of 'normal feudal resources' open to the king had begun to go into decline, the king had to push for more wealth, especially in the form of land, to make sure his supporters were able to prosper in the most important political institution of the kingdom, the peerage in parliament. Unsurprisingly, then, the potential of forfeited lands began to become far more interesting to those in power.

This growing importance of the royal right of forfeiture over the later Middle Ages can be broken down into two main areas, both primarily, though as we have seen not solely, connected with the treason legislation developing in the same period: the scope of crimes for which estates were to be confiscated, to be discussed here; and the fate of the estates once they were taken into the king's possession, which will be examined in the next section. In terms of the scope of crimes now open to forfeit, in the first half of Edward III's reign a continuous debate rumbled on between the king and the landowning community over what crimes warranted forfeiture in the first place and which then meant forfeiture to a vassal's immediate lord and which forfeiture to the king.[109] Though the debate had already been ongoing in the previous two reigns, as we have seen, why this monarch's government pushed the expansion of the right to crisis point is difficult to tell. Most obvious was Edward's realisation that, in the face of both problems with the nobility over the past two decades and the damage potentially done to the monarchy by his father's deposition, he had to take a much firmer hand with internal dissent. This, along with the fact that the lands which this king gained hold of as a result of this widened definition of treason could be used to further enhance the power of his supporters for both war abroad and political power at home,[110] all made Edward III in particular believe an aggressive royal policy towards both treason and forfeiture was the approach to take. Whatever the cause or causes, the controversy between king and landowning classes over the definition and scope of treason (and forfeiture) reached a climax with the statute of 1352, a piece of legislation arising from both short-term grievances by parliament and longer-term developments noted above (for the statute, see p. 42). This statute stated which crimes were treasonous, warranting forfeiture to the king, and which were only felonies, to be held by the king for a year and a day and then returned to the convicted's feudal lord or lords. Further, the statute effectively stopped judgement on the 'king's record',[111] and reinforced the point that all treason and similarly serious trials and questions of jurisdiction concerning the same should be held in parliament. But though such penalties now had a clearer definition and delineation – especially excluded riding armed, robbery and kidnapping from 'great' treason – the tenure of lands open to royal forfeiture was still rather vague. Because of the emergence and expansion of relatively novel varieties of land tenure involving third parties, especially enfeoffments-to-use and entails, some decision had to be made as to how lands so held were to be treated – namely, since more than just the accused had rights over them, whether they were open to forfeiture or not.

These issues, along with Richard II's attitude towards forfeitures,[112] and his more general stance on monarchical power ('the law is in the breast or mouth of the king'[113]), were to cause controversy in his reign, both at the time and among modern historians,[114] but by the end of the century we see what was in effect a victory for the monarchy in the face of attempted restriction, most types of tenure thereafter being made open to forfeiture to the king.[115]

The last stage in the theoretical development of the royal right of forfeiture can be seen in the rise of forfeiture connected with attainder (also discussed in Chapter 1). According to Rogers, attainder stemmed from the king's supporters 'capturing' the process of the appeal (as used by the Appellants in 1388) for royal purposes in the late 1390s[116] – a process which would turn out to be very useful against the king's enemies, living or dead.[117] Bellamy, Hicks and Lander have all written on the subject and, according to the latter, attainder 'was a procedure that had the virtues of speed and simplicity. All that was necessary to condemn opponents was the reading of a bill in the parliament chamber, the mere acquiescence of the Commons and its acceptance by the king.'[118] With such ideas in common currency, then, it was a relatively short jump to legally founded summary justice. However, its importance to the story of the shift from in effect temporary confiscation to a more full-blooded definition of forfeiture lies in the fact that – aside from obviously making lands potentially more quickly and easily confiscated by the king's government in the first place – with the development of attainder, through the process of the 'tainting of the blood', it was made more difficult for claimants related to a forfeitee to get his lands back, let alone be allowed representative or 'due' process to take place. In all instances, the downfallens' names were now disgraced and so were those of their line – namely, those most likely to attempt to pursue the issue through the courts. Thereafter, the only way for an individual to get a reversal of sentence was either at the king's (or sometimes parliament's) mercy, or through a change of monarchs – and sometimes not even then.[119] Attainder, in other words, in theory at least, helped to protect the rights of those individuals over their newly granted forfeited lands, or at least make it more difficult for their previous holders to gain reseisin.

Forfeiture in practice, 1322–1455

Lo, the king of this country – the Lord preserve him! –
Sends word to you by me, as suits his pleasure,
That none, on pain of blinding, be so bold
As to strike a single stroke or to move any nearer
To lead his host, or think himself so regal
That he may by his prowess disturb the king's peace.

For this is the custom here, and always shall be:
If a baron is so bold as to rise with his banner
Within the bounds of the kingdom, save only the king,
That man shall lose his land and later his life.[120]

These lines of the mid-fourteenth-century poem *Winner and Waster* show how serious and public the issue of treacherous activity and royal forfeiture had now become, and how severe the physical and material penalties.[121] Indeed, it was not just the legal controversies over what were forfeitable offences or which lands were open to be seized by the king's officials which were at issue. Making forfeiture a more serious and controversial proposition was the actual treatment of individual properties once under royal control. If Edward I can be said to have taken the first steps towards the more violent, longer-term forfeitures of the later Middle Ages by his manner of execution of Celtic traitors, Edward II took bounds by not only executing a considerable number of those English nobles who had stood against him at Boroughbridge in 1322,[122] but also seizing *en masse*, and in a more forceful and permanent manner than for the last two centuries, their connected estates. Though many of the confiscated properties remained with royal custodians – according to *Scalacronica* Edward II kept 'for himself whatever he was able to grab of the lands forfeited by the aforesaid barons',[123] the connected income swelling the totals of the chamber and exchequer for the period[124] – it was ominous that a considerable amount of property was also allowed to 'migrate' to the elder and younger Despensers under long-term, if not permanent, conditions.[125] Indeed, though most long-term grants were from the estates of dead Contrariants,[126] these were nonetheless often very lucrative properties. On 24 March 1322, a grant was made to Hugh Despenser the younger of the Lancastrian manor of Bisham (Berks.) to be held in fee,[127] and, on a grander scale, in early 1323, among a number of other long-term (life or longer) grants to the Despensers,[128] the king made an even more encompassing permanent grant to the younger Despenser of 'all the castles, manors, towns, lands and tenements of all those who lately rose in war against the king in Glamorgan, Morgannou and Wentelok in Wales, and of their adherents'.[129] About the same time, the king also gave Hugh the younger the castle of Carreg Cennen and the land of Is Cennen for life, late of John Giffard's estate,[130] and a bit later, also from the Giffard estate, the manor of Rockhampton (Glos.),[131] both helping to develop further his contentious Welsh and Marcher estate. Similarly, there were a number of long-term or permanent grants to members of the royal family, individuals who, considering Edward II's otherwise tempestuous relationship with most of the nobility, he had to make sure to keep onside: in July 1322 arrangements were made for the king's younger son 'wishing to provide for John de Eltham . . . after his own [Edward II's] death', giving him the castle, manor and honour of Tutbury, again part of Lancaster's estate, in fee.[132] John of Brittany, earl of Richmond and a grandson of Henry III, was granted the manor of Hart and the town of Hartlepool, late of the Contrariant Roger de Clifford, as well as John Mowbray's manor of Woodhall and the town of Thirsk (Yorks.), and the manor of Caythorpe (Lincs.), late of Roger D'Amory, all to be held by 'the said earl and the lawful heirs of his body'.[133] And though nowhere near the arrangements for the Despensers and the royal family, there were a number of long-term grants of Contrariant lands to royalist nobility and gentry as well – such as the August 1324 in fee grant to Miles de Verdon of Roger Mortimer of Wigmore's manor of Dissard (Meath).[134] Likewise, on 25 March 1322 the earl of Arundel was granted in tail male 600 marks' worth of land for 'good service rendered and to be rendered', namely all lands of, again, John Mowbray and other rebels in the Isle of Axholme, the Badlesmere manor of Shifnal (Salop) and Roger Mortimer's (of Chirk) castle, manor and land of Chirk and Dolforwyn, and the lands of Kerry and Caedewen.[135] All this then marked a clear shift from the royalist policy in the aftermath of Evesham, though even then there was initially, as we have seen, an attempt to move towards long-term confiscation. This time, however, with so clear and forceful a victory, so many executions afterwards and so defined a postwar policy, the implementation of the post-Boroughbridge policy was far more effective.

And, with the next political upheaval, the Usurpation of 1326, long-term forfeited-land use by the crown expanded further still, again focused around favourites and the most important royals. In particular, the Minority regime redistributed the massive estates of the Despensers, Arundel and others who had remained faithful to Edward II to enrich themselves and their cronies. Maybe partly because the *de facto* grantors, Mortimer and Isabella, were quite often the recipients as well, the term of tenure for grants from forfeited lands remained longer – keeperships or 'during pleasure' grants being replaced with those under life, entail, tail male,[136] or sometimes, though not often, permanent 'in fee' terms. Some estates were, at least in part, fragmented, such as the entailed grant of the manor of Mileham (Norfolk), forfeited by the earl of Arundel in 1326, to the above-mentioned John of Eltham, now the increasingly close confidant of the young Edward III and so a good way to keep a hold of the king.[137] Other lands were granted out in larger blocks, though again to members of the extended royal family. For instance, in 1327, the earl of Norfolk, the half-brother of Edward II, was given 1000 marks of land and rent entailed – including manors in Oxfordshire, Berkshire, Buckinghamshire, Cheshire, Gloucestershire, Essex and Lincolnshire – mainly forfeited by Despenser the elder in 1326 and granted by the king and 'all the council' in parliament.[138] Similar grants were also made to the earl of Kent, another half-brother of Edward II, and despite being a fervent royalist in the early 1320s[139] – all to make sure those most able to cause problems, especially in terms of counterclaims to the throne, were clearly onside with the Minority regime. Possibly the most famous instance of such longer-term granting, however, were the permanent grants of Despenser lands to Mortimer himself. These included not only the lucrative lordship of Denbigh, but also many of the earl of Arundel's other lands in Wales and on the Marches,[140] all of which would help to justify his promotion to the newly created earldom of March in 1328; moreover, to make the earldom, the title of which was also granted either entailed or in fee,[141] sustainable in the long term the landed endowment also had to be granted as such. Thereafter, though the 1328–9 Bedford rebels were dealt with less harshly by the Minority regime, and their lands not regranted *en masse*, this was probably because of the limited amount of time between the order to seize their lands and the rebellion's end – at best no more than a couple of weeks.[142] Nonetheless, the regime went back to form when it came to its treatment of the now downfallen earl of Kent's estate, a large portion of which was granted entailed to Geoffrey de Mortimer, perhaps the earl of March's son by his wife Joan – including the castle and manor of Donington (Leics.), the manors of Lechlade and Siddington (Glos.), Woking (Surrey), Caistor (Lincs.), Ryhall (Rutland), Keevil (Wilts.), Ashford in the Peak and the wapentakes of Risley (Derby.), Plumtree and Ollerton (Notts.) as well as the reversion of the manor of Beelsby (Lincs.), with remainder, in case of failure of issue, to the earl of March.[143] The Minority regime, as the Despenser 'tyranny', were intent on redistributing lands of their enemies as permanently as possible, not only enriching themselves but also making any resurgent 'old royalism' very difficult.

Having become an increasingly important part of long-term royal patronage policy by the end of the 1320s, during Edward III's reign this potentially controversial source of forfeited land further moved to become the cornerstone of his largesse programme – some of which again went to the royal family, but more was concentrated on members of the established nobility such as William Latimer, the son of Hugh Despenser the younger, also Hugh, and most importantly a smaller group of 'new men'.[144] Indeed, the lands of Mortimer, Isabella and their henchmen (including John Maltravers and Simon Bereford), as well as many of the Despenser properties held by Mortimer and Isabella, were all used as long-term patronage to those sixty-eight men Edward III raised to parliamentary peerage, some of whom would be promoted to the baronage such as Gilbert Talbot, Roger Swynnerton and John Darcy, and some also elevated to earldoms later in the decade such as William Montagu and Robert Ufford.[145] For both 'old' and 'new' nobility alike, though, more permanent (though rarely 'in fee') grants, especially tail male, seem to be the way for Edward to give out forfeited lands for the first decade of his independent rule, as when, in the summer of 1331, he granted in tail male parts of the Maltravers and Bereford estates to John Neville, a member of an established noble family and a participant in the Nottingham coup – and again, granted, unlike in previous centuries, with the assent of a representative assembly, in this case, parliament.[146] And even when the original term had ended, such grants usually remained away from the forfeitee and his family. In February 1336 Ralph Ufford was granted in tail male, for his service in Scotland and elsewhere, the Maltravers manors of Childrey (Berks.), Philipston and Wimborne (Dorset), which escheated on the above-mentioned John Neville's death without direct male heirs.[147] Some of the largest grants, though, were those from the Mortimer estate. For instance, in 1331, William Montagu, one of Edward III's closest advisors and a key player in the Nottingham coup, was granted entailed Denbigh, cantrefs of Rhos, Rhufiniog and Carmarthen and the commote of Dinmael in Wales, originally part of the Lancastrian estate.[148] More importantly, though some land was initially reintegrated into the royal demesne, such as when the Mortimer lordship of Chirk was annexed to the crown 'forever' after the Nottingham coup,[149] even in this instance the estate was, after a while, granted out again: in this case to the earl of Arundel in fee in the mid-1330s, with the notable clause 'that if the premises shall at any time be recovered against the earl or his heirs by judgement of the king's court, compensation shall be made'.[150] These and other forfeitures, including those from the Scottish wars, would help fund Edward III's patronage programme throughout the first half of his reign – though with the general political stability of the reign as a whole after the Nottingham coup, and the defeat of the Scots at Neville's Cross in 1346, by the mid-1340s forfeited lands connected with the French war, especially alien priories, would come to play a much bigger part.[151]

Edward III himself helped limit criticisms of his use of forfeited lands partly by balancing his use of such lands with the decreasing, though still relatively available, 'traditional' sources of patronage such as wardships and marriages as well as annuities and offices. Partly, also, he avoided too much controversy by making many grants conditional, if still of generally much longer terms than previously, and, differing from many earlier and later kings, choosing competent and generally congenial men who tended not to upset the established nobility – unlike Gaveston and the Despensers.[152] However, Edward III's successors were, on the whole, not nearly as able or as fortunate in such respects. Encouraged to a degree to rely, when available, on forfeited lands more than Edward and previous kings because of the growing impact of various legal devices on feudal incidents as the later Middle Ages progressed,[153] and the continued concentration of lands in fewer and fewer hands as the later Middle Ages continued,[154] nonetheless when using confiscated properties as patronage during their reigns, not only did these kings, especially Richard II and Henry VI, usually choose men who were of little worth to the kingdom as a whole, but they also failed to give any substantial patronage to the established nobility, instead concentrating it on a very small group of favourites. Perhaps the only place where such monarchs learned from their predecessor, at least to a degree, was in the policy of not granting out estates in fee, though most grants were long term, on parchment at least (life or entailed). When it came to Richard II's treatment of the Appellants in 1397, this monarch took total forfeiture to its extreme, sentencing them to death or exile, and dividing up their estates among a group of his favourites. For example, aside from the lands he annexed to his own 'Principality' of Chester,[155] some of the earl of Arundel's estates was divided up among four of his newly promoted men, Huntingdon, Nottingham, York and Percy.[156] The earl of Warwick's estate was redistributed, in what has been seen as a clear attempt to 'break up the socio-political units long established under the Beauchamps' – Warwick Castle going to the duke of Surrey, and other lands in the West Midlands and Gloucestershire going to the earl of Salisbury and Thomas Despenser.[157] Richard II was quite deliberate in his break-up of the latter estate, granting parts far and wide: take, for instance, the life grant to the king's esquire, William Audele, of two messuages and the pessage of Southampton; to the king's knight, John Bushy, a tail male grant of the manor of Kirtling (Cambs.); and a tail male grant to another king's knight, Henry Green, of the manors of Cosgrove and Preston Capes (Northants), and the reversion of the manor of Kibworth (Leics.).[158] The duke of Gloucester's estates did not fare much better, and the remaining Arundel and Warwick estates and rights were also at least partly fragmented and regranted under life or entailed terms.[159] Notably, about the same time that these and other forfeitures and regrants were going on, as mentioned above, Richard was also making authoritarian and extremely telling statements about his ideas of royal rights over forfeiture – for instance, 'that the life of any one of his lieges, and his lands, tenements, goods and chattels are at his will without any [process of] forfeiture'[160] – and, going from his actions, he intended to live up to them. In practice, moreover, through a number of royal writs in the late 1390s, it was clear that this king had little time for the protection offered by enfeoffments-to-use either, especially those connected with the Appellants and their heirs:[161] unsurprisingly, then, as we have already heard, by the end of the fourteenth century enfeoffments-to-uses and entails were both included in forfeitures by traitors.[162]

Richard's successor, Henry IV, initially took a more measured approach towards his opponents' estates, probably due to the nature and violence of his accession and the weaknesses of his claim. However, faced with continual rebellions, by 1404 this king realised that a hard line was the only way to defend his hard-won throne, and so he too had adopted 'increasingly sweeping and inclusive forfeitures of the traitors' estates', especially those of, or connected with, the Percy family.[163] One of the key, though unlikely, rebel allies of the Percies, Thomas Mowbray, had his estate spread far and wide, mostly under life or longer grants: Mowbray's castle, manor and lordship of Framlingham went to Prince Henry,[164] and his castle and town of Swansea in the lordship of Gower ('as much as is in the king's power') went to the earl of Warwick.[165] The earl of Northumberland also had his lands redistributed, with some smaller pieces going to lesser players such as John Robynson, 'one of the yeomen of the king's chamber', and the king's knight, Robert Umfraville, a loyal career soldier very active on the northern border.[166] And though there was an eventual rehabilitation of various families involved, mainly through service,[167] it was often a longer, more complicated process than had been faced in the high Middle Ages.[168] The heirs of another rebel of the period, the Lollard John Oldcastle, never saw any of his estate or his title, but more surprisingly it would take eighty years before the 1403 attainder of the earl of Worcester was reversed,[169] and John Beauchamp of Kidderminster, who fell in 1400, died without heirs after twenty years of being attainted.[170] Similarly, after the 1415 Southampton Plot, though Cambridge's and Lord Grey's estates were, according to Allmand, 'kept within their family circles',[171] both Cambridge and Le Scrope's families would have to wait for over a decade before the estates were returned to the direct male heir;[172] and the duke of Suffolk's heirs, though he was brought down in 1450 by the king's enemies rather than on royal orders, would never get back his earldom of Pembroke.[173] Reseisin, in other words, was often a long and tortuous process in these as in many other cases, and almost never brought the individual or his family back to their former positioning, if it quite often did their landed estate.[174] Thereafter, though a little beyond our period, some nod to a milder approach towards forfeitures was again implemented by Henry VI's government when dealing with the temporarily defeated Yorkists: however, this was mainly because, in this case at least, it was in the crown's interests for patronage 'not to be dispersed in the form of ill-considered rewards to numerous supporters'.[175] Nonetheless, the estates involved were often granted to life-tenure royal stewards, mainly courtiers, for the foreseeable future – even if with the profits probably going direct into the royal coffers. Thereafter, though eventual reversals did become more common (64 per cent of attainders of all levels of landowners in the reigns of Henry VI, Edward IV, Richard III and Henry VII were reversed, and 84 per cent of those of the nobility), they still could take many years to bring about: the attainders of the early 1460s, for example, often not being reversed until the 1470s.[176] The tradition of long-duration grants of forfeitures set in the fourteenth century was a hard one to break, unsurprising considering the growing dependence, actual and psychological, on such lands by kings looking for patronage since that time.

Overall, then, this increasingly harsh attitude towards landed estates, as well as the persons, of downfallen nobles, combined with the continuation of the trend towards longer-term, if rarely permanent, regrants made forfeitures all the more important, and contentious, an issue by the later Middle Ages – and one which, as we will see in the penultimate chapter, took up more and more of both the administration's, and parliament's, time. Even those lower down the social scale now realised that a noble family's forfeiture usually meant for a longer time than hitherto by the later Middle Ages, and often saw fit to take advantage of the situation. For instance, there were a series of reversals and attempted reversals, often themselves undoing reversals and regrants of Edward III's minority government: as when, in the early 1330s, Iorwerth, the chamberlain of Thomas, earl of Lancaster, requested the restoration of certain bailiwicks and rents he had held of the earl, which had been taken from him in 1322, restored at some point later in Edward II's reign, and then taken away again during the Minority and given to Roger Mortimer.[177] Again, early in Edward III's reign there was the land granted by Thomas Multon to John de Rye, which Thomas of Lancaster then disseised him of illegally – and which then forfeited to the king after Boroughbridge; accordingly, the claims concerning the land were reopened at the beginning of the new reign.[178] And, later in the century, when the earl of Arundel forfeited in 1397, those who had lost out initially to his family, in this case William and Florence Thornhull over the manor of Sandford (Salop), saw it as the right time to petition the king to get it back.[179] However, probably the estates most open to such actions were those seized and otherwise accumulated by the earl of Winchester and Hugh Despenser the younger during their period of dominance in the mid-1320s. After the fall of the Despensers and their associates in 1326 and the forfeiture of their estates, both inherited and acquired by various means, their land was again open to claims from previous owners – which could put a damper on any future use by the government, especially for the sake of patronage. For instance, in the first year of the new king's reign, William de Odiham petitioned king and council that though Edward I had granted him custody of the park of Odiham, to hold for life after the death of Robert Parker, it was seized by Despenser the younger, as so often, by extortion.[180] Similarly c. 1327, Richard Wyke claimed that he was ejected from various tenements in Windlesham by Hugh Despenser the elder, among others, in which he now planned to claim his right.[181] In the same year the daughters of John de Keu claimed forty acres of land in Sherrington (Wilts.) seized by the elder Despenser, claiming it with respect to their poverty and long disseisin.[182] Even religious houses which had lost lands to the Despensers or others were now in a position to reclaim them, as when c. 1328–9 the prior of Lewes claimed back certain lands connected with Melton Mowbray church and which Despenser the younger's wife had been given by Edward II as a result of a supposed breach by the priory of the Statute of Mortmain.[183] If the later medieval period was especially hard on the higher noble estates when it came to punishment for transgressions against the king or those in power, it was also a time when individuals lower down the order could look to profit. For every bad turn or fortune for one earl or baron, there could be several good ones for, say, county knights looking to add to their landed holdings.

But this return to an Anglo-Saxon/Anglo-Norman seriousness when it came to the forfeiture had other effects on later medieval England. Firstly, as Hicks notes for Edward IV's reign,[184] forfeited land granted in such a manner gave the newly raised supporters and favourites a real stake in the continuation of their benefactor's regime. Whether it be Edward III's new men, Richard II's favourites, or the individuals of varying qualities who inhabited the courts of Henrys IV, V and VI, all had an important interest in seeing the penalties inflicted stand as long as possible. Moreover, because royal patronage was now increasingly coming at the expense of other, downfallen, landowners, and in an increasingly public forum, it was also politicising the issue as it had never been before. It is notable that, in the period before Edward II when kings were criticised for having favourites, it was not primarily for the land patronage given out (though complaints were noted about wasting the king's money and offices) but instead the way these people had risen and/or how they were acting (e.g. Henry I's new men, Poitevins, Savoyards, etc.); whereas during and after this reign, though criticism continued to be connected with the background and behaviour of favourites, the actual nature of the patronage (especially land patronage) being granted out became much more of an issue. Conspicuous in this regard, one of the earliest coherent and structured attempts at an official process of resumption of royal patronage, especially in connection with parliament, dates to the Ordinances of Edward II's reign[185] – around the time when so many aspects of falls from grace (not just treatment of land, but also trials and the body) had begun to change – a process which would become increasingly popular in the fifteenth century.[186] Finally, as for the recognised importance of Edward III in the development of the idea of a 'proper' long-term use of forfeited and other lands discussed above – as arguably a paradigm of sensible royal patronage – one of the allegations made against Richard II in 1399 was that he was giving away the royal patrimony, a patrimony bequeathed him by his grandfather; and, in 1404, the Commons went so far as to demand a resumption of grants since 40 Edward III

$(1367)^{187}$ – possibly because it was seen that this was the last time that the king's rights in this area had been used responsibly.

Loss of worldly goods, 1066–1461

Land, however, was but one aspect of a noble's identity, which, while important socially and economically, was not often visible to one's peers on a day-to-day basis. Rather, material wealth was also a key part of identity, and could be fuel for derision if not kept up-to-date, or worse, lost. Take the following story from Jacques de Vitry:

> I have heard how, when a certain covetous knight ate at the court of a certain noble, and asked after dinner for his mantle, which his servant had laid among the other garments, then, seeing that it could not at once be found, he began to revile him before all that stood by, saying: 'Son of a —, bring my mantle forthwith! Knowest thou it not?' The servant, offended and moved to indignation, answered in all men's hearing, 'Lord, I know it well; I have known it these seven years past; yet I have not yet been able to find it.' The other knights hearing this, began to laugh and scoff at this covetous knight, who was covered with confusion.[188]

In today's consumer society, it might seem accepted that keeping one's possessions new and looking fashionable is a benefit, but for a society increasingly influenced by the nature and trappings of status, both material and cultural, being perceived to be wealthy and successful was crucial to political and social survival, let alone acclaim. The popularity of books of manners and etiquette, Raymond Lull's *Book of the Order of Chivalry* and Geoffrey de Charny's *Book of Chivalry*, to name but two, points to the importance of the rules and symbols of class, and social order, in the Middle Ages, and especially the later medieval period – as did, of course, the Sumptuary Legislation of 1363,[189] and even, it could be argued, labour legislation.[190] To neglect such matters, even to the smallest degree, was to risk at best mockery and/or worse, social exclusion. Thus, when examining the medieval aristocratic outcasts and their families, one should not forget the impact of the often sudden deterioration of their personal material position. Take the inventory of moveables of the earl of Arundel upon his execution in 1397:

> One bed of blue satin embroidered with 'faucons' of gold and ten hangings with pieces from a tapestry with the arms of Arundel and Surrey and one 'frette', three curtains of blue taffeta, one 'sile' with one 'tester' of sandal emblazoned with lions of gold, one covering of scarlet embroidered with lions of gold, one coverture of ermine, ten carpets with pieces from a tapestry with lions; three curtains of sandal emblazoned with lions of gold, one bed of blue satin and red

panel, ten hangings of the same . . . of worsted panel, three curtains of blue taffeta and red panel, one bed with golden embroidered of 'crabbes' and the arms of Arundel, four red hangings of pieces of tapestry with the arms of Arundel, three curtains of red sandal, one bed of embroidered of gold with 'un parke'; seven red hangings with pieces of tapestry with the arms of March.[191]

Arundel's downfall, then, not only took away his, and his family's, wealth and position, it also removed his identity in the eyes of others, high and low – it took away how people would first judge him, and how, at least in part, he would have judged himself. If various forms of bodily penalty were the most painful of physical punishments, and temporary or permanent loss of estates the most financially damaging, then the forfeiture of personal property was perhaps the most psychologically damaging for the fallen noble and his family – and a daily reminder of their loss.[192] Grants connected with Arundel's fall were so comprehensive as to be almost intentionally humiliating to the memory of the fallen and his family, especially when they were given to social lessers, most notably two of Richard's career favourites, John Bushy and Henry Green, who, on 26 September 1397, were granted the utensils and other materials of one of Arundel's London residences 'except silver vessels, and also the barge late of Thomas, earl of Warwick, with all its tackle, which belong to the king by the forfeiture of those earls'.[193] Thus, the handling of personal goods could be more than punitive – it could be vindictive. Henry V's treatment of the chattels of one of the Southampton plotters was especially vengeful, granting in December 1415 to the 'king's servitors' and yeomen of his chamber, Robert Cliderowe and David Cawardyn – in other words, relatively lowly men – some of Henry le Scrope's goods, including such personal items as a 'long coat of scarlet furred with "broune grey", a half-length coat of scarlet furred with miniver, a long coat of green with sleeves lined with "tarteryn" and the body with "carde", a long coat of black velvet with the body furred with old "marteryns" and the sleeves lined'.[194] Sometimes, confiscated goods were treated with greater contempt by the monarchy, simply granted *en masse* to those first on the scene of a downfall – as after the battle of Evesham in 1265 when the occupiers of the lands of the Montfortians were often initially granted the goods and chattels connected with them,[195] and when Edward de Kethe was granted all the goods which he could take of William Wallace's.[196] One cannot help but think of the dismay such cavalier treatment of personal goods in particular must have had for both the downfallen and his family.

In the late fourteenth and early fifteenth centuries in particular, we have an abundance of confiscations of personal possessions, more than likely emphasising, along with the increasing number of comprehensive falls from grace and the amounts of bureaucracy surrounding them, the growing noble preoccupation with the trappings of status, and the hurt it was likely to cause when they were removed. It was especially painful when armour and horses were confiscated, not only removing one of the main physical manifestations of knighthood, but also any chivalric pretensions, and even, it could be argued, claims to masculinity.[197] We have already seen the completeness with which the earl of Arundel lost his possessions in 1397, and these, it should be noted, also included his implements of war – a loss then not just to him, but also his family, and especially his son, who had, after his father's fall, suffered an abusive custodianship by the duke of Exeter, and run away to live in poverty on the Continent.[198] In particular, we find that Arundel's armour and harness – symbols of both knighthood and manhood – including a pair of black knives with the arms of Arundel on it, had been confiscated, and were on their way to John Torre, the king's armourer.[199] Similarly, on 6 May 1400, Nicholas Saxton was ordered to confiscate 'all manner of armour which belonged to John late earl of Huntingdon, John late earl of Salisbury and Thomas Shelle, "chivaler," who made forfeit to the king, wheresoever and in whosesoever hands it may be found, and to cause it to be brought to the treasurer with all possible speed'.[200] This seizure of armour and implements of war, then, was not only a case of confiscation – it was often both a personal and a familial affront. Equally, the confiscation of townhouses and their contents was not just, or even, it could be argued, primarily a case of property deprivation: it was also a deep blow to a noble's, and his family's, pride and prestige – especially in London and Westminster, where nobles were expected to conduct business, entertain and impress their peers, and attend parliaments.[201] But the impact of townhouse confiscations could also be more long term and profound. The forfeitee's family, without a London base, added to the fact that they had often lost the head of the family, would have a very hard time re-establishing contacts and position. After Evesham, Henry III granted in perpetuity to Roger de Leybourn the Westminster houses of Peter de Montfort, slain in the battle of Evesham.[202] De Montfort, though not related to Simon, was one of his most important advisors – in 1264 even acting as a negotiator with the king of France to try and arrange a peace treaty between the warring factions in England – and for a while after his fall it looked like his family would be completely disinherited and have all their goods confiscated, especially without any physical base from which to press his case at the King's Court. However, probably more as a result of the *Dictum of Kenilworth* and the *Statute of Marlborough* than any direct efforts of his family, his eldest son did eventually recover most of his father's lands.[203] Not so lucky was the family of Bartholomew de Badlesmere after Boroughbridge in 1322, who had all his properties within Aldgate Ward taken into the king's hand and granted in tail male to the earl of Arundel, and whose son would have to wait until after Isabella's usurpation to reclaim his father's London estate.[204] Though the loss of London properties and contents may not have been the key to later hardships faced by disgraced nobles and their families, no longer retaining a fashionable foothold at the political centre of the kingdom probably did not help matters either.

Finally, along with valuable household possessions, jewels and plate were also among the first forms of moveable personal wealth that kings confiscated, not only because of their value, but also because they were useful forms of currency in times of trouble.[205] The fall of Piers Gaveston in 1312 has left us considerable evidence concerning easily moveable wealth, including various forget-me-nots given by the queen mother and even the queen, but also large quantities of diamonds, rubies, emeralds and sapphires, as well as various items of silver and gold.[206] Later in the reign, such moveable wealth was again to become an issue. On 22 February 1322, the sheriffs and bailiffs of Glouce-stershire and Somerset were ordered to aid an enquiry 'touching all jewels, coined money and other goods of Maurice de Berkele, Hugh de Audele the younger and other contrariants in those counties'.[207] In some cases, such jewels could then disappear from view, and be very difficult for either king or forfeitee to retrieve. Despenser jewels and precious metals were missing, or at least unaccounted for, well into the 1330s[208] – years after both Hughs' executions in 1326. The Despenser line faced much such loss, possibly the result of a family tendency to hoard moveable wealth in case of changes in circumstances: later, some of the jewels of a Hugh Despenser of Richard II's reign were ordered recovered from his executors in the middle of Henry IV's reign[209] – close to a decade after his downfall.[210] Currency and financial holdings of those in disgrace of the king were also avidly pursued. In particular, there was the pursuit of money deposited at home or abroad by those out of favour: the deposits of Falkes de Bréauté with the Templars in the 1220s which were pursued through letters to Pope Honorius III;[211] and in the 1320s, the recognisances due the Despensers and the earl of Arundel,[212] as well as the loss of Despenser money kept with Italian and other bankers in the 1320s.[213] In such circumstances, those who had previously lost out to the downfallen would often then try to reclaim money or obligations from his estate. For instance, a group of individuals headed by Stephen Abingdon took advantage of the forfeiture of the earl of Arundel in 1326 to try to get the reversal of recognisances held over them: now the earl was dead and the regime changed, Abingdon and his associates saw this as the perfect time to reassert their rights in the matter.[214]

In a few instances, wealth could be so completely stripped from an individual that, even if he did not lose his life, he had to beg for his livelihood. At its worst, the effect of the loss of all wealth was visible in the plight of dispossessed Lancastrians after Edward IV seised the throne in 1461. Of those who retreated to the Continent, Philippe de Commynes reported, though probably not without hyperbole, that some were 'in such great poverty that beggars could not have been poorer'.[215] The exiled Lancastrian duke of Exeter was, according to Commynes, found 'walking barefooted behind the duke [of Burgundy's] train, begging his livelihood from house to house without revealing his identity'.[216] And it was not only nobles that faced such personal shame, bereft of finery and luxuries, but also their wives, widows and families. In particular, while there were an increasing number of legal provisions protecting wives' of rebels rights,[217] the assumption remained that any moveable chattels which the woman brought into the marriage became the property of the husband[218] – and therefore often irretrievably forfeited upon his fall. Finally, if a man needed social trappings to emphasise his success, a woman needed them possibly even more simply to retain the illusion of status and position; such losses could otherwise have serious consequences for a noblewoman's life, as can be seen from the mid-fifteenth-century tract *The Lament of the Duchess of Gloucester*:

> Sum tyme I was in riche aray,
> Ther myght no princes be my pere;
> In clothys of gold and garmentys gay,
> Me thowght ther was no thyng to dere.
> I purchast fast from yere to yere,
> Of poore men I had no pite.
> Now ar my wittys all in were –
> All woman may be ware by me.[219]

The words put in the Duchess's mouth by the unknown poet were very apt – even if many would argue that she, let alone her husband, never warranted such a fate.

Overall, then, loss of both goods and land, temporary or more long lasting, accepted or controversial, was extremely detrimental to the noble and his family – and even if not long term or permanent, or meant to be, was still a cruel blow to income status and place in society of any noble worth his salt. That said, the growing use of forfeited lands for longer-term patronage to the king's supporters or new favourites, as well as their increasing use for funding supporters in, or into, the parliamentary peerage, meant that not only were such lands lost for a time to disgraced nobles, but it also became a lot harder to get them back. For most of the high Middle Ages – especially after the Anarchy and the settling down of inheritance rights – when an individual fell from favour for whatever reason, the estates rarely stayed away for very long. Usually given to temporary keepers, or kept by the king's government, the lands involved were usually fairly easily returnable – and indeed were returned in most instances within a couple of years. However, by the later Middle Ages a change had occurred, mainly in line with Bracton's ideas about forfeiture, though also looking back to Anglo-Saxon and Anglo-Norman precedent. Confiscated lands were now granted away under much more permanent terms – life, entailed and sometimes in fee. And, though hardly ever staying away from the original grantee or his family for the full term, they usually did stay away for a number of years or decades, rather than simply a few months or a couple of years – in the meantime usually becoming an increasingly integral part of another's estate. Finally, it was often more difficult to get the lands back off the individuals they had been granted to in the interim, especially with parliamentary attainder, and indeed parliamentary sanction, in effect disenfranchising the families of those who had fallen.

The best way to account for this change in the treatment of forfeited lands, a change which appears to have happened around the reign of Edward I, is by acknowledging, as has been done above, a number of key interrelated factors – the increasingly harsh treatment by this king of traitors and others who crossed him; the development of a land-based parliamentary peerage and the need to fund supporters within it; and, of course, the decreasing number of lands and other rights coming into the king's hands due to several reasons, including the rise of various devices designed to avoid having to give the king his rights, though also even perhaps, if more arguably, the delayed fallout from the loss of Normandy in 1204 and all the attendant rights that went with it. With these (and doubtless other) factors in play, there was a greater emphasis put on any land which *did* come back into the king's hands through what-ever means (but especially through forfeiture), emphasis which would be further intensified by the growth of the ideas of attainder and resumption (both of which can, in various forms, be dated back to at least Edward II's reign)[220] over the course of the later Middle Ages. This emphasis would make the treatment of forfeited lands become all the more controversial, and fought over, by the later Middle Ages. Finally, the loss of goods and chattels throughout this period, especially fashionable and valuable ones, took away not just the luxuries of the noble, but also the way he manifested his superi-ority to the rest of society. Poets may well moralise about the dangers of materialism and obsession with worldly goods, as in this early fifteenth-century verse:

As þe see doþ ebbe *and* flowe,
So fareþ þe world hyder *and* pedere.
A3en þe wynd they sayle *and* rowe
To gadre worldys gooddis to-gedere.

At þe last it goþ, y wot not whyder,
As ende of web out of slay.
And hem-self stoden so slydere
How it is wiþ hym, y kan not say.[221]

but those same goods were often a key indicator of worldly success in the Middle Ages, and not to show off meant, to others at least, that one was in social, if not economic and political, decline. This loss of personal possessions was to become increasingly thorough over the later Middle Ages, often leaving the disgraced noble with only the basics of survival within their class, if that. Whether by design or simply the effect of increasingly efficient royal administration, when an individual forfeited in full, he *would* often find most of his goods taken, and, by the later medieval period at least, often granted to other people, including old enemies as well as social inferiors. In other words, if execution was physical death, then forfeiture of lands and chattels could well be economic and social extinction, and increasingly so as the later Middle Ages progressed and the upper classes became more and more concerned with material wealth as an indicator of status – especially with the continued rise of chivalric culture and the construction of increasingly ornate manor houses, but also with the more general need to stay above the ever-aspirational gentry and merchant classes. Finally, such processes, it should be noted, could also make the downfallen all the harder to trace whatever the period, the loss of one's landed estates and possessions sometimes being so detrimental as to help erase the individual from the historical record. Chandler's assessment of the case of Roger and Arnulf, who forfeited to Henry I in 1102, well illustrates this point:

> When he took Roger and Arnulf's lands, the king deprived them of more than property. He deprived them of the one thing which gave them identity and importance, and he thereby rendered them nearly invisible to the public record and of no great interest to chroniclers, even the one (Orderic) who was almost a family historian. Every decision they had made in their adult lives had been based on land – keeping what they had, acquiring more or finding a more pliable lord from whom to hold it. No land, no inheritance – this is why they seem almost to vanish after 1102.[222]

Possession of an estate in all its guises, in other words, might not have been everything in the Middle Ages, but it was a very important part of identity, and without it, the individual quickly fades from the historical record.

Notes

1 J. Kail, ed. *Twenty-Six Political and Other Poems from the Oxford MSS. Digby 102 and Douce 322* (London, 1904), pp. 60–1.

2 Though see the Ferrers case in the previous chapter for an exception.

3 Perhaps the most famous example being the forfeiture of the Lancastrian estate from September 1398 to September 1399, by which time, going from 1394–5 income estimates, Henry of Bolingbroke would have lost about £10,000. A. Goodman, *John of Gaunt: The Exercise of Princely Power in Fourteenth-Century Europe* (Harlow, 1992), p. 341.

4 *The Old English Rune Poem: A Critical Edition* M. Halsall, ed. (Toronto, 1981), p. 91.

5 See above, pp. 58–9; Pollock and Maitland, *English Law*, i, 51; on the connection of *laesa majestas* and *Lex Julia Majestatis* and Anglo-Saxon treason laws, see Forbes, 'Laesa Majestas', 359ff.

6 Laws of Alfred, clause 4, *EHD c. 500–1042*, p. 410; Chaney, *Kingship*, p. 207; Loyn, *Governance of Anglo-Saxon England*, pp. 65–6.

7 *EHD c. 500–1042*, pp. 446, 463. Though these later two law codes note also the option of ordeal or wergild, or just ordeal (Cnut).

8 A. Harding, *A Social History of English Law* (Harmondsworth, 1966), p. 17. For capital punishment see Chapter 2.

9 Chaney, *Kingship*, p. 209.

10 Pollock and Maitland, *English Law*, i, 52; for the threefold ordeal, clause 30 of Æthelred's law code of 1008 and clause 57 of the laws of Cnut see *EHD c. 500–1042*, pp. 446, 463.

11 Chaney, *Kingship*, pp. 207ff.

12 M.K. Lawson, *Cnut: The Danes in England in the Early Eleventh Century* (Harlow, 1993), pp. 208–9; Loyn, *Governance of Anglo-Saxon England*, p. 46.

13 Lawson, *Cnut*, pp. 208–9; also see S.D. Keynes, 'Crime and Punishment in the Reign of King Æthelred the Unready', in I.N. Wood and N. Lund, eds. *People and Places in Northern Europe 500–1600* (Woodbridge, 1991), 77–8.

14 Lawson, *Cnut*, p. 209.

15 Stafford, *Unification and Conquest*, pp. 62, 146.

16 Though, as we will see, later provisions would at times be made for jointures, a wife's inheritance and other such tenures. See pp. 123n.115, 160.

17 P. Wormald, *The Making of English Law: King Alfred to the Twelfth Century* (Oxford, 1999), Volume I; vs. Pollock and Maitland, *English Law*.

18 Swanson notes the 'sheer mobility of individuals' at the time. R.N. Swanson, *The Twelfth Century Renaissance* (Manchester, 1999), p. 9. Powell notes a more active impact of both Roman and canon law. Powell, *Kingship, Law and Society*, pp. 30–1; also see Chapter 4 on more general developments in law, politics and government.

19 Williams, *English and the Norman Conquest*, p. 7.

20 See Williams, *English and the Norman Conquest*, Chapters 2–3.

21 R. Fleming, *Kings and Lords in Conquest England* (Cambridge, 1991), p. 178.

22 Williams, *English and the Norman Conquest*, Chapter 3.

23 See p. 160.

24 A feeling not unknown to William when dealing with rebels. See also p. 186.

25 *Ecclesiastical History of Orderic Vitalis*, ii, 351.

26 Barlow, *William Rufus*, pp. 89–90.

27 D.R. Bates, 'The Character and Career of Odo, Bishop of Bayeux 1049/
    50–1097', *Speculum* 50 (1975), 10.

28 F. Barlow, 'William of St Calais, *c*. 1030–1096', *DNB* (Oxford, 2004); though
    some question over Mowbray's fate: see Barlow, *William Rufus*, pp. 168–9.

29 *ASC* (1088E).

30 For the following, see Barlow, *William Rufus*, pp. 92–3, 167–9.

31 Bartlett, *Norman and Angevin Kings*, p. 211.

32 Green, *Aristocracy*, pp. 261–2; Henry of Huntingdon, *History of the English People*,
    p. 38.

33 C.W. Hollister, 'Henry I and Robert Malet', *Viator* 4 (1973), 121.

34 For treatment of the lives and bodies of rebels, see Chapter 2.

35 Green, *Government of England*, pp. 55–69, 180–1.

36 *Ecclesiastical History of Orderic Vitalis*, vi, 17. The count of Mortain's estate, as
    that of Odo of Bayeux in the previous generation, was broken up 'possibly
    because it would have been too dangerous to regrant them as a whole'. Green,
    Government of England, p. 181.

37 Henry of Huntingdon, *History of the English People*, p. 52.

38 *ASC* (1112E).

39 R.W. Southern, 'The Place of Henry I in English History', *Proceedings of the British
    Academy* 48 (1962), 150–1; C.W. Hollister, 'Henry I and the Anglo-Norman
    Magnates', in R.A. Brown, ed. *Battle Conference II* (Woodbridge, 1980), 98;
    though how novel many of these sources are is open to question. Green,
    Government of England, pp. 190–1.

40 *Ecclesiastical History of Orderic Vitalis*, vi, 17; most recently, see Hollister, *Henry I*,
    pp. 327–48.

41 Green, *Aristocracy*, p. 262. For example, Green points out that Waleran of
    Meulan's lands were confiscated in 1124, but returned within five years.

42 Green, *Aristocracy*, pp. 262–3.

43 *EHD 1042–1189*, p. 407.

44 *EHD 1042–1189*, pp. 400–2.

45 R. de Aragon, 'The Growth of Secure Inheritance in Anglo-Norman England',
    JMH 8 (1982), 384–6; more generally for inheritance in this period, J. Hudson,
    Land, Law, and Lordship in Anglo-Norman England (Oxford, 1997), esp. Part II and
    Chapter 9.

46 *Treatise called Glanvill*, p. 91.

47 See Warren, *Henry II*, esp. pp. 332–48.

48 From Warren, *Henry II*, pp. 136–8.

49 *CP* vii, 531.

50 Crouch, 'Breteuil, Robert', *DNB* (2004).

51 *Ranulfi de Diceto Opera*, i, 385; *Gesta Regis Henrici Secundi*, i, 73; according to Wareham
    a £466 fine. A. Wareham, 'The Motives and Politics of the Bigod Family,
    c. 1066–1177', *ANS* 17 (1994), 240–2; see also Chapter 2, p. 56.

52 *Gesta Regis Henrici Secundi*, i, 127; for Framlingham's thorough demolition, see
    R.A. Brown, 'Framlingham Castle and Bigod 1154–1216', *Proceedings of the Suffolk*

Institute of Archaeology (& History) 25 (1951 for 1950), 137–8. Though Framlingham's destruction was 'no different from the treatment which the King's most loyal supporters received'. Wareham, 'Bigod Family', 241–2.

53 T.F. Tout, 'Hugh, Fifth Earl of Chester (1147–1181)', rev. Thomas K. Keefe, *DNB* (Oxford, 2004); *CP* iii, 167; also see A.T. Thacker, 'Introduction: The Earls and Their Earldom', *Journal of the Chester Archaeological Society* 71 (1991), 14. See also p. 134 on Hugh's travels while in royal captivity.

54 *Dialogus de Scaccario* C. Johnson, ed. and trans. (London, 1950), p. 76.

55 J.E. Lally, 'Secular Patronage at the Court of Henry II', *BIHR* 49 (1976), 159; Green also notes for the period as a whole that 'it would no longer have been considered acceptable to remove lands from a family permanently except for the most grave reasons, and armed rebellion against the king was no longer among them'. Green, *Aristocracy*, p. 263; more generally of Henry II's rather tight approach to patronage, see Keefe, *Feudal Assessments*, pp. 106–8.

56 Clanchy, *Memory to Written Record*, pp. 58–62.

57 Clanchy, *Memory to Written Record*, pp. 168–71.

58 W.L. Warren, *King John* (London, 1961), pp. 185–8.

59 S.D. Church, *The Household Knights of King John* (Cambridge, 1999), pp. 93–4.

60 Warren, *King John*, p. 241.

61 *EHD 1189–1327* H. Rothwell, ed. and trans. (London, 1975), p. 81.

62 Carpenter, *Minority of Henry III*, pp. 46–7.

63 Turner, *King John*, p. 259.

64 *Rot. Litt. Claus.*, i, 286.

65 *Rot. Litt. Claus.*, i, 250–1.

66 E.g. *Rot. Litt. Claus.*, i, 240; for more land grants, see Church, *Household Knights*, pp. 91–3 footnote 108.

67 *Rot. Litt. Claus.*, i, 287, 288.

68 Church, *Household Knights*, p. 93.

69 *Memoriale Fratris Walteri de Coventria* W. Stubbs, ed. (London, 1873), ii, 239.

70 Carpenter, *Minority of Henry III*, pp. 41, 45–6, 56–60.

71 Bartlett, *Norman and Angevin Kings*, pp. 59–60.

72 Knowles, 'Resettlement', 26.

73 *CPR 1258–66*, 529.

74 *CCharR 1257–1300*, 56.

75 *CCharR 1257–1300*, 56.

76 See p. 93.

77 Numerous entries: *CCharR 1257–1300*, 56–8.

78 *SR* i, 12–18; Knowles, 'Resettlement', 29.

79 Powicke, *King Henry III*, pp. 536–7.

80 *CPR 1266–72*, 73.

81 For details of redemption agreements, especially term payment schedules, see E368/41–3.

82 J.R. Maddicott, 'Follower, Leader, Pilgrim, Saint: Robert de Vere, Earl of Oxford, at the Shrine of Simon de Montfort, 1273', *EHR* 109 (1994), 644–5.

83 Knowles, 'Resettlement', 32–3.

84 Powicke, *King Henry III*, p. 554.

85 Bracton, *Laws and Customs*, ii, 335.

86 *Britton*, i, 90.

87 For example, adjustments of *Novel Disseisin* during Edward I's reign. Prestwich, *Edward I*, pp. 271–2.

88 See Bellamy, *Treason*, pp. 3–5.

89 See Bellamy, *Treason*, pp. 15–16.

90 A. Musson, *Medieval Law in Context: The Growth of Legal Consciousness from Magna Carta to the Peasants' Revolt* (Manchester, 2001), p. 237; also see Kaeuper, *War, Justice and Public Order*, pp. 229–31.

91 See pp. 58–9 and 88–9.

92 Musson, *Medieval Law*, p. 237.

93 Prestwich, *Edward I*, pp. 273–4. And, of course, for grants to the Church with the Ordinance of 1228 as well as the Statute of Mortmain (1279).

94 S.F.C. Milsom, *Historical Foundations of the Common Law* 2nd edn (London, 1981), pp. 116–18.

95 J.M.W. Bean, *The Decline of English Feudalism 1215–1540* (Manchester, 1968), pp. 233–4.

96 Bean, *English Feudalism*, Chapter 3.

97 See Given-Wilson, *English Nobility*, pp. 137–53.

98 Bean, *English Feudalism*, p. 234.

99 SR i, 289–90; RP ii, 141, 356; iii, 57, 74; G.L. Harriss, *King, Parliament and Public Finance in Medieval England to 1369* (Oxford, 1975), Chapter 7; C. Given-Wilson, *The Royal Household and the King's Affinity: Service, Politics and Finance in England 1360–1413* (New Haven and London, 1986), pp. 130–8.

100 Most recently Musson and Ormrod, *Evolution of English Justice*, pp. 108–9; for debate over aspects of this, especially timing, see Ross, 'Forfeiture for Treason'; Clarke, 'Forfeitures and Treason'.

101 Though 'purchase from lesser men was commoner'. See G.A. Holmes, *The Estates of the Higher Nobility in Fourteenth-Century England* (Cambridge, 1957), pp. 7–8.

102 As Bartlett points out, no one knew in 1204 that the loss of Normandy would be permanent, and the duchy would still be an issue for kings throughout most of Henry III's reign: official recognition of this loss did not come until the Treaty of Paris of 1259. Bartlett, *Norman and Angevin Kings*, p. 27.

103 Powell and Wallis, *House of Lords*, pp. 303–15; Bothwell, *English Peerage*, Chapter 1.

104 Pronay and Taylor, eds. *Parliamentary Texts*, p. 81.

105 Powell and Wallis, *House of Lords*, p. 296.

106 R.R. Davies, 'Mortimer, Roger (V), First Earl of March (1287–1330)', *DNB* (Oxford, 2004); Bothwell, *English Peerage*, passim. Carlisle, Winchester and March were also new earldoms, and therefore doubly in need of further endowment. On these earldoms, see Prestwich, *Plantagenet England*, pp. 362–3.

107 Bean, *English Feudalism*, pp. 100–1.

108 *SR* i, 256.

109 J.G. Bellamy has examined this issue in depth: Bellamy, *Treason*, Chapter 4.

110 Bothwell, *English Peerage*, Chapter 3.

111 Musson and Ormrod, *Evolution of English Justice*, p. 27; also see Ormrod, *Political Life*, p. 76. Though in fact this had stopped some decades before. See above, p. 41.

112 See p. 108.

113 J. Dunbabin 'Government', in J.H. Burns, ed. *The Cambridge History of Medieval Political Thought c. 350–c. 1450* (Cambridge, 1997), 492.

114 Clarke, 'Forfeitures and Treason'; Ross, 'Forfeiture for Treason'.

115 Though notably the inheritances, dowers and/or lands held in jointure of traitors' wives were on occasion protected (sometimes in theory, sometimes in practice and sometimes both) from the full rigours of forfeiture by the fifteenth century. See R.E. Archer, 'Rich Old Ladies: The Problem of Late Medieval Dowagers', in A. Pollard, ed. *Property and Politics* (Gloucester, 1984), 20.

116 Rogers, 'Parliamentary Appeals', 124; though Hicks sees attainder as part of a much longer development. Hicks, 'Attainder, Resumption and Coercion', 28.

117 See also above, pp. 44–5.

118 Lander, *Crown and Nobility*, p. 128.

119 On reversals, see Chapter 5.

120 *The Alliterative Morte Arthur: The Owl and the Nightingale and Five Other Middle English Poems* J. Gardner, ed. (London, 1973), p. 120.

121 For more on this connection, see J. Scattergood, '*The Tale of Gamelyn*: The Noble Robber as Provincial Hero', in Scattergood, *Reading the Past*, 107–8. Though, of course, blinding by this time was a thing of the past for nobles. See pp. 59–60.

122 *CP* ii, Appendix C, for those at Boroughbridge.

123 T. Gray, *Scalacronica 1272–1363*, A. King, ed. and trans. (Woodbridge, 2005), pp. 90–1. Especially after March 1324 when, while all estates worth less than £40 continued to be put on short-term leases, those over £40 were to be 'restocked with animals and exploited directly by royal keepers'. Fryde, *Tyranny*, p. 83.

124 M.C. Buck, 'The Reform of the Exchequer', *EHR* 98 (1983), 257; for a study of the fate of some Welsh border estates in this period, see S.L. Waugh, 'The Confiscated Lands of the "Contrariants" in Gloucestershire and Herefordshire in 1322: An Economic and Social Study', University of London PhD (1975), esp. Part I.

125 Fryde, *Tyranny*, Chapters 6 and 8. For evidence of temporary grants, see C257/8/30.

126 Fryde, *Tyranny*, pp. 108–9.

127 *CCharR 1300–27*, 441.

128 E.g. *CCharR 1300–27*, 442, 443, 444, 446, 448, 449, 450, 451, 452, 461, 463, 464, 466, 467, 469.

129 *CCharR 1300–27*, 451.

130 E40/4886.

131 E40/937.

132 *CCharR 1300–27*, 448.

133 *CCharR 1300–27*, 441, 443; a similar grant made to Richmond in May 1322. *CCharR 1300–27*, 443; for another tail male grant to a royal family member, see those of Mortimer lands to the earl of Kent. *CCharR 1300–27*, 442.

134 Though this was notably Irish rather than English lands, and perhaps worth less in practice. *CCharR 1300–27*, 469. Other examples include *CCharR 1300–27*, 441, 446, 450.

135 *CCharR 1300–27*, 441–2.

136 For example, the massive life grants which Isabella arranged for herself after Edward's deposition. B.P. Wolffe, *The Royal Demesne in English History: The Crown Estate in the Governance of the Realm from the Conquest to 1509* (Athens, OH, 1971), pp. 232–5.

137 *CCharR 1327–41*, 53; E40/5570.

138 *CCharR 1327–41*, 3–4.

139 Though he would be a firm backer of Isabella by the time of the revolution. For Eltham see Waugh, 'John, Earl of Cornwall (1316–1336)', *DNB* (2004).

140 *CCharR 1327–41*, 55.

141 See G. Ellis, *Earldoms in Fee: A Study in Peerage Law and History* (London, 1963), p. 47.

142 *CFR 1327–37*, 116–17; G.A. Holmes, 'The Rebellion of the Earl of Lancaster', *BIHR* 28 (1955), 84–9.

143 *CCharR 1327–41*, 176.

144 Bothwell, *English Peerage*, Appendix 3; J.S. Bothwell, 'Edward III, the English Peerage and the 1337 Earls', in Bothwell, ed. *Age of Edward*, 35–52.

145 For examples, Bothwell, *English Peerage*, Appendices 3 and 5.

146 *CCharR 1327–41*, 230–1.

147 *CCharR 1327–41*, 352.

148 *CCharR 1327–41*, 210.

149 *CPR 1330–4*, 109.

150 *CPR 1334–8*, 519.

151 Bothwell, *English Peerage*, Appendix 3.

152 J.S. Bothwell, 'Edward III and the "New Nobility": Largesse and Limitation in Fourteenth Century England', *EHR* 112 (1997), 1132–4.

153 For the enfeoffment-to-use's growing importance, see Bean, *English Feudalism*, Chapters 3 and 4.

154 Given-Wilson, *English Nobility*, p. 124.

155 Saul, *Richard II*, p. 393.

156 Saul, *Richard II*, p. 382.

157 A. Gundy, 'The Earl of Warwick and the Royal Affinity in the Politics of the West Midlands, 1389–1399', in M. Hicks, ed. *Revolution and Consumption in Late Medieval England* (Woodbridge, 2001), 67; for examples of long-term grants (life or longer) see *CPR 1396–9*, 200–1.

158 *CPR 1396–9*, 195–6, 218, 226.

159 E.g. numerous small grants: *CPR 1396–9*, 194–7.

160 *RP* as quoted in W.H. Dunham and C.T. Wood, 'The Right to Rule in England: Depositions and the Kingdom's Authority, 1327–1488', *AHR* 81 (1976), 745; see also p. 103.

161 C245/27/16, 17, 18, 19, 20, 21–5, 27, 32–4, 40, 41, 43; C245/28/3, 6, 20.

162 Most recently Musson and Ormrod, *Evolution of English Justice*, pp. 108–9.

163 A. Dunn, 'Henry IV and the Politics of Resistance in Early Lancastrian England, 1399–1413', in L. Clark, ed. *The Fifteenth Century III: Authority and Subversion* (Woodbridge, 2003), 13, 15.

164 'For life or so long as they are in the king's hands'. *CPR 1405–8*, 23, 26.

165 *CPR 1405–8*, 44.

166 *CPR 1405–8*, 43, 50; H. Summerson, 'Umfraville, Sir Robert (d. 1437)', *DNB* (Oxford, 2004).

167 A. Dunn, 'Exploitation and Control: The Royal Administration of Magnate Estates, 1397–1405', in Hicks, ed. *Revolution and Consumption*, 31.

168 See also Chapter 5.

169 *CP* x, 47–8; xii: 2, p. 842.

170 *CP* ii, 46.

171 Allmand, *Henry V*, p. 77.

172 *CP* ii, 495; xi, 567.

173 *CP* xii: 1, pp. 447–8.

174 Dunn has argued that, for the period 1389–1413, 'there was no great tenurial revolution, and that the vast majority of magnate inheritances survived intact, or were reassembled with little difficulty' (Dunn, *Magnate Power*, p. 182). This is undoubtedly true, but that inheritances survived or were reassembled, especially as a reaction to Richard II's policy of fragmentation, does not alter the fact that by the fourteenth century such inheritances of fallen individuals were being granted away under longer terms than ever before, and were also often staying away for longer periods – a fact which could not but have had a real impact upon the king, the fallen and those in receipt of the estates. See also Chapter 5.

175 Griffiths, *Henry VI*, p. 825.

176 Lander, *Crown and Nobility*, pp. 136–7 and Appendix C; Hicks, 'Attainder, Resumption and Coercion', pp. 17–20.

177 SC8/180/8979.

178 C245/3/44.

179 E28/4/69.

180 C245/3/1 Edward III; SC8/160/7986; SC8/165/8217; though, according to the VCH, this became 'part of Queen Isabella's dower in 1327'. *VCH Hampshire*, iv, 90; on Odiham in this period, also see P. MacGregor, *Odiham Castle 1200–1500: Castle and Community* (Stroud, 1983), p. 100.

181 SC8/16/796.

182 SC8/17/842.

183 C257/15/4.

184 Hicks, 'Attainder, Resumption and Coercion', 19.

185 For resumption and its implementation as a result of the Ordinances of 1311, see Harriss, *King, Parliament and Public Finance*, pp. 160–75.

186 C49/50/29 Hen VI (*RP* v, 217–24); C49/30/7 33 Henry VI; *RP* v, 328; despite attempts to limit its scope. C49/29/14 31–2 Hen VI; *RP* v, 267–8; C49/30/8 33 Henry VI Repealing of Act of Resumption of 31 Henry VI; *RP* v, 329–30.

187 Brown, 'Commons and the Council', 18–19.

188 Jacques de Vitry, 'The Stingy Knight', in G.G. Coulton, ed. and trans. *Life in the Middle Ages* (Cambridge, 1967), iii, 28; for the importance of dress, see F. Piponnier and P. Mane, *Dress in the Middle Ages* (New Haven and London, 1997), esp. pp. 124–6; Crouch, *Image of Aristocracy*, pp. 247–51.

189 *SR* i, 378–83.

190 Statute of Labour (1351) and its reissues tried to control wages and therefore potentially consumption.

191 E154/1/22; for the earl's possessions, also see *CIM* 1392–9, esp. 107–15; for a comprehensive look at the earl's forfeiture, see L.F. Salzman, 'The Property of the Earl of Arundel, 1397', *Sussex Archaeological Collections* 91 (1953), 32–52; also see Roger Mortimer, earl of March, at Hundon (Suffolk). E154/1/23; SC8/221/11037: for the earl of Warwick's forfeited goods (see also *CCR* 1396–9, 163–4). For other articles on forfeited goods, see C.L. Kingsford, 'Two Forfeitures in the Year of Agincourt', *Archaeologia* 20 (1920), 71–100; H.A.L. Dillon and W.H. St John Hope, eds. 'Inventory of Goods Belonging to Thomas, Duke of Gloucester, and Seized in his Castle at Pleshy, Co. Essex, 21 Richard II (1397)', *Archaeological Journal* 54 (1897), 275–308.

192 On the Continental origins of chattel seizure, especially connected with outlawry or banishment, see J. Goebel, *Felony and Misdemeanour: A Study in the History of Criminal Law* (Philadelphia, 1976), pp. 238–42; M.V. Clarke gives a good overview of the so-called 'Book of Forfeitures' of 1388. Clarke, 'Forfeitures and Treason', 115–23; on such loss more generally, see Mertes, *Noble Household*, pp. 102–3.

193 *CPR 1396–9*, 198. A double blow because Arundel had earlier referred to Bussy as one who 'was always false'. J.L. Gillespie, 'Bussy, Sir John (*d.* 1399)', *DNB* (Oxford, 2004).

194 *CPR 1413–16*, 378. Le Scrope's personal property, excluding lands, was probably worth *c.* £6000. See T.B. Pugh, *Henry V and the Southampton Plot of 1415* (Southampton, 1988), pp. 117–20.

195 E.g. *CPR 1258–66*, 493.

196 C47/22/9/36.

197 For recent commentary on knightly lifestyle, see M. Bennett, 'Military Masculinity in England and Northern France *c.* 1050–*c.* 1225', in D.M. Hadley, ed. *Masculinity in Medieval Europe* (London, 1999), 79–82; A. Ayton, *Knights and Warhorses: Military Service and the English Aristocracy under Edward III* (Woodbridge, 1994), esp. Chapter 2.

198 G.L. Harriss, 'Fitzalan, Thomas, Fifth Earl of Arundel and Tenth Earl of Surrey (1381–1415)', *DNB* (Oxford, 2004); *CP* i, 245.

199 E163/6/13; for Arundel's armour and weaponry, see also Salzman, 'Property of the Earl of Arundel', 46–9.

200 CFR 1399–1405, 56.

201 Barron calculates there were about thirty greater lay aristocratic townhouses in London on the eve of the Dissolution. For the importance of the townhouse, see C.M. Barron, 'Centres of Conspicuous Consumption: The Aristocratic Town House in London, 1200–1550', *London Journal* 20 (1995), 1–16; Woolgar, *Great Household*, pp. 47, 80–1.

202 CCharR 1257–1300, 55.

203 D. Carpenter, 'Montfort, Peter de (*c.* 1205–1265)', rev. DNB (Oxford, 2004).

204 CCharR 1300–27, 446.

205 M. Campbell, 'Gold, Silver and Precious Stones', in J. Blair and N. Ramsey, eds. *English Medieval Industries: Craftsmen, Techniques, Products* (London, 1991), 108.

206 Hamilton, *Gaveston*, pp. 119–27; also see R.A. Roberts, 'Edward II, the Lords Ordainers, and Piers Gaveston's Jewels and Horses, 1312–1313', *Camden Miscellany* 15 (3rd Ser. 41) (1929), v–viii, 1–22.

207 CPR 1321–4, 74; CP i, 372–3.

208 C255/3/3/3–6; CPR 1334–8, 367; CPR 1338–40, 63.

209 C49/47/13 (7 Henry IV).

210 For other writs concerning forfeitures in Richard II's reign, see C255/3/5/8–25.

211 SC1/2/105; SC1/2/111.

212 E163/4/29.

213 See E.B. Fryde, 'The Deposits of Hugh Despenser the Younger with Italian Bankers', *EcHR* 2nd Ser. 3 (1951), 344–62.

214 KB27/269/38; CCR 1327–30, 47, 50 for the rest of the story.

215 Philippe de Commynes, *Memoirs: The Reign of Louis XI 1461–83* M. Jones, ed. and trans. (Harmondsworth, 1972), p. 180; though Lander notes Commynes' tendency to exaggerate. See Lander, *Crown and Nobility*, p. 140.

216 Though, when recognised, he was given a small pension. Commynes, *Memoirs*, p. 180.

217 A. Crawford, 'Victims of Attainder: The Howard and de Vere Women in the Late Fifteenth Century', *Reading Medieval Studies* 16 (1990), 61–2; J. Ward, *English Noblewomen in the Later Middle Ages* (London, 1992), pp. 44–9; Archer, 'Rich Old Ladies', 17–20.

218 Though, in reality, other considerations including propriety, affection and private arrangements often came into the equation. J. Senderowitz Loengard, '"Plate, Good Stuff, and Household Things": Husbands, Wives and Chattels in England at the End of the Middle Ages', *The Ricardian* 13 (2003), 340.

219 *Historical Poems*, p. 177.

220 See pp. 44–5, 100–1.

221 Kail ed., *Twenty-Six Political Poems*, pp. 14–15; italics in original.

222 V. Chandler, 'The Last of the Montgomerys: Roger the Poitevin and Arnulf', *HR* 62 (1989), 14.

4

Life in the wilderness:
the English noble in disgrace

Weland well knew about exile;
that strong man suffered much;
sorrow and longing and wintry exile
stood him company; often he suffered grief
after Nithhad fettered him, put supple bonds
of sinew upon the better man.

Deor[1]

He knows this who is forced to forgo his lord's,
His friend's counsels, to lack them for long:
Oft sorrow and sleep, banded together,
Come to bind the lone outcast;
He thinks in his heart then that he his lord
Claspeth and kisseth, and on knee layeth
Hand and head, as he had at otherwhiles
In days now gone, when he enjoyed the gift-stool.

The Wanderer[2]

The exiles of these Anglo-Saxon poems suffer greatly from being far from kin and hearth, their worlds make no sense, their lives lived alone. Mercy comes only from God, and that is the only mercy they can hope for. Both physically and psychologically, they are cast out, distanced from all that they hold dear. All religions, all societies, to one degree or another acknowledge the placing of the individual outside their ranks. In the Bible, Jesus is outcast for much of his life, either psychologically, from Jewish society, or during his time in the wilderness. He is, in many ways, a form of wayside marker for all outcasts – to paraphrase the gospels, 'he who is exile, let him come unto me' – and therefore the starting point for understanding the mental and moral terrain of those excluded from medieval society. Many of the Apostles followed this path, as later did the likes of the legendary Arthur, exiled, as some would have it, in Brittany: the last, greatest king of the Britons who would one day return to lead his people from servitude. The Wanderer and Weland also lived lives of exile, as did Geoffrey of Monmouth's Brutus, Robin Hood, Fulk Fitz Waryn, King Horn and a number of the Round Table knights in *Morte D'Arthur* – Malory himself was in a form of exile when he was said to have written it, in prison for plotting against Edward IV.[3]

There is a substantial amount written about such characters, about the individual outside the law, outside society or outside communion, in romances, poems and religious tracts. Even today, the idea of the outsider is one which is ubiquitous within Western popular culture; so much so that the rebel can be seen as one of its mainstays, though usually in a negative manner – where would the modern world be without James Dean or Sid Vicious, Mae West or Marilyn Monroe? However, in the Middle Ages, the image of the outsider, though common, was not nearly as hackneyed, or as tacitly accepted. It was far more difficult for the excluded to 'make his own world' and still be considered a success, or even survive. If an individual was 'outside', it tended to be a deadly serious situation – and every attempt had to be made to get back 'in', even if it ended up being into a different society from which he had been ostracised. According to the underlying rationale in stories, songs and poems such as those connected with Robin Hood and Fulk Fitz Waryn, this was the result of another key characteristic of medieval outsiders, their nobility. For though outsiders in modern works of fiction are usually romanticised with some form of 'moral' nobility, in medieval literature the figure of the outsider usually had literal nobility – i.e. he was a member of an economically, legally or socially defined aristocracy – and the fact that he was now excluded from the society which had previously both supported and fêted him made the issue all the more serious. In reality, moreover, though it was far more difficult, and seemingly rare, for those from the lower orders to survive exclusion from the generally exploitative yet also usually protective ranks of medieval society (e.g. village, manor, gild or mystery), the noble outcast had his own equally serious problems, not the least of which was the often highly focused animosity of king or government, as well as the animus of the people whom he had ruled, obstructed or persecuted during the height of his powers. Those individuals a disgraced noble had used or abused on the way up, or while in power, might well show an equally keen interest in his new, more straitened, circumstances.

Excommunication

To start with, there was official spiritual exile, excommunication, a process developed by the Church but appropriated by monarchs and their governments throughout Europe during the high Middle Ages, a process which Pollock and Maitland called 'ecclesiastical outlawry'.[4] It must of course be remembered, at base, that all positions of grace in medieval life came, to one degree or another, from God. As Ullmann discusses for a somewhat earlier period:

> This theocratic form of government was also demonstrated by the king conceding to his subjects, as a matter of royal grace, offices and rights which they otherwise would not have had. The underlying idea was that all power came from God through the king who then distributed parts of it to his subjects. This was the essence of the all-important principle of concession, according to which the subjects received offices, functions, rights, etc, as a matter of concession, as an effluence of royal favour.[5]

This state of grace, then, could also be retracted by the Church, and, through it, by kings – most effectively through excommunication. Throughout our period, as well as religious prohibitions, canon and civil law put substantial controls on the excommunicate's legal and feudal status, including restrictions on services owed to excommunicates by their feudal vassals, the status and continuation of familial relationships, as well as the right to take part in civil litigation or criminal trials.[6] Despite going through a series of adjustments in the high Middle Ages, and despite being, in theory at least, a 'warning rather than a punishment',[7] these and similar limitations potentially weakened the individual's legal, social and even economic position by theoretically (for 'greater' excommunication at least) cutting him off from all dealings with other Christians. Moreover, the royal administration also came to reinforce the importance of excommunication in both theory and practice, especially as used against those disgraced in the king's eyes. Reissues of Magna Carta have clauses threatening excommunication for infringements of the document:[8] a development thought in part to stem from Archbishop Langton's ideas about limited monarchy,[9] and possibly the increased presence of papal power in the realm after John's peace with the pope, though also more than likely a result of the monarchy's more general willingness to back the penalty up with secular power.[10] Indeed, by the high Middle Ages, there was a set Church/state procedure for dealing with all but the most powerful of excommunicates, namely 'the royal chancery at the request of the residential bishop would issue to the local sheriff a writ for the capture and detention, until absolved, of any person who had remained excommunicate for more than forty days',[11] and in fact between 1250 and 1435 almost 17,000 excommunications were 'signified to the secular arm for arrest' for England as a whole.[12] Though at times contentious, as in the case of 'criminous clerks' in Henry II's reign and the problems with the election of the archbishop of Canterbury after the death of Hubert de Walter in 1205, nonetheless excommunication became a more politically forceful act in the high Middle Ages. Some excommunications, if important enough, were even pronounced in parliament, or at least a gathering of the great and the good in Westminster Hall – for example the May 1253 excommunications by the archbishop of Canterbury in the presence of Henry III and his nobles of those accused of breaking clauses of Magna Carta.[13]

Most noble excommunications of our period were connected with large-scale uprisings, such as the Barons' Wars of 1215–17 and 1264–5, a time when the king needed as much authority, and as many sanctions, against his enemies as possible. According to the *Historia Anglicana*, excommunications during the 1215–17 disturbances were issued at royal request,[14] as, of course, had been the papal nullification of Magna Carta itself.[15] The papal legate Pandulf, who was responsible for this series of excommunications, was also responsible for later such acts: for instance, in 1220–1, for the second excommunication of William de Fortibus, earl of Albemarle, in connection with attacks on the castles of Newark, Sleaford, Kimbolton and Fotheringhay, known at the time as 'the war of Bytham', and started by de Fortibus having left the king's court at Oxford without permission.[16] Indeed, when papal legates were on hand, as they tended to be throughout Henry III's reign, they were almost always the agents by which such excommunications were sent out, clearly for the sake of that extra bit of authority though also usually at direct royal behest. Immediately after the battle of Evesham, Ottobon, the papal legate, excommunicated the earl of Leicester and all his 'supporters and accomplices',[17] and again, in 1266, he excommunicated those who had yet to accept the king's peace.[18] When papal legates were not available, however, most orders for excommunications went from the pope to the local diocesan, as when, during disturbances in the spring of 1234, Pope Gregory IX ordered the bishop of Ely to excommunicate those individuals involved.[19] High-ranking English churchmen were often used for such purposes, especially for dealing with straying nobles, and were put under both papal and royal pressure accordingly. As early as 1075, excommunication was used by Archbishop Lanfranc against Roger, earl of Hereford, already alluded to in Chapter 1, though the archbishop was not listened to:

> Therefore I have cursed and excommunicated you and all your adherents by my authority as archbishop; I have cut you off from the holy precincts of the Church and the assembly of the faithful, and by my pastoral authority I have commanded this to take effect throughout the whole land of England. I can free you from this bond of anathema only if you seek my lord the king's mercy and if you render satisfaction to him and the other men whose property you have unjustly seized.[20]

And, in 1225, it was again the archbishop of Canterbury who pronounced excommunication against Falkes de Bréauté, besieged in Bedford Castle by the king's forces, and offering pardons to those who helped bring about the fortification's surrender.[21] Even Henry II, co-instigator of one of the most serious royal clashes with the medieval Church, was not above using excommunication, or the threat thereof, against his enemies – as when the newly crowned king arranged for the bishop of Hereford to excommunicate Roger of Gloucester, earl of Hereford, over a dispute concerning the castle of Gloucester.[22] The importance of excommunication as a weapon against recalcitrant nobles lessened to a degree in the later Middle Ages, probably connected with other problems the Church was facing at the time – including the Babylonian Captivity (1305–77) and the Great Schism (1378–1417) – though partly also because both Edward I and Edward II 'had not only withdrawn assistance from, but actually prohibited, excommunication of their servants and tenants-in-chief',[23] an act which at the same time as strengthening previous royal controls,[24] also clearly weakened the device for future use. Nonetheless, despite such precedent, official exclusion from the ranks of the faithful remained an important weapon against 'all that destroyeth the peace of England and traitors that be false or consent to treachery against the king or the realm',[25] as well as, increasingly, a way to combat heresy, as Henry V would find when dealing with John Oldcastle and the Lollard knights.

Imprisonment

But it was not just ecclesiastical sanction which impacted upon a downfallen noble and his family: it was also, and often far more importantly, loss of freedom, and especially, in some cases, the enforcement of new living conditions. Of course, if you are at the sharp end of almost any society, imprisonment is a desperately hard affair. Chaucer's image of prison life in the *Romance of the Rose* was not that far off the mark for many in the Middle Ages:

> As man in prisoun sett
> And may not geten for to et
> But barly breed and watir pure
> And lyeth in vermyn and in ordure.[26]

And the fourteenth-century Holkham Bible's vision of imprisonment through the story of St John the Baptist was not much better (see Fig. 8). But this was generally the sort of treatment meted out to the lower orders rather than members of the nobility, however errant they may have become. Medieval aristocrats were very rarely held in conventional royal prisons whatever the period – 'common gaols for common suspects', as R.B. Pugh called them[27] – but instead often, in the shorter term at least, in the nearest available secure place. For instance, in 1336, Hugh de Frene, an undistinguished member of the upper gentry though later summoned to the Lords,[28] abducted Alice,

8 BL Additional 47682, f. 21: Holkham Bible Picture Book, John the Baptist entering prison; England, c. 1320–30.

countess of Lincoln, widow of Thomas of Lancaster and one of the most important unmarried widows in Edward III's kingdom, from Bolingbroke Castle,
Lincolnshire.[29] When caught, they were both imprisoned in Somerton Castle,
which the couple had just seized, and were held separately therein, though
they later tried to escape together at least once.[30] Similarly, one could be kept
at the nearest available place not just for convenience sake, but also as a
counter in diplomatic efforts. In the autumn of 1141, in aiding Matilda to
escape from her enemies, Robert of Gloucester was caught by the king's forces
at Stockbridge. At first he was imprisoned in Rochester Castle, but was then
removed to Winchester in order to help the royalists bargain for the release of
King Stephen, caught earlier in the year – which indeed came to pass, the
king being released on 1 November and Robert on 3 November.[31] However,
the more problematic the prisoner, regardless of his rank, and the longer the
potential term of imprisonment, the closer to the centre of royal authority
he would be kept. Robert Mowbray, a participant in the rebellion of 1095
against William Rufus, was initially imprisoned in Windsor Castle, though
it is unclear whether he remained captive there for the next two to three
decades.[32] Likewise, after the defeat of the Contrariants at Boroughbridge
in 1322, Roger Mortimer submitted to royal authority, and was immediately
sent to the Tower of London.[33] Even when the monarch was on the move, as
Henry II was after the events of 1173–4, he made sure to keep his imprisoned
disgraced nobles close to him, bringing a number of the recent rebels across
in his train when he went to Normandy.[34] Hugh, earl of Chester, was
particularly well travelled in this regard, being moved from Dol, where he had
been captured, to Falaise, then to England (for imprisonment, probably in
Devizes), then back to Barfleur, Caen and finally ending up returning to Falaise
– all the time roughly mirroring his captor king's movements.[35]

However, though imprisonment of nobles was taken seriously, it could rarely
be called hard or overzealous, though there were exceptional cases – especially when the king or the regime in power wanted something in particular,
or in times of civil war. In one case, complete isolation from potential allies
was the approach taken: one of the prisoners Henry II moved with him
to Normandy was William the Lion, the Scottish king as well as earl of
Huntingdon, captured outside Alnwick in July 1174. According to Dunbabin,
this move 'increased the pressure on the defeated monarch. There could be
no hope of a Scots raiding party helping William to escape from Falaise. He
had no alternative but to accede to Henry's terms, harsh as they were.'[36] Other
times the torment was both psychological and physical. Desiring control
of Devizes Castle, King Stephen had Roger of Salisbury treated harshly,
'oppressing him by torturing him with starvation and putting a rope round
the neck of his son, who had been the royal chancellor, as if to hang him'.[37]

Similarly, the Mortimers, Audleys and Lord Berkeley all suffered close imprisonment after the battle of Boroughbridge in 1322 – according to one account, so that Despenser the younger 'might slay them, without any cause but a coveting of their estates'.[38] Further, physical impediments were also intermittently used on nobles to keep control of them – mainly, in all likelihood, down to the insecure nature of castle imprisonment, as well as the initial tendencies of retinues and allies to attempt to rescue the imprisoned by one means or another.[39] According to Orderic Vitalis, as a consequence of his plot against Henry I, Ranulf Flambard, a key administrator and erstwhile rebel against the king, was kept in fetters in the Tower;[40] and, in Matthew Paris's chronicle, Hubert de Burgh was brought to the Tower of London, bound and bloody, after one of his run-ins with Henry III.[41] Nevertheless, though treatment of the imprisoned nobility could be hard, usually it was not – issues of humanity aside, there was also the increasing protection offered by the development of the idea of noble rights and 'dignity', especially as displayed in public, and the problems stirred up when a monarch or regime was seen to ignore them.[42] The much reported abuse of William de Braose's wife and eldest son by King John, said to have been starved to death while imprisoned,[43] even if true, was not a common occurrence for nobles, and caused much comment at the time. If a noble did die while in custody, his own state of health, and especially his age, were often to blame. After Boroughbridge, when Hugh Audley (of Stratton Audley) died in captivity in Wallingford Castle, he was in his late fifties, having lived a hard life, including a considerable amount of royal service abroad and on the Welsh borders, and had already been imprisoned at least once before by the French;[44] and, about the same time, Roger Mortimer of Chirk, another very active campaigner in his youth but now in his early seventies, died, though in this case, it has to be said, also after 'severe' imprisonment.[45] Nonetheless, though such events may not have been lamented by the nobles' captors, by the same token rarely do they seem to be sought. The major exceptions to this statement are, if true, the fate of Thomas of Woodstock, the duke of Gloucester, who died in royal captivity in Calais in September 1397, and, of course, at the highest level, the treatment while imprisoned of Edward II – and more than likely Richard II also. These, however, may simply also be more general indications of the increasingly violent nature of the times, as we have already seen with the changing nature of physical punishments in Chapter 2.

Rather, captivity for nobles could be relatively unobtrusive,[46] usually more in the form of an enforced visit than imprisonment *per se*.[47] According to the *Gesta Normannorum Ducum*, after Tinchebrai in 1106 the individuals involved, including Robert Curthose and the count of Mortain, were held in 'free custody' by Henry I until the end of their lives.[48] Curthose, brother of

Henry, was kept comfortably, 'more like a noble pilgrim than a foreign captive',[49] for the remaining twenty-eight years of his life, first in Devizes and Cardiff – learning Welsh and composing poetry while imprisoned.[50] Robert Mowbray, another rebel of the period who also had a decades' long captivity, itself an indication of relatively lenient treatment, ended up becoming a monk at St Albans before his death[51] – showing at least some accommodation to religious inclination, an option also notably allowed Henry of Essex in the latter half of the twelfth century.[52] Even those most definitely out of favour could often expect relatively lenient treatment: indeed, such imprisonment could be relatively humane, *despite* the attitude of the disgraced noble himself. Roger, earl of Hereford, involved in the Earls' Revolt of 1075, was well treated by William I, though in this case Roger, by his continued bad behaviour, gave up any hope of release. At one point the king even made him a present of expensive robes ('cloak and silken tunic and mantle of ermine skins from distant parts'); however, on receiving them, Roger ordered that they be piled up and burned.[53] The king's response to this act was amazingly measured: 'It is a proud man who insults me in this way, but by God's glory he shall never leave my prison as long as he lives.' Though the king still felt some compassion for the earl thereafter – he is said to have ordered Roger's freedom though never carried it out[54] – the latter remained in prison, and his lands in the king's hands, for the rest of his life. At the end of our period, John Oldcastle, whom most in authority viewed as a heretic, was treated with a considerable degree of leniency while captive in the Tower of London, being allowed to continue to publicise his ideas[55] – though Henry V then made the mistake of giving Oldcastle private time to do penance, during which he effected his escape.[56] And humane treatment did not have to stop at the perpetrator. The families of disgraced men could end up being treated well, despite the possible threat of returns to earlier allegiances. Edmund Mortimer, the young earl of March and a potential claimant to the English throne, was imprisoned along with his brother Roger in 1399 in Windsor Castle by Henry IV and ended up being raised with some of the king's children at Berkhampstead.[57] A century and a quarter earlier, Amaury de Montfort, the younger and very bookish son of Simon, was in enough comfort while imprisoned in Corfe Castle in 1276 to compose two largish theological treatises.[58] Boyle describes de Montfort's imprisonment as 'quite mild', with eight valets, four grooms and a single guard.[59] Finally, in terms of actual accommodation while imprisoned, most nobles were probably placed in upper rooms or apartments, rather than dungeons, of royal or royalist castles – whether in the Tower, Windsor, Winchester or further afield such as Nottingham and Devizes.[60] Overall, then, whatever the specific form of imprisonment, nobles and their families, especially those involved in political crimes, were almost always segregated from, and treated differently than, other malefactors. Ideas of status, even in disgrace, were not just saved for the heads on London Bridge.[61]

At times, prisoners were sure enough of their position to ask the king for small though useful favours, as when Llewellyn ap Rhys, a long-term Welsh captive in the Tower, petitioned for a robe, a new bed and other amenities early in Edward II's reign, which the king saw fit to grant him.[62] Wives likewise tried to live up to their marital responsibility to care for their husbands, often asking for the amelioration of their disgraced spouses' circumstances, as when, in March 1390, Constance, wife of Thomas Fauconberge, petitioned the king

> that her husband, imprisoned in Gloucester castle at great charge to his friends, which is not duly expended upon him, he being in great destitution and misery through defective regimen (*regiminis*), be delivered up to the governance of John de Felton, knight, and William de Hilton, baron of Hilton, if it be not against his will.[63]

Rather, the disgraced, imprisoned individual could be harsher on himself than any royal keeper, especially psychologically.[64] While Earl Waltheof was imprisoned after the failed revolt of 1075, according to 'Florence of Worcester', though still protesting his innocence, he lamented his other wrongdoings and his fate and hoped to appease God by 'vigils, prayers, fasting and alms'.[65] Though probably as much poetic licence on the chronicler's part as an actual record of Waltheof's feelings, it was still a good indicator of the type of mental torments a noble prisoner could go through, especially one who, through his own bad judgement, had thrown away a life of privilege and instead faced shame, dispossession and, perhaps, execution. At least according to one poet's account, the duke of Gloucester went through similar soul-searching when imprisoned in 1447, to die in short order: 'For shame and angwishe off which, Ieloussye / I-toke hym sone after, & soo lowe brought hym downe / that In short while after I-caused him to dye'.[66] That said, owing to the lack of security of prisons at the time and the tendency for 'prisoners of state' in particular to escape,[67] among other reasons, imprisonment of the most problematic disgraced nobles quite often made way for either banishment or, more commonly, execution in the fourteenth and fifteenth centuries. Nonetheless, for most of our period, captivity was one of the main ways to punish a wayward noble, especially one over whom the king's government felt the necessity of retaining control.

Escape, outlawry and banishment

Lord Roger Mowbray has taken to flight; he has fought chivalrously; what reason has he for staying? All those who are still fighting are his foes, and if they can capture him, he will have no assurance that the king of England will not wreak his will on him. And Lord Adam de Port, a most valiant baron, fled with him. Off they go at full speed. It is well for them – God is their protector – that they were not caught up with by anybody. Truly, if Adam de Port had not taken a good lead, he would have lost everything that day; but that was not God's will, God who is the omnipotent king; it would have been too much to bear, for he is a very valiant man.[68]

As with these lords in the aftermath of the failed revolt of 1173–4, the threat of imprisonment (light or otherwise) or execution often encouraged nobles to try to get away from their would-be captors, if not from England altogether. Some nobles managed to forestall their sentence in the first place by escape, though not all were ultimately successful: when making for the Continent after a failed revolt in 1400, the earl of Huntingdon found that 'as often as he assaied to take the se, so often was he bore of with the wynde', being ultimately pushed to the Essex shore.[69] As a result of this meteorological bad fortune, he was caught and held prisoner at Pleshy, and executed by popular demand somewhat pointedly 'at the spot where [the duke of] Gloucester had been arrested, on his advice, in 1397'.[70] Even outside (and inside) help did not guarantee a successful getaway – as when 'certeyn men let make keyis of many dores in the castelle of Wyndesore' to help the earl of March escape in 1404, possibly for the sake of leading him to rebels in Wales. Unfortunately for them, the conspirators were pursued, and the smith who made the keys beheaded.[71] Other nobles, captive or in danger of becoming so, were more successful in their escape attempts, though this was often as much to do with bravery, forethought and connections abroad as with luck. Hereward the Wake 'and all who could flee away with him',[72] managed to escape the siege of Ely by William I, and spent the next few months harrying the area, including perhaps the sack of Peterborough Abbey.[73] A few years later, again in East Anglia, the 1075 rebel Earl Ralph de Gael escaped the lengthy siege of Norwich by the earls Warenne and Clare, left his wife, Emma, to defend the castle and made it to a boat and across to Brittany – his wife then arranged the surrender of the castle, and the safe conduct of herself and the garrison to the Continent.[74] Indeed, despite many failures, escape, when successful, was usually through some form of subterfuge. After being imprisoned in the Tower for around a year and a half following Boroughbridge,[75] Roger Mortimer escaped by drugging his guards, making them quite ill.[76] According to one source, he then slipped

> not through the door of his chamber, because it was barred with many casks and bars, but another way, through a break in the wall, he came into the kitchen of the palace of the king; through which exiting quickly, he came to one of the walls of the castle; thence through ropes, to the way of a ladder ingeniously made, provided by a certain friend, and to himself secretly conveyed, he came in no

way afraid to another wall of the castle. And thus, blessed Peter, held in the chains of Nero, led by an Angel, he got over the first and second wall, at last, with great difficulty he came to the river.[77]

Having made it to the banks of the Thames, he found the skiff, left by arrangement, and headed for the Channel – though the king's intelligence clearly thought he was headed for Wales, as all horse and foot were raised in west and south Wales.[78] Avoiding the hue and cry and other such precautions being arranged throughout southern England and especially in the coastal ports,[79] the fugitive noble made it across the Channel, and upon landing on the Continent[80] went to the French court where he remained until taking part in the invasion of 1326. At other times, escape was attempted at least partly by force, often with help from the concerned noble's retinues, though a direct attack on a castle was usually deemed unfruitful. In February 1323, an Oyer and Terminer commission was set up to investigate those persons who 'seditiously entered the castle of Walyingford, co. Berks., wherein Maurice de Berkeleye and Hugh Daudele, the elder, and other prisoners were detained, and held it against the king; as the king now understands that the said Maurice and Hugh and the other prisoners consented thereto, and kept the castle against the king jointly with the said persons'.[81] Though the attempt by force failed, as did most such direct attacks or seizures of castles in the Middle Ages, it still showed the extent to which at least some allies and supporters would go to free a disgraced man from punishment.

For such nobles, especially those 'on the run' or about to be so, the threat of outlawry could come into play. Usually for acting against a monarch's judgement, outlawry was constantly a theme in the public consciousness – perhaps to some degree a reaction to increasing royal government interference in the lives of ordinary people on a day-to-day basis. Whether in stories and songs of Hereward, Fulk Fitz Waryn, Gamelyn or, of course, Robin Hood,[82] the individual outside the law was a common, and usually popular, figure. Without a doubt, the image of the down-on-his-luck outlawed noble in particular was a standard literary device,[83] at least partly to emphasise the pathos of a tale, though also because of his popularity as a powerful symbol against an increasingly authoritative and exactive government. And in reality royal governments, at times at least, did feel it a necessity to outlaw individual nobles, or even a section of the nobility *en masse*, especially when there was no other immediate way of punishing them. For instance, later in the reign of King John, the fugitive William de Braose was outlawed 'by the ancient process in the county court' for not being able to pay a 40,000 mark fine to regain the king's goodwill, and ended up fleeing to France to join his son Giles – his wife and another son, as we have already learned, having not been so lucky.[84]

John favoured the use of outlawry throughout his reign, outside the period of civil war as well as during, with at least two other higher nobles, Eustace Vescy and Robert Fitzwalter, being outlawed because of the plot of 1212 against the king.[85] In the next reign, in November 1233, Henry III ordered the sheriff of Wiltshire to outlaw Hubert de Burgh for breaking out of prison with the help of the rebel earl of Pembroke's retinue,[86] and at the other end of the reign, there was one of the most famous cases of mass outlawry in the period, when all the 1265 rebels who had not surrendered themselves to the king's forces were outlawed: somewhat predictably, these individuals then seized and fortified Kenilworth, raiding the area for months to come, with others remaining hidden around St Edmunds.[87] Aside from, of course, those nobles mentioned in the *Song of Lewes*, even some of the lesser-known rebels of this period made it into contemporary poetry. John Giffard of Brimpsfield – whose descendant was also to face outlawry and execution during the 1322 rising – though originally an insurgent against Henry III, after Lewes in 1264 became a rebel against the de Montfort administration, and escaped to the Forest of Dean, collecting other like-minded men about him: 'To the Forest of Dene Sir Joh wende tho, / And turnde age Sir Simonde and procurede other mo'.[88] Such extreme reactions were unsurprising considering that outlaws resisting arrest could be killed without any judicial process until early in Edward III's reign,[89] though this rarely actually happened to members of the higher nobility. By the mid-fourteenth century, moreover, other pro-cedures against the outlaw were softening: the outlaw did not as a matter of course, according to Keen, forfeit permanently, nor was anyone who killed him free from prosecution for murder. Nonetheless, he was still an outcast, and had no legal defence of his possessions or his person from those who would harm him.[90] Over the course of the Middle Ages, moreover, outlawry's usage expanded considerably to deal with not only felony and treason, but also criminal trespass and, eventually, civil suits,[91] and was increasingly used against disgraced nobles who failed to come in after an uprising, not just in the mid-1260s, but also in the post-Boroughbridge period, the early 1400s, and even against John Oldcastle and his supporters in the 1410s – though of course in the latter case with the charge of heresy mixed into the bargain.[92] Placing an individual outside the law was one of the harshest non-physical punishments for a rebel – especially considering the potential fate of his wealth, land and status, all of which would now be outside royal protection.

Nonetheless, as witness the months prior to the *Dictum of Kenilworth* of October 1266, as well as the period after Boroughbridge, many problems could arise for the royal administration, especially in the area of law and order, if it forced too many powerful individuals outside the legal framework. Outlawry, then, usually occurred only when an individual could not be caught and punished otherwise – which was rare with high-profile nobles, some of whom conceivably thought it beneath them to run away in any case.[93] Rather, banishment was a more common punishment for members of the increasingly structured and powerful aristocracy, and, some would argue, a way for the government to deal with those previously at the apogee of medieval society without imprisoning or executing them. In the laws of England as copied by Roger Hoveden in the twelfth century:

> But as to a murderer, traitor or criminal of that description, although the king shall pardon them as to the life and limb, they shall on no account with the sanction of the law remain in the country; but shall immediately make oath that they will go to the sea-shore within a time prescribed to them by the justice, and will immediately, as soon as they find a ship and a fair wind, cross the seas. And if, being forsworn, they shall afterwards remain in this country, whoever shall be able to find them, may execute summary justice on them without judgement pronounced.[94]

And, in the next century, the legal treatise known as 'Bracton' was clear that banishment was but another form of punishment: 'The kinds of punishment visited upon malefactors are these. Some take away life or member, some entail the abjuration of a city, borough or county, others abjuration [of the realm], permanent or temporary.'[95] Again, banishment and exile, as outlawry, was a favourite theme of medieval literature, especially in the fifteenth century, in part at least a result of the personal experiences of social exclusion through imprisonment of writers such as Thomas Malory and George Ashby.[96] But even prior to this, banishment and exile were ever-present in contemporary culture. Not only were the scriptures and religious commentaries, as well as increasingly accessible classical texts (e.g. the *Iliad* and the *Odyssey*), full of references to those forced out of accepted society, but in England, as far back as the Anglo-Saxon and early Norman periods, poets turned again and again to banishment and exile as a theme to their work – as seen at the beginning of this chapter.[97] Moreover, the heavily romanticised story of one of the last Anglo-Saxon rebels against Norman rule, the *Gesta Herwardi*, devotes a large portion of its time to Hereward's period exiled on the Continent – an account which had at least some basis in fact.[98] Even the twelfth-century writer Geoffrey of Monmouth had Britain originally founded by an exile of Rome (Brutus),[99] and the Arthurian stories becoming popular throughout the later Middle Ages were full of gallant, and not so gallant, knights, being sent into exile either for their misdeeds, or to prove themselves. Many of these stories, indeed, have assimilated the trappings of contemporary ideas of banishment – as when, in Malory's *Morte D'Arthur*, King Mark banished Sir Tristram from Cornwall for sleeping with the wife of Sir Segwarides:

Then the king asked him upon his faith what he was, and what was his name. 'So God me help', said he, 'my name is Sir Tristram de Liones; now do by me what ye list.' 'Ah,' said King Mark, 'me repenteth of your recovery.' And then he let call his barons to judge Sir Tristram to the death. Then many of his barons would not assent thereto, and in especial Sir Dinas, the Seneschal, and Sir Fergus. And so by the advice of them all Sir Tristram was banished out of the country for ten year, and thereupon he took his oath upon a book before the king and his barons. And so he was made to depart out of the country of Cornwall; and there were many barons brought him unto his ship, of the which some were his friends and some his foes.[100]

Banishment and exile were as interesting for stories then as they are now, especially when they were punishments for the sins or transgressions of those previously at the apex of medieval society.

But banishment was not the same punishment in the mid-fifteenth century as it was in 1066. Initially, between the Norman Conquest and Magna Carta, banishment, as many other punitive processes, lacked any standardised legal format, and such exclusions that did take place 'had little connection with the ordinary workings of the legal system'[101] – despite the laws as copied in Hoveden.[102] However, this began to change as early as Henry I's reign, with the beginnings of the idea of the royal power over abjuration (often seen as an offshoot of outlawry), initially for the sake of allowing repeat offenders out of sanctuary by forcing them to leave the realm.[103] Gradually broadening its scope, throughout the reigns of Henry III and Edward I, *abjuratio regni*, or abjuration of the realm, played a major part in some very important orders for expulsion. Initially for people who had taken sanctuary in churches, or otherwise put themselves under ecclesiastical jurisdiction, though gradually broadening out, abjuration essentially allowed the individual to swear to leave the realm of his own free will, never to return – one offered this option was advised to accept it, otherwise face trial and possible execution. In 1191 Roger Mortimer was accused by the justiciar William Longchamp of being part of a conspiracy with the Welsh, forced to give up his castles and abjure the realm, though in this case it appears that the exile was only for a few years.[104] But the most famous case of the move from sanctuary to potential abjuration is that of Hubert de Burgh in 1232, ordered to leave England within fifteen days. However, in this case Henry III changed his mind, possibly thinking that de Burgh would be even more of a problem if free abroad, and ordered the sheriff of Essex to arrest him if and when he left the chapel.[105]

A more instructive and complete case from a little earlier in the century was that of Falkes de Bréauté in 1224. According to Walter of Coventry, de Bréauté realised that his position was untenable after the capture of Bedford Castle, and put himself on the mercy of the king.[106] Handed over to the bishop

9 BL Royal 14 C. VII, f. 119: Matthew Paris, *Historia Anglorum*, Hubert de Burgh seeking sanctuary at Merton Priory; England (St Albans), 1250–9.

of London's custody until the next meeting of the royal council, de Bréauté then decided publicly to abjure the realm and crossed to Fécamp, where he was taken captive and led to the king of France – who in turn imprisoned him.[107] This was obviously not what de Bréauté had intended; nevertheless the process itself shows a certain degree of latitude of punishment on the part of the English king at least. Likewise, when faced with his baronial critics having the upper hand in the early 1260s and when he was effectively besieged in the Tower, Henry III had to accept as one of their terms the banishment of many of his alien courtiers,[108] despite his clear wishes to the contrary. An even more politicised version of abjuration, if only from the royal court, began to appear in the later Middle Ages, as when, in 1376, Alice Perrers was banished from the king's council by order of the Good Parliament of 1376;[109] and in 1388, a number of Richard II's courtiers, including lords Beaumont, Burnell, Camoys, Lovell and Zouche, as well as a number of noblewomen, were forced to 'swear that they would leave the [i.e. Richard II's] court and not return without the permission of Parliament'.[110] Though not as serious as banishment from England, such an act did cut these individuals off from the main venue of power and wealth in the kingdom.

More generally, by the later medieval period, banishment was becoming increasingly serious, increasingly connected with trial and punishment for political offences, and increasingly secularised. As noted by Meredith:

> Before the reign of Henry III, banishment had often been imposed without trial, as a result of an agreement between the king and a rebel, or as an act of the king's arbitrary will. The political banishments in the reigns of Henry III and Edward II [however] were imposed as formal judicial sentences, pronounced by the king in council or in parliament.[111]

Moreover, no longer were banishments primarily connected with sanctuary and 'free will' abjuration, at least in this period: now they were seen as 'the proper punishment for the offences that were said to have been committed, and not as a substitute for the penalty of death'.[112] As such, banishment was also increasingly a process which could legitimately be forced on a king by his nobility when they wanted to remove a favourite, but were not yet willing, or in a position, to push for execution. In the case of the second banishment of Gaveston in 1308, the barons pushed the issue, though not too far – threatening excommunication of Gaveston if he ever returned to England, but allowing provisions for himself and his wife in exile:[113] this was done 'after much circumlocution, since they [the barons] could not agree to anything else'.[114] In late 1310, more fierce and detailed strictures about Gaveston's future were to emerge, that once in exile he was 'never to return, nor should he thereafter be styled nor be an earl, nor be admitted to any county which might be under the king's dominion'.[115] Banishment from the kingdom was indeed a popular first resort for the nobility when dealing with Edward II's favourites prior to Boroughbridge. In 1321, the edict of banishment was published against the elder and younger Despensers at the pressure of the barons,[116] not yet willing to draw blood again to get rid of Edward II's unwanted favourites. Remaining family members could also be of considerable trouble to both the ruling elite and, as we will see, those who had gained hold of the properties in the meantime: thus, probably for similar reasons, all of the relatives of Gaveston, according to the canon of Bridlington, were to be banished, and other Gascons connected with his household removed from the king's service through the Ordinances of 1311, itself a form of vocational exile.[117] Finally, despite such baronial uses, banishment could obviously be used by kings themselves as well as by their critics – though by the later fourteenth century, at least at the level of the nobility, it was again often either as a form of hard mercy, or to protect favourites from the hatred and designs of the more established nobles, rather than a form of effective punishment *per se*. At Richard II's pressure, John Cobham was impeached in the Shrewsbury parliament of January 1398 for being on the deputation to the king during the Merciless Parliament of 1388, and sentenced to be hanged. However, this was commuted, on the condition that he be banished to the Isle of Jersey for the rest of his life – a mercy he did not apparently ask for.[118] Around the same time, as we will hear in more detail a little later, the earl of Warwick also faced such punishment, though his fate was to the more desolate and isolated Isle of Man.[119] There could, however, be more positive uses of banishment: Henry VI and his advisors used exile as a means to try to protect the duke of Suffolk, 'the result of an attempt to save him from the wrath of the Commons in Parliament and outside who regarded him as a traitor', and gave him a number of weeks to prepare[120] – though as we have already seen, this did not in the end save him from a brutal, summary execution at sea.

Places of exile

Outlawry, banishment or versions of voluntary exile were often the options for those not wishing to, or unable to, come back under the king's command. Some nobles, of course, looked or opted for extended banishment/exile in their own country – though this could be a very difficult affair as there were clear penalties from early on for any trying to help them:

> if any person shall gratuitously harbour them for a single night only he shall be fined according to the greater law of the English or of the Danes, on the second occasion twofold, and for the third offence he shall be adjudged to be the associate and accomplice of malefactors.[121]

Pronouncements could be similarly pointed when it came to aiding the ruling regime's exiled enemies in England: according to the Ordinances of 1311 a 'sentence of excommunication was solemnly pronounced by the Archbishop of Canterbury upon all who should receive, defend, or entertain him [Piers Gaveston] in England after the aforesaid fixed limit of time'.[122] The fact that bounties were also offered made any potential harbourer's position twice as difficult as well as dangerous. In September 1326 a bounty of £1000 was put on the head of Roger Mortimer, as well as a promise of a pardon for any other transgressions against the king, for anyone capturing Mortimer upon his return;[123] and a price was also put on John Oldcastle's head after he fell into revolt during Henry V's reign, an amount which was later claimed by Ieuan and Gruffudd, two sons of Sir Gruffudd Vaughan.[124] That said, some potential abetters thought it worth the risk, obviously feeling that personal loyalties outranked royal commands – some of the remaining rebels after Evesham and Boroughbridge were helped by inhabitants of the countryside, as were Oldcastle and John Maltravers, the latter aided by a number of members of the peerage despite being officially out of favour due to his suspected role in the death of Edward II. Indeed, at some point in 1334 or 1335, this exiled henchman of the downfallen Minority regime had slipped back across to England, as in April 1335 Edmund Bereford was granted a pardon by the king's council for receiving Maltravers, 'lately banished from the realm'[125] – as were Thomas and Maurice Berkeley, William de Whitfield, all long-time associates, and the abbot of Malmesbury.[126] But not all such exile was imposed from without. Other periods of internal exile, however brief, were self-inflicted, especially when there was no urgent need for the individual involved to leave the country. A noble might just retire to his estates until political crises had passed, rather than continue to fight what might be, at the time, an unwinnable battle. In 1385 when trouble was brewing between Richard II, his courtiers and the duke of Lancaster, Lancaster decided it wisest to regroup, and so withdrew to his castle of Pontefract[127] – as had, seventy-odd years earlier, Thomas, earl of Lancaster, after the failure of the post-Bannockburn settlement and the resurgence of Edward II's power.[128]

But if a disgraced noble did not want to remain in, or return to, England, or thought it unwise or potentially unhealthy to do so, there was always foreign exile. Some banishment and exile was ordered by the king to, effectively, unnamed places abroad – in other words to get them out of the kingdom, no matter to where. Most poetically, and vaguely, when Falkes de Bréauté was sentenced to be exiled forever, he was ordered, on 26 October 1224, to quit the realm as soon as possible: to facilitate this, Earl Warenne was to take him to the coast and, having put him on board ship, 'to commit him to the winds and the sails'.[129] But of course the most famous banishments of the period to vague or unspecified locations were undoubtedly those of the dukes of Hereford and Norfolk. Thomas Mowbray, duke of Norfolk, was banished for life in the late 1390s as a result of his dispute with Henry Bolingbroke, duke of Hereford, over accusations of treason (see Fig. 10).[130] Told to pass his exile in the Holy Roman Empire, Bohemia, Hungary or on pilgrimage and 'never go or dwell anywhere else in Christendom', he faced a choice wide enough to

10 BL Royal 18 E. II, f. 362: John Froissart, *Chroniques de France et d'Angleterre,*
King Richard II banishes Henry Bolingbroke and Thomas Mowbray, duke
of Norfolk; S. Netherlands, c. 1460–80.

be almost unspecified.[131] Hereford, on the other hand, was banished for ten
years, but again specifying no particular place to go.

That said, whether by personal preference or by the king's will, most
disgraced men thought it wisest to head for the Continent rather than risk
staying in the British Isles, however well from their enemies they might hide.
Sons of rebels were especially well advised to leave the kingdom, given
the tendency for rebel blood, however diluted, to stir up anger and vengeance
among old foes. After de Montfort's death at Evesham, his son, also named
Simon, understandably had grave doubts about his future: according to
Maddicott, 'after the battle he saw his father's head go by on a spear and
withdrew, heartbroken, to Kenilworth'.[132] At first he decided to stay and fight,
laying waste the area around Kenilworth,[133] before ultimately taking part in
the seizure of Axholme. However, he was captured and taken prisoner by Prince
Edward while apparently trying to arrange a truce, and taken thence to London.
Ever resourceful, like his father, Simon the younger then decided to abandon
the cause for the present, and managed to escape from Edward to 'partibus

transmarinis',[134] going there, according to the *Brut*, in order to 'seek aid from his relations and friends'.[135] Other members of de Montfort's family suffered more variable fates, though all were eventually spread to the European winds. De Montfort's wife, Eleanor, retired to a convent in France founded by her sister-in-law and lived off an English exchequer annuity there for the rest of her life;[136] his son Guy went to Sicily (with his younger son, Simon, later to join him), and there married the daughter and heir of the Count de la Bere (though this was not to be the end of the brothers' story, see p. 159);[137] while the elder Simon himself in his earlier years had, in 1238, used Rome as a place of haven and potential aid after various rumours and accusations arose, including financial mismanagement and that de Montfort had slept with Eleanor, the king's sister, before their marriage.[138]

Disgraced nobles also used the Continent as the springboard for life in exile further afield – and often as not, further east. Most notably, though in many cases going on crusade was linked with loyalty to the monarchy, there were some important exceptions. For his part in the rebellion of 1088 against William Rufus, Odo, bishop of Bayeux and earl of Kent, was banished from England forever, losing all his English possessions as a result – though, in this instance, he only went across to Normandy and joined Robert Curthose's administration.[139] Having spent the first part of the 1090s concentrating on the care of his see, Odo then decided to heed the pope's call for crusade at Clermont – though the would-be crusader did not make it very far, dying of disease in Palermo in January 1097.[140] Similarly, once it was clear that Peter des Roches had lost a curial power struggle with Hubert de Burgh in the mid-1220s, he decided that it was safer to opt for crusade in the Holy Land with the bishop of Exeter instead, in which activity he seems to have had a considerable degree of success, helping to refortify many of the crusader strongholds including Jerusalem.[141] Even the effective end of serious crusading by the first half of the fourteenth century did not stop some nobles from considering taking the cross, or at the very least going on pilgrimage abroad. John of Gaunt ostensibly did so after falling out with his nephew, King Richard, in 1385;[142] and the future Henry IV considered going on crusade while living in exile in Paris in the late 1390s, perhaps thinking to relive his youthful exploits as crusader and pilgrim throughout most of Europe and the Middle East earlier in the decade – though in this case Henry appears to have been talked out of the plan by Gaunt.[143] Thomas Despenser, on the other hand, would continue to toy with the idea of crusading throughout the late 1390s, again probably aware that this might be the best option considering the increasingly untenable political situation for Richard II's erstwhile supporters.[144] Taking the cross, in other words, either as a warrior or as a pilgrim, though not the easiest of options and often ultimately ending in death much farther from home than otherwise necessary – as Thomas Mowbray was to find when on pilgrimage during his exile in the later 1390s[145] – was nonetheless an obvious, yet also honourable, way for a Christian knight to free himself from an otherwise bad state of affairs at home.

Finally, there were the difficult decisions facing female relatives, whatever their men decided to do once in disgrace. While male relatives usually had a fairly clear decision between fight or flight when the situation had hit crisis point, wives in particular often found it wiser to follow their disgraced menfolk into exile once it was clear that they were not coming back into favour any time soon – especially as they could otherwise often face captivity, either under house arrest or in a local religious house.[146] Some judged the situation before they acted and took a measured approach. When initial problems with their husbands' political careers had flared up, a few wives, quite reasonably, fled to sanctuary. When Hugh de Burgh was imprisoned by Henry III in the early 1230s, his wife, Margaret, shorn of personal possessions, fled for sanctuary to Bury St Edmunds, and wisely stayed there safely until peace was arranged[147] – though notably in this case with ample provision also being made for her.[148] To others, the situation was serious enough to mean leaving the kingdom for the foreseeable future, as in the case of Agnes de Grandmesnil, whose new husband made the mistake of disregarding Henry I's expressed will by attacking Enguerrand l'Oison, and was forced into a wandering exile.[149] In the next century, in 1258, the wife of exiled foreign favourite William de Valence, the earl of Pembroke, though allowed to stay in England with even some financial help from the king's council, ultimately decided that such arrangements were inadequate, and went to join her husband in exile in southern France.[150] And, less than a decade later, upon the defeat and death of Simon de Montfort in 1265, his widow, Eleanor, despite being Henry III's sister, was clearly in a rather tricky situation; after a brief delay, however, as noted above, Prince Edward allowed for her and her daughter to go into 'dignified retreat in exile in France', where she became a nun at Montargis – later also receiving a £500 life exchequer annuity, though unsurprisingly only for so long as she remained in exile.[151] However, many wives and widows of disgraced nobles would have little choice in their fates, and little such provision, and would often face, both quickly and eventually regretfully, the necessity of following their husbands into exile. The Anglo-Saxon poem *The Lament* captures the mood of one such woman:

My lord asked me to live with him here [in exile];
I had few loved ones, loyal friends
in this country; that is reason for grief.
Then I found my own husband was ill-starred,
sad at heart, pretending, plotting

murder behind a smiling face. How often
we swore that nothing but death should ever
divide us; that is all changed now;
our friendship is as if it had never been.[152]

Following one's spouse into exile might have often been the best option for
survival for some women – but it did not mean that they had to like it, and
a number, as we will see at the end of this chapter and in the next, chose to
fight the situation by one means or another instead.

Life in exile

Many a time hath banish'd Norfolk fought
For Jesu Christ in glorious Christian field,
Streaming the ensign of the Christian cross
Against black pagans, Turks, and Saracens:
And toil'd with works of war, retired himself
To Italy; and there at Venice gave
His body to that pleasant country's earth.

These lines of the bishop of Carlisle in Shakespeare's *Richard II*, inscribed
on a plaque over the supposed pieces of the tomb of Thomas Mowbray, duke
of Norfolk,[153] gives the idealised view of the fate of the banished noble,
one full of acts of bravery and piety: but what was the reality? What did the
outcast noble do while 'in the wilderness', at home or abroad? To start,
some aristocrats committed themselves to internal exile, or at the very least
ostracism, for the long term – mainly, it would seem, in order to keep their
cause alive, lest by leaving they were seen to forfeit their rights. Hereward
the Wake is perhaps the most famous internal exile of the early period, if we
discount the legend of Robin Hood, though even here 'there is little reliable,
and much suspect, information' about the Anglo-Saxon said to have continued the fight against the Normans in East Anglia in the decade after the
battle of Hastings.[154] However, there were many such internal exiles throughout the Middle Ages, mainly if the individual, or individuals, involved had
more to lose by going abroad than staying. We have already talked about the
Lancastrian tendency to go into self-imposed internal exile on their estates in
the fourteenth century,[155] and towards the end of our period, after John Oldcastle
escaped from confinement in October 1413, he remained in hiding, plotting
and fomenting revolt for the next four years, despite attempts to make him
give up in exchange for a pardon, and despite a price upon his head.[156] And
such troublemaking was not just an individual pastime. On a larger scale, 'the
Disinherited' of the post-Evesham settlement spent their time hiding in the
countryside, attacking the king's forces when and where they could:

Certain of the disinherited who had hidden themselves at St Edmunds, on the morrow of Palm Sunday marched out of the said town in great array, and entering the marshland, made their attack against Lynn in Easter Week: but the inhabitants resisted vigorously, and they retired frustrated. On the Vigil of the Pentecost [15 May], when the disinherited had collected in the town of Chesterfield, and having no concerns, some scattered about, and others out hunting, suddenly the royal troops came upon them and, attacking them, killed some, captured others, and routing the rest, retired victorious with a great booty. Meanwhile, the remaining disinherited again drawing together in bands, established themselves in many places in the thickest parts of the woods; and it was harder to fall in with them than with a bear that had lost its cubs; for they ravaged the whole country for all that they wanted.[157]

Some of the most important rebels such as Robert de Ferrers, earl of Derby, especially hated by Henry III and Prince Edward, and one of the heads of a nascent group of 'Disinherited', spent the post-Evesham period raiding the country with retainers and malcontents, occupying, stealing and burning properties and goods of men such as William de la Launde at *Caldelawe*, Alsop and Snelston (Derby.).[158] Similarly, John de Ville continued resistance to Henry III's government, leading a large band of discontented nobles to Axholme, and later to battle with the royalist forces at Chesterfield in May 1266, thereafter holding out in the Isle of Ely for most of 1266–7.[159] Such men were later joined by one of Henry III's most important, if fickle, noble supporters, the earl of Gloucester, in 1267 – apparently disgruntled with his part in the land settlement,[160] and now posing as the champion of the Disinherited. Gloucester went so far as to occupy London with the remaining dispossessed lords until sufficient satisfaction was made (see Fig. 11). Many of these men, especially the richer of them, had of course the option to escape abroad, but while avoiding the immediate danger, they knew that such a plan of action was also a recipe for longer-term suffering, if not complete disinheritance. Unsurprisingly, then, such an attitude of resistance also pervaded those Contrariants who had avoided capture after Boroughbridge in 1322: John Maltravers and members of the Percy family escaped after the battle, and spent their remaining time as free men attacking the estates of the earl of Winchester and his followers in southern England.[161] And, in the year leading up to Boroughbridge, when Roger Mortimer was on the run, he supposedly became involved in conspiracies to destroy the properties of both the earls of Winchester and Arundel, among others;[162] though in this case in the end he made the crossing to France after a period of imprisonment in the Tower. Both periods 'on the run', however, may well have helped to soften up parts of the country for Isabella's invasion a few years later.

11 Bodleian Library MS Douce 180, f. 87: *Douce Apocalypse*: the arms of Clare
in the army of Satan; England, c. mid–late thirteenth century. A manuscript in
Edward I's possession in the 1270s, 'this heartfelt moralisation of the heraldry
of the king's opponents was the logical, if unfortunate, outcome of a policy
which had advertised heraldry as a sign, not of rebellion, but of loyalty'.
P. Binski, *Westminster Abbey and the Plantagenets* (New Haven and
London, 1995), p. 86.

Indeed, many out-of-favour nobles, as well as those lesser landholders
tied to them,[163] made a point of trying to make life as difficult as possible in
the kingdom for the monarchy or those who had arranged their exclusion.
The author of 'Fulk FitzWarin' was not far off for many exiled men when he
said: 'During the entire time that he was a banished man neither Fouke nor
any of his followers did damage at any time to any one, *save the King and his
knights* [author's italics]'[164] – though usually if others got in the way, then
so be it. Aside from Mortimer's doings discussed above, the events of the
earlier part of the 1320s more generally tend to bear this out. In January 1322,
a proclamation went out to the sheriffs in England against the Contrariants,
in particular for taking and burning:

> the town of Briggenorth, whither the king had sent certain of his servants
> to make his purveyances there, and who attacked the king's servants aforesaid,

beating and wounding some of them and slaying others, and who afterwards took in like manner the castles of Elmele and Henle, which are in the king's hands, and beat and wounded his men and servants therein, and took and carried away certain of them, and slew others, and burned the gates and houses of the aforesaid castles, detaining the said town and castles against the king, and who stole the garments, jewels, beasts, and other goods and chattels of the king's men and subjects in the surrounding parts, slaying certain of the said men and detaining others in prison until they made grievous ransoms.[165]

Around the same time, Edward II was also getting reports in from Morgan ap Mareddud concerning the rebel earl of Hereford's attempts to control Brecon,[166] yet another of a series of affronts to Despenser power in the area.[167] Then, in February 1322, orders went out to all sheriffs to raise the hue and cry against the Contrariants, especially for taking control of castles and towns.[168] Activities of the followers of rebels yet to be captured, or recaptured, by Edward II's forces in this period were still causing concern in March 1326, when an Oyer and Terminer commission was sent out to deal with 'the persons who with John de Moubray and Roger de Clyfford, rebels and traitors, and others, came with banners unfurled to Burton on Trent, co. Stafford, and prevented the king's men and servants from passing through that town, killed some of them and committed other crimes in that town', and around the same time 'besieged the castle of Tykehill, co. York, killed the king's servants there, plundered the men of the town and committed other crimes'.[169] Indeed, sometimes, for a variety of reasons including local sympathies overriding royal duties, sheriffs and other local officials did *not* follow royal orders, thus helping the rebels and outlaws even further: for example, the sheriff of Northampton was chastised for letting the Contrariants journey in, and stay in, his county unopposed after the hue and cry had been raised.[170] The king accordingly ordered the sheriff to put out spies for the Contrariants, and promised to keep the sheriff himself under surveillance, and to punish him with similar penalties to those meted out to his enemies if he continued to fail to do his job. Even women could be involved in such obstinacy: in January 1326 Edward II ordered the seizure of Wigmore Castle, where Margaret, Lady Mortimer and mother of Roger, sometimes lived 'and at which place as well as at Worcester she was accustomed, as the king is informed, to hold meetings of suspected persons, for which reason the king has commanded her to be removed from Worcester to the abbey of Elnestowe by Bedford'.[171] Obviously Mortimer himself was not the only one who schemed and plotted, and one would not be at all surprised if those 'meetings of suspected persons' of Mother Mortimer were in some way connected with her then-exiled son. The 'exile' within England, then, was in both a potentially dangerous and a potentially powerful situation – in limbo when it came to help from the king's government, or often anyone else for that matter, though also rather difficult to bring under royal control.

Nevertheless, some disgraced individuals only stayed in the kingdom until they had found enough money to leave, and then headed off to find aid for their cause abroad: before leaving for Rome to gain the backing of the pope for his problems with Henry III in the late 1230s, Simon de Montfort spent his time, 'extorting an immense amount of money from every possible place; so from one citizen of Leicester, Simon Curlevache, he extracted 500 marks'.[172] And, indeed, those in exile abroad could cause even more problems for kings or those governing in their names than those who had stayed on in England – so if one wanted to continue to cause trouble and yet remain healthy (and willing to risk forfeiting his right by leaving the 'field of battle'), it was often best to disappear for the present. Aside from the famous case of Henry Bolingbroke returning from exile to claim the throne in 1399, the history of the period is littered with expatriate troublemakers of varying sorts. In the late eleventh century, while Ralph de Gael, earl of Norfolk, was in Denmark soon after the Earls' Revolt of 1075, he arranged to invade England with a force of 200 ships, but despite such ambitious arrangements, in the end failed to accomplish anything.[173] Similarly, in 1105, after William de Mortaigne had been deprived of his lands, 'wherever he had the power, did injury to the king's property and men, on account of his own estates which he had lost in England'[174] – as, of course, did Odo, the exiled earl of Kent, who continued to plot against William Rufus from Normandy while also holding his brother, the future Henry I, captive.[175] Many rebels and their families, indeed, nursed a long-standing hatred of the causes of their downfall, and acted upon it from Continental or other bases when and where possible. In the twelfth century, in the run-up to the Anarchy, Geoffrey Talbot, a banished and very bitter opponent of Stephen, planned his revenge, an ill-fated plan as it would turn out:

> He had been banished from England, and he was preparing to breathe out everywhere the poison of his furious hatred and to do every cruel deed that a frenzied and unbalanced mind is wont to imagine. But by God's judgement his malice was turned against himself, because while he was planning to slaughter some and injure others he himself was first captured and very closely confined in chains and barely escaped a sentence of condemnation.[176]

In the late 1260s, Simon de Montfort the younger was rumoured to have plotted against Henry III's regime while on the Continent, as well as intermittently negotiating for his return, though both these schemes were ultimately unsuccessful.[177] His brother, Amaury, was also out to cause trouble for the English king, in particular by arranging the marriage of his sister with

Llewellyn, prince of Wales, a betrothal with clear political implications considering Edward I's problems with the Welsh at the time: however, the couple were captured at sea on their way to Wales by the men of Bristol and given over to Edward.[178] And during Edward II's reign, there was the high-profile case of the Despensers' exile in the early 1320s. When Edward was forced to banish them by parliament, and the barons in particular, there was, according to Fryde, 'no precedent' for doing so in such a manner for members of the nobility.[179] Nonetheless, while the elder Despenser left for Bordeaux, the younger Despenser remained at sea, menacing the communications and interests of his enemies with the help of royalists in the Cinque Ports. He even went so far as to raid Southampton, and, according to the *Vita*:

> He became a sea monster, lying-in-wait for merchants as they crossed his path. He was a master of the seas, their merchandise and chattels, and no ship got through unharmed. He attacked a great Genoese ship, commonly called a dromond, killed the crew, and appropriated to himself the vast wealth that he found in it.[180]

Edward II's reign, to be sure, seemed to encourage hateful exiles. Later in the decade, some of the most famous exiles to grace the Parisian court – including Queen Isabella, Prince Edward and the earl of Kent[181] – would, of course, plot and plan and eventually bring an army on their return. As a prelude to this, according to Geoffrey le Baker, the recently arrived exile Roger Mortimer wheedled his way into the queen's favour, as the bishop of Exeter was to notice with much spite, his position having been usurped by this upstart and 'other exiles'.[182] This is not to say that Edward II was unaware of what the growing band of exiles at or near the French court were thinking of doing; even as early as October 1324, Hugh Despenser ordered John Sturmy, admiral of the Northern Fleet, to seek out and attack any fleet led by Mortimer from Holland and Zeeland.[183] Unsurprisingly, then, kings were also not hesitant in trying to stop such situations before they started, as outlined in Bracton's laws concerning aid of exiled individuals;[184] and more specifically, when in November 1323 Edward II made clear to the widow of Thomas of Lancaster that she was neither to communicate with nor aid the fugitive Roger Mortimer.[185] A few generations earlier Henry III even requested that the French king Louis IX not support or assist Simon de Montfort while the latter was on the Continent,[186] little good it ultimately ended up doing him.

There were also cases of those who, instead of solely set on stirring up trouble for the king or government, used various forms of exile to their advantage, and not always in ways also deliberately detrimental to the interests of the regime which exiled them. Bishop Odo, aside from causing problems for

William Rufus, spent much of the 1090s rebuilding the estates of Bayeux Cathedral, as well as restoring the monastery of St Vigor – though it should be noted that he was not ultimately terribly successful in either.[187] And, according to the *Vita Edwardi Secundi*, Piers Gaveston and his household spent their Irish exile denuding the country of much of its worth: 'he converted to his own use and devoured, with the king's express consent, all the revenues of that land which pertained to the king of England. And so the last state was worse than the first.'[188] Alternatively, as we will see in more detail in the next chapter, in the 1330s and 1340s John Maltravers passed his time more constructively, gradually trying to work his way back into Edward III's favour through acting as an unofficial royal servant/envoy while in exile on the Continent.[189] Likewise, whether a case of exile or more gentle censure by the ruling clique,[190] Richard, duke of York's stay in Ireland in the late 1440s was not poorly spent, building up connections there – connections which would in part help sustain the Yorkist cause in the late 1450s. In order to help them survive abroad, some exiled nobles were even able to gain or retain protection of the English king or governing regime, depending on their relationship before the exile. William de Valence, sent into exile in 1258 along with other Poitevins as a result of the Provisions of Oxford clauses against foreign favourites, was given a 3000 mark annuity, and allowed to have his estate and its income put under the control of his retainers with the latter revenues being deposited at the New Temple – a set-up, which, according to one recent commentator, was 'a remarkable arrangement that permitted his return'.[191] And, as mentioned above, Edward II constantly worked for the interests of Gaveston and the Despensers after they had been forced out of the country by the baronial opposition,[192] going so far as to ask the abbot of Glastonbury to search his chronicles to see if there was any precedent for Gaveston's, or perhaps the Despensers', exile.[193] Indeed, when sent to Ireland, Gaveston was allowed to leave with a large household, and by order of the king 'the whole land was subjected to his authority and power'.[194] Just because one was exiled, did not mean that one's career, or lifestyle, necessarily stopped – so long as one had the right backing.

Even those who had been exiled by the regime in power as enemies of the monarchy and kingdom could at times experience outbursts of royal favour, however unexpected. Though in the late 1390s the Appellant earl of Warwick was exiled to the Isle of Man,[195] the king saw fit to order the earl of Wiltshire, his custodian, not to be overly harsh on his prisoner but to cause him to be there kept in 'moderate and honourable custody'.[196] He was committed to life banishment, with a fixed annuity of 500 marks but under the watchful eye of a warder, 'thus, tempering the wine of justice with the oil of clemency'[197] – though, according to Adam of Usk, the annuity did not

seem to have been paid and Warwick and his wife were deprived 'of everything, even down to their shoestraps'.[198] However, even if initially the case,
this situation did not last for long: in November 1397, the king granted back
some personal possessions to Warwick and his wife, a kindness not always
shown:

> Two beds, one 'trussyngbed', six pairs of sheets, sheets for heads and feet,
> pillows, etc. for the same, two dozen plates, one dozen salts of silver, one basin
> and one ewer of silver, suitable napery, one vestment complete for a chaplain
> with all the fittings for an altar, a missal, a chalice, cruets and 'paxbrede', and
> vessels and other things needful for the kitchen with 'clothsekkes' and 'bare-
> hides,' the raiment and furs and all gear and goods appointed for the body and
> chamber of the said Margaret, pearls and jewels excepted.[199]

Thus, though exile was meant to be a punishment, it was sometimes, at least
for the higher nobility, not meant to be inhumane. Thomas Mowbray, duke
of Norfolk, also forfeited and banished for life in the late 1390s, still felt
sure enough of his position to petition the king for £1000 a year from his
former estate and certain moveable goods in his banishment.[200] Richard II was
indeed quite accommodating in arranging for Mowbray's banishment, especially considering his role as Appellant in the 1380s as well as his part in the
intrigues since 1397, not only allowing for contrary winds pushing him back
to shore without penalty, unlike later would-be exiles, but also arranging for
the 'rainment' of Mowbray and his household, and a boat for the passage
to the Continent – though the latter notably at Mowbray's own expense.[201]
Mowbray and his retinue of thirty servants left England in October 1398,
but unfortunately he died in Venice of the plague on his way to/from the
Holy Land in September 1399[202] – thus perhaps denying him the later career
attributed him by the 'Mowbray Stone' at the beginning of this section.
Nonetheless, despite the ill luck of some, there appears generally more of
an attempt to provide for exiled individuals as time went on, or at least
ameliorate their circumstances, the relatively thoughtless banishments of the
eleventh and twelfth centuries comparing generally unfavourably with the more
considered acts of the fourteenth and early fifteenth centuries.

Mostly though, whether in exile in the British Isles or abroad, it was not
unusual for the noble to slip into bitterness or depression, living a lonely life
far from family and usually ultimately abandoned by retainers. A noble might
become racked with guilt and dismay, as John Maltravers was said to have
been, fleeing into exile in Germany, and remaining there for a long time, filled,
according to one chronicler, with remorse[203] – presumably ostensibly for his
supposed part in the deaths of both Edward II and the earl of Kent, though
undoubtedly also for the life of privilege he had lost. Others kept faith, and

continued to plan, usually in vain, for a comeback. In the early 1400s, the earl of Northumberland spent the last few years of his life moving between safe havens in Scotland and Wales, always plotting further uprisings against Henry IV but never being successful, and ultimately being killed, decapitated and quartered at the battle of Bramham Moor in 1408.[204] Most exiles, however, either at home or abroad, were merely trying to stay alive, even if not necessarily in as extreme a situation as those described in Philip de Commynes's *Memoirs* mentioned earlier.[205] When the Earl Warenne and William de Valence, the king's brother, came to St Edmunds in order to hunt out the king's enemies in 1266, 'abruptly summoning before them the town's abbot and burgesses, they charged them with favouring the king's enemies since, without any impediment, the outlawed barons stored and sold the fruits of their ravages and robberies there'.[206] Likewise, upon being expelled from England in 1102, Roger the Poitevin retired to his wife's castle of Charroux, there leading a rather lonely existence, and, having no lands of his own in the area, was 'without legal existence in his refuge'.[207] And though his brother Arnulf was more active in exile, and had a greater sense of purpose, both were, in essence, landless men, to a large degree dependent on the goodwill of others.[208] In the end, it was not unknown for an exiled noble to die in poverty, or at least extremely straightened circumstances. After Robert de Vere, duke of Ireland and favourite of Richard II, had brought the Appellants' wrath down upon him, he ended up dying in some financial distress on the Continent;[209] according to Walsingham, he died in Louvain, troubled in mind and in much poverty.[210] But for one of the most poignant tales of misfortunes upon exile one must again return to that of Falkes de Bréauté. After his downfall at the hands of Henry III's minority government in 1224, Bréauté spent the remainder of his life in pitiful conditions in France and Rome, first imprisoned by Louis VIII at Compiègne, as noted above, and then trying to mount a legal defence of his actions while in England to the pope.[211] However, while travelling to England in the summer of 1225, continuing to fight for his reinstatement, Bréauté was caught and imprisoned in Burgundy, though the pope managed to gain his release. Having failed to regain his estate and position in England, Bréauté first resided at Troyes, but was exiled from France for refusing to do homage to Louis VIII, whereafter he returned to Rome, dying apparently of food poisoning in 1226.[212]

Exile, then, forced or otherwise, did not necessarily mean prosperity or safety, and some exiles further found their lives deliberately cut short by old enemies or otherwise damned. After the duke of Gloucester was forcibly taken to Calais in the late 1390s, he found himself the target of semi-judicial murder. The murder has been talked about earlier; however, the run-up to it was just as ominous:

When the Duke of Gloucester had been taken into the castle of Calais and found himself shut in there and deprived of his attendants, he began to feel very afraid. He said to the Earl Marshal: 'Why have I been spirited out of England and brought here? You seem to be treating me as a prisoner. Let me take a walk through the town and see the fortifications and the people and the sentries.' 'Sir,' replied the Earl Marshal, 'I dare not do as you ask, for my life is answerable for your safekeeping. My lord the King is a little displeased with you at the moment. He wishes you to stay here and put up with our company for a time. You will do that until I receive further instructions, which I hope will be soon. As for your own displeasure, I am very sorry about it and I wish I could relieve it. But I have my oath to the king, which I am bound in honour to obey.'[213]

On a slightly different note, the younger Simon de Montfort had joined his brother Guy by 1270, another refugee from the baronial cause's failure in England now in the service of Charles of Anjou, a man responsible for the recent conquest of a large part of southern Italy. Soon thereafter, however, Simon and Guy gained infamy for the death in a church in Viterbo of Henry of Almain, son of Richard of Cornwall, their cousin and the one they blamed, along with his father, for the brutal death of the elder de Montfort.[214] Towards the brothers themselves, fate thereafter took ultimate vengeance: later that year the younger Simon would die in a castle near Siena, 'like Cain, cursed by God, a wanderer and a fugitive'.[215] As for Guy, according to many later commentators, Dante himself imagined his punishment for this crime in Hell:

A little farther on the centaur stopped beside a people who seemed to issue from that boiling stream as far as the throat. He showed us a spirit on one side alone and said 'That one clove, in God's bosom, the heart which on the Thames still drips with blood'.[216]

If the connection is correct, it also shows that this exile at least left an impression on one of his new countrymen.

Those left behind

There is then the question of what happened to those left behind by the disgraced (and/or dead) noble, unable or unwilling to depart with him. One reaction was passive acceptance of one's fate, and thereafter grateful receipt of any assistance offered. Charitable acts towards noblewomen and other relatives here will be defined as that which is granted, by the government's initiative or on humble request, immediately or soon after the fall of an individual from grace by the regime which caused it – unless there is clearly more 'active' evidence to the contrary (mainly through various forms of later petition and other legal action), in which case it will be dealt with in the more 'independent' response of relatives in the next chapter.[217] In the case of spouses, though noble rebels themselves were often executed in the later Middle Ages, and in theory at least forfeiture would come to take precedence over entail, enfeoffment-to-use and dower rights (all potentially of assistance to relict women), not only were lands held of their own inheritance as well as jointure generally excluded, but in practice rebel wives could at times be treated more moderately for almost all the medieval period by the regime in power – though this of course would depend on how much the government wanted the lands and/or wealth involved and how much anger there was against the disgraced noble.[218] At the extreme end, of course, there were sometimes unwarranted abuses: Crawford relates the fate of Lady Oxford in the later fifteenth century 'imprisoned, threatened and brow-beaten, stripped of her lands and left to die in a convent' – though she was 'perhaps the most unfortunate' of female victims of the Wars of the Roses.[219] For the most part, however, the ruling regime's attitude towards those left behind was more lenient throughout our period, though at some points more forgiving than others. And though the Bractonian line of the family of an 'attainted' man being 'legally dead' had generally prevailed in theory in the twelfth and thirteenth centuries,[220] even here there were a few leniencies with some legal basis from at least Henry II's reign – in this case in connection with unlawful death:

> If any such [malefactors] shall have wives living in this country, and any one of the relatives of the person murdered shall say they were accomplices in the crime, they shall make proof of their innocence by the judgement of God; and if the mercy of God and their own innocence shall save them, they may continue to be lawful persons with their dowries and marriage portions. But children who, before commission of the crime, were born or begotten, are not to lose their lawful rights for a crime committed after they were begotten, nor are they to be deprived of their right of heirship.[221]

Such provisions could also be around in practice from very early on. The Conqueror himself, faced with the rebellion in 1075 of the earls of Hereford, Norfolk and Huntingdon, took away the rebels' lands and titles – though notably, as mentioned earlier, William granted back most of Waltheof, earl of Huntingdon's inheritance to his wife, and she appears to have kept her status as countess.[222] And though there was no comprehensive overturning of the sentence against Huntingdon, some land did also return as a result of royal favour to the men whom the couple's eldest daughter married: namely, Simon de Saint Liz and, more importantly, David, king of Scotland, both of whom were to become in turn earls of Huntingdon.[223] For Huntingdon's female relations, however, especially before the settling down of inheritance rights, such grants were clearly more a matter of royal grace than noble right – as they probably also were when Henry I perhaps made provision for Sibyl of Falaise, apparently the illegitimate daughter of Robert Curthose, after the latter's death in 1134.[224] However, though the evidence is somewhat patchy, such cases seem to be the exception in the late eleventh to mid-thirteenth centuries – though this state of affairs probably reflected the low number of executions in the period as well as the impact of the relatively quick return of forfeited lands, especially after the Anarchy and the Barons' Wars of 1215–17, more than any deliberate harshness on the monarchy's part. Rather, though initially few arrangements had been organised for 'relict' women,[225] officially at least, by early 1266, what has been called 'increasingly systematic efforts' were made for wives and widows of the defeated at Evesham.[226] This in practice often included dower rights, as well as 'possession of the lands and tenements of their own inheritance and marriage, and a varying proportion, between one-quarter and one-third, of the lands of their husbands, to be held for life'.[227] As early as 20 February 1266, Elizabeth de Colevill was granted 'by way of grace and humanity' the lands late of her husband in Aubourn (Lincs.) 'for the maintenance of herself and her children, for her life, by the title of a free tenant'.[228] Similarly, Elizabeth de Marescal was reseised by Henry III's government of lands of her husband, William, in Charlton, Norton, Whittlebury (Northants) and connected properties which had previously been granted out by the king to others as forfeitures of war, 'for the maintenance of herself and her household for her life by the title of a free tenement'.[229] Substantial – though not uncontroversial – provision was, then, quickly made for the women and children of rebels, especially from inheritances and dowers; other examples include the provision for the wives and widows of Robert FitzNicholas, Thomas de Estleye and Henry de Hastings.[230] As we have seen, the royal administration even granted Eleanor de Montfort, the widow of Simon, a largish annuity, as well as arranging for some provision for the de Montfort family more generally after Evesham – a deal negotiated by the French king, Louis IX.[231] By the second half of the thirteenth century, then, just as with some of the wives of banished nobles, there was a firmer precedent of accommodation to rebel relicts, thereby strengthening the position of disgraced nobles' wives more generally.

Though the next king to face a major rebellion, Edward II, was nowhere near as generous, and some would argue bordering on harsh to rebels' wives, including use of imprisonment,[232] he was still known to make some immediate provision for the most important of spouses. As a precursor, in 1308, possibly realising that to be too harsh on a royal favourite might be unwise, the barons had allowed Gaveston £200 per annum for himself in exile – and £100 per annum for his wife 'if she were willing to leave the country with him'.[233] Later royal policy, then, may have at least partly reflected the barons' treatment of Gaveston's wife – though, that said, it may also have been an early forerunner of an unofficial policy of not humiliating the greatest rebellious noble families of the land too much in the public eye lest it impacted upon the reputation of the upper ranks as a whole.[234] Whatever the case, during the 1320s, various rebel wives could at times be treated relatively humanely, despite the fact that their husbands had taken part in Boroughbridge and were often facing imprisonment and/or execution afterwards, and despite even the Despensers' avarice towards their estates. The widow of John Giffard, a Contrariant executed in 1322, was given King's Stanley (Glos.), a joint enfeoffment with her husband;[235] and more notably, there was Edward II's treatment of the earl of Lancaster's widow, Alice. Though initially forced to quitclaim many lands through pressure from the Despensers, by the end of 1322 Alice had been given back at least part of her estate for her sustenance for life, as well as being allowed to keep the title of countess of Salisbury and Lincoln.[236] The king was also willing to arrange physical as well as legal protection for the countess, ordering the sheriffs and bailiffs of Lincolnshire to 'be attendant upon and aiding' her, with the posse of the county if necessary, 'the king having heard that certain men with armed force are marching to where she is staying awaiting an opportunity to abduct her'[237] – though of course keeping the countess single was as much in the king's interest as hers.[238] Following this trend, Isabella and Mortimer's regime could be moderately generous when it came to wives of noble rebels, if not many others. After the death of the earl of Arundel in 1326 at their hands, the Minority regime granted to Alesia, his widow, until other provision could be made to her, the manors of Mapledurwell, Burton and Farlington (Hants), Stanford (Berks.), Rotherfield (Sussex), Marston (Wilts.) and Fairford (Glos.), as well as, in the next year, £220 from the City of London, and other lands to replace lands earlier granted to her, but which were then returned to Hugh Despenser the younger's widow.[239] More positively, after the Minority regime's downfall, as is well known, the policy was a more general and far-reaching one of mercy to the old regime's servants, and this often extended to their wives: even the often forgotten wife, then widow, of Roger Mortimer himself, Joan, had provision arranged for her, her ladies and her children, all of whom were living in Ludlow Castle in the early 1330s,[240] as did Agnes Maltravers, another victim of the Nottingham coup – though both women were also, as we will see in the next chapter, far more active in arranging provisions for themselves and their families.[241] Similarly, if a bit lower down the scale, the wife of the supposed regicide Sir Thomas Gourney received a number of manors to help support herself and her children while he was on the run abroad.[242] Indeed, all these acts of generosity were notably for families intimately connected with the deposition and murder of Edward III's father – showing, if nothing else, how some monarchs separated the actions and fate of the individual from those of the rest of his family.

Evidently, then, much of the policy towards women 'left behind' in the fourteenth and fifteenth centuries was dependent on the character of the regime in power. However, though Richard II's regime was not as generous with the relicts of his disgraced nobles, especially during the period of his tyranny, he rarely forgot the relicts and other relatives of favourites brought down by his nobility. Wives could even be taken care of while their husbands were in exile – as was the earl of Oxford's estranged wife by a chastened Richard II. In October 1389 Philippa was granted, with the assent of council, a 100 mark annuity – which was later raised to 300 marks – as well as, in 1398, getting the dower portion of her husband's estate.[243] Blood links could also help in this regard: the fact that Philippa was the granddaughter of Edward III probably did not hurt her chances when it came to getting back her jointure lands soon after her husband's fall in 1388.[244] To his credit, though, his successor was again more ecumenical in his favour to relicts, being charitable to those of his enemies as well as his friends. Early in the reign of Henry IV, John Look, Margaret de Rempton and Thomas de Ansey were ordered to give up issues of the manor of Deeping (Lincs.), forfeited by Thomas Holland, earl of Kent, in 1400 after an attempt to topple Henry IV, to Joan, his widow, for her sustenance for life.[245] As a result of the same rebellion, Henry granted for life to Constance, widow of Thomas Despenser, various forfeited lands and goods in Oxfordshire, Buckinghamshire, Nottinghamshire, Warwickshire and Wales – as well as several of their more precious chattels, and the wardship of the body of his heir.[246] It did again, however, help one's cause if one had fallen by the hands and at the will of those other than the king. In Henry VI's reign, when the duke of Suffolk was murdered in 1450, and certain lands granted taken back into the king's hands, his wife, Alice Chaucer, was treated with a fair degree of generosity, being quickly given all her late husband's property until the majority of their son, freed from arrear payment connected with the land, and later even confident enough to go on the offensive concerning some of her husband's previous land claims,[247] a growing tendency among noblewomen which we will see much more of in the next chapter. Finally, it was not just lands or annuities which were given back to a wife or widow, but all-important family possessions and other goods, including crops, again crucial not just for the ability to keep up appearances, but in some cases for simply keeping the family fed and clothed. After the duke of Exeter's death in 1400, his wife, Elizabeth, as well as being given a grant of 1000 marks a year for her sustenance,[248] was given back a number of personal possessions, as well as household goods for daily survival.[249] Earlier, in the summer of 1322, grants to the widow of the earl of Lancaster included all the hay, corn and grass in her recently restored Midlands and southern manors.[250] Such possessions, personal and domestic/agricultural, then, as noted in the last chapter, were often just as important as land itself to a woman's survival, especially one otherwise at least partly disenfranchised from her social rank and often her support network as well.

Aside from wives and widows of dead or exiled disgraced individuals and their dependent offspring, other relations could also be taken care of, depending upon the character and determination of the king involved – and especially in the fourteenth and fifteenth centuries.[251] After his execution in 1322, John Giffard's mother was granted back Syde manor (Glos.) for life, though by the 1330s the reversion had been settled on Thomas Berkeley;[252] and after Roger Mortimer's forfeiture in the same year, the king ordered that his mother be given back the lordship of Radnor, part of her dower – which only after her death was to forfeit to the king.[253] On a less grand scale, though still very useful, in May 1391, Matilda, countess of Oxford, mother of the exiled Robert de Vere, was granted licence to fell and sell wood to the value of 400 to 500 marks at a time 'for her better support' from her dower lands in Oxford, which were to revert to the king on her death.[254] Though this licence had to be restated later in the summer of 1391,[255] it showed some concern for the relatives of fallen nobles,[256] especially if they had not fallen at the royal behest. Later in the decade, an heir of Richard II's exiled earl of Warwick, Katherine Beauchamp, a nun at Shouldham Priory, was granted forty marks a year at the exchequer because she could not enjoy parts of her inheritance,[257] doubtless having been granted out to some of Richard II's favourites.[258] Male relatives could also receive such favourable treatment, though unless there *was* an overturning of the sentence, this was less common and usually more passive on the part of the administration.[259] Nonetheless, Edmund Mortimer, a claimant to the throne and therefore a threat to Henry IV, was, along with his brother, allowed a 300 mark annuity for their maintenance while imprisoned in Windsor Castle from the lordship of Clare.[260] Most such charitable deeds to remaining males, however, seem to have taken a less active manner. In one case, though getting no land grants or annuities, both the father and the son of the accused were allowed to keep on functioning as full land-holders and participants in local affairs despite the latter's exile from the realm. In 1336, John Maltravers the elder took part in a case of unjust disseisin of *Golafreston* in the King's Bench against John Coteral,[261] and in the spring of 1339 was granted licence to enfeoff-to-use a number of his lands, arranging for them to descend to his nephew upon his death – a very wise move considering the uncertain position of his exiled son at the time. Notably, this grant had the clause attached: 'notwithstanding any escheat or other profit which may fall to the king in the future by reason of the forfeiture of John

Mautravers, son of John Mautravers the elder'.[262] Further, while his father was still out of favour, Maltravers the Younger's son also claimed an interest in the Berkeley estate at King's Stanley and Rockhampton, and felt able to petition the king concerning the wardship of the heir of Maurice Berkeley.[263] Thus, overall then, perhaps also in part due to the increasing number of ways for landowners to control the descent and fate of their estates – which could at times push kings into a position of more leniency despite themselves – as well as the growth of chivalric culture in the same period and the concurrent fashion of adoration of a certain class of women,[264] there appears to have been something of an, albeit at times intermittent, amelioration of the position of those 'left behind' by the deaths or exiles of nobles of the mid-thirteenth to mid-fifteenth centuries.

Therefore, once an English noble was outside royal or governmental favour, both his existence and that of his family almost always changed dramatically. Not only were his lifestyle and political affiliations severely curtailed, but also his whole view of himself and his place within the world. It was, then, not just political or economic 'death' but also often social and hierarchical destruction as well. In the high Middle Ages, excommunication, increasingly used by the Church in this period on behalf of friendly monarchs, was often the starting point of a serious downward fall from favour – as with the 1215 rebels and 1265 holdouts – though by the later Middle Ages, perhaps in part because of the weakening position of the Church but also the growing power of the monarchy itself, this treatment became less common. Similarly, though imprisonment was a common fate for errant nobles in the high Middle Ages – it must be noted, however, that it was for the most part not very harsh, often bordering instead more on the idea of house arrest – again it became a bit less popular with monarchs and regimes in the later fourteenth and fifteenth centuries, especially when it came to higher nobles. Whether because of the growing power of the nobility as a class, or the growing fear of what a rebellious noble could do if he escaped, by the later medieval period truly problematic nobles were increasingly either executed or, if some clemency was shown, banished for the most serious of crimes – though the latter, as we have seen, also had its problems.

Indeed, though outlawry was always an option, and its definition and implementation expanded dramatically, usually by the later medieval period at least, if a noble was involved, some agreement was sooner or later arranged, either official or unofficial, and the individual either was sent into, or ran into, exile. As a result, not only was banishment used more and more as a serious penalty, often in place of imprisonment though not as serious as capital punishment, it also became increasingly regulated, and thereby more utilised by both kings and nobles when they wanted to get rid of, but were not in the position or did not desire to execute, problematic nobles. Banishment in its widest sense could be from court or kingdom, and so could be either internal exile or exile abroad, whether in the rest of the British Isles, or on the Continent or further afield. Whatever the form, the downfallen noble could spend his time in any number of ways: causing problems for the king or those who had sent him into exile in the first place, going off to Rome or on crusade, or, more commonly, spending his life as comfortably as possible, and dying with varying degrees of bitterness in a foreign grave. However, by the fifteenth century at the latest, banishment too had become clearly problematic, mainly, as has been pointed out, 'because the exiles kept returning', and the only way really to remove political undesirables from the kingdom was to execute them[265] – hence yet another reason for the increasing number of executions in the later Middle Ages. Henry IV himself well knew what banished higher nobles could do, and of course, though a bit out of our period, the Wars of the Roses would find exiled nobles, and at least one exiled king, causing many problems for those in power.

Finally, though wives and families were rarely forcibly sent to the execution block or into exile, they did often initially also pay for their husbands' or fathers' transgressions. Usually they were turned off their lands, and often thereafter encouraged to leave the kingdom as well. However, as the later medieval period continued, kings, or even those acting in their name, developed something of a conscience – or were forced by precedent and fashion – to ameliorate the plight of the spouses and families of downfallen nobles, and made some sort of provision for them, especially in the form of partial return of estates or the payment of annuities. Nonetheless, the fuller development of the idea of attainder in the middle of the fifteenth century, and especially the attainting of the blood of the family of the rebel, again started to make the lots of spouses and children of rebels a harsher one. It could even be argued that the development of attainder, as well as the development of trial by peers for noblewomen in the 1440s, were at least in part a reaction to the strengthened position of the disgraced's family by this time – in part the result of both the growing customary charity towards relicts and, as we will see in the next chapter, the increasing importance of wives and widows in the fates of families and their estates.[266] Poets and artists (for the latter, see the discussion of the development of depictions of fortune's wheel in the Conclusion), as well as lawyers, recognised this change, making the downfall of women themselves a theme for their work, as with the disgrace of Eleanor de Cobham, the wife of the duke of Gloucester, in 1441. Ostensibly tried for witchcraft, though possibly part of moves to bring down her husband,[267] her fate again brought the muse back to at least one contemporary poet:

Thys ladye was soo proude & high of harte
that she hur-selffe thought pereles of estate,
And yet higher fayn she wold haue starte
Butt sodenlye she fell, as was hur fate.[268]

Redemption, for such individuals at least, especially after the rise of attainder and despite later provisos for the sake of relicts and others left behind, would often come more through the mercy of the king or those controlling the throne rather than any ideas of right or precedent.

Notes

1 K. Crossley-Holland, ed. and trans. *The Anglo-Saxon World: An Anthology* (Oxford, 1984), p. 7.

2 M. Alexander, *Old English Literature* (London, 1983), p. 113.

3 P.J.C. Field, 'Malory, Sir Thomas (1415x18–1471)', DNB (Oxford, 2004).

4 Pollock and Maitland, *English Law*, i, 478.

5 W. Ullmann, *A History of Political Thought: The Middle Ages* (Harmondsworth, 1965), p. 55.

6 E. Vodola, *Excommunication in the Middle Ages* (Berkeley, 1986), pp. 59–69, 70–111; F.D. Logan, *Excommunication and the Secular Arm in Medieval England* (Toronto, 1968), pp. 13–14.

7 R.T. Hill, 'The Theory and Practice of Excommunication in Medieval England', *History* 42 (1957), 2; or 'medicinal': Logan, *Excommunication*, p. 15.

8 D.L. D'Avray, 'Magna Carta: Its Background in Stephen Langton's Academic Biblical Exegesis and its Episcopal Reception', *Studi Medievali* 38 (1997), 424.

9 D'Avray, 'Magna Carta', 423–32.

10 There were, of course, different levels of excommunication: categorised as 'major' and 'minor'. Logan, *Excommunication*, p. 14.

11 Logan, *Excommunication*, p. 17 and ff.; for excommunication backed up by secular power, also see R.C. Fowler, 'Secular Aid for Excommunication', *TRHS* 3rd Ser. 8 (1914), 113–17; R.N. Swanson, *Church and Society in Late Medieval England* (Oxford, 1989), pp. 180–1.

12 Logan, *Excommunication*, pp. 66–8.

13 BL Additional Charter 75748.

14 *Bartholomew Cotton's Historia Anglicana* H.R. Luard, ed. (London, 1859), p. 103.

15 *Annales Monastici*, iii, 43. Though initially, on 18 June 1215, between the making of the first and final copies of Magna Carta, the pope issued a bull apparently backing the document and threatening to excommunicate any who did not accept it within a certain time. SC7/52/25.

16 *Annales Monastici*, iii, 63; *Memoriale Fratris Walteri de Coventria*, ii, 247–8; B. English, 'Forz, William de, Count of Aumale (1191x6–1241)', DNB (Oxford, 2004).

17 *Chronica Buriensis*, p. 33.

18 *Chronica Johannis de Oxenedes* H. Ellis, ed. (London, 1859), p. 233.

19 *Royal Letters Illustrative of the Reign of Henry III*, i, 556.

20 *Letters of Lanfranc*, p. 123.

21 According to Falkes's testimony. *Memoriale Fratris Walteri de Coventria*, ii, 265.

22 *CP* vi, 454 footnote g.

23 P. Heath, *Church and Realm 1272–1461* (London, 1988), p. 330.

24 Most importantly, since the Conquest, excommunications of tenants-in-chief, especially royal officers, were not to be executed without royal licence. Pollock and Maitland, *English Law*, i, 478–9.

25 John Mirk's *Instructions for Parish Priests*, as in Heath, *Church and Realm*, p. 331.

26 *Riverside Chaucer*, p. 716 ll. 2755–8.

27 R.B. Pugh, 'The King's Prisons before 1250', *TRHS* 5th Ser. 5 (1955), 1.

28 He also had a few royal grants in the first half of the 1330s, including a small annuity continued from the Minority period, a Mortimer manor in wardship and the control of Cardigan Castle. E403/253 (12 November 1330); *CPR 1330–4*, 31; *CFR 1327–37*, 401.

29 For Alice Lacy, see Maddicott, 'Thomas of Lancaster, Second Earl of Lancaster, Second Earl of Leicester, and Earl of Lincoln', *DNB* (2004).

30 *CPR 1334–8*, 282; *CFR 1327–37*, 473; J.G. Ruddock, *Boothby Graffoe and Somerton Castle* (Lincoln, 1980), p. 21.

31 D. Crouch, 'Robert, First Earl of Gloucester (*b*. before 1100, *d*. 1147)', *DNB* (Oxford, 2004).

32 W.M. Aird, 'Mowbray, Robert de, Earl of Northumbria (*d*. 1115/1125)', *DNB* (Oxford, 2004); *CP* ix, 706.

33 Trokelowe, *Chronica*, p. 111.

34 Crouch, 'Breteuil, Robert de', *DNB* (2004).

35 Tout, 'Hugh, Fifth Earl of Chester (1147–1181)', rev. Keefe, *DNB* (2004).

36 J. Dunbabin, *Captivity and Imprisonment in Medieval Europe 1000–1300* (London, 2002), pp. 83–4.

37 Henry of Huntingdon, *History of the English People*, p. 73.

38 *Literae Cantuarienses*, iii, 409.

39 For discussion of the implements of captivity, see Dunbabin, *Captivity and Imprisonment*, pp. 32–4.

40 *Ecclesiastical History of Orderic Vitalis*, v, 311–13.

41 M. Paris, *Historia Anglorum* F. Madden, ed. (London, 1869), iii, 267.

42 See also Chapter 2.

43 Warren, *King John*, p. 185.

44 *CP* i, 347–8.

45 L. Smith, 'Mortimer, Roger (IV), First Lord Mortimer of Chirk (*c*. 1256–1326)', *DNB* (Oxford, 2004).

46 Dunbabin, *Captivity and Imprisonment*, pp. 114–20.

47 And for prisoners of rank, this was by personal guards rather than common jailors. R.B. Pugh, *Imprisonment in Medieval England* (Cambridge, 1968), p. 162.

48 *Gesta Normannorum Ducum*, ii, 223.

49 Dunbabin, *Captivity and Imprisonment*, p. 115.

50 K. Thompson, 'Robert, Duke of Normandy (*b*. in or after 1050, *d*. 1134)', *DNB* (Oxford, 2004).

51 Aird, 'Mowbray, Robert', *DNB* (2004).

52 Amt, 'Essex, Henry of', *DNB* (2004); see above, Chapter 1.

53 *Ecclesiastical History of Orderic Vitalis*, ii, 319.

54 *CP* vi, 450.

55 Though this was a double-edged sword for Oldcastle. Allmand, *Henry V*, pp. 295–6.

56 Capgrave, *Chronicle*, p. 306.

57 *CPR 1401–5*, 108.

58 L.E. Boyle, 'E *Cathena et Carcere*: The Imprisonment of Amaury de Montfort, 1276', in J.J.G. Alexander and M.T. Gibson, eds. *Medieval Learning and Literature* (Oxford, 1976), pp. 381ff.

59 Boyle, 'E *Cathena et Carcere*', 385.

60 Pugh, *Imprisonment*, pp. 125–7; Dunbabin, *Captivity and Imprisonment*, pp. 38–9.

61 See pp. 77–8.

62 SC1/19/43; also see *Calendar of Ancient Correspondence Concerning Wales* J.G. Edwards, ed. (Board of Celtic Studies, Cardiff, 1935), pp. 98–9.

63 *CPR 1388–92*, 228.

64 Also see Dunbabin, *Captivity and Imprisonment*, pp. 118–19.

65 Florence of Worcester, *Chronicon*, ii, 12.

66 Robbins, ed. *Historical Poems*, p. 186.

67 Bellamy, *Crime and Public Order*, p. 178.

68 Fantosme, *Chronicle*, p. 137.

69 Capgrave, *Chronicle*, p. 276.

70 D.A. Crook, 'Central England and the Revolt of the Earls, January 1400', *HR* 64 (1991), 404.

71 Capgrave, *Chronicle*, pp. 288–9.

72 ASC (D1072).

73 D. Roffe, 'Hereward (*fl.* 1070–1071)', *DNB* (Oxford, 2004); Douglas, *William the Conqueror*, p. 222.

74 C.P. Lewis, 'Warenne, William (I) de, First Earl of Surrey (*d.* 1088)', *DNB* (Oxford, 2004); Williams, *English and the Norman Conquest*, p. 63.

75 E.L.G. Stones, 'The Date of Roger Mortimer's Escape from the Tower of London', *EHR* 66 (1951), 97–8.

76 *CCR 1323–7*, 13–14; though, according to *The Anonimalle Chronicle*, there are many different accounts of this event. C. Given-Wilson, *Chronicles: The Writing of History in Medieval England* (London and New York, 2003), p. 10.

77 Trokelowe, *Chronica*, p. 146; see also Walsingham, *Historia*, i, 174; Pugh, *Imprisonment*, pp. 221–2.

78 Four days later the earl of Winchester was ordered to capture Mortimer 'with power to punish all persons not aiding him by incarcerating them and seizing their lands and goods'. *CPR 1321–4*, 335.

79 *CCR 1323–7*, 132, 133.

80 He initially found harbour in John de Fienles's lordship of Picardy. *CCR 1323–7*, 140–1.

81 *CPR 1321–4*, 257.

82 As seen in M.H. Keen's *The Outlaws of Medieval Legend* (London, 1987); G. Seal, *The Outlaw Legend: A Cultural Tradition in Britain, America and Australia* (Cambridge, 1996), pp. 19–31; for Hereward, see J. Hayward, 'Hereward the Outlaw', *JMH* 14 (1988), esp. 293–7.

83 For examples, see Keen, *Outlaws*, pp. 28, 40, 93, 177–8; also see the beginning of this chapter.

84 Turner, 'Briouze, William (III) de (*d.* 1211)', *DNB* (2004).

85 R.V. Turner, 'Vescy, Eustace de (1169/70–1216)', *DNB* (Oxford, 2004); M. Strickland, 'Fitzwalter, Robert (*d.* 1235)', *DNB* (Oxford, 2004).

86 *Royal Letters Illustrative of the Reign of Henry III*, i, 429.

87 Knowles, 'Resettlement', 25–30.

88 Keen, *Outlaws*, pp. 194–5.

89 R.B. Pugh, 'Early Register of English Outlaws', *American Journal of Legal History* 27 (1983), 319; Seal, *Outlaw Legend*, p. 20.

90 Keen, *Outlaws*, p. 10.

91 From 1409 to 1412 there were 162 felonies, 133 trespasses, 3 treasons and 3 uncertain charges. Pugh, 'English Outlaws', 325.

92 J.A.F. Thomson, 'Oldcastle, John, Baron Cobham (*d.* 1417)', *DNB* (Oxford, 2004).

93 Bellamy also points out that nobles were only outlawed on 'very rare occasions' – though the above discussion shows that this might be, to a degree, overstated. Bellamy, *Crime and Public Order*, p. 73.

94 *Annals of Roger de Hoveden*, i, 549.

95 Bracton, *Laws and Customs*, ii, 298.

96 R. Epstein, 'Prisoners of Reflection: The Fifteenth-Century Poetry of Exile and Imprisonment', *Exemplaria* 15 (2003), 159–98; for Malory, see above, p. 129.

97 For discussion of early exile literature, see e.g. E. Kelemen, '*Clyppan* and *Cyssan*: The Formulaic Expression of Return from Exile in Old English Literature', *English Language Notes* 38 (2001), 1–19; C. Hares-Stryker, 'Adrift on the Seven Seas: The Medieval Topos of Exile at Sea', *Florilegium* 12 (1993), 79–98.

98 E. Van Houts, 'Hereward and Flanders', *Anglo-Saxon England* 28 (1999), 222–3.

99 Geoffrey of Monmouth, *The History of the Kings of Britain* L. Thorpe, ed. and trans. (Harmondsworth, 1966), pp. 55–75.

100 T. Malory, *Le Morte D'Arthur* J. Cowen ed. (Harmondsworth, 1986), i, p. 420.

101 K.F. Meredith, 'The Penalty of Banishment in Medieval France and England', University of Virginia PhD (1979). Most of the following discussion of the development of 'political' banishment in later medieval England comes from Meredith, Chapters 9 and 10; also see W.R. Jones, 'Sanctuary, Exile and Law: The Fugitive and Public Authority in Medieval England and Modern America', in W.R. Jones et al., *Essays on English Law and the American Experience* (Arlington, 1994), 19–41.

102 See above, p. 141.

103 Jones, 'Sanctuary, Exile and Law', 23–6. For the process of abjuration, see Bracton, *Laws and Customs*, ii, 382–4.

104 J.F.A. Mason, 'Mortimer, Hugh (II) de (*d.* 1181?)', *DNB* (Oxford, 2004); CP ix, 272.

105 West, 'Burgh, Hubert de', *DNB* (2004).

106 *Memoriale Fratris Walteri de Coventria*, ii, 254.

107 See also below, pp. 146, 158, 207.

108 H.W. Ridgeway, 'Henry III (1207–1272)', *DNB* (Oxford, 2004).

109 Holmes, *Good Parliament*, p. 137.

110 See J.L. Leland, 'The Abjuration of 1388', *MP* 15 (1994), 115.

111 Meredith, 'Banishment', 542–3.

112 Meredith, 'Banishment', 543.

113 *Chronicle of Lanercost*, p. 187; see below, pp. 161–2.

114 *Vita Edwardi Secundi*, p. 5.

115 *Chronicle of Lanercost*, pp. 193–4.

116 Wilkinson, 'Sherburn Indenture', 1–28; Fryde, *Tyranny*, pp. 48–9; also see Trokelowe, *Chronica*, p. 110.

117 *Chronicles of the Reigns of Edward I and Edward II* W. Stubbs, ed. (London, 1883), ii, 40.

118 *Chronicle of Adam of Usk*, pp. 38–9; also see Walsingham, *Ypodiigma Neustiae*, p. 379.

119 See below, pp. 156–7, 186.

120 Virgoe, 'Death of William de la Pole', 489–92.

121 *Annals of Roger de Hoveden*, i, 549; on outlawry and helping outlaws, see also Bracton, *Laws and Customs*, ii, 361–2.

122 *Chronicle of Lanercost*, pp. 193–4.

123 CCR 1323–7, 650–1.

124 CCR 1419–22, 196.

125 CPR 1334–8, 89.

126 CPR 1334–8, 111.

127 Goodman, *John of Gaunt*, pp. 101–2; on this dispute, also see *The Westminster Chronicle* L.C. Hector and B.F. Harvey, ed. and trans. (Oxford, 1982), pp. 110–14, 120; Walsingham, *Ypodiigma Neustiae*, pp. 340–1.

128 Maddicott, *Thomas of Lancaster*, Chapter 6.

129 See CP iv, 318 footnote a.

130 Also see ECR, p. 13.

131 C49/67/31; RP iii, 383–4.

132 For de Montfort the younger's life after Evesham, see J.R. Maddicott, 'Montfort, Sir Simon de, the Younger (1240–1271)', *DNB* (Oxford, 2004).

133 *Annales Monastici*, ii, 369–70.

134 *Eulogium Historiarum sive Temporis*, iii, 135.

135 *Brut Y Tywysogion, or Chronicle of the Princes* J. Williams, ed. (London, 1860), p. 354.

136 E. Hallam, 'Eleanor, Countess of Pembroke and Leicester (1215?–1275)', *DNB* (Oxford, 2004).

137 *Annales Monastici*, iii, 259.

138 Paris, *Chronica Majora*, iii, 479–80. On the substance of these accusations, see above, p. 28.

139 See *ASC* (1088E); Bates, 'Career of Odo', pp. 18–20.

140 D. Bates, 'Odo, Earl of Kent (d. 1097)', *DNB* (Oxford, 2004).

141 C. Tyerman, *England and the Crusades 1095–1588* (Chicago, 1996), pp. 98–101; N. Vincent, 'Roches, Peter des (d. 1238)', *DNB* (Oxford, 2004).

142 Tyerman, *England and the Crusades*, p. 123.

143 A.L. Brown and H. Summerson, 'Henry IV (1366–1413)', *DNB* (Oxford, 2004).

144 M. Lawrence, '"Too Flattering Sweet to be Substantial"? The Last Months of Thomas, Lord Despenser', in J.S. Hamilton, ed. *Fourteenth Century England IV* (Woodbridge, 2006), 153.

145 See below.

146 Crawford, 'Victims of Attainder', 72. Though, as Dunbabin points out, 'Ladies of the highest rank, unless they posed a very real threat to the captor powers, generally received fairly liberal terms as prisoners.' Dunbabin, *Captivity and Imprisonment*, p. 116.

147 *Chronica Buriensis*, pp. 7–8. A Close Roll mandate (CCR 1231–4, 161) of 16 October 1232 ordered the capture of Margaret when she left St Edmund's Liberty. Notably, de Burgh may have also been planning to divorce Margaret. W.W. Scott, 'Margaret, Countess of Kent (1187x95–1259)', *DNB* (Oxford, 2004).

148 CCR 1231–4, 161, 296, 378.

149 *Ecclesiastical History of Orderic Vitalis*, iii, 135; S.M. Johns, *Noblewomen, Aristocracy and Power in the Twelfth-Century Anglo-Norman Realm* (Manchester, 2003), p. 17.

150 H.W. Ridgeway, 'Valence, William de, Earl of Pembroke (d. 1296)', *DNB* (Oxford, 2004).

151 Hallam, 'Eleanor, Countess of Pembroke and Leicester (1215?–1275)', *DNB* (2004); Maddicott, *Simon de Montfort*, pp. 369–71.

152 Crossley-Holland, ed. and trans. *Anglo-Saxon World*, p. 56.

153 N. Pevsner, *The Buildings of England: Cumberland and Westmorland* (Harmondsworth, 1973), pp. 110–11 and plate 34. Though, according to Given-Wilson, the 'Mowbray Stone' is more likely to have been associated with Bolingbroke. C. Given-Wilson, 'Mowbray, Thomas (I), First Duke of Norfolk (1366–1399)', *DNB* (Oxford, 2004).

154 Roffe, 'Hereward (fl. 1070–1071)', *DNB* (2004).

155 See p. 146.

156 Allmand, *Henry V*, pp. 296, 302–3; also H.G. Richardson, 'John Oldcastle in Hiding, August–October, 1417', *EHR* 55 (1940), 432–8.

157 Florence of Worcester, *Chronicon*, ii, 197.

158 KB26/175/70b; KB26/175/140b.

159 O. de Ville, 'John de Ville: A Neglected Rebel', *NH* 35 (1998), 29–32.

160 Knowles, 'Resettlement', 30–1.

161 Fryde, *Tyranny*, p. 151.

162 KB27/255/before second section, m. 1; Davies, 'Mortimer, Roger (V)', *DNB* (2004).

163 As well as, in the lesser gentry's case, profiting from the disturbances: S.L. Waugh, 'The Profits of Violence: The Minor Gentry in the Rebellion of 1321–1322 in Gloucestershire and Herefordshire', *Speculum* 52 (1977), 843–69.

164 *Fouke le Fitz Waryn* S. Knight and T.H. Ohlgren, eds. (TEAMS On-line).

165 CCR 1318–23, 511–12.
166 SC1/19/129; *Calendar of Ancient Correspondence Concerning Wales*, p. 101.
167 J.S. Hamilton, 'Bohun, Humphrey (VII) de, Fourth Earl of Hereford and Ninth Earl of Essex (*c.* 1276–1322)', *DNB* (Oxford, 2004).
168 CCR 1318–23, 512.
169 CPR 1324–7, 287.
170 CCR 1318–23, 519.
171 CPR 1324–7, 206.
172 Paris, *Chronica Majora*, iii, 479–80.
173 CP ix, 573–4.
174 *Annals of Roger de Hoveden*, i, 197.
175 Bates, 'Odo, Earl of Kent', *DNB* (2004).
176 *Gesta Stephani* K.R. Potter, ed. and trans. (London, 1955), p. 38.
177 Maddicott, 'Montfort, Simon de, the Younger', *DNB* (2004); see also below, p. 159.
178 J.R. Maddicott, 'Montfort, Amaury de, Styled Eleventh Earl of Leicester (1242/3–*c.* 1300)', *DNB* (Oxford, 2004); Gray, *Scalacronica*, p. 9.
179 Fryde, *Tyranny*, p. 49.
180 *Vita Edwardi Secundi*, pp. 115–16; also Trokelowe, *Chronica*, p. 110; Fryde, *Tyranny*, p. 49; according to one source, 'the king kept Despenser the son in the realm, at sea'. *Anonimalle Chronicle*, p. 101.
181 Fryde, *Tyranny*, pp. 159, 180–1. Waugh, 'Edmund, First Earl of Kent', *DNB* (2004).
182 *Chronicon Galfridi le Baker*, p. 20.
183 SC1/54/12; also see P. Chaplais, ed. *The War of Saint Sardos (1323–5)* (London, 1957), pp. 72–3; also see Fryde, *Tyranny*, p. 144.
184 Bracton, *Laws and Customs*, ii, 361–2.
185 CP vii, 687.
186 SC1/2/59: also see P. Chaplais, ed. *Diplomatic Documents 1101–1272* (London, 1964), i, 229–30.
187 Bates, 'Career of Odo', 18–19.
188 *Vita Edwardi Secundi*, p. 6; for a more positive view of Gaveston's time in Ireland, see Hamilton, *Gaveston*, pp. 53–66.
189 C. Shenton, 'Maltravers, John, First Lord Maltravers (*c.* 1290–1364)', *DNB* (Oxford, 2004); J.S. Bothwell, 'Agnes Maltravers (d. 1375) and Her Husband, John (d. 1364): Rebel Wives, Separate Lives and Conjugal Visits in Later Medieval England', in Hamilton, ed. *Fourteenth Century England IV*, 88; CP viii, 581–5.
190 A. Cosgrove, 'Anglo-Ireland and the Yorkist Cause', in A. Cosgrove, ed. *A New History of Ireland*, Volume II: *Medieval Ireland 1169–1534* (Oxford, 1987), 562.
191 Ridgeway, 'Valence, William de', *DNB* (2004); also see H.W. Ridgeway, 'William de Valence and His *Familiares*, 1247–1272', *HR* 65 (1992), 240.
192 *Vita Edwardi Secundi*, pp. 116–17.
193 See Given-Wilson, *Chronicles*, p. 73.
194 *Vita Edwardi Secundi*, p. 6.

195 Monk of Evesham in Given-Wilson, ed. and trans. *Chronicles of the Revolution*, pp. 61–2; Walsingham, *Ypodiigma Neustiae*, pp. 377–8.

196 *CCR 1396–9*, 346.

197 Given-Wilson, ed. and trans. *Chronicles of the Revolution*, p. 96.

198 *Chronicle of Adam of Usk*, p. 35; there is some debate about the earl's demeaning behaviour at the trial. C. Given-Wilson, 'Adam of Usk, the Monk of Evesham and the Parliament of 1397–8', *HR* 66 (1993), 331.

199 *CCR 1396–9*, 163–4.

200 C49/67/31; *RP* iii, 383–4.

201 *CCR 1396–9*, 339; *CPR 1396–9*, 420, 439.

202 Given-Wilson, 'Mowbray, Thomas (I), First Duke of Norfolk', *DNB* (2004).

203 *Chronicon Galfridi le Baker*, p. 34; or perhaps, according to other sources, in exile in the Low Countries instead. Shenton, 'Maltravers, John', *DNB* (2004).

204 For a recent survey of the Percies' importance, see A. King, ' "They have the Hertes of the People by North": Northumberland, the Percies and Henry IV, 1399–1408', in G. Dodd and D. Biggs, eds. *Henry IV: The Establishment of the Regime, 1399–1406* (Woodbridge, 2003), 139–60; Bean, 'Percy, Henry', *DNB* (2004).

205 See above, p. 116.

206 Florence of Worcester, *Chronicon*, ii, 197.

207 Chandler, 'Montgomerys', 6–7.

208 Chandler, 'Montgomerys', 11–13.

209 Though perhaps not as much as Walsingham indicates, a result of obtaining some of the instalments of his ransom of Jean de Penthièvre. A. Tuck, 'Vere, Robert de, Ninth Earl of Oxford, Marquess of Dublin, and Duke of Ireland (1362–1392)', *DNB* (Oxford, 2004).

210 Walsingham, *Ypodiigma Neustiae*, p. 364.

211 For the following, see D.J. Power, 'Bréauté, Sir Falkes de (d. 1226)', *DNB* (Oxford, 2004).

212 Divorced by his wife and perhaps died by eating a poisoned fish. For Falkes's end, also see D.H. Kennett, 'Falke de Bréauté: Henchman of King John', *Bedfordshire Magazine* 14 (1974), 282.

213 Froissart, *Chronicles*, p. 430.

214 N. Vincent, 'Henry of Almain (1235–1271)', *DNB* (Oxford, 2004); F.M. Powicke, 'Guy de Montfort (1265–71)', *TRHS* 4th Ser. 18 (1935), 7.

215 *Flores Historiarum* as quoted in Maddicott, *Simon de Montfort*, p. 371.

216 Dante, *The Divine Comedy: Inferno*, ed. and trans. C.S. Singleton (London, 1971), p. 127.

217 There is a slightly artificial divide between this and the section on petitioning women of the next chapter: I have tried to keep the divide as clear as possible, though there is also always the issues of overlap of cases (being a mixture of charity and petitioning) as well as record survival: either way, however, both sections' ultimate aim is to show the increasing role of women in the fate of families and estates. See also Chapter 5, pp. 200–6.

218 See Ward, *English Noblewomen*, pp. 44–9 on the position of rebels' wives and widows. Though by the later fifteenth century there was a harshening of

attitudes towards the rebels' wives, including the fact that noblewomen could be tried as peers of the realm after 1441/2, which while offering similar rights as men in this instance, also showed that they were now beginning to be charged with the most serious of crimes. For a case study of this harsher treatment at the end of our period, see Crawford, 'Victims of Attainder', 59–74; *RP* v, 56; see also Chapter 5.

219 Crawford, 'Victims of Attainder', 72; she also was later granted a £100 annuity during her husband's life, and Lander puts forth evidence of other humane treatment to her. Lander, *Crown and Nobility*, pp. 140–1.

220 Crawford, 'Victims of Attainder', pp. 61–2.

221 *Annals of Roger of Hoveden*, i, 550.

222 F.S. Scott, 'Earl Waltheof of Northumbria', *Archaeologia Aeliana* 4th Ser. 30 (1952), 208.

223 See Lewis, 'Waltheof, Earl of Northumbria', *DNB* (2004); *CP* vi, 639–42.

224 Thompson, 'Robert, Duke of Normandy', *DNB* (2004).

225 I am using 'relict' in its contemporary sense, according to the *Oxford English Dictionary*.

226 Knowles, 'Resettlement', 28; probably also connected with marriage and blood ties between the two sides. C.H. Knowles, 'Provision for the Families of the Montfortians Disinherited after the Battle of Evesham', in P.R. Coss and S.D. Lloyd, eds. *Thirteenth Century England I* (Woodbridge, 1986), 127.

227 Knowles, 'Resettlement', 28.

228 *CPR 1258–66*, 558.

229 *CPR 1258–66*, 602.

230 *CPR 1258–66*, 533, 557, 558; Knowles, 'Families of the Montfortians', 124–7.

231 Knowles, 'Families of the Montfortians', 127.

232 Fryde, *Tyranny*, p. 79; Knowles, 'Resettlement', 28; Knowles, 'Families of the Montfortians', 127.

233 *Chronicle of Lanercost*, p. 187. Though, of course, it was Edward II who helped Gaveston's family after his execution. Hamilton, *Gaveston*, pp. 100–1.

234 See Chapter 2.

235 Langston, 'Giffards', 126.

236 Though notably with remainder to Despenser the younger and heirs when she died. *CCharR 1300–27*, 451; on Lancaster's wife, see Maddicott, 'Thomas of Lancaster', *DNB* (2004). *CPR 1321–4*, 180, 181. In the same period, she was granted a 500 mark annuity in case anyone legally evicted her from her dower lands. *CPR 1321–4*, 183. Though, as we will see in the next chapter, some of these returns also came more through her own pressure and petitioning.

237 *CPR 1321–4*, 215.

238 Even wives of followers could at times be provided for, as in the case of the widow of Bartholomew Badlesemere's retainer, John Penreth, who was given the manor of another Contrariant to ease her family's destitution. Fryde, *Tyranny*, p. 79.

239 *CPR 1327–30*, 42, 271.

240 *CPR 1330–4*, 13.

241 See next chapter, pp. 202–3, 204–5; Bothwell, 'Agnes Maltravers', 80–93.

242 CPR *1330–4*, 89.

243 CPR *1388–92*, 117; Tuck, 'Vere, Robert de', *DNB* (2004).

244 Ward, *English Noblewomen*, p. 45.

245 KB2₇/587/section 2 m. 15.

246 CPR *1399–1401*, 204–5, 223–4, 226. Though she also seems to have put some pressure on the administration to regain her lands (see pp. 203–4), and apparently later went into revolt. R. Horrox, 'Despenser, Constance, Lady Despenser (*c.* 1375–1416)', *DNB* (Oxford, 2004).

247 C49/29/17 (31–2 Henry VI); R.E. Archer, 'Chaucer, Alice, Duchess of Suffolk (*c.* 1404–1475)', *DNB* (Oxford, 2004); though this leniency may in part be the result of a 3500 mark loan made to Henry VI for sending an army to France, as well as, of course, Suffolk's good relations with the king. M. Anderson, 'Alice Chaucer and her Husbands', *Publications of the Modern Language Association of America* 60 (1945), 39–40.

248 CP v, 199.

249 CPR *1399–1401*, 206, 244.

250 CPR *1321–4*, 182.

251 See above.

252 *A Catalogue of the Medieval Muniments at Berkeley Castle* B. Wells-Furby, ed. and trans. (Bristol, 2004), i, 487–8; *VCH Gloucestershire*, vii, 228–9.

253 CPR *1321–4*, 266.

254 CPR *1388–92*, 404.

255 CPR *1388–92*, 462.

256 Though Matilda herself alienated lands and wasted what remained. J. Ross, 'Seditious Activities: The Conspiracy of Maud de Vere, Countess of Oxford, 1403–4', in Clark, ed. *Fifteenth Century III: Authority and Subversion*, 27–8.

257 CPR *1396–9*, 357, 411; E28/5/27.

258 See Chapter 3.

259 Rather, adult male relatives at least had to be more active if they wanted the family estate back. See next chapter.

260 CPR *1399–1401*, 380.

261 KB27/303/112.

262 CPR *1338–40*, 238–9.

263 CPR *1348–50*, 240

264 See also p. 180.

265 Meredith, 'Banishment', 544–6.

266 See this chapter, pp. 159–64 and next chapter, pp. 200–6.

267 G.L. Harriss, 'Eleanor, Duchess of Gloucester (*c.* 1400–1452)', *DNB* (Oxford, 2004).

268 Robbins, ed. *Historical Poems*, p. 184; for this and similar verse on the duchess's fall, see Scattergood, *Politics and Poetry*, pp. 152–4.

5

Returning to favour:
the search for redemption

You have restored to me the brother I so sorely missed and me to the most affectionate of brothers. You have restored their parent to my children and my children to me. You have given me back rank, status, fortune, a noble common-wealth, and, a source of delight second to none, my country. In a word, you have given me back myself.[1]

As Cicero found over a thousand years before the start of our period of study, not all men's lives ended because of their political and social demise, nor were they or their families all permanently disinherited. Men and their families fell, but they also could find their way back to forms of royal grace, economic and/or political position. Though the route was rarely without diversions and problems, a fair number of downfallen nobles and their families returned to some degree of status and favour. Unsurprisingly then, redemption, including return from exile, was an increasingly popular literary and cultural theme throughout the Middle Ages.[2] With a firm basis in the Scriptures, ideas of deliverance and salvation were to influence the culture of the Middle Ages, especially through the image of the Virgin Mary and the teachings of St Paul. The importance of Mary in the life of Christ, emphasised by the growth of the cult of the Blessed Virgin, could not but have had a profound impact upon medieval man. Royalty and nobility in particular not only founded a growing number of chapels (especially Lady Chapels in parish churches)[3] throughout England and Europe dedicated to Mary as the Middle Ages progressed, but also commissioned missals, psalters and diptychs, all helping to emphasise the resurrection of Christ, and through Christ, the redemption of Man. As for the teachings of St Paul, these were also to prove a crucial factor, especially the concept of individual, rather than just collective, redemption through faith in Christ – as Paul himself experienced on the road to Damascus. This idea, first influencing the writings of the Church Fathers, was also glossed and expanded regularly throughout the medieval period, both in works of Anselm, Abelard and Aquinas and in lives of the saints themselves, from

St Augustine to St Francis and beyond. However, individual, as well as collective, redemption not only showed up in theological texts and hagiographies but also in more accessible media, for example mystery and miracle plays, romances and other secular works such as *Sir Gawain and the Green Knight* and, more generally, the various reworkings of the Arthur legend:[4] just as places at the Round Table at times could be vacated, so too at times could they be reclaimed. The chance of redemption, then, just as fall and damnation, was ever in the medieval mind, and none more so than for those who had fallen from great heights.

Returning to royal favour

Also, it was asked of them [Richard II's judges] how those who had procured the aforesaid statute, ordinance and commission [of the Wonderful Parliament of 1386] ought to be punished. To which they unanimously replied that they deserved capital punishment, namely death, *unless the king wished to grant them grace in that respect* [author's italics].[5]

Probably the easiest, though also potentially most dangerous, way to return to favour with a monarch was to beg his forgiveness directly and/or in person. Depending upon the king, as well as the disgrace in question, this could be a very tense affair, especially considering the mercurial temperaments of some medieval English monarchs: Henry I had, according to some chroniclers at least, one noble thrown over castle battlements to his death and others blinded or mutilated;[6] and John, as we have already heard, was said to have starved the wife and son of William de Braose to death. Henry II was known for his rages at the mere thought of treachery, in one case apparently throwing off his garments and tearing at the rushes on the floor,[7] Richard II's outbursts clearly illustrated the tension points of his career,[8] and even Edward III in a fury sacked a number of his administrators in late 1340, believing they were not giving him proper support for the war in France.[9] With such a reputation, deserved or not, of severe, even manic, reactions, was it really such a good idea to petition the king directly or even in person when out of favour? Nevertheless, some nobles thought it worth the risk, particularly if they had close, especially blood or political, links with the monarchy. When Richard of Poitou, the future Richard I, realised that he might not be included in the Peace of 1173–4, 'coming in tears, he fell prone upon the ground at the feet of his father [Henry II], and begging pardon, was received back into his father's heart'.[10] And when Prince John in turn faced Richard I in person after his revolt during the period of Richard's captivity by the Holy Roman Emperor, John was weeping and repentant. The king in this case again showed mercy, though at the same time patronising his younger brother with the line: 'You are a child. You have had bad companions.'[11] Later in the period, a couple of years after the Nottingham coup, probably gauging the time as right after the overthrow of Mortimer and Isabella, Hugh Despenser, son of the younger Hugh, petitioned king and council that he be freed from prison as he had already been pardoned execution for holding Caerphilly Castle – in this case the council deciding that if there was no other reason for him to be in prison, then he ought to be released, if, of course, it was pleasing to the king.[12] Even Hubert de Burgh, after a tumultuous summer of problems with the king, dared to throw himself on the king's mercy in person in October 1232, and ended up receiving back most of his inherited and purchased lands (except those lands given him by the king) within a couple of years, the lands mainly having been kept in the royal possession in the meantime.[13] Nonetheless, asking or begging for mercy directly, or even a hearing, from the king was at best a hit and miss affair, and one could end up with the opposite of the result desired, however initially responsive the king might have been. After the rebellion of 1075, according to the *Anglo-Saxon Chronicle*, Earl Waltheof 'travelled across the sea, and confessed, and asked forgiveness and offered treasures. But the king made light of it until he came to England – and then had him taken afterwards.'[14] Despite pleading for mercy from William I, Waltheof was thrown into prison, later to be executed.[15] Similarly, in early 1234, when a furious Henry III demanded that the rebellious earl of Pembroke come to him with a rope around his neck to beg mercy, one has to wonder about the form that forgiveness would take.[16] Finally, Baldwin Redvers, faced with the fall of Carisbrooke Castle which he had seized from the royalists at the beginning of Stephen's reign, appeared in person to petition for clemency; however, in this case, the king ignored his pleas, and Redvers was forced to leave the kingdom and go into exile – despite also the pleas of his wife, who came barefoot, bareheaded and weeping out of the castle begging for royal leniency.[17]

That said, unless one was a prince of the royal blood, if the disgrace involved was not overly serious, or there were other reasons for petitioning the king directly, it was often wiser to persuade a third, preferably more important, party to plead on one's behalf – if nothing else such a method offered a buffer if things went wrong. In some cases, help could come from another noble, or at times a group of them. In 1202, it was William Longspee, earl of Salisbury, who despite besieging the outlawed Fulk Fitz Waryn in Stanley Abbey, was the one who in the next year gained a pardon for both Fitz Waryn and his followers.[18] Likewise, after Evesham, when Ralph Basset obtained a pardon it was through pressure from other supporters of the king in the Midlands.[19] Indeed the Lords could even act as a unit in aid of a disgraced individual, so long as he was, or was on the edge of becoming, one of their own. In the spring of 1332 during a heated dispute in front of the king between John de Grey of Rotherfield (enjoying moderate favour and later in the decade to be raised to a peerage) and Lord William de la Zouche of Ashby (the brother of Lord Mortimer of Richard's Castle),[20] Grey made the mistake of beginning to remove his knife from its scabbard, a deed for which he was sent to prison – though, by the Lords pleading with the king for mercy, he was pardoned soon after.[21] Queens and noblewomen were also often useful conduits through whom to gain favour and mercy, being outside the mainly male political culture of the period but usually worshipped by the chivalric one – as most famously seen in the case of Queen Philippa and her petition to Edward III for mercy for the burghers of Calais in 1347. Even if their own husbands had fallen into disgrace, powerful women would nonetheless often be able and willing to petition for the sake of others. In late October 1265, the countess of Leicester, widow of Simon de Montfort, still thought she had enough royal goodwill left as the king's sister to risk asking Henry III for some of the members of her household to be pardoned,[22] despite the more general dispossession of her husband's supporters at the time. Again, when Roger Mortimer fell from favour for the first time in late 1306, having left Edward I's service without licence, he thought it wisest to have Queen Margaret plead his case in front of the king.[23] This role of intermediary was often crucial, especially for more serious offences, and especially after rebellions: after Boroughbridge, Joan, wife of Bewes de Knovill, petitioned Queen Isabella to encourage Edward II to free her husband from imprisonment in York Castle, the king responding that he would consider the matter;[24] by 1324 Knovill was definitely free as he was returned as a Knight of the Shire for Wiltshire for the Great Council held in that year,[25] and by 1325 he was petitioning to get parts of his estate back.[26] Likewise, others outside the relatively restrictive bounds of the feudal military masculine ethos could also be useful when searching for means through which to obtain pardon. Just as churchmen could be used to get erring nobles back on the straight and narrow, petitioning for the sake of an already fallen noble could come from the ecclesiastical elite, as when, in 1282, Archbishop Peckham pleaded with Edward I to free Amaury de Montfort, Simon's son[27] – who was released later in the year, on condition that he abjure the realm.[28] A century earlier, during Henry II's reign, Roger Mowbray, one of the main 1173–4 rebels and with a mixture of potential grievances against the king,[29] asked the archbishop of Canterbury to plead his case, though in this case wisely encouraging him to argue forcibly with the offer of a grant.[30]

Other disgraced nobles found return to favour through their own actions, behaviour or general demeanour. Simple good service could retrieve position and estates – playing up to superiors, especially when one is in trouble, is by no means a modern phenomenon:

Those who have submitted to the conditions of service for the sake of recovering their inheritance – although they are ground down by toil of one kind or another, and suffer insults of every description – yet bear everything with steadfast minds so long as they have a firm desire to recover their inheritance and are supported by a sure hope.[31]

For example, in 1345, John Maltravers submitted himself to Edward III's mercy at the port of Swyn in Flanders, and later in London, asking that since he was convicted and banished unheard in 1330, that he be allowed to put his case in parliament.[32] Under normal circumstances, considering his connection with the deaths of the earl of Kent and Edward II, Maltravers would have been insane to consider such a petition, especially in person. However, the errant henchman of the Minority regime had spent much of the last twenty years carefully rebuilding his reputation in the king's eyes (especially through his continual royal service abroad on various foreign commissions and embassies (including as negotiator with Jacob Van Arteveldt)), and this went a long way to getting his petition a favourable hearing.[33] By the mid-1340s Maltravers (as well as his son John) was in a secure enough position to be able to start making moves in order to get a parliamentary reversal of his 1330 sentence and to get his estate back.[34] Some individuals, however, had to fight more fiercely for redemption and/or reintegration – or at least use strongarm tactics. First noted in the last chapter, Gilbert de Clare, the earl of Gloucester, one of the later rebels of the Barons' Wars of the 1260s, was forced to show up in London on Palm Sunday with a large retinue and take possession of the city's defences before any sort of rapprochement was seriously considered.[35] Peace negotiations were initiated between king and earl and, by mid-June, an agreement was arranged, the earl swearing on the altar in St Paul's that he would never bear arms against the king, save in self-defence.[36] That said, by the same token other men seemed determined to throw such favour away, however hard it was initially to arrange. The interplay between Gaveston and his baronial critics during Edward II's reign makes a good case study of this. To start, the comment of the *Vita Edwardi Secundi* on Piers Gaveston's 1307 return from an exile arranged by Edward I says as much: 'An astonishing thing, that he who had lately been an exile and outcast from England should now be made ruler and guardian of the realm.'[37] Nevertheless, in this case Gaveston's critics generally held their tongues, however outrageous his subsequent behaviour. When Gaveston returned to England after his second exile in 1308, again according to the *Vita*, 'none of the barons now dared to raise a finger against him, or to lay any complaint about his return . . . So he who had twice been condemned to exile, returned exulting and in state.'[38] Later on, to reinforce his favourite's again deteriorating position still further, Edward II ordered the sheriff of York to publish that Gaveston 'lately exiled contrary to law and custom, in which exile he was named other than good and loyal, has returned to the kingdom by the king's order and is ready to justify him-self before the king, wherefore the king holds him good and loyal'.[39] True to form, however, Gaveston acted even more obnoxiously than usual upon his return, including forcing a Lancastrian retainer out of the royal household, on which *Vita* pointedly commented: 'Wherefore look to yourself, Piers, for Lancaster will pay you like for like';[40] and he was exiled for a third time in November 1311. In other words, returns to grace with the larger political community could easily be thrown away if the one so favoured did not take care, as Gaveston found on Blacklow Hill several months later.

What we have been talking about up to this point were generally unofficial if often public attempts at returns to favour with either king or ruling regime. However, for the most part, some form of official pardon, as well as more general forgiveness, could and should have also been arranged by the disgraced noble with the king as well – even if at times it was given less than graciously. In theory, if the person requested pardon for a clearly serious transgression, at least according to the twelfth-century chronicler Roger of Hoveden, the king was to act as follows:

> If a person guilty of a capital offence shall ask the king's mercy for his crime, in his fear of death or of loss of limb, the king may, by the law of his dignity, pardon him if he pleases, even though he be deserving of death. The malefac-tor, however, shall make redress, so far as he shall be able, for the offence of which he has been guilty, and shall give sureties that he will keep the peace and observe the laws; and if such sureties shall not be forthcoming, he shall be banished the country.[41]

Moreover, there was also a clear set of rules when it came to pardons for people already under arrest. Again, the 'Laws of Henry II', as recorded by Hoveden:

> The king has also another prerogative of mercy as to those who are under arrest. For wherever he shall come, whether into city, borough, castle, vill, or even in the road, if a person shall be under arrest, it is in his power, by a single word, to release him from such arrest. The person released shall, however, make satis-faction to the person against whom the crime was committed.[42]

In practice, however, the process of official pardoning was far more fluid, especially for members of the nobility. In 1232, according to Matthew Paris's gloss on the events of that year, Henry III showed mercy to Hubert de Burgh in memory of his service to John as well as Richard I.[43] In de Burgh's case, though, his final official forgiveness came as part of a group pardon. In 1234, according to Roger Wendover, the king 'who longed for peace at any price' had all 'exiles' summoned under a safe conduct of the realm's prelates to see him at Gloucester, to receive his pardon and their estates back – including de Burgh and all his associates: 'the king received these men with the kiss of peace, and returned to them all their rights'.[44] That said, kings were not to grant pardons inconsistent with their oaths, or in an overly free manner;[45] and, as the period continued, an increasing number of pardons for nobles and others had to be obtained through the judiciary, parliament or with council advice. After the standoff in 1297 with Edward I over taxation and the French war, the earls of Norfolk and Hereford and their followers were issued a full pardon for their actions in the autumn parliament.[46] In the next reign, for his part in the problems in South Wales in 1320–1, John Giffard of Brimpsfield received a parliamentary pardon for both himself and his followers for 'all homicides, robberies, felonies, trespasses, etc. committed in the "pursuit"'.[47] Similarly, after the overthrow of Edward II, Geoffrey le Scrope was pardoned and restored to the young king's favour as 'on the testimony of prelates, earls, barons, and other persons of credit that, according to his ability, he bore himself well and faithfully towards the late king and his people'.[48] But pardons could also, of course, be forced on a king by his baronial critics, as was the case in 1215, in Magna Carta clause 62:

> We have remitted and pardoned fully to all men any ill-will, hurt, or grudges that have arisen between us and our subjects, whether clergy or laymen, since the beginning of the dispute. We have in addition remitted fully, and for our own part have also pardoned, to all clergy and laymen any offences committed as a result of the said dispute between Easter in the sixteenth year of our reign [i.e. 1215] and the restoration of peace.

Nevertheless, behind all this it must again be remembered that control over pardoning ultimately lay, in theory at least, with the king: according to Bellamy, 'Pardons were granted not just by justices or parliament, but by the king himself, it being a prerogative he retained largely unimpaired in this period.'[49] In other words, the monarch had a clear, unquestionable right to issue royal pardons, even for the most serious of crimes, and further, the right to a pardon could not simply be assumed.[50]

And whatever the case, whether it be the money that Ralph Basset of Sapcote had to pay to get his lands back after Evesham,[51] or the financial penalties of the Bedford rebels of 1328–9, payment in one form or another was often connected with official pardon for unacceptable behaviour. One of the few statutory statements of what a pardon was worth to the king's government was made in 1389–90, with treason, among other crimes, if pardoned, being fined at £1000 for a duke, 1000 marks for an earl and 500 marks for a baron or banneret;[52] in other words, what was perceived to be a year's income from their lands, roughly mirroring amounts put forth by the *Modus Tenendi Parliamentum* of the 1320s – though it still of course remained an option for the king not to be bought out of his rights.[53] Nonetheless, when successful, arrangements for personal returns to favour could be quite gracious and sometimes even generous, especially when it came to members of the royal family. When Henry II announced the settlement of the 1173–4 rebellion, though ringed with clauses protecting royal interests, there was also the realisation that some form of peace had to be brokered with the nobles, and especially his sons. The terms included an annuity of £15,000 for Henry the Young King as well as two castles in Normandy 'at my pressure'; to Richard, his next eldest, the revenues of Poitou 'and two castles from which he cannot harm me'; and to Geoffrey, his third son, half of the revenues of Brittany. According to the *Chronicle of Thomas Wykes*, the agreement was arrived at through mediation between the elder and younger Henrys, in which, in exchange for receiving pardon for guilt publicly acknowledged, the younger Henry would agree to a threefold pledge not to upset his father again: by oath, by noble warrantors and by hostages.[54] Other nobles who returned to Henry II's allegiance were to get the estates *ante bellum* back under this scheme – except those who had to make separate arrangements owing to the importance of their role, most notably the king of Scotland and the earl of Leicester, and usually excluding strategic castles which were demolished lest they become a venue for trouble again.[55] Henry III's regime could appear equally generous at times in dealing with the rebels of 1264–5:

> August 26, 1265: . . . And although the king ought to deal with them, generally and severally, judicially rather than mercifully, yet, of his inborn benevolence he has thought fit to counsel them, commanding them, as they would not be reputed public enemies, or be disinherited or lose their lives, as lately their accomplices deservedly did, that they go out of the said castle and deliver it to the king without delay.[56]

Clearly, however, there was always a certain amount of *real politik*, as well as mercy, coming into such situations, the victors realising that it was unwise to ostracise or exclude such powerful individuals in the longer run – though in this case, as it would turn out, the penultimate royal settlement, which involved total forfeiture, sparked widespread resistance and would force the king into issuing the *Dictum of Kenilworth*. Indeed, in such cases, before the days of police forces and standing armies, it would have been hard for a government to operate if it had not issued at least some such pardons after periods of unrest. A similar case of the monarchy facing up to the reality of a situation were the pardons for the group of nobles (including Lancaster and Warwick) involved in the death of Piers Gaveston in 1312, almost all of which were complete, despite Piers's close relations with the king; in essence it was a general pardon covering the barons, though they in return agreed to make no further moves against Gaveston's erstwhile supporters.[57] Again, Edward II, as Henry III and Prince Edward, was really not in the position to do any other, a situation further enforced by the English loss at Bannockburn a couple of years later. And, aside from Roger Mortimer and a few henchmen, Edward III pardoned most of the members of the overthrown Minority regime in 1330, knowing well enough that he could not alienate masses of the nobility, however much they had disgraced the monarchy previously. For instance, on 8 December 1330, Oliver de Ingham, a peer of the realm and one of the more important followers of Mortimer and Isabella, was pardoned by Edward, 'in consideration of service to the late king and the king in the duchy of Aquitaine'.[58] However, Edward III, as Henry II, put a variety of controls on his subsequent goodwill to previous opponents, especially when it came to future grants,[59] and so rarely saw any substantive negative effect from this leniency. In other cases, the main limitation on royal pardons or parliamentary pardons in the name of the king was that they were less than inclusive, or the determination behind such mercy less than enduring, especially as a result of changing circumstances: the pardons of 1388, for instance, though coming from those in control of the government rather than the king, were generally comprehensive in their nature, though not necessarily in who they included.[60] Along the same lines, Henry IV's regime, though originally quite – arguably overly – merciful to Richard II's supporters, within a few years, facing numerous revolts around the country, had to take a much firmer line when it came to mercy to his foes,[61] a lesson which Henry V remembered when dealing with the Southampton plotters of 1415, none of whom was pardoned.

However, it must also be remembered that one other process could bring a disgraced noble back to favour: the indisposition or change of a regime, both directly and/or through the actions of one's supporters, a point somewhat more evident in the fourteenth and fifteenth centuries than the twelfth and thirteenth. Just as, for a variety of reasons noted in Chapter 1 (especially increasing division between court and anti-court parties as a result of developing ideas of set baronial interests, and increasingly mechanistic and comprehensive administrative arrangements for punishment and forfeiture), when regimes were indisposed or fell in the later Middle Ages they tended to take more people with them than in the high Middle Ages, so too could change of political climate in the later Middle Ages also bring about the resurrection of many other fortunes. This could, in some cases, be the result of a temporary change of political situation, which nonetheless would help individuals out of bad circumstances. For instance, in 1321, according to the *Vita*, the Despensers 'returned from exile, because their reconciliation and reception into the king's peace at his mere will was to be published in England. They returned to England, I say, because the king knew that they had been banished out of malice.'[62] This return, of course, was the result of a recent resurrection of royal power, a resurrection sealed by the victory of the royalist forces at Boroughbridge in 1322. Thereafter, whether the 1327 pardoning of the deposed Edward II's erstwhile opponents, Edward III's forgiveness of the families of the Despensers, Arundels and the earl of Kent after the coup of 1330, or even the reversal of the sentences of the Good Parliament of 1376 once John of Gaunt had regained control, all offered a way, though often fraught, back to favour within the kingdom. One of the most famous examples of this process was the resurrection of a number of careers upon Henry of Bolingbroke's invasion of England in 1399, mainly in order to secure much needed further support. There was, for instance, the ever-variable fate of Thomas Beauchamp, earl of Warwick, an exile on the Isle of Man, recently discussed by Alison Gundy:

> As soon as news of his landing at Ravenspur reached them [Warwick's affinity], they sprang into action on behalf of their lord. Horses and men were dispatched to rescue Warwick from the Isle of Man. Members of the affinity were then sent around the country to seize Warwick's lands, whilst Richard Beauchamp, with Walter Power, rode to Cheshire to meet Bolingbroke. Meanwhile, Bolingbroke himself had signalled his intentions towards Warwick and his attitude towards the settlement of 1397 by throwing down the badges placed on the gate of Warwick castle by Surrey. Although some members of the Warwickshire gentry did attempt to raise troops for Richard, the grounds-well of opinion, carried by the Warwick affinity, favoured Warwick and Bolingbroke.[63]

Though his last years were out of the political limelight, Warwick's ultimate end did show the sometimes positive impact of national crisis on the lives of individual nobles.[64] Finally, official pardons could also arise through a change in the monarch's personal circumstances. When William I realised he was dying, and so more than likely for the sake of his soul, he released from imprisonment Odo, bishop of Bayeux and earl of Kent, and the earls Morcar and Roger, among others,[65] despite being some of the most important rebels against his kingship. Clearly, however, whether the monarch was coming to the end of his reign or not, the timing of such requests could be everything: it was often wise to seek peace from the king or those in power as early as possible, especially if it was clear that the fortunes of one's own side were on the wane, as Fulk d'Oyri was to do even before the baronial defeat at the battle of Lincoln in 1217.[66]

Nonetheless, though such attempts were made to return to favour, some settlements were never carried out, or at least not in the spirit of the agreement or in full – as in the early 1230s' deal between Henry III and the ever-errant earl of Pembroke, despite being a son of William Marshal, one of the most loyal royalists of the previous reign and the early Minority.[67] Likewise, the relations between this king and Hubert de Burgh were so strained that even truces were only begrudgingly agreed to:

> Then Hubert, put in tight place, and having no other remedy, asked for a truce to consider the aforesaid matters, asserting that these were great and harsh charges which the king alleged against him. And so a truce was agreed, though scarcely granted by the king in his anger, up to the Exaltation of the Holy Cross. In great dismay Hubert left London for the priory of Merton.[68]

De Burgh, indeed, was to fall from power soon thereafter anyway, as we have already seen, though later he was to return to his estates if not his power and position.[69] Whatever the medium, then, not all overtures for peace and reconciliation, permanent or more temporary, were graciously received or fully implemented. And even when such official promises were obtained, they were not always kept. In 1397, the pardon granted to the earl of Arundel in 1394 for various treasons and insurrections was rescinded, according to one chronicler, because it 'was grauntid in preiudice of him and of his croune'.[70] That said, Arundel was desperate, for obvious reasons, to argue for the validity of any pardons previously granted. He claimed:

> the benefit of his pardon, protesting that he had no desire ever to withdraw himself from the king's grace. But the duke of Lancaster, who was also steward, said to him, 'That pardon is revoked, traitor'. 'Truly you lie,' replied the earl, 'never was I a traitor'. 'Why then did you seek a pardon?' the duke asked him. 'To silence the tongues of my enemies, of whom you are one,' retorted the earl, 'and to be sure, when it comes to treason, you are in greater need of a pardon than I am.'
> Then the king said to him, 'Answer the appeal.' To which the earl replied, 'I see it clearly now: all those who accuse me of treason, you are all liars. Never was I a traitor. I still claim the benefit of my pardon which you, within the last six years, when you of full age and free to act as you wished, granted to me of your own volition'. 'I granted it provided it were not to my prejudice,' the king said to him. Whereupon the duke of Lancaster said, 'Therefore the grant is worthless.' But the earl replied, 'In truth, I was as ignorant about that pardon as you were – and you were abroad at the time – until it was willingly granted to me by the king.'[71]

This was, of course, also connected with a larger refusal of Richard II in 1397 to honour the pardons to Appellants given out in 1388,[72] and so the earl was clearly fighting a lost cause. In this case it was a matter of immediate political and personal need, thus not all requests for, or even recognitions of, official pardons (just as more general attempted returns to favour) were successful

or ultimately effective – especially when too evidently connected with treasonous activity or other threats to monarchical power.[73] Even so, such an attempt
was often worth a try, especially as one could not expect to survive, let alone
thrive, outside the king's favour for long. As a result, at the most base level,
some such requests seem to have descended into little more than attempts at
bribery: in December 1265, the Ferrers earl of Derby tried to buy himself
back into the king's good favour with the gift of a gold drinking cup and a
payment of 1500 marks – nonetheless, considering his past, and the fact that
the monarchy had other plans for his earldom of Derby, the earl would remain
in fact well outside royal favour for the rest of his life.[74]

Martyrs and posthumous forgiveness

Even those who had died in the process of their political, economic and/or
social demise could come back to some form of favour, despite what their
critics may have felt a few years before. One of the clearest indications that
a family was coming back into royal favour was the honourable reinterment
of a disgraced noble's body. In the late 1070s, a couple of weeks after
Waltheof's remains had been hastily buried where he fell at Winchester,[75] 'by
the providence of the Lord, his body was raised from the earth, and removed
with great honour to Croyland, where it was honourably entombed in the
church'.[76] Though this was not expressly at the royal will, the fact that the
Crowland monks were allowed to do it at all, and especially then to move
the body all the way from Hampshire to Lincolnshire, must assume some sort
of tacit royal agreement on the matter.[77] In addition, kings sometimes felt uncom-
fortable about their previous treatment of disgraced nobles and would try,
keeping on eye on their own interests of course, to lessen the indignity.
Henry III and Prince Edward were said to have been very upset by the death
of Simon de Montfort,[78] whatever their recent relations. Though by the time
Edward came to deal with the issue, de Montfort's various extremities had
already been divided up and sent to different parts of the kingdom, nonetheless, he ordered de Montfort's trunk to be given a Christian burial before
Evesham Abbey's high altar.[79] Henry III attended the funeral, and later
allowed a mortuary chapel to be erected around de Montfort's tomb. Similarly,
Edward III continued arrangements for a chapel for pilgrims set up to Thomas
of Lancaster in March 1333 at the place of his execution, Pontefract, started by
the Minority government,[80] and despite Lancaster being the main troublemaker
in his father's reign. In a fairly clear case of concern for his memory, Edward
also took control of the chapel away from Robert de Weryngton, appointed
by Queen Isabella, because Edward considered a married man unfit for such
a spiritual office.[81]

12 British Museum MLA 1984, 5–5, 2: Pilgrim badge: the execution of Thomas of Lancaster; England, mid-fourteenth century.

Such posthumous rehabilitation, however, often came not only at the wish of the king, but also through the often more subtle negotiations of churchmen. In April 1268 Ottobon, the papal legate, absolved de Montfort and the baronial rebels from earlier excommunications,[82] one of the last chapters in the return of the rebel nobles into the commune of the realm, and crucial for the healing of wounds done to medieval society in this period. As a final act of forgiveness, more poignant because it could have easily gone unnoticed, kings sometimes continued to honour the wishes of those fallen from favour, as when Henry III confirmed grants of land and money by de Montfort and the earl of Winchester to the abbey of Preaux 'so that the said nuns be not further wearied by labours and expenses through his default whereby the king may have to take himself grievously to the sheriff'.[83]

Though, as Simon Walker points out, not all who met untimely ends had cults develop around them – the most notable exceptions being Piers Gaveston (despite Edward II's best efforts), Thomas of Woodstock and Humphrey of Gloucester[84] – there was still often a degree of royal, as well as of course popular, veneration towards even the most hated of royal enemies.[85] And this veneration could quickly turn into cult worship. Over the twelfth and thirteenth centuries, Waltheof's tomb at Croyland became a site of local worship, apparently helped along by the abbey's financial needs, and inspiring various medical miracles: 'For there, by the mercy of God, the blind received their sight, the deaf their hearing, the lame the power of walking, and the dumb the power of speech.'[86] Though of little political significance – one commentator has called him a 'depoliticised saint' by the early twelfth century[87] – news of Waltheof's sainthood also spread far, and even shows up in Icelandic sources.[88] Other cults retained their political affiliations.[89] One of the most famous, and well developed, was unsurprisingly that of the cult of de Montfort himself.[90] According to the 'Lament of Simon de Montfort', probably composed some time in the early fourteenth century:

> I am driven to sing, my heart wills it, in sorrowful language,
> all with tears was made the song concerning our gentle barons,
> who for the peace so long after suffered themselves to be destroyed,
> their bodies to be cut up and dismembered, to save England.
> Now is slain the precious flower, who knew so much of war, the
> Earl Montfort, his hard death the land will deeply lament . . .
>
> But by his death the Earl Montfort gained the victory,
> like the martyr of Canterbury he finished his life;
> the good Thomas would not suffer holy Church to perish,
> the Earl fought in a similar cause, and died without flinching.
> Now is slain . . .[91]

The song continues to talk in a similar manner about the rest of the rebels, though de Montfort's posthumous fame was to be the greatest, and even reached the notice of Scottish Border chroniclers.[92] Further south, according to one source, when a chaplain began a service in memory of de Montfort soon after his death, 'such was the air of serenity, nor indeed any cloud appeared in the sky, and scarcely with many candles lit, [nonetheless, soon thereafter] he had to terminate the mass, on account of the density of the darkness'.[93] Florence of Worcester notes the many miracles surrounding the death of de Montfort,[94] and there were a number of wondrous events recorded by Rishanger as well, including the healing of those stricken with delirium, heart disease, paralysis and dumbness, and even the resurrection of the recently deceased.[95] Unsurprisingly, this cult's popularity was to continue well into the fourteenth century, with Edward II having problems with 'pilgrims' venerating the remains of some of de Montfort's followers still hanging on the gibbet in Bristol[96] – a touchy subject considering Edward's own troublesome relations with his nobility. Again, an early Hugh Despenser, an ally of de Montfort in the 1260s, had miracles attributed to his tomb, something which his ill-fated, though also clearly more self-interested, descendants in Edward II's reign rarely seem to have had happen:

> For God gave many miracles of the undoubted holiness of Hugh: at his tomb the blind received their sight, the lame walked, and many were the wonders which God performed for him; a privilege which he had obtained from God, for he was always truly just, to the best of his ability, as far as regards his dealings, both towards God and man, a course from which he could never be withdrawn. So therefore, after his death, God worked divine wonders through him; for during his whole life, up to the hour of his death, he always held the accurate line of truth. [97]

Thomas of Lancaster was also to benefit from such martyrdom, despite initial royal efforts to the contrary.[98] The *Brut*'s description of his last hours having been likened to Christ's journey to Calvary,[99] at the place of his execution, 'because of the miracles which it is said God works in his honour, there is a great concourse of pilgrims';[100] and, according to a more recent commentator, 'no sooner was his body laid in the church of St John's Priory, than these same people [those citizens of Pontefract who had pelted Thomas with mud] began to flock to his tomb and to acclaim him as a martyr and a worker of miracles'.[101] There was even an attempted canonisation of Lancaster, argued for by his brother and the Commons in 1327 after the deposition of Edward II,[102] and the phrase 'St Thomas of Lancaster' was used at least once in petitions to the king and council thereafter.[103] However, this was considered inappropriate by many, at least according to the fifteenth-century chronicler John Capgrave, 'for it was seid comounly that he schuld nevir be canonised onto the tyme that all the juges that sat upon him were ded, and al her issew'.[104] That said, considering the strength of emotion towards Lancaster in some quarters, it is unsurprising that there were claims that canonisation did take place c. 1389/90.[105]

Similarly, along with miracles, political prophecy was also an important part of later medieval martyrdom,[106] and overlaid the potential resurrection of disgraced nobles almost as much as religion did. Such 'political saints' could cause problems for the king, even those over whose fate he had felt otherwise some remorse. After the death of the earl of Arundel in 1397, as we have heard, he was so venerated by the masses that Richard II, becoming increasingly disturbed by this veneration as well as his own nightmares, ordered his place of burial to be concealed. Indeed, the stories of the head and body of Arundel having come back together so upset Richard that he ordered an exhumation to check the facts of the matter first:

> So on the tenth day after the burial the king sent some dukes and earls at four o'clock in the morning to get the earl's body dug up and see if the head had been joined back to the body, as the people said it had. When the body was dug up, the nobles found the story was untrue and reported all this to the king. But he was not satisfied with this experiment and ordered the Augustinian friars to take down the signs which had been set up around the body and to hide his burial at once under the floor.[107]

Though interest in Arundel's cult was short lived, the last references to miracles dating to 1404,[108] prior to this point such veneration, including the talk of his body and head coming together – a very symbolic act and a sign of political interest[109] – was bound to cause Richard II great worry. Thus, this sort of worship and connected prophesising was perceived to be a serious threat to royal power, and political prophecy in general was also legislated against.[110] Henry III's government was so concerned about such cults and prophecies connected with de Montfort that a clause was included in the *Dictum of Kenilworth* that

> the Lord Legate will utterly prohibit, under the Penalties of the Church, any Man from holding Simon Earl of Leicester for a Saint or Just One, for that he died under excommunication, according to the Doctrine of Holy Church. And that the vain and foolish Miracles related of him by certain Persons, shall not pass any Man's Lips. And that our Lord the King will strictly enjoin the same prohibition, under Pain of temporal Punishment.[111]

Even so, though it might be going too far, as Walker suggested, to say that political saints were more important as a 'point of contact' between the populace and monarchs than as a threat,[112] the obvious popularity at all levels of society meant that such cults often had to be forborne. The great, such as the earl of Oxford, and the less so, such as Letitia Lamede, a dropsy sufferer who had to be brought from London to Evesham in a wheelbarrow, as well as dozens of others, venerated de Montfort, and kept his cult going for decades.[113] In the later 1320s, Thomas of Lancaster even had a religious Latin office composed in his honour: 'Rejoice, Thomas, the glory of chieftains, the light of Lancaster, / who by his death imitatest Thomas of Canterbury; / whose head was broken on account of the peace of the Church, / and thine is cut off for the cause of the peace of England; / be to us an affectionate guardian in every difficulty.'[114] Like it or nor, kings had to face the fact that such veneration of the greatest of their critics was often part of the later medieval religious and political landscape.

Reversal of judgements and return of estates

The king's wrath *is* as the roaring of a lion; but his favour *is* as dew upon the grass. (Proverbs 19:12, italic in original)

As we have already seen in Chapters 2 and 3, both the physical and the material punishment for disgrace became more serious, and more permanent (at least in regranting if not always in actual duration), as the later Middle Ages continued. Whether because of the decreasing value of other feudal resources returning to the monarchy and the concurrent growing importance of forfeited lands, the increasing severity of treason laws, or even the growing publicity around 'falls', the individual or family desiring redemption faced an increasingly complex road to social and economic recovery by the later Middle Ages. That said, it must be remembered that, for the first two centuries after the Conquest, any reversal of judgements, as with pardons, came mainly from the king himself or his immediate council, sometimes in consultation with a small group of officials, but mainly still based on royal authority alone. There were some early instances of this, such as an attempt by Odo of Bayeux's nephew, William, count of Mortain, to claim his uncle's earldom of Kent after the latter's demise[115] – though it proved to be abortive, the estate remaining in royal possession, and still referred to as the land of Odo, bishop of Bayeux, in the second half of the twelfth century.[116] Nonetheless, when some of the combatants of the Anarchy were brought back into acceptable society and received back their estates, it was primarily by the will, authorisation and on the orders of Henry II, as it was after the various revolts led by Henry's sons.[117] Similar royal, or executive, initiatives were set in motion in 1217 by Henry III's guardians, in the 1230s after the fall of des Roches and de Rivallis, and even after Evesham in 1265 by an administration increasingly dominated by Prince Edward – Knowles, for example, notes the many instances of fathers, brothers, sons and even father-in-laws and stepfathers petitioning for estates in the aftermath of Evesham, including Philip Basset for his son-in-law, Henry Despenser, and the earl of Hereford for his son.[118] However, it is an indicator of the future that a number of the final restorations after Evesham, though only affirmations rather than individual reversals themselves,[119] took place in a full parliament (1271).[120] Indeed, by the early fourteenth century, marking yet another stage in parliament's growing importance, most actual reversals of judgement against disgraced individuals started to take place in parliament or some form of large common council, which not only publicised the reversals more, but also potentially made them more controversial.

Perhaps the most important early instance of this changing venue for revivals of fortunes was the reversal of judgements of 1322 in the first parliament of Edward III's reign in February and March of 1327,[121] one of the most important acts of Edward's early minority. It must be noted that while some of the most powerful people, such as Henry of Lancaster,[122] had been in the position to petition the king, council and/or parliament to get lands back before the Despensers were toppled in 1326, most had to wait until the parliament of 1327. Henry himself had to hold off until 1327 until he could assume a reasonably sympathetic response, as he did concerning lands of his brother – including Halton Castle and Congleton (Ches.) – which he should have inherited after Boroughbridge, but which went to the widow of his brother Thomas, who was then forced to disgorge them to the Despensers.[123] And, a bit lower down the social scale, the Berkeleys, minor favourites of the new regime and one of whom was to be the warder of the deposed Edward II, also pursued their lands lost in previous reigns with varying degrees of vehemence and success in 1327, though in some cases they needed to reacquire hold of relevant deeds in the first place.[124] Nonetheless, not all the 1327 reversals had immediate impact, however backed by the new regime: much of the Giffard estate remained tied up with administrators throughout most of Edward III's minority, only later diverted to Isabella and Mortimer's favourite John Maltravers through legal chicanery.[125] Some cases involved not just the forfeitees, but also their grantees, which could delay matters further: the heir of Bartholomew Badlesemere tried to get back the manor of Well (Herts.), which the latter had granted entailed to William Bereford. Bereford had, however, died without heirs, and, as he held other lands of the king, these all came back to royal custody, and remained there when Badlesmere forfeited after Boroughbridge in 1322. However, with the 1327 reversal of sentences, the heir of Badlesmere's appointed holder (Elene de Dynarston) did eventually gain hold of the property.[126] Even relatively unimportant claims could be revived if the time was thought right, confusing and delaying the final 1327 settlement even further, as when Simon de Bereford revived a new claim over the goods of the manor of Iselhampstead (Bucks.), which Matilda de Boteourt also claimed, and which had come into the king's hands because of the fall of the Despensers in 1326.[127]

However, the parliamentary reversals themselves during Edward III's minority, the first recorded mass set of individual reversals in the history of the institution, not only emphasised the growing authority of parliament to all, but also set the precedent for how to deal with the aftermath of the next major crisis, the Nottingham coup. One of the most important cases was in the winter of 1330/1, when Richard, son of Edmund late earl of Arundel, executed in 1326, was restored to all his father's lands by the king in parliament except for those of the king's gift or under obligation to others.[128] Other restorations were made by the king, parliament and/or Great Council. In one instance, in January 1331, Glamorgan and Morgannon in the March of Wales were restored in front of king and council to William de la Zouche of Mortimer, supposedly an ally of the earl of Kent, Eleanor his wife and their heirs, with the phrase: 'made to ease the king's conscience'.[129] Again, on 16 February 1331, a grant was made to Ebulo le Straunge and Alice his wife, the widow of Thomas of Lancaster, with the assent of the whole council in parliament, of the castle and cantred of Builth in Wales, and the manor of Bisham (Berks.) to hold for the life of his wife – though this time also 'in return for a release to the king and his heirs of the right of the said Alice in the castles, towns, manors and lands which before her marriage she surrendered to the late king and the Despensers, and which escheated to the king by the forfeiture of the latter'.[130] Even the reseisin of certain lands of Roger Mortimer for the sake of his son, Edmund, was discussed in parliament in September 1331, though notably it was recognised by all that such 'grace' should ultimately come only from the king on such a touchy subject.[131] Nonetheless, by the early 1330s, it was not just through formally or informally petitioning the king or those controlling the throne that one gained a reversal, but usually through a mixture of this and seeking reversals in parliament, which was especially important considering the extra authority it could also give Edward III's fledgling regime.

And this tendency for parliament to be the generally accepted venue for the official reversal of falls and judgements, having been firmly established in the 1320s and early 1330s, continued throughout Edward III's reign and beyond, the reversals of some of the downfallen individuals and families of the 1330 Nottingham coup taking place in the mid-1350s, including most famously the Mortimers and the Maltravers – in theory the result of the rewritten treason legislation of the early 1350s, though also through renewed good service to the monarchy.[132] All the reversals of the judgements of the Good Parliament of 1376 took place in a parliament of the next year, including those of Lord Neville,[133] as did the reversals of the grants to the 'Duketti' after the usurpation of Richard II in 1399.[134] By the end of the fourteenth century, parliament had become the *sine qua non* of the public phase of political resurrections and estate reversals: the king might have the final say, but without the authorising stamp of parliament, their legitimacy in the eyes of the larger political community and the country as a whole were more open to question. Parliament indeed by this time was also the primary institution for the resumption of royal grants and therefore *had* to be part of the reversal process in order to return estates. This idea of a legal tool of parliamentary resumption, a crucial part of the way for forfeitees to get back their lands, was initially one forced upon the king in order to control the king's finances, which dated back at least to the Ordinances of Edward II's reign (clause 7), but which came to the fore in the reigns of Henrys IV and VI.[135] Thereafter resumption quickly became part of the 'give-and-take of the late-medieval constitution',[136] allowing late medieval kings not only more control over finances, but even more power to give lands to supporters – as well as take them away and regrant them to their original owners, or others. Moreover, the controversiality of such grants in the first place, coming as they often did from forfeitures, made both changes and reversals even more into an affair of both polity and policy, one which parliament began to take seriously – especially as a result of pressure from the Commons in the years 1377 to 1390 and 1399 to 1406.[137] Notably kings and disgraced individuals usually realised the increased importance of parliament in the fate of estates, and acted accordingly, going to parliament whenever possible. In 1403/4, when the increasingly rebellious earl of Northumberland was restored to his lands, it was in full parliament[138] – especially important considering his still problematic position, a position which would later ultimately lead to his death in 1408. In turn in 1414, when the minor Henry Percy petitioned Henry V in parliament to restore to him the estates and rights of the earl of Northumberland, he also requested that his right to inherit might be enacted in parliament, which the king granted, though notably only with regard to lands entailed rather than in fee simple.[139] And in 1421, Thomas Montagu, son of the earl of Salisbury, another casualty of the revolution of 1397–1400, petitioned Henry V in parliament that he might again become full heir to his father with all associated rights, and reverse all grants made of his father's forfeited lands[140] – though having regained his estate and full rights, the judgement against his father was not to be overturned until 1461.[141]

However, this is not to say that monarchs could not still make and unmake grants primarily under their own authorisation in the later Middle Ages, or that in most cases, depending of course on the political situation and the present strength of both monarchy and parliament, the ultimate decision could not lie with them and/or their minority or immediate council. For instance, in 1327/8 William and Sibyl Graunson petitioned the king and minority council to get back the manor of Tytherley, then under royal administration, but which had previously been wrestled from their control, along with a fine, by the elder Despenser, in exchange for getting their Contrariant son out of prison in Windsor.[142] Again, Gilbert Talbot petitioned the king and minority council that not only should he be freed from £2200 in financial bonds forced on him by Edward II and the Despensers in exchange for his life and lands, and which officers in the new administration continued to hound him about, but also concerning other money which had been levied from himself and his mother by one Gilbert de Asshe with the help of the Despensers.[143] At some point after the Nottingham coup of 1330, Hugh and Margaret Audley petitioned the king and council to gain back the advowson of the church of North Luffenham (Rutland), which the earl of March, by misinforming Edward II, his father, appropriated during the Minority for his own nominee;[144] as, though on a larger scale, did Henry of Lancaster to the king over some outstanding claims going back not just to the deposition, but also to the death of his brother, Thomas of Lancaster.[145] There was even some royally inspired clemency to the son of the earl of March right down to the details. In October 1331, Edward III, under his own authorisation, granted to Edmund Mortimer, 'in enlargement of the late restitution to him of the castle and manor of Wyggemore', and various other lands which his father, the earl of March, had held in Wales, 'of the oxen and cattle of the ploughs and carts, with the armour, brazen pots, basins, and other domestic utensils, as well as the tapestries, curtains and beds made with the arms of the said Edmund, which were seized into the king's hands in the castles and lands'.[146] That said, as with the period 1327–30, most regrants of land in the post-Nottingham coup period were at least authorised by both king *and* council, probably showing the still insecure nature of the king's position in the aftermath of his father's deposition. This was especially true when granting back lands to families of his father's favourites, such as the heir of Hugh Despenser the younger,[147] which, though not nearly as controversial as it would have been if done in 1327, still needed perhaps a somewhat wider authority than the king alone. In any case, through king direct, king and council, or king and parliament, some nobles quite wisely – so as not to upset the king and the present owners – were willing to hold off receiving back their lands and/or rights until after the lives of the present holders. In 1415, Richard Beauchamp, later earl of Worcester, through the right of his wife, Isobel, the posthumous daughter of Thomas, Lord Despenser, forfeited and executed in 1400, claimed lands of the Despenser estate, but agreed to wait until the death of Despenser's brother-in-law, the duke of York, before taking seisin.[148] Likewise, whether because, until the mid-fourteenth century at least, parliament's authority had yet to be fully accepted in this area, or for other reasons, some nobles thought it wisest to make deals with those individuals from whom their land was being returned, lest they or their families face problems in the future. For example, in 1355, Roger Mortimer, doubtless with Edward III's influence, managed to retrieve the lordship of Chirk from the earl of Arundel, but also arranged for compensation to be paid to Arundel in either money or land within two years of the return of the lands – and if the forfeiture be confirmed, for Mortimer to arrange for Chirk to come back to Arundel.[149] Petitioning was as much about tactics and managing both the situation and the monarch – as well as his council and sometimes parliament – as the legal niceties of the case, and the petitioner always had to remember this fact.

Nonetheless, whatever the personal inclination of the king, and his final will, parliament was the official public venue for reversals of disgraces by the later Middle Ages, and the place for disgraced nobles to find official reinstatement not just with the king, but with the political community as a whole. However, by the fourteenth century it was also increasingly commonplace, and increasingly necessary, for those newly redeemed to go to the lawcourts to regain physical possession of the lands involved: though the parliamentary or governmental reversals gave one general legal authority to reclaim one's estates, and orders would go out to this effect to those concerned, it was usually necessary to chase up recalcitrant holders of one's forfeited lands in the lawcourts. Indeed, many of those who gained from the fall of others were not always keen to give up their gains, especially when their grants had been made only for the duration of a period of civil war. Even when such grants and regrants had been the result of a decision of the king and/or his council rather than in concert with the king's parliament or the royal courts, especially before the latter had become the main judicial venues for such processes, such resistance could be a serious issue. In April 1218 there was a writ from the sheriff of Sussex to the king's council informing the latter that there were problems with a reseisin of Robert Marion after the wars of 1215–17: 'I have received writs which, without delay, order me to give to the said Robert such seisin of all his lands with appurtenances in your jurisdiction, which he held before the war and thence was disseised on occasion of the war'; which the sheriff duly did – however, Robert Mortimer and Ralph Tirel would not let him hold it in peace.[150] Another such instance comes from the career of Falkes de Bréauté. In June 1217, de Bréauté himself wrote to the justiciar Hubert Burgh that members of the earl of Hereford's retinue had taken control of the manor of *Gerdeslee* of the earl of Huntingdon's estate, and refused to vacate it, even on the command of the sheriff of Northamptonshire – and stated that while he would not do anything without de Burgh's counsel, his patience was nonetheless coming to an end.[151] Likewise, the returns of 1266–7 had to have an eye to the erstwhile owners of the land, and the *Dictum of Kenilworth* has a clause dealing with any, presumably both rebels and those who lost out as a result of the agreement, who refused to abide by the award.[152] And when parliament and the courts had started to gain firm control over such events, they could still fail to settle refusals or rebellions against seisin – an issue which, despite being the most powerful men of the land, the Despensers had to face from their return from exile in late December 1321 until their final fall in 1326.[153] Similarly, when, in 1327, Henry, earl of Leicester, was granted back various lands forfeited after Boroughbridge by both himself and his brother, Thomas of Lancaster, there were still other claimants to rights of the estate, not all of them particularly important, but still an irritant to one trying to establish one's overall claim: one case indeed was simply over tolls connected with the manor of Melbourne and earldom of Leicester, which nonetheless also formed part of a larger legal battle with the widow of Robert Holland, a newly emerged enemy of the Lancastrians.[154] Some court cases sowed the seeds for even more dissension, as when, in the later 1320s, Richard, heir of the earl of Arundel, claimed the manor of *Kyneleye* (Kinlet, Salop?) was entailed to him and his wife though various agreements with his father, forfeited and executed in 1326; however, the earl of Kent, the uncle of Edward III and at that time in favour with the Minority regime, also claimed the manor, saying that it had been granted to him entail by the king.[155]

Indeed, just because a noble was granted back rights by the king, parliament and/or the courts, it did not mean that they would later go uncontested, and could revive again and again. As an example, there was the case of Martley manor (Worcs.), which had been held since Henry III's reign by the Despensers.[156] However, a year after the elder Despenser's fall in 1326, the reversion of the manor (it was then held for life by Alice Burnell) was granted in fee, at the request of the earl of Kent, to John Wyard.[157] By the late 1330s, the son of Hugh Despenser the younger had regained possession of the manor, which was then to remain with the family until the 1360s.[158] However, one of the granddaughters of John Wyard and her husband, John de Herle, took control on the basis of the 1327 grant, and despite the Despensers having had physical possession for over three decades.[159] The descendants of Herles had regained full seisin by 1385, and their heirs retained the manor until the sixteenth century.[160] In other instances, petitions and resulting cases went *back* years, and yet were still claimed, and successful. For instance, in June 1321, the justices of the eyre in London were ordered to allow the earl of Lancaster to have various liberties of the city and suburbs of London, as he claimed they pertained to the honour of Leicester.[161] These claims went back to the grant of Henry III to his son Edmund towards the end of his reign, which had been taken from the forfeited lands of Simon de Montfort. Indeed, some such cases spanned many decades, as with the lengthy case of the estate of John Giffard of Brimpsfield.[162] Giffard died in rebellion in 1322, but in 1327 the judgement against him, along with many others, was reversed. Since Giffard was dead, a dower portion of the land went to his widow: the rest, however, was disputed by the descendants of the two surviving sisters of Giffard.[163] In March 1329, despite many coming forward to claim the estate as heirs, the king's government decided that, as there were no legitimate heirs to most of the estate, it escheated to the king. More than likely politically motivated, the Minority regime (in Edward III's name) then granted 'so far as the king can', apparently through a form of legal fiction, Giffard's lands out in fee to one of its key supporters and Isabella's household seneschal, John Maltravers, who in turn enfeoffed his son, also named John, with Giffard's lands and rents.[164] However, after Maltravers's fall in 1330 there was an attempt by Giffard's remaining heirs to get the lands of John Giffard back,[165] though during the 1330s the bulk of this estate ended up in the hands of Maurice Berkeley.[166] In the early 1350s, the judgement on Maltravers was reversed and he was granted back his estate, including most of the Giffard lands: soon after, however, the heirs of John Giffard attempted to claim back lands in Shrewton, Ashton, Giffard, Stapleford, Elston and Orcheston St George (Wilts.) against Maltravers and others.[167] Estates, in other words, were never as secure as they had been before the initial forfeiture, and though the land might be returned to a noble, the question of ownership, once opened, was thereafter very difficult to silence.

The role of female relatives in the fate of estates and families

Once again must not forget the role of the women of rebel nobles in the fortunes of disgraced families: in particular, in many ways, the actions of the wives and widows were often the most crucial in getting some, if not all, of a family's estates back. As we have already seen in the last chapter, spouses of disgraced individuals could often, though by no means always, be on the receiving end of charitable treatment from those in power who had caused the downfall in the first place, if only as passive recipients. Moreover, as such treatment became increasingly accepted as the norm as the later Middle Ages continued, it also put women in a somewhat stronger position, few later medieval kings being willing completely to ignore the rights of the disgraced's female relicts, no matter how hated their menfolk may have been. Women, however, were also far more active and forceful than this in attempted resurrections of fortunes, pursuing estates and rights with whoever would listen. In the twelfth and thirteenth centuries, of course, there was a tradition of women physically supporting their husbands when in rebellion or disgrace with the ruling regime, including the countess of Chester and the countess of Lincoln during the Anarchy, Petronella, countess of Leicester, during Henry the Young King's revolt and, of course, the case of Simon de Montfort's wife, Eleanor, during the Barons' Wars of the 1260s.[168] Nichola de la Haye was said to have defended her husband's castle 'manfully',[169] while Juliana, wife of Eustace de Breteuil, was sent by her husband to protect his town of Breteuil against Henry I; Juliana, however, was betrayed by burgesses and forced to jump from the town walls 'shamefully with bare buttocks' – an 'unlucky Amazon', Orderic Vitalis called her.[170] However, by the later medieval period, though such activities at times continued – for example, the defence of Leeds Castle (Kent) against royalist forces by the wife of Bartholomew de Badlesemere in autumn 1321,[171] and more famously Margaret Paston's defence of her husband's manor of Gresham (Norfolk) against Lord Moleyns in the late 1440s[172] – protection of estates and families usually took on a more legal bent, in part owing to the growing importance of legal activity in society in general, though also because of the changing position of noblewomen, especially in terms of land tenure and even responsibility for estates.[173]

When it came to the defence of estates through legal or otherwise official channels, petitioning the king, royal family and council was often the first port of call. Usually some groundwork had to be laid before such acts were contemplated, as when Edward I ordered his chancellor to do justice to the countess of Leicester's attorneys (his aunt but also the widow of Simon de Montfort), as he had received her back into the king's favour.[174] Though few of the 1265 rebel wives were in such a position, most depending upon charity on the part of the administration,[175] the countess was thereafter moderately effective, both for her own sake and for those of her children; and, according to the Dunstable Annals of 1273, she also regained her dower lands by her first husband, William Marshal, the earl of Pembroke[176] – though the latter must have been arranged from her exile at the Dominican convent at Montargis, France, where she had been since late 1265.[177] Eleanor was able to use such favour for others as well, as when, soon after Evesham, the countess successfully petitioned Prince Edward to reseise a number of her family's followers.[178] Then there was the case of the Contrariant women, after the battle of Boroughbridge being in a very tenuous position but nonetheless sometimes willing to put up a fight for their, and their families', interests – though usually ending up with terms forced on them by the Despensers as well.[179] In 1323 Acelyne, widow of the Contrariant John Giffard of Brimpsfield, petitioned the king and council for lands of her husband, held by him or by them in joint enfeoffment or of her inheritance, to grant for the term of her life,[180] a forward thing to do since Giffard himself had been one of the main peerage Contrariants, so much so that he had warranted execution. In the same year, Margaret, widow of Edmund Mortimer, and the mother of Roger Mortimer who also forfeited after Boroughbridge, petitioned the king for her dower lands, which appear to have been taken in by the escheator when her son rebelled.[181] More importantly, Alice, the wife of Thomas, earl of Lancaster, as we have already heard, the recipient of a fair amount of quickly given if 'provisoed' charity from Edward II,[182] within a short time of Boroughbridge felt brave enough to petition the king to get back the manors of Wainfleet, Wrangle, Stepyng, Ingoldmells, Thorseby and other lands in Lincolnshire, which she had held entailed of Edward I[183] – though of course this was also part of a deal made with the Despensers.[184] However, it must be remembered that such requests could be premature, if only by a few months – as when, in March 1326, only half a year before the downfall of the Despensers, Elizabeth de Burgh, the lady of Clare, protested the forced loss (through imprisonment and threats) of her Usk inheritance in South Wales upon the demise of her husband, Roger D'Amory, after Boroughbridge in 1322.[185]

Noblewomen who were less powerful, wiser, or both, often bided their time before they petitioned. Obviously, an especially popular time for women, as for downfallen men if they had survived, to petition the king and/or council to receive estates, or at least dowers and inheritances back, was after the downfall of a regime. The change of government in 1327 was again one of the busiest times for such activity in our period, especially as this was when the Contrariants' wives started petitioning for reseisin in earnest – including Margaret, widow of Bartholomew de Badlesmere, and Aline, widow of John Mowbray.[186] For example, in 1327 Margaret petitioned the king's council for a redivision of her brother Gilbert de Clare's estate, of which she was coheiress and which Hugh Despenser had forced the partition of without any reference to or provision for Margaret while she was in prison.[187] Aline and John de Bohun (the future and only Lord Bohun of Midhurst), both heirs of William de Braose, petitioned the king and council to regain seisin of the manor of Wickhambreaux (Kent) which they claimed that Hugh Despenser the elder had taken from de Braose without any substantive recompense.[188] Aline also made similar claims concerning the lordship of Gower, which she said had been taken from her, Elizabeth de Burgh and others by imprisonment and a fraudulent novel disseisin assize, by Hugh the younger this time.[189] Even women who arguably had a part or stake in the downfallen regime were nonetheless willing to try their luck, especially if the new government seemed relatively benevolent, as Edward III's did after 1330. Surprisingly, though she had already been well treated by the king, Roger Mortimer of Wigmore's widow, Joan, was also well in on the act as early as 1331/2, petitioning for a number of the couple's lands in England and Ireland to go to her, her son or grandson under various tenures.[190] Later, in September 1334, almost four years after the execution of Roger Mortimer, she was still petitioning the king concerning various lands which the couple held in Ireland.[191] This is all very surprising and aggressive coming from a woman so intimately connected with one of the individuals believed responsible for the death of the present king's father. That said, such petitioning by women continued throughout the fourteenth and early fifteenth centuries – even with such daring precedents and despite often being to the regimes that had overthrown their husbands. For instance, in 1404, Isabel, the widow of William le Scrope, the earl of Wiltshire, who had been executed on the orders of Henry Bolingbroke during his invasion in 1399, petitioned to get arrears of a royal annuity paid to her, and that she should continue to have the same sum in the future – or if this was not possible, to be re-endowed with her husband's lands.[192] And Henry V, as Henry IV and Edward III, was also clearly perceived to be something of a soft touch, at least when it came to such matters, and well worth petitioning, whatever one's past affiliations. On 18 October 1414, a grant was made at the petition of Joan Cobham, wife of the fugitive John Oldcastle, of a London inn and all goods connected with it, to Thomas Brook and Richard Cliderow, in-laws, who were to hold the property to her use.[193] Again, in the early 1420s, Joan petitioned for seisin of the manor of Burnham (Norfolk), which she had held in jointure with her first husband and was lost because of the forfeiture of Oldcastle and granted to John Rodenhale and others.[194] Nonetheless, whether in strong or less strong positions, the main point was for the women involved to get back everything they could, as they were never sure how long such favour would last, as seen in the widow of the earl of Kent's petition in 1330–1 to regain the goods, chattels, crops and cattle held at her husband's manors, especially those at Ryhall (Rutland).[195] For similar reasons, empowering new spouses as well as themselves through the medium of dead husbands' estates was always, if possible, a good idea as an extra defence for women and their families. After the execution of John de Holland, duke of Exeter, in January 1400 as part of the first rising against Henry IV, his widow, Elizabeth, the daughter of John of Gaunt and the king's sister, married one Sir John Cornwall, and around the same time successfully petitioned the king and council for 1000 marks per annum for her maintenance, later granted various chattels from their estate, and finally, as a couple, were given a number of lands of both the forfeited Holland estate and of Elizabeth's dower.[196]

That said, this regaining of rights through petitioning was not automatic. Women often had to pursue the matter quite vigorously, as when Constance, widow of Thomas Despenser, lobbied the king in 1400 to have delivered to her various muniments and documents dealing with the estate of her husband which were at present under the control of the treasurer and chamberlain.[197] And, though the disgraced noble was usually willing to fight it out in the courts as well, and even parliament, if he was in a situation to be able to, often it ended up being his wife, and especially his widow, who pushed forward a reversal and, more importantly actual seisin of the land, in these venues. Of course, at least in the twelfth and thirteenth centuries, wives of rebels, especially those still living, were in a relatively unregulated position, and were far more limited in their legal actions than had their husbands been either free or dead – though this was to change for the better by the later fourteenth century, in part because of the rise of jointures, entails and uses, but also thanks to some specific provision for spouses made in the 1390s.[198] That said, in the later Middle Ages in particular, female relatives, and especially widows, of disgraced individuals also had to fight for their and their family's rights in the courts and other official and semi-official venues, as well as petitioning king and parliament – securing possession as well as right just as their men had to do.[199] Again, the ever crucial period of the late 1320s and early 1330s was a particularly active time when it came to women and offspring pursuing their rights in the courts. Margaret, the earl of Kent's widow, spent most of the early 1330s either re-establishing rights (along with her son)[200] – or protecting them in the lawcourts either from other legal claimants[201] or, on some occasions, from use of force used by local landowners.[202] In the same period, Margaret, the widow of the Contrariant Bartholomew de Badlesmere, executed after Boroughbridge, a woman already experienced in petitioning the Minority regime in order to get what she wanted, in the aftermath of the Nottingham coup continued this aggressiveness, taking the archbishop of Canterbury to court over her husband's forfeited manor of *Hatfield* (Hothfield by Charing?) (Kent) over which she claimed right.[203] Some women were so insistent on their rights that they went to parliament, the ultimate authority bar the king and his council, for the return of lands. In the first year of Henry IV's reign, Elizabeth, widow of William Montagu, earl of Salisbury, and entitled to some of the estate of his executed nephew John (d. 1400), petitioned the king and council in parliament for its return, including the castle and manor of Hawarden, the manor of Bosley and *Reston* (Ches.), the castle, town and lordship of Mohaut (Welsh March), and Christchurch Twynham, Ringwood, Swainston, as well as other manors and lands, many in Hampshire.[204] Indeed, Elizabeth was very busy trying to get her family's lands back in this period: in the case of Wodeford manor arguing right through dower against one Katherine de Faulkener, a woman granted the property by the king.[205]

Often the wives and widows of disgraced men used a mixture of petitioning those in power and legal action at various levels and in various forms – as shown in the case of the wife of the exile John Maltravers, one of the main henchmen of the Minority regime and implicated in the death of Edward II. After the Nottingham coup of 1330, Agnes Maltravers made a concerted attempt to protect her husband John's lands from loss to other claimants by, among other strategies, withholding crucial documents connected, in one case, with the estate of John Giffard, parts of which were granted during the Minority to John Maltravers but then went into limbo when he forfeited in 1330.[206] This was indeed a woman determined to protect and rebuild her, and her husband's, lands whatever the means. Initially, in the weeks after the Nottingham coup, she petitioned the king and council directly for full right of the dower lands from her first two husbands, seized by the escheator upon John Maltravers's fall.[207] When this brought no action, Agnes approached Edward III's queen, Philippa of Hainault. Though it was not uncommon for individuals, and especially women, to petition the queen, the fact that her husband had been condemned for the death of the king's uncle (the earl of Kent), as well as implicated in the death of Edward II himself (the present king's father), made it a bold move on Agnes's part. Nevertheless, on 26 February 1331, at the request of Queen Philippa, Agnes Maltravers was granted back 200 marks' worth of land which she held in dower or in jointure with John de Nerford.[208] The following day, this time approved by the king and his council and presumably connected with the earlier petition, she was further granted the knights' fees and advowsons of Nerford's lands.[209] Next, in March, the queen arranged for Agnes to have back all the dower lands connected with her first marriage, that to John de Argentein, and those in jointure with her second husband, Nerford: all approved by king and council.[210] In the autumn of the same year, Agnes arranged for enlargements of the grants which Queen Philippa had arranged for her, namely that the lands were to be granted for her life rather than until other provision could be made[211] – a clear victory for her claims over her dower lands. Agnes was not afraid to fight for her estate and her husband's estate in court either, for example taking to the Common Pleas, among others, Henry le Botiller, for breaking her close and trees at Barkham (Berks.), an individual who, along with his brother, had previous claims to the manor and was obviously trying to intimidate her off it.[212] Though such passion and determination usually came about as the result of the death of a husband, rather than simply exile or outlawry, it still shows how far women could go to protect their family's, and their own, interests.

Whatever the aim, the road was rarely easy to either regain or retain lands, especially for such women, limited as they still were when it came to both legal rights and social and political position. A good final case study of such a problematic return to favour, or at least estates, is the case of the manor of Thaxted (Essex), between two wives, one widowed, of Contrariants, which remained unsettled for decades.[213] Initially Thaxted was part of the Clare inheritance, but with the death of Gilbert de Clare, earl of Gloucester, at Bannockburn in 1314, the inheritance was divided up between the Clare coheiresses, with the manor apparently going to Margaret, wife of Hugh de Audley.[214] However, the widow of the Contrariant Bartholomew de Badlesmere claimed that, before his death, Gilbert de Clare had granted the manor to her and her husband in jointure, while Margaret, the wife of the now former Contrariant Hugh de Audley, claimed it had only been granted to Bartholomew for his life, with reversion to her.[215] Initially, after the reversal of judgements of 1322 in 1327, the lands were returned to Badlesmere's widow, but thereafter Margaret de Audley restated her legal claims, and apparently had Thaxted seized by force.[216] At some point in late 1327/early 1328 the manor was taken into the king's hands by reason of the said claims after Margaret de Badlesmere petitioned parliament, and she was then given possession of it during Hugh de Audley's rebellion in 1328–9.[217] Once Audley had gained the king's pardon, however, he petitioned to get the manor back,[218] with Margaret de Badlesmere putting forth a counterpetition to regain seisin.[219] As a result of chancery proceedings, a commission of twenty-four knights looked into who held the manor before the confiscation because of Audley's part in the Bedford rebellion, which returned that Audley and his wife did hold the land, and the evidence that Badlesmere's widow also held right was denied in part because of the failed identification of her seal on the document produced as evidence:[220] by the time of his death in 1347, Audley and his wife clearly had control of the manor for some time.[221] However, with the end of the direct Audley line in that year, the rights of Badlesmere's widow seem to have been reasserted, and the manor was claimed by her heirs.[222] Women, in other words, considering their otherwise legally, socially and economically restricted position as relicts of disgraced men (even with all the legal advances of the period), could nonetheless be among the most determined campaigners for the return of estates.

The long road to recovery

As should, then, be becoming clear, and especially as the medieval period continued, quite often it was women, through one means (growing position as recipients of royal charity after the downfall of husbands) or another (petitions, court and parliamentary cases, etc.), who started, and sometimes even finished, the push to get reseisin of estates, if not rehabilitation of the disgraced male himself. Often being in effect the 'last person standing' – by their husband's death, pariah status or by exile, or even by a woman's own supposed infirmity of body (especially in connection with the idea, if not the reality, of being usually unable to mount serious political, legal or military threats) – could then be a very good thing for a family. But whether by women or 'relict' male relatives, or of course by the disgraced man himself, it must be remembered that such fights back were not always successful. Though de Bréauté's son did get some lands back after his father's fall in the mid-1220s, Falkes himself never did, and, after having his castle of Bedford besieged, and escaping to the papal court to plead his case concerning his ill-treatment by Henry III, he died in exile in Rome in 1226.[223] As late as 1232, the king's government – now officially under the control of Henry – continued to dismember to the smallest detail the once large estate de Bréauté had amassed, for instance granting to Nicholas de Nevill, a royal clerk, in perpetuity 'the meadow in Bidenham, called Martinesholm, formerly belonging to Falkes de Bréauté and now the king's escheat, to hold by rendering therefor yearly at Easter one pound of cummin'.[224] We have already discussed the Ferrers's failed attempts to get back their lands after 1266, ultimately instead being given to Henry III's son Edmund (as in Chapter 2), but there were increasingly in the later Middle Ages many other notable examples of partial or whole estates not being returned as, most famously, William Montagu's petitions to Edward III to regain the honour of Denbigh in the late 1350s, 1370s and 1390s show.[225] Originally granted in the early 1330s to William Montagu's father, the first earl of Salisbury, an individual who had helped Edward take control of the kingdom during the Nottingham coup, these lands were then lost under Montagu's son – a less likeable individual, at least for Edward III. Instead, Edward brought Roger Mortimer's grandson back to court in the 1350s, to the title of earl of March and to the lands of his grandfather's estate, many of which had in the meanwhile been granted to the Montagus.[226] On a smaller scale, John Maltravers did not end up getting back his moiety of the manor of Stapleford (Wilts.), which he had forfeited in 1330, despite much legal activity to the contrary – rather it ended up going to the Sturmys, a family with a strong recent previous claim.[227] And, in 1342, when the King ordered Alice, countess of Lincoln and the widow of Thomas of Lancaster, to justify her hold on parts of her estate, it was found that they did not include lands Lancaster had claimed from the forfeitures of the Templars – Lancaster had held them prior to Boroughbridge but they did not pass to Alice in the tenurial readjustments of the later 1320s.[228] Similarly, after Richard II's fall in 1399 and Thomas Beauchamp, earl of Warwick's reinstatement, though the latter received back most of his lands, he never had the lucrative lordship of Gower returned to him.[229] Likewise in the early fifteenth century, when the earl of Northumberland's heir was restored to his grandfather's estates, according to Bean, 'his inheritance was much inferior to that enjoyed thirteen years before by his father and grandfather'.[230] And title as well as land could be permanently brought to an end as a result of a downfall. When the earl of Wiltshire was executed upon the invasion of Henry Bolingbroke in the summer of 1399, his earldom was declared extinct – though notably the declaration of extinction in this instance was at the request of the earl's father, so that his heirs did not suffer the ignominy and restrictions of forfeiture.[231] Thus, it must be emphasised that, though individuals or their families were restored to their lands, it did not necessarily mean that they were restored completely, or to the same degree – a trend which would continue long beyond our period, with reversal 'not necessarily imply[ing] complete restitution' well into the sixteenth century.[232] Similarly, just because an individual *was* being brought back into favour, did not mean that the king might not continue to grant out his family's lands for a considerable time to come. When Hugh Despenser the youngest was being brought back into favour in the late 1330s, this did not stop Edward III from granting parts of his father's forfeited estates to some of his more favoured nobles.[233] Or the king could also hang on to pieces of the land so obtained indefinitely, effectively attaching the land to the royal demesne. Early on, in May 1234, when Gilbert de Marshal, the earl of Pembroke, and Hubert de Burgh were brought back into favour, it was notable that in both cases lands were kept back for the king, including the Marshal's castles of Striguil and Dumas in Ireland, to ensure the continued loyalty of both men – and though Pembroke regained control of his properties fairly quickly thereafter, de Burgh ended up losing his castles permanently.[234]

Even when lands were returned, which was more often the case, because of a variety of procedures mentioned earlier (including attainders and granting out for longer than previous terms) and complications (including the increasingly litigious nature of the English landowning classes) by the later Middle Ages, reversals of sentences and restoration could take a much longer time,[235] often counted in decades rather than years. The Despensers, Mortimers and Montagus are all examples of this trend but it was also the case with another family who had also taken part in the events of the 1320s, the Mowbrays. In the early years of Richard II's reign John Mowbray, earl of Nottingham, took legal action against the earl of Warwick over Swansea Castle and the lordship of Gower, which he claimed were denied him because of errors going back to judgement against his grandfather after Boroughbridge in 1322.[236] The restoration of a later John Mowbray to the duchy of Norfolk in the fifteenth century was an equally long-drawn-out affair, which was to last almost three decades, including a dispute with the Beauchamp family as well as many other complications, and was only finally decided by an initiative from the Commons in parliament.[237] And the Percies, as we have already seen, were another such case in the fifteenth century, taking many long, insecure years to get back to power and a degree of respectability after a series of rebellions against Henry IV.[238] Reversals of judgements could in some cases take many decades, and often had to await a change of dynasty, as in the case of Thomas Lumley's restoration.[239] Thomas was grandson of Ralph Lord Lumley, one of the rebels of the Epiphany Rising of 1400 executed by the people of Cirencester, his estate thereafter being declared forfeit.[240] However, Thomas had to wait until the Yorkists usurped the throne in 1461 before he could successfully petition for a reversal of sentence and get the lands and lordship back. Moreover, such restoration was further limited by growing restrictions on the disgraced's rights, in particular the process by which they came to be restored. In a couple of high-profile cases, as Archer notes, 'Henry V made the legal point firmly by dismissing the earl of Salisbury's pleas in 1414 that he had a right to be restored to his father's dignities and again in 1416 by *creating* Henry Percy, earl of Northumberland, not simply restoring him.'[241] This, along with the fact that the king (and parliament) was now regularly revoking the rights to appoint attorneys, as in the case of the duke of Hereford and the duke of Norfolk when in exile,[242] and the 'corruption of the blood' caused by the process of attainder, furthered weakened the position of a disgraced noble and his family, and laid his estate rights even more open to abuse. Indeed, some wives and widows, while usually feeling to stick with one's husband or his family was the best chance of survival, knew that in some cases there was little hope of getting any sort of reinstatement for their disgraced spouses and instead arranged what they could for themselves. At its most extreme, this could mean remarriage and removal into the 'right' side of the political spectrum. After his imprisonment by William Rufus as a result of the failed revolt of 1095, Robert de Mowbray's wife gained an annulment of their marriage from Pope Paschal II and married Nigel D'Aubigny, a close associate of the new king Henry I.[243] Likewise, Alice, relict of Thomas of Lancaster, was more than willing to abandon her erstwhile lover and husband, Hugh de Frene, once it was clear that she could otherwise face long-term imprisonment as a result of her connection with him.[244] Though spousal loyalty tended to be the norm, even in the case of rebellion, at times this could be pushed to breaking point.

Overall, in the words of Joel Rosenthal:

> The process of recovery could be very long, and the chances of each successive step forward made dependent upon the degree of loyalty demonstrated at the previous plateau of advancement.[245]

An attempted return to grace, in other words, was not meant for the impatient, or the faint of heart. Nonetheless, whatever the specific instance, there were various routes to attempt to return to grace, with various inherent dangers as well as advantages. One could request royal or government forgiveness oneself, one could ask well-connected friends or supporters to arrange it, or a downfallen individual could decide to work his way back into the king's favour primarily through his own efforts. Following on, but connected with this, pardoning was the next official recognition of this regained favour. Pardon and forgiveness for individuals who had fallen from grace, both for themselves and for getting back their lands, became an increasingly regulated, politicised issue as the Middle Ages progressed. In the high Middle Ages, it tended to be a prerogative of the king, or at best the king and a small council, to forgive such individuals and return to them their wealth. By the later Middle Ages, however, pardons and returns of estates, while still mainly decided by the king or those controlling the throne, usually were approved by parliament and/or great councils, and were consequently a much more publicised, and therefore potentially controversial, issue than they had been before. Add this together with the now set rights concerning inheritance, the declining potency of royal feudalism, the fact that the estates involved had often been granted more clearly as long-term patronage, and the continued rise of attainder, and it is unsurprising that such reversals were all the more contentious and in need of justification than even before, especially in parliament. The fact that the idea of resumption of royal grants of whatever source and type became inextricably linked with the power of parliament by the beginning of the fifteenth century made it clear how important, though also how difficult, such processes could be. Finally, other unofficial and/or official forgiveness in the form of posthumous cults, and sometimes political sainthood, also began to grow up around previously disgraced individuals, thus allowing them at least some posthumous redemption. Mainly the case after the murder and canonisation of Becket, these processes nonetheless set the tone for the afterlives of some of the most vocal of later medieval critics of royal policy.

However, aside from the disgraced men fighting to get their estates back themselves, one other major factor came to play an important part in the potential resurrection of fortunes, the role of women. Usually turned off their lands and out of their estates upon the fall of their men in the high Middle Ages, very soon after, kings, or even those acting in their names, developed a conscience, were forced to do so by precedent, or even at times influenced by the examples of chivalry, and (as we saw in Chapter 4) made some sort of charitable provision for the females left behind, whether it be an annuity, or a grant of some of their lands (especially their dower) back for the remainder of their lives. At first this was an informal arrangement, though over the later Middle Ages some of these provisions began to gain the force of tradition and law. But as shown in the present chapter, it was not just a passive role that noblewomen played in order to get their estates back. Though they had also mounted physical defences of estates in the high Middle Ages, such women were as well much more legally active, particularly in the fourteenth and early fifteenth centuries. By the later Middle Ages, they often felt confident enough of their position to petition kings, and often queens, for the amelioration of their husbands' circumstances – as well as fighting back for the sake of themselves and their families both within the royal court and without. Along with pursuing rights and rehabilitation in the lawcourts and parliament, the women of disgraced men were often an important way for families not only to keep property and other claims alive, but also to push their way back into a certain degree of favour, or at least economic solvency. That said, though at times regaining some status, the restored noble family would still often be considered somewhat suspect, by the king or by those who brought them down in the first place, and on the whole would never quite reach the heights they had previously attained. There were exceptions within the nobility, of course – the Mortimers and the de la Poles, to name two of the more important,[246] though only the de la Poles can be said to have had even more power than they had before. Returning to some semblance of position, therefore, was not nearly the same as returning to power, especially when one had incurred the wrath of the most powerful in the land. The quote from Cicero which started this chapter may have had the upbeat tone it did in the first flush of a joyous return, but though some of the ideas present are also applicable to the later medieval case, the theme of return to previous strength of position is often not. Rather, in many ways, when it came to estates, position and influence, both the English nobility and the English monarchy could have been said to have been living by a less emphatic version of Robert Kennedy's maxim centuries before he uttered it: 'Mostly forgive your enemies – but never forget their names.'

Notes

1 *Cicero: Back from Exile: Six Speeches upon His Return* D.R. Shackleton Bailey, ed. (Chicago, 1991), p. 5.
2 For the Anglo-Saxon period, see Kelemen, '*Clyppan* and *Cyssan*', 1–19.
3 S. Friar, *A Companion to the English Parish Church* (Stroud, 1996), pp. 252–3.
4 See the return of Sir Gawain to court. *Sir Gawain and the Green Knight* B. Stone, ed. and trans. (Harmondsworth, 1962), pp. 124–5; also J. Scattergood, '*Sir Gawain and the Green Knight* and the Sins of the Flesh', *Traditio* 37 (1981), 347–71; for ideas of redemption in contemporary and modern literature, see Murdoch, *Adam's Grace*, Introduction and Chapter 3.
5 *RP* iii, 233.
6 Hollister, *Henry I*, pp. 73–4; Hollister, 'Mutilation', 330–4.
7 Warren, *Henry II*, pp. 210–11.

8 As above, pp. 27–8 and below, p. 192.

9 Ormrod, *Edward III*, pp. 14–15.

10 *Chronica Magistri Rogeri de Houedene* W. Stubbs, ed. (New York, 1964), ii, 67.

11 From Turner, *King John*, pp. 46–7.

12 SC8/42/2091; CPR *1330–4*, 246; RP ii, 61; for earlier pardon of execution (20 March 1327), see SC8/42/2092; *Calendar of Ancient Petitions Relating to Wales* W. Rees, ed. and trans. (Cardiff, 1975), pp. 59–60; though not his lands: CPR *1327–30*, 39.

13 S.F.H. Johnson, 'The Lands of Hubert de Burgh', EHR 50 (1935), 431–2; West, 'Burgh, Hubert de', DNB (2004).

14 ASC (1076D).

15 *Annals of Roger de Hoveden*, i, 158; Lewis, 'Waltheof', DNB (2004).

16 D.J. Power, 'Marshal, Richard, Sixth Earl of Pembroke (*d.* 1234)', DNB (Oxford, 2004).

17 R.H.C. Davis, *King Stephen* 3rd edn (London, 1990), pp. 22–4; *Gesta Stephani* (1955), pp. 20–30.

18 M. Strickland, 'Longespée, William (I), Third Earl of Salisbury (*b.* in or before 1167, *d.* 1226)', DNB (Oxford, 2004).

19 H.W. Ridgeway, 'Basset, Ralph (*c.* 1220–1279?)', DNB (Oxford, 2004).

20 CP xii: 2, pp. 957–60; perhaps over a seizure of a wagon, horses and some goods by Grey. CPR *1330–4*, 203.

21 CP vi, 145–6; CFR *1327–37*, 298; CCR *1330–3*, 446; H. Summerson, 'Grey, John, First Lord Grey of Rotherfield (1300–1359)', DNB (Oxford, 2004).

22 *Royal Letters Illustrative of the Reign of Henry III*, ii, 294–6.

23 CCR *1302–7*, 481–2.

24 SC8/55/2731.

25 CP vii, 348–9.

26 Going from land petitions: SC8/264/13152; SC8/275/13705.

27 *Registrum Epistolarum Fratris Johannis Peckham* C.T. Martin, ed. (London, 1882), i, 287–90; D.L. Douie, *Archbishop John Pecham* (Oxford, 1952), 202–5.

28 Maddicott, 'Montfort, Amaury de', DNB (2004).

29 H.M. Thomas, 'Mowbray, Sir Roger (I) de (*d.* 1188)', DNB (Oxford, 2004).

30 See CP ix, 371 footnote a.

31 Eadmer, *Vita Anselmi* R.W. Southern, ed. and trans. (London, 1962), p. 94.

32 CPR *1343–5*, 535, 541–2.

33 Bothwell, 'Agnes Maltravers', 88.

34 CPR *1345–8*, 532; C81/333/19777; CPR *1348–50*, 239–40; Shenton, 'Maltravers, John', DNB (2004); Bothwell, 'Agnes Maltravers', 80–93.

35 See C.H. Knowles, 'Clare, Gilbert de, Seventh Earl of Gloucester and Sixth Earl of Hertford (1243–1295)', DNB (Oxford, 2004).

36 Florence of Worcester, *Chronicon*, ii, 200; for negotiations between king and earl, including the parts played by the pope and the French king, see CPR *1266–72*, 70–3, 144–5. For these later relations, see S. Lloyd, 'Gilbert de Clare, Richard of Cornwall and the Lord Edward's Crusade', NMS 30 (1986), 46–66.

37 *Vita Edwardi Secundi*, p. 3.

38 *Vita Edwardi Secundi*, p. 7.

39 'Note that this form was made by the king himself, and that he took the writs as soon as they were sealed and put them on his bed.' CCR *1307–13*, 448–9.

40 *Vita Edwardi Secundi*, p. 8.

41 *Annals of Roger de Hoveden*, i, 549; for pardon after outlawry, see Bracton, *Laws and Customs*, ii, 369–73.

42 *Annals of Roger de Hoveden*, i, 549.

43 Paris, *Historia Anglorum*, ii, 351.

44 *Roger de Wendover Flores*, iii, 89. Though, in point of fact, de Burgh did end up losing some of his properties permanently. See p. 208.

45 S. Grupp, 'Some Historical Aspects of the Pardon in England', *American Journal of Legal History* 7 (1963), 56, 58.

46 Powell and Wallis, *House of Lords*, p. 238.

47 Butler, 'Brimpsfield Giffards', 81–2; CP v, 646.

48 CPR *1327–30*, 28.

49 Bellamy, *Crime and Public Order*, p. 192.

50 For the continued importance of the pardon through Richard II's reign, see H. Lacey, '"Mercy and Truth Preserve the King": Richard II's Use of the Royal Pardon in 1397 and 1398', in Hamilton, ed. *Fourteenth Century England IV*, 124–35.

51 SC1/8/22.

52 SR ii, 68–9; though there is some question of enforcement. Bellamy, *Crime and Public Order*, p. 195.

53 There is also some overlap with the concept of fining, as in Chapter 2 – but for the most part the divide between money paid as punishment and money paid for pardon is fairly clear.

54 *Annales Monastici*, iv, 36–7.

55 *Ranulfi de Diceto Opera*, i, 394–5; also *Annales Monastici*, iii, 21–2; for the 1174 peace, see Warren, *Henry II*, pp. 136–40; see also above, pp. 93–4.

56 CPR *1258–66*, 488.

57 Trokelowe, *Chronica*, pp. 80–1; though there was also a grant for the king in return. Hamilton, *Gaveston*, pp. 104–7.

58 CPR *1330–4*, 22.

59 Bothwell, *English Peerage*, pp. 140–3.

60 J.L. Leland, 'Unpardonable Sinners? Exclusions from the General Pardon of 1388', *MP* 17 (1996), 181–95.

61 For a still useful overview of this period, see E.F. Jacob, *The Fifteenth Century* (Oxford, 1993), Chapters 1 and 2.

62 *Vita Edwardi Secundi*, p. 121.

63 Gundy, 'Earl of Warwick and the Royal Affinity', 70.

64 A. Tuck, 'Beauchamp, Thomas, Twelfth Earl of Warwick (1337x9–1401)', *DNB* (Oxford, 2004).

65 *Annals of Roger of Hoveden*, i, 168–9; Bates, 'Odo, Earl of Kent', *DNB* (2004).

66 B. Golding, 'Simon of Kyme: The Making of a 1214 Rebel', *NMS* 27 (1983), 36.

67 *Annales Monastici*, i, 90; for the long-running strife between Henry III and Pembroke, see Powicke, *King Henry III*, pp. 125ff.

68 Roger of Wendover, *Flores Historiarum* H.O. Cox, ed. (London, 1841–4), iv, 247.

69 See pp. 182–3.

70 ECR, p. 9; J.G. Bellamy, 'The Northern Rebellions in the Later Years of Richard II', *BJRL* 47 (1964–5), 269–70.

71 The Monk of Evesham in Given-Wilson, ed. and trans. *Chronicles of the Revolution*, pp. 58–9.

72 Bellamy, *Treason*, p. 175.

73 There were some statutory controls placed on treason pardons in the later fifteenth century. Bellamy, *Treason*, pp. 174–5.

74 CPR 1258–66, 517–18; Maddicott, 'Ferrers, Robert', *DNB* (2004).

75 *Ingulph's Chronicle of the Abbey of Croyland* (London, 1854), p. 145.

76 Florence of Worcester, *Chronicon*, ii, 12; see also *Annals of Roger de Hoveden*, i, 158; Lewis, 'Waltheof', *DNB* (2004).

77 Perhaps also because of the rapid depoliticisation of Waltheof's cult. See below.

78 Trokelowe, *Chronica*, pp. 19–20.

79 C. Hole, *English Shrines and Sanctuaries* (London, 1954), p. 101; see also above, Chapter 2.

80 CPR 1327–30, 317.

81 CPR 1330–4, 415.

82 Florence of Worcester, *Chronicon*, ii, 201. Though this may in part have been a result of their failure, and a shift to use of secular power. Logan, *Excommunication*, p. 54.

83 CPR 1266–72, 309–10.

84 S. Walker, 'Political Saints in Later Medieval England', in Britnell and Pollard, eds. *McFarlane Legacy*, 80–1.

85 Walker, 'Saints', 77–106.

86 *Ingulph's Chronicle*, p. 241 and ff.

87 C. Watkins, 'The Cult of Earl Waltheof at Crowland', *Hagiographica* 3 (1996), 111.

88 F.S. Scott, 'Valdjofr Jarl: An English Earl in the Icelandic Sources', *Saga Book of the Viking Society of Northern Research* 14 (1955 for 1953), 78–94; more recently, Lewis, 'Waltheof', *DNB* (2004).

89 On political sainthood, see J.M. Theilmann, 'Political Canonisation and Political Symbolism in Medieval England', *JBS* 29 (1990), 241–66.

90 See C. Valente, 'Simon de Montfort, Earl of Leicester, and the Utility of Sanctity in Thirteenth-Century England', *JMH* 21 (1995), 27–49; Maddicott, 'Follower, Leader, Pilgrim, Saint', 641–53; J.C. Russell, 'The Canonisation of Opposition to the King', in J.C. Russell, *Twelfth Century Studies* (New York, 1978), 252–5.

91 'The Lament of Simon de Montfort', in T. Wright, *Political Songs of England* P. Coss, ed. and trans. (Cambridge, 1996), pp. 125–6.

92 *The Chronicle of Melrose* J. Stevenson, ed. and trans. (Lampeter reprint, 1991), pp. 107–20.

93 Trokelowe, *Chronica*, p. 19.

94 Florence of Worcester, *Chronicon*, ii, 196.

95 *Chronicle of William de Rishanger*, pp. 67–110.

96 Hole, *Shrines*, pp. 102–3.

97 *Chronicle of Melrose*, p. 107. Probably as a result, Tewkesbury Abbey, where the tomb is located, became very closely associated with the Despenser family. R. Morris, 'Tewkesbury Abbey: The Despenser Mausoleum', *Transactions of the Bristol and Gloucestershire Archaeological Society* 93 (1975 for 1974), 142–6.

98 Hole, *Shrines*, pp. 105–6.

99 Given-Wilson, *Chronicles of the Revolution*, p. 36.

100 *Chronicle of Lanercost*, pp. 234–5; see also J. Edwards, 'The Cult of "St" Thomas of Lancaster and its Iconography', *YAJ* 64 (1992), 103–22; J. Edwards, 'The Cult of "St" Thomas of Lancaster and its Iconography: A Supplementary Note', *YAJ* 67 (1995), 187–91. The hill was renamed St Thomas' Hill. Hole, *Shrines*, pp. 104–5.

101 Hole, *Shrines*, p. 104.

102 C65/1 in *The Parliament Rolls of Medieval England, 1275–1504* C. Given-Wilson, gen. ed. (Woodbridge, 2005).

103 SC8/17/820.

104 Capgrave, *Chronicle*, p. 253.

105 Capgrave, *Chronicle*, p. 253; A. Makinson, 'Thomas of Lancaster: The Turbulent Earl', *History Today* 10 (1960), 703.

106 E.g. L.A. Coote, *Prophecy and Public Affairs in Later Medieval England* (Woodbridge, 2000), p. 18.

107 *Chronica Maiora of Thomas Walsingham*, p. 301; also see above, pp. 72–3.

108 Walker, 'Saints', 81.

109 See Chapter 2.

110 See R. Taylor, *The Political Prophecy in England* (New York, 1911), pp. 104–5.

111 SR i, 13.

112 Walker, 'Saints', 98.

113 Maddicott, 'Follower, Leader, Pilgrim, Saint', 646–51; above, p. 191.

114 Wright, *Political Songs*, p. 268.

115 William of Malmesbury, *Gesta Regum Anglorum* R.A.B. Mynors, ed. and trans. (Oxford, 1998), i, 721.

116 CP vii, 129 and footnote d.

117 See Warren, *Henry II*, pp. 59–65, 136–49.

118 Knowles, 'Resettlement', 27–8.

119 Though parliament did also set up the committee to compose the *Dictum of Kenilworth*, as well as the more general pardon and idea of reversals as set forth in the Statute of Marlborough. Powell and Wallis, *House of Lords*, pp. 198–9.

120 *Annales Monastici*, ii, 110.

121 SC8/156/7769; RP ii, 5ff.; CCR 1327–30, 101–2. For parliament reversals, see the various versions of the January 1327 parliament offered by *The Parliament Rolls CD-ROM* (Given-Wilson, gen. ed.).

122 E.g. over Chartley (Staffs.). SC8/174/8675; more generally SC8/56/2776, which also pithily reminded Henry of his elder, troublemaking brother Thomas; also see SC8/124/6156 (for the petition for the castle, town and county of Lancaster).

123 SC8/56/2766; for other petitions by Lancaster and Robert Holland during the Minority, see SC8/57/2806-7; RP ii, 18; C81/155/1908; C81/200/6443C; CCR 1327-30, 286-7.

124 SC8/14/694; SC8/171/8512.

125 Langston, 'Giffards', 127-8.

126 C245/3 4 Edward III; CIPM vii, 85.

127 KB27/273/89.

128 CPR 1330-4, 41, 194; RP ii, 55-6; though regaining his father's moveable goods was less successful. See C. Given-Wilson, 'Wealth and Credit, Public and Private: The Earls of Arundel 1306-97', EHR 106 (1991), 3-5.

129 'And in consideration of their having entered into a recognisance in £10,000 before the chancellor, the treasurer and the Parliament, notwithstanding that the king is not bound to make such restitution until satisfied of £50,000 wherein they became bound to obtain pardon for a theft by Eleanor of a very great quantity of jewels and other goods at the Tower of London'. CPR 1330-4, 51; CP xii: 2, p. 959.

130 CPR 1330-4, 74; later extended to life in the case of the castle. CPR 1334-8, 10, 34.

131 RP ii, 62.

132 See Holmes, Estates, pp. 14-17; Shenton, 'John Maltravers', DNB (2004).

133 Holmes, Good Parliament, Chapter 6.

134 Dunn, Magnate Power, pp. 78ff.

135 B.P. Wolffe, 'Acts of Resumption in the Lancastrian Parliaments, 1399-1456', EHR 73 (1958), 583-613.

136 S.J. Gunn, 'The Act of Resumption of 1515', in D. Williams, ed. Early Tudor England (Woodbridge, 1989), 88-90.

137 Given-Wilson, Royal Household, pp. 130-8.

138 Capgrave, Chronicle, p. 285.

139 SC8/23/1134; RP iv, 37: also see SC8/85/4250; the entailed land clause was also connected with the attempt in the mid-1420s by Henry le Scrope of Masham's heir to get back some of his brother's lands after the botched Southampton Plot of 1415. SC8/85/4235; RP iv, 287-8.

140 SC8/24/1160; RP iv, 141b-2b; also see earlier request for judgement reversal because of error. SC8/23/1122; RP iv, 17-19.

141 C81/611/2885; CPR 1399-1401, 466; CP xi, 392-3; M. Warner, 'Chivalry in Action: Thomas Montagu and the War in France, 1417-1428', NMS 42 (1998), 147-8; S. O'Connor, 'Montagu, Maud, Countess of Salisbury (d. 1424)', DNB (Oxford, 2004); A. Curry, 'Montagu, Thomas, Fourth Earl of Salisbury (1388-1428)', DNB (2004).

142 SC8/49/2437.

143 SC8/75/3711.

144 SC8/31/1514B.

145 SC8/56/2768; CPR 1330-4, 19.

146 CPR 1330-4, 193.

147 CPR 1330-4, 241.

148 SC8/32/1575; CCR 1413-19, 339-40; CPR 1413-16, 286; T.B. Pugh, 'Despenser, Thomas, Second Lord Despenser (1373-1400)', DNB (Oxford, 2004).

149 E40/4882.

150 Royal Letters Illustrative of the Reign of Henry III, i, 13.

151 Royal Letters Illustrative of the Reign of Henry III, i, 4.

152 SR i, 15.

153 As seen in the many cases of trespass and similar crimes perpetrated against the Despensers as recorded in the King's Bench rolls for the period. KB27/262/40 & ob; KB27/262/67 & ob; KB27/265/50; KB27/265/57; KB27/257/93, 930b & 107; KB27/258/26, 260b, 27 & 270b; 590b, 540b, 470b; KB27/259/29; KB27/259/32, 33 & 34; KB27/252/730b; KB27/253/400b.

154 C255/12/3; for Melbourne, also see J.W. Leedom, 'Lady Matilda Holland, Henry of Lancaster and the Manor of Melbourne', *American Journal of Legal History* 118 (1987), 118-25.

155 KB27/274/1070b: appears to have ended up with the earl of Kent: CPR 1327-30, 322.

156 VCH Worcestershire, iv, 292.

157 CPR 1327-30, 180.

158 Hugh entailed this manor, among others, on himself, his wife and his heirs in 1344/5. C143/269/9; CPR 1343-5, 268.

159 C44/3/13; exemplification: BL Additional Charter 75476.

160 Birmingham City Archives, MS 3688/259; VCH Worcestershire, iv, 293.

161 CCR 1318-23, 310.

162 Langston, 'Giffards', 126-8.

163 KB27/270/119; also see C44/1/3; CP v, 647-9.

164 CCharR 1327-41, 116-17. In part, at least, through the agency of John Caillewe (CPR 1327-30, 527); also C47/59/3/75; Langston, 'Giffards', 126-8.

165 KB27/283/151. This dispute among them over who had ultimate right, closeness of blood, etc.

166 CPR 1334-8, 42; CFR 1327-37, 423. Expanded in 1339 and 1340. CPR 1338-40, 400, 446.

167 C44/2/13; for Maltravers's Inquisition Post Mortem, see CIPM xi, 452-5.

168 For women active in such a way as recorded in the twelfth-century chronicles, see Johns, Noblewomen, pp. 17-25; for Eleanor see Hallam, 'Eleanor, Countess of Pembroke and Leicester', DNB (2004).

169 From Johns, Noblewomen, p. 24.

170 From Johns, Noblewomen, p. 18.

171 Fryde, Tyranny, pp. 50-1.

172 J. Ward, ed. and trans. *Women of the English Nobility and Gentry 1066-1500* (Manchester, 1995), p. 121.

173 E.g. 'Rules of St Robert', in Ward, ed. and trans. *Women of the English Nobility*, pp. 128–32.

174 SC1/7/91.

175 See last chapter.

176 *Annales Monastici*, iii, 258–9.

177 Hallam, 'Eleanor, Countess of Pembroke and Leicester (1215?–1275)', *DNB* (2004).

178 SC1/8/23.

179 See Fryde, *Tyranny*, pp. 109ff.

180 SC8/112/5596; Langston, 'Giffards', 126; for Giffard in 1321–2, see Butler, 'Brimpsfield Giffards', 75–97.

181 SC8/63/3110; CPR 1321–4, 266; the majority of her estate does not seem to have been returned to her until 1328. CP ix, 283.

182 See last chapter.

183 C49/33/14 (18 Edward II); SC8/56/2754; for other petitions by the countess around this time, see also SC8/56/2752–3; more generally, see R. Somerville, *History of the Duchy of Lancaster*, Volume I: *1265–1603* (London, 1953), i, 33–4.

184 CP vii, 687–8.

185 G.A. Holmes, 'A Protest Against the Despensers', *Speculum* 30 (1955), 207–12; F.A. Underhill, *For Her Good Estate: The Life of Elizabeth de Burgh* (Basingstoke, 1999), pp. 30–2; J. Ward, 'Elizabeth de Burgh, Lady of Clare (d. 1360)', in C.M. Barron and A.F. Sutton, eds. *Medieval London Widows, 1300–1500* (London, 1994), 30; J.K. Knight, 'Usk Castle and its Affinities', in M.R. Apted, R. Gilyard-Beer and A.D. Saunders, eds. *Ancient Monuments and their Interpretation* (London, 1977), 147.

186 C257/14/8 and 6.

187 SC8/32/1559 (c. 1327); also see CFR 1327–37, 30–1, 35, 41; CCR 1327–30, 136, 563–4; also see J.R. Maddicott, 'Badlesmere, Sir Bartholomew (c. 1275–1322)', rev., *DNB* (Oxford, 2004).

188 SC8/157/7805; RP ii, 436.

189 SC8/173/8631.

190 SC8/61/3027; C81/191/5599 (6 Edward III); SC8/173/8638; CCR 1330–3, 110, 489, 503.

191 C81/217/8176.

192 SC8/22/1076; though she did not get his lands back, she did receive an annuity of £100 at the exchequer. CPR 1401–5, 466; for earlier grants to her in this period, some of which had not been fulfilled, see CP xii: 2, pp. 733–4 and footnote.

193 CPR 1413–16, 248; Thomson, 'Oldcastle, John, Baron Cobham', *DNB* (2004).

194 Oldcastle: SC8/29/1406–7; RP v, 401–3; CPR 1422–9, 90; KB27/274/1070b.

195 C257/16/11 (4–5 Edward III).

196 E28/27/57; A. Goodman, 'Elizabeth of Lancaster (1364?–1425)', *DNB* (Oxford, 2004); CP v, 199–200 and footnote.

197 E28/25/2 (Henry IV).

198 Crawford, 'Victims of Attainder', 61–2; Ward, *English Noblewomen*, pp. 44–9; Archer, 'Rich Old Ladies', 20; and above, pp. 123n.115, 160.

199 See last section.

200 KB27/283/88.

201 E.g. Windlesham and Bagshot (Surrey), both claimed in 1331 by Richard Wyke, who claimed he had been unfairly deseised of the lands by the Despensers. KB27/286/1020b; for other examples, see KB27/290/90; CPR *1330–4*, 178 (petition to king and council); during the Minority period and the early 1330s, there was a spate of such cases, usually claiming duress, extortion and unjust disseisment in the 1320s by the Despensers. e.g. SC8/15/743; SC8/17/848; SC8/58/2871; SC8/81/4001; KB27/286/48ff.

202 E.g. in the mid-1330s, the abbot of Kirksted's men raided her lands at Stiklewood (Lincs.). KB27/290/90.

203 KB27/290/430b; KB27/293/58; earlier, in 1329, perhaps to emphasise her rights, Badlesemere's widow claimed, through the said manor, the role of the chamberlain during Archbishop Mepham's enthronement – though, according to Haines, 'Mepham would have nothing from her.' R.M. Haines, 'An Innocent Abroad: The Career of Simon Mepham, Archbishop of Canterbury', *EHR* 112 (1997), 566.

204 E175/6/31 (1 Henry IV); Dunn, *Magnate Power*, pp. 136–7.

205 C245/29/31; also see C245/29/41.

206 KB27/299/81; Bothwell, 'Agnes Maltravers', 86–8.

207 SC8/63/3108; Bothwell, 'Agnes Maltravers', 83.

208 CPR *1330–4*, 84, 89–90.

209 CPR *1330–4*, 120.

210 CPR *1330–4*, 106.

211 CPR *1330–4*, 215.

212 CP40/284/95; KB27/286/107.

213 For background, see K.C. Newton, *Thaxted in the Fourteenth Century* (Chelmsford, 1960), pp. 3–4.

214 E. Simcoe, *Short History of the Parish and Ancient Borough of Thaxted* (Saffron Walden, 1934), p. 9.

215 CCR *1327–30*, 183–4; SC8/31/1513; CCR *1330–3*, 363.

216 CCR *1327–30*, 250.

217 SC8/41/2039; KB27/274/19; KB27/275/18.

218 SC8/41/2039.

219 SC8/94/4663.

220 C44/1/4.

221 CIPM ix, 56.

222 C47/9/27; M. Arman, *A Short History of Thaxted Church* (Thaxted, 1982), p. 8.

223 Despite a letter from the pope to Henry II which basically argued that his past royal service outweighed his offences. *Memoriale Fratris Walteri de Coventria*, ii, 272–4; see also Chapter 4 for de Bréauté.

224 CCharR *1226–57*, 169.

225 C47/10/35; SC1/38/106; also RP iii, 7b, 58–60; Holmes, *Estates*, p. 19 footnote 3.

226 For this, see Bothwell, *English Peerage*, pp. 122–4.

227 C44/2/4; C143/192/7; C143/236/9; E142/71/12; VCH Wiltshire, xv, 256–7.

228 C257/8/25.

229 Tuck, 'Beauchamp, Thomas, Twelfth Earl of Warwick', DNB (2004).

230 J.M.W. Bean, 'Henry IV and the Percies', History 44 (1959), 227.

231 CP xii: 2, pp. 733–4.

232 Lander, Crown and Nobility, p. 151.

233 E.g. CCharR 1327–41, 427.

234 CPR 1232–47, 48, 65–6, 70. Richard de Burgh was likewise fined £3000 for
     Connaught, though still had other lands detained from him, and was forced to
     give hostages. CPR 1232–47, 73.

235 See also Chapter 3.

236 KB138/109.

237 R.E. Archer, 'Parliamentary Restoration: John Mowbray and the Dukedom of
     Norfolk in 1425', in Archer and Walker, eds. Rulers and Ruled, 99–116.

238 J.M.W. Bean, The Estates of the Percy Family 1416–1537 (Oxford, 1958), pp. 69ff.

239 For other examples, see Chapter 3, pp. 109–10.

240 RP v, 486–7.

241 Archer, 'John Mowbray and the Dukedom of Norfolk', 101–2.

242 C49/67/21.

243 Aird, 'Mowbray, Robert de', DNB (2004).

244 SC8/64/3163.

245 J.T. Rosenthal, Patriarchy and Families of Privilege in Fifteenth-Century England
     (Philadelphia, 1991), pp. 55–6.

246 For the post-1354 Mortimer estate, see A. Dunn, 'Richard II and the Mortimer
     Inheritance', in C. Given-Wilson, ed. Fourteenth Century England II (Woodbridge,
     2002), 159–70.

Conclusion:
the medieval aristocrat,
'wheels of fortune' and 'falls of princes'

Regnabo, regno, regnavi, sum sine regno.[1]

Let no one trust in the continuance of happiness, nor take fortune's constancy for granted, nor strive to remain for long in a set place on the revolving wheel.[2]

Falling from grace, medieval style

We have now seen the rise, fall and sometimes resurrection of fortunes of members of the medieval nobility. The reasons for loss of royal goodwill and support were many and varied, including a lessening or termination of personal interest by the king (friendship, romance, etc.), political or economic expediency, machinations by 'new' nobles or by 'old', betrayal of king or of kingdom, royal family infighting, or even the downfall of the monarch himself. Once the king – or those acting in his name – had identified this state of affairs, events could proceed in any number of ways. First and unsurprisingly, there was usually some form of indication to the individual himself, whether it be simple omission from seasonal festivities or witness lists, various types of warning shots, or more pointed indicators, such as sharp words at court, decline in patronage, or even failure to be summoned individually as a peer of the realm. Whatever the case, if these went unnoticed, or even if they did not, there were also usually more official sanctions in the form of oral or written royal orders, trials and condemnations. In the early period, these tended to take the form of direct royal commands to the nobles involved, though, as the Middle Ages continued, more formal procedures developed – both ordinary in the form of the functioning of the king's chancery, courts, council and parliament, and extraordinary, especially in the development of legally based, yet summary, judgements. In either instance, aside from the stripping of offices and powers as a prelude to more formal trial, there was often some attempt to avoid a 'scene', and first get the noble to come in of his own free will. If this was unsuccessful, it was sometimes necessary to hunt down fugitive nobles, and to remind the population of the consequences if they continued to help such men. Either way, in presence or *in absentia*, this was usually the last stage before various forms of royal justice were exercised. In the high Middle Ages, when such trials took place at all, this usually meant judgement by the king himself, or those firmly under royal control, and the trials themselves were generally brief and relatively select affairs compared to such events in the later Middle Ages. Indeed, rather than any period-wide uniformity in the nature of royal trials of nobles, a somewhat more unifying theme for most of the Middle Ages was another form of judgement coming down from God – though this time not through the king, but through shows of martial ability. Both individual and mass trial by battle were, throughout our period, an important way for disgraced nobles to meet their fate. That said, by the later Middle Ages, probably influenced by the growth of parliament itself, more formal and legalised, and less violent, forms of trial and judgement were also beginning to be developed for disgraced nobles. Though initially, in the later years of Edward I's reign, and throughout the troubled years of Edward II's, this mainly took the form simply of public pronouncement of guilt and sentence, by the middle of Edward III's reign there began to be accepted ideas of both the use of evidence and standardised judicial procedure, including trial by peers, an aristocratic version of the earlier development of trial by jury for the rest of society. Along with the Statute of Treasons (1352), impeachment, appeal and most notably the rise of the process of attainder, these developments came to demarcate, and to a degree define, the disgraced noble's experience of royal or governmental justice in the later Middle Ages.

When a man reached this level of disgrace, as seen in Chapters 2, 3 and 4, he was facing increasingly grave consequences. First, there was financial punishment: the payment of fines or the agreement to bonds for good behaviour – slaps on the wrist, severe or otherwise, for those who strayed outside the king's (or those governing in his name) favour. Though initially falling out of use as a penalty for the upper end of society, by the thirteenth century monetary fines were not only a key first port of call for the punishment of nobles, but also an increasingly important part of royal income. After this point, however, things became more painful for the noble, both physically and in terms of status. In the Anglo-Saxon period, both mutilation and execution were used for the most serious of crimes, though usually only after the possibilities of the wergild had been exhausted. However, after the first decade of the Norman Conquest, there was a general slowing of the execution of nobles, which extended to William Rufus and Henry I's reigns – though notably both these kings, and especially the latter, were generally quite fond of the use of mutilation to get their points across. Thereafter, though, until the early

1300s, mutilation and execution were rarely used against delinquent members of the English aristocracy – they might die on the battlefield, but for this period at least they tended not to face the gallows or the executioner's axe. However, probably for a mixture of reasons, including increasingly harsh treason laws, the growing influence of Celtic practice and the needs of kings, by the fourteenth century execution, and mutilation, was again in use. By this time, though, in place of maiming of those still expected to live, there was mutilation of those doomed to die, if they were not corpses already. Indeed, the use of the body as a textual message to those who wished to cause problems for the king or question monarchical authority hit a high point during the first decades of the fourteenth century, though for various reasons extreme abuse of bodies before death would become less popular later on in our period. Finally, though closeness to the king in blood or other ways could ultimately cause the body to be treated with a degree of respect, for others, both their bodies and the dignities of rank continued to be dishonoured to the highest degree, leaving followers and would-be avengers with little doubt as to their own fates if they continued to back the cause of the departed.

With the harming or destruction of the person, moreover, we have seen the ruination of his legacy. The Anglo-Saxons had used the idea of land and chattel forfeiture, increasingly permanent, alongside wergild and execution, as a way to punish individuals involved in serious acts against king, kingdom and public order, an attitude which spilled over into the reigns of the early Anglo-Norman kings – though this punishment was somewhat unevenly used until hitting an apex with Henry I's exploitation of forfeited lands, most notably for the sake of his 'men raised from the dust'. Thereafter, however, whether because of the growing importance of inheritance, a dislike of the destabilising influence of the Anarchy on land tenure, or even the roughly concurrent softening of physical punishments, for the next century or so forfeiture became usually, in fact, short-term estate confiscation. Whether Henry the Young King's rebellion in 1173–4, the revolt of the barons against King John in 1215–17, the ultimate outcome of the events of 1265–6, or any number of smaller incidents in between, when land went into the king's hands, very rarely was it taken away for any length of time, nor was it granted away with any degree of permanency, when it was at all. However, as with bodily punishment and probably due to an equally wide mixture of reasons, forfeiture of estates went through another sea change in the late thirteenth/early fourteenth centuries, after which time, when lands were taken away from disgraced men, they tended to be taken away for longer periods, if rarely for good, and regranted under more permanent terms as royal patronage in the meantime. In practice, though such grants usually ended up being reversed by one means or another, properties stayed away from their disgraced owners for longer periods than previously (sometimes even counted in decades), and often, through the attainting of blood in the late Middle Ages, there was the emphatic disinheritance of their heirs as well. Indeed, though lands rarely remained away from a family permanently, they now stayed away long enough for a memorable dent to be inflicted upon the family's wealth and position, and made it all the more difficult to get them back. The practice of disinheritance had, in other words, been given new 'punch' in the fourteenth and fifteenth centuries, often in connection with the needs of those in power, though also by a variety of legal processes and restrictions, most notably the early versions of attainder developing in the same period. Finally, a sting in the tail of a noble's fall from grace was that all his worldly goods, from ermine cloaks to embossed shields and ceremonial swords, were usually confiscated, with some goods then being given to servants or social lessers. In the most serious of cases, a later medieval fall from grace could mean, for a generation at least, the near complete eradication of most rights and privileges which had put the noble above the mass of humanity in the first place.

The consequences of such falls could, then, effectively downgrade, if not destroy, any previous privileged position. Not only were one's lands, offices and possessions usually redistributed to others, as administrators or as owners, but it was uncommon, after an initial spurt of support in the immediate aftermath of a downfall from grace, if most of one's former allies and supporters did not gradually disappear to more profitable pastimes – after a while, if one was lucky, one would retain one's inner retinue, if unlucky not even that. Indeed, though there are notable exceptions, for the most part we come across little evidence of sustained fightback by retainers *once* an individual has definitely fallen, or similar sustained activity on their behalf. Moreover, as today, the populace as a whole loved to see the mighty brought down, even better if it was in as bloody a manner as possible. This was reflected in the popular songs and poems used throughout this book, as well as in the works of chroniclers, who, as has been noted, often took particular pleasure in watching the great laid low – especially when they were not seen, either because of birth or behaviour, to have deserved their good fortune in the first place. Kicking a man when he was down was as common then as it is now. And, even if one did manage to survive the initial fall, life in disgrace was still psychologically hard if not always physically harsh. First, there could be the stigma of excommunication or outlawry, both of which put the individual outside religiously or legally acceptable society. Though outlawry had only limited usage for members of the nobility, and excommunication was to become a less powerful threat by the later Middle Ages when the problems of the international Church started to impact on the position of ecclesiastical power in England, both were to be an important way of sending, and keeping, the exiled noble outside of acceptable society. More common, however, for members of the nobility – especially those considered dangerous – was time spent in captivity of varying degrees of severity, sometimes under house arrest, more frequently in one of the king's castles or those of one of his supporters, or in the Tower of London. Though this was rarely as severe as for the lower orders, and in some instances disgraced nobles continued to live a relatively comfortable life while in the king's captivity, it was still another way in which not only a noble was punished, but also how he would be kept out of society, and out of further trouble. However, if the individual was not able to be caught or kept, or if imprisonment were not deemed appropriate, there was banishment and exile, which again developed into a more legalised and publicised process over the course of our period, and one particularly popular for getting difficult nobles out of the way without killing them. Though some nobles managed thereafter either to continue to cause problems for the king, or to better their position abroad or in the outer reaches of the British Isles, many in such circumstances simply slipped into obscurity and/or poverty, and spent their remaining years in bitterness and regret, something which those they left behind – male or female – were also often to face to one degree or another. Though the effectiveness of both banishment and imprisonment would come into question in the later fourteenth and fifteenth centuries, for most of our period both punishments still remained an important way of dealing with problematic nobles.

That said, the relics of exiled and deceased individuals could at times end up being treated charitably if not always generously, especially as the later Middle Ages progressed, and would often also petition and fight (in council, court and parliament) their way back to some degree of wealth if not position – both for their own sakes and for those of their kindred. Indeed, though almost never the primary victims of falls, women were often a crucial part of the ultimate salvation of families' fortunes, if not their disgraced menfolk themselves, as we saw in the last two chapters. Men could petition and work their way back into the king's good favour, or have the more dubious honour of returning to a more general grace though posthumous forgiveness, martyrdom or even political sainthood, but as seen in the reversal of judgements and the return of estates, it was also women who had considerable success, or at the very least presence, in this regard. Men did find more official and 'legal' ways of returning to grace, position and power as the later Middle Ages continued than simply the king's goodwill alone, especially with the rise of parliament and the increasing use of the courts for land litigation, but the fact that women were often the last individuals of importance and maturity active, either legally or literally, for the immediate family, often meant the onus of arranging some return to estate and position, or even just provision for survival, lay in the first instance with them – if at times in reality this meant only through the charity of the ruling regime. Nonetheless, with the increasingly bloody and long-term nature of falls of individuals as well as estates, even this became more difficult. Though families usually regained some degree of position and favour, very rarely, especially in the later Middle Ages, was it the same as what they had had before. There are exceptions to this statement,[3] the most famous of all of course being Henry Bolingbroke, but for the most part, once individuals and families had fallen, especially by the later Middle Ages, it was quite difficult to return to their former glory.

Kings, nobles and the national stage

On a mowntayne, a sete may not be hyd,
Ne lordis werkis in no degre.
A lordis werkis, wiþ comouns is kyd,
Þat he doþ most in preuete.
Gouernour of kyngdom or Cyte,
After þey lyue, men deme so.
For eche a werk, god ȝeueþ a fe.
Eche man be war, er hym be wo.[4]

So what do such cycles of disgrace, ostracism and sometimes redemption tell us about the larger medieval scene? Were the individuals involved just failures at the political and social game, who can tell us how not to survive at the top end of medieval society but little else? Or do their fates, both damned and redeemed to varying degrees, also reveal something more about the late medieval world, of the changing mentalities of kings and nobles, of the medieval populace as a whole? The five 'larger' themes from the preceding chapters that stand out in particular and which should be considered again when thinking about these questions are: the increasingly formal, pointed and public processes against disgraced nobles, including trial, punishment, sentences and reversals; the growing importance and at least theoretical tenurial permanence of confiscated lands in royal patronage; the increasing use of violence, and banishment; the growing role of women in the fate of families and estates; and the continued presence of trial by battle in various forms. The significance of each individually has already been discussed, but it is also important to look at them together to understand more about the changes going on in both the tone and nature of the later medieval polity. In conjunction, they all help, to a degree at least, explain the darkening hue of the later medieval scene. For with a greater public knowledge of the disgraces of the high and mighty, watching them stripped of their lands and their lives after having been marched, or dragged, defeated through the streets of

London and other major towns, as well as often the necessity of having women fight back for the fates and estates of families (rarely a truly accepted thing in a supposedly chivalric society), not only made the public in general feel more and more that nobles could be just like them in their varying fortunes, but also that the medieval hierarchy was by no means a static entity, even at the highest levels.[5] This in turn not only caused more potential stress on a social system already under a considerable degree of pressure,[6] but also did nothing to discourage – on the contrary often helped to fuel – the growing mood of *schadenfreude* in the kingdom as a whole when a noble did fall, especially one who had been newly raised or empowered. For instance, Andrew Harcla's fate was used as a warning by the judge, Sir Anthony de Lucy, as reported in the *Brut*, of climbing above one's station:

> And our lord the king's will is that the order of knighthood, by which thou undertookest all thine honour and worship upon thy body, be all brought unto nought, and thy state undone, so that other knights of lower degree may after thee beware.[7]

And at a higher, though still popular, level a little later in the fourteenth century, Geoffrey de Charny's quotation of the 'proverb of the ancients', 'he that climbs higher than he should falls lower than he would'[8] also emphasises this. The fact that the idea was also abroad among the lay preachers of the day that often the most hated kind of parvenus 'will not deign to look upon their inferiors or the poor, save from a distance and from the tips of their eyes'[9] again says as much about the mentality of those outside power (though not necessarily rank) as those still within it in the later Middle Ages, indicating a mixture of envy and abhorrence which was well satisfied when such individuals did ultimately fall. Finally, add this to the fact that, of all popular cults around nobles in the later Middle Ages, not one major cult was set around a new or newly empowered individual, also shows the mentality of the populace towards those who had pushed themselves upwards: for instance, Simon de Montfort, Thomas of Lancaster, the earl of Arundel and even the Anglo-Saxon earl Waltheof, all had cults rise around them, but it is very hard to find popular cult veneration of Piers Gaveston, Andrew de Harcla, Michael de la Pole or any other of those that Richard II pushed up the ranks. All of this essentially negative feeling was increasingly voiced in the growing amount of vernacular poetry and prose of the later Middle Ages as seen throughout this book – the tone of which was often one of happiness, or at least self-righteousness, at the misfortunes of others, especially those who had raised themselves to great heights. In other words, the further outside actual power one was, the more reactionary became one's view of medieval society for all, rather than for just those outside one's own section of it. In addition, this more critical tone could not but affect how those in power perceived themselves and the continued security of their positions. If it was clear to all and sundry now that no one, despite the strictures of the Church and various ideas about a structurally static, organic body known as medieval society, was necessarily permanently 'safe' in their position within that society, the fight was thereby made more vicious for those protecting their position, even filtering up to the way that kings treated their nobles – as well as the way nobles treated their kings. If, in other words, a noble or monarch got into a fight in the fourteenth and fifteenth centuries, because of the number of eyes looking on, as well as the potential permanence of his fall, he had to make sure that when he hit, he hit hard, far harder than when there was some idea, at least, that though members of the upper classes may err, the threat was not nearly so great of them being erased from the economic, social and political map.

As a result of these pressures, in themselves arising from the stresses and strains made evident throughout this work, the two main institutions involved – monarchy and nobility – tended to act differently when trouble arose between them as the later Middle Ages continued. In terms of the monarchy, though kings or those controlling the throne tended to become more violent towards erring nobility in the later medieval period, they also made more of an effort to rationalise and package that violence for both an increasingly vocal political community and the wider populace. Whether it be through statements in parliament, church and chronicle, or through writs read at markets and county courts, or even how the disgraced's body was disposed of, the important thing now was, once the problematic individual had been dealt with, to present the proceedings as forcibly as possible – not only to justify the actions of the monarchy, but also, as far as possible, to prevent future problems connected with the issue at hand. In other words, the monarchy knew that a festering perceived ill was a dangerous one, and that unless dealt with quickly and assuredly, it could cause no end of problems for those running the kingdom. As for the nobility, they too had to react to the fact that the relationship between themselves, the king and the rest of society was changing, and respond to the best of their ability. However, since they usually had far less in the way of resources and venues to influence larger noble and, indeed, public opinion to push their case, they initially instead had to resort more to clear, forceful statements of concerns to deal with such situations. We see the evidence of these statements first in Magna Carta and connected documents, followed by those of the Paper Constitution, the Provisions of Oxford and Westminster, Remonstrances of 1297 and the Ordinances of 1311 – most of which, while increasingly being developed during the course of parliamentary sessions, also gained notice and currency above and beyond such sessions as separate, independent entities. However, thereafter, it is also not-able that subsequent to Edward II's reign there were few such coherent major noble statements of intent, and definitely few of such fame or wide reference. Part of this may be simply, of course, that the points raised by these earlier statements had become part of the noble vocabulary in parliament, and so there was no further need to emphasise them overtly; part also may be that the development and growing power of a parliamentary peerage itself also in effect addressed many of these points. But it could also be argued that, when the nobility perceived that serious problems had arisen, and/or their rights infringed, by the later Middle Ages the increasing amount of procedure, business and power of parliament as an institution tended to overlay, if not dilute, the forcefulness and unity of any programme thereby pushed by them, let alone anyone else. Whether in 1340–1, 1386 or in the early part of the reign of Henry IV, or any number of other smaller incidents noted throughout this book, when noble interests were perceived to be threatened either individu-ally, severally or as a group, they now first made their points in parliament, as part of the developing parliamentary process and as part of the parliamentary record – and *not* as a clear forceful statement of group interest as produced earlier, one which had often transcended the circumstances, whether in parliament or outside, that produced it. Indeed it is notable how, starting in the later fourteenth century, it is the parliaments that are remembered, and by names given at the time or afterwards – The Good Parliament, The Bad Parliament, The Wonderful Parliament, The Merciless Parliament, etc. – rather than any unified 'documents of intent' that nobles or Commons pushed *per se* during them. However, this fact also meant such programmes or causes that the nobility *did* desperately want to push – programmes or causes which had been, or they realised otherwise would be, lost or made ineffective in the procedure and business of a parliamentary session – could easily become extra-parliamentary and thereby less controlled in practice. Thus, once parliament had gained the reputation as the place for at least semi-rational, if increas-ingly regulated, political debate, noble initiatives outside parliament – having gradually lost the long-developed, and hard-won, necessary sophistication of earlier pre- and extra-parliamentary discussion through continued depend-ency on that institution for dialogue between nobility and king – became all the more heated and violent. The clashes of 1322, 1326, 1330, 1387, 1399 and in the reigns of Henry IV and VI can all be argued to be points at which parliament had been perceived to have failed to offer a way to resolve issues between rulers and ruled, and thereafter, with the tradition of at least some degree of rational non- and extra-parliamentary debate of the high Middle Ages dimmed, a more angry, violent and bloody form of dialogue developed. Both nobility and monarchs, in other words, were becoming increasingly dependent on parliament as a place to work out grievances in the later Middle Ages, and when the institution was not used for one reason or another, the level of debate degenerated, and the chance of violent action increased.

Indeed, if we look even more broadly, the question at the base of much of this book is an age-old and very fundamental one: namely, why did English history get so much more divisive, and bloodier, in the later Middle Ages, especially among the upper echelons? Part may be the interaction of the above factors which in turn brought certain fundamental problems to the fore and as a subject for (often acrimonious) discussion and debate among the larger populace as well as the participants themselves. Part also might be, as mentioned in Chapter 3, the need for kings to be able to control and promote individuals in an increasingly stratified, hierarchical but also resource-limited society, by the use of fear at times, though also more and more through royal largesse, which in turn put mounting pressure on royal administrations to find new resources of varying types wherever and whenever they could. But there was also the fifth 'larger' theme of this book which we have yet to return to, the issue of trial by battle, especially battle between groups, which, though not changing to any degree in its execution, did shift in two other important ways that not only encouraged and speeded up the changes in the other four areas (trial and sentencing, estate confiscation, violence and banishment, and the role of women), but also darkened the political landscape at the national level. Firstly, when it came to mass disobedience and rebellions at least, it is notable how, in the high Middle Ages, it was often a member of the king's immediate full-blood family who led it – whether William Rufus, Robert Curthose in the period 1088–1106, Henry II's sons several times during his reign, or John against his brother Richard. In other words, major revolts in this period tended to be a close royal family affair. However, by the later Middle Ages, the leaders of such revolts tended to be more distantly linked, though often still related to the ruling monarch – Simon de Montfort was the brother-in-law of Henry III; Thomas of Lancaster and Henry of Derby were cousins of the foci of their rebellions, Edward II and Richard II. All these men, instead of being led by renegade members of the immediate royal family and fighting their cause, had their own ideas about what they were rebelling against, and increasingly represented the interests of their social group, the higher nobility, as a whole. Whether it be the right of the nobility to security of tenure, access to and counsel of the king, or even more general ideas about noble mores and how they fit within the kingdom as a whole, these men no longer followed would-be kings as much as represented the interests of their class. Indeed, many rebel or restive noble fomenters were even less clearly linked with the king than those mentioned above: for instance, those involved in the crisis of 1297, and during the rebellions of the early years of Henry IV's reign, had comparatively little royal blood in them. Though by no means conclusive, and only a section – if a large and influential one – of those who fell from grace, the fact that those who led rebellions against the king, or at least fell out of favour with him, tended to be more and more distantly connected with the monarchy by blood as the Middle Ages progressed, and more vehement about their own rights, might again help explain why the treatment of downfallen individuals and their followers became more harsh and heartless. After all, even in the Middle Ages, it was far less problematic for kings to deal harshly with a cousin or other more distant relation, or someone who married into the family, who had ideas increasingly at odds with the interests of the monarchy, than with one's own brother or son. If nothing else, and even if conventional bonds of close blood did not matter, there were also the strictures against murders within the family in the Bible (e.g. Cain and Abel) and throughout Canon Law, as well as the impact of the revival of classical culture at the time (e.g. stories of Romulus and Remus), rules and cautionary tales which were ever present, increasingly visible and ever hard to ignore.

Connected with this point, but more generally, it is remarkable that, when nobles did disobey or rebel against the king in the first century or so of our period, as individuals or groups, they usually did so not just under the auspices of a prince or other individual with strong claims to royal blood, but one usually after the throne or another major part of the royal inheritance as a result.[10] Robert Curthose, Matilda, Henry of Anjou, Henry the Young King, Richard and John were all the leaders of revolts aimed at usurping kings from their throne or other major rights (especially on the Continent) in the first century or so after the Norman Conquest, and they were all closely related to the king by blood. However, as early as the Barons Wars' of 1215–17, and definitely by 1264–5 and de Montfort's rebellion, nobles had not only started rebelling without anyone of full royal blood leading the armies, it was usually, initially at least, without claims to the throne or other parts of the royal inheritance clearly enunciated – and this was a trend that was to continue into the fourteenth and fifteenth centuries. The crisis of 1297 was not about overthrowing the king; the Contrariants did not revolt in 1322 with any clear aim to replace Edward II; nor, in the case of Richard II, did the Appellants in 1388 or, though more arguably, Henry of Derby when he first landed at Ravenspur. The only insurrection threatening the governance of the kingdom itself which did have direct claims on the throne or similar royal rights was Isabella's invasion of 1326, though even here, the nobility, aside from Mortimer, mainly took a passive rather than active part in events. Only in the fifteenth century, with a second royal deposition confirming the precedent, did replacement of the monarch in particular again immediately become a key issue from the beginning in such events – as witness the Southampton Plot of 1415 and the Wars of the Roses. Thus, not only did lack of strong bonds of royal blood matter in the fates of those who had fallen out of favour with the king or their followers by the later medieval period, but conceivably the lack of clear regal claims may also have made later medieval downfallen rebels more open to abuse by their victors. It was far easier, looking from the government's point of view, to deal harshly with noble rebels in the later Middle Ages without the power of a royal leader or a clearly defined legitimate claim to royal rights, than with rebels of the high Middle Ages, who not only had royal blood clearly on their side, but also clearly focused claims on the monarchy itself. If nothing else, high medieval monarchs' overly harsh treatment of royal blood and royal supporters of whatever line might stir up problematic ideas with the ascendant Church in the period, one clearly against execution at any level, but especially in connection with those related to God's anointed. Finally, if kings themselves *could* face bloody deposition because of the growing ideals and powers of the nobility, were their nobles, in a group or individually, to expect anything less? If the wheel of fortune, powered by society's changing expectations and needs, began to spin more quickly and violently for the monarchs, as we see from so many wheel of fortune manuscript illuminations (see next section), why not also for their nobles? There is therefore, again, as with many other questions examined in this book, no *one* simple answer as to why the nature of later medieval politics darkened so perceptibly, but darken it did, and this change was not lost to the wider world.

From the wheel of fortune to the fall of princes: the arts, historicism and the substantiation of a late medieval paradigm

Lich fals Fortune, which turnyth to and fro
To make folkis, whan thei most cleerli shyne
In ther estatis onwarli to declyne.[11]

One should not put trust in the benefits of fortune, which are not earned, for fortune is fickle and is destined to come to an end.[12]

At the start of this work, we talked about the wheel of fortune, its various meanings and permutations, and how it has manifested itself throughout the succeeding centuries. If we were to characterise the presence of the wheel of fortune now, rather than arguing historical events or chance as the main issue involved, we might instead change our whole view of what 'fortune' was supposed to represent. One could argue that 'fortune', either on or off the wheel, represented not a personification of variable fate, but medieval society itself, and that when that society was 'on' the wheel, as it mainly was in the early Middle Ages, it represented the fact that external events such as wars and raiding frequently threatened to undermine the social structure and those within it. By the high Middle Ages, however, when there had been a certain amount of political and economic stabilisation of Europe as a whole, one's own society (England, France, etc.), as personified by fortune, was usually now in a secure enough position to be 'off' the wheel and instead turn it itself, judging the actions and influencing the lives of individuals.[13] The individual's life, in other words, could be more influenced by one's own society than by larger processes, an idea which would also be popular with an increasingly secular and 'national' age. Limited free will (as represented by the individual's actions on the wheel) within a 'national' societal context (as represented by the turner fortune controlling the wheel), in other words, had gained a far greater degree of independence than when fortune itself (as representing society) had been on the wheel. To developing ideas of free will, destiny and society's ability to influence them, and the reality of such ideas within an increasingly fluid social hierarchy, the wheel and its turner must have become inextricably intertwined.[14]

The product of this fusion was to help further the wheel of fortune's dovetailing with, and ultimate partial superseding by, another important motif of the later Middle Ages, that of the fall from grace, and in particular the idea of the 'fall of princes'. Of course this theme had also been around in various forms for a long time in both artistic expression and political commentary, as we have already seen. In classical myths, Prometheus' fall from grace was all painful, as was Icarus' all final. In the Bible, Lucifer, Cain and Judas of course stand out as some of the most notable victims of declines in grace, but there are also lesser falls as well – for example, Jacob, David and even, at times, Moses. In the case of English mythology, perhaps the most prevalent image is Lancelot's fall because of his relationship with Guinevere, and the fall of Camelot itself. The idea of the destruction of a social system, be it court or kingdom, comes up again in Gildas's *Destruction of Britain*, as it does in Nennius, and Bede's *Ecclesiastical History*. Even *Beowulf* and the *Battle of Malden* both deal with this idea of a break of faith and the resulting fall, as discussed in the introductory section of this book. Much of this was brought together at the very beginning of our period by Geoffrey of Monmouth's *History of the Kings of England*, which weaves together both the classical myths of falls from Aeneas onwards and the Arthurian legends of the Anglo-Celtic world into one great tapestry of free will and fate. However, never had this more negative theme of 'falling from grace' taken so firm a position as the main subject of secular works of literature and art as in the fourteenth and fifteenth centuries – rather than one of many. Boccaccio, Chaucer, Gower, Lydgate and

Hoccleve all have 'falls' as major themes, often for massive works, and to an appreciative public always wanting more. In many ways, the increasingly dominant image of the individual now slipping on the wheel in the later Middle Ages, ready to fall off, or indeed falling off, is echoed in the many characters in the 'falls of princes' (and literature with similar themes) which began to become popular in the fourteenth and especially fifteenth centuries, from Dante's *Inferno* and Hoccleve's *Regiment of Princes*, to *Musing on Mutability* and beyond.[15] Just as fortune (as representing medieval society) slipped and slid like a 'lumberjack on a log' in the early Middle Ages,[16] so princes and aristocrats slipped and slid upon what medieval society as a whole, as well as those in power, expected of them by the late Middle Ages. Throughout this work, indeed, we have watched nobles fumble as they tried to control themselves on the increasingly unstable sphere of political and societal expectations. One could even argue that, because of the many political, social and economic changes going on within later Medieval England in particular, English society at least morphed to such a degree that individuals on the downward swing, or now 'fall', were an increasingly common and public occurrence, just as it had previously been with a variety of European societies themselves (as represented by images of fortune) when they had tried to stay on the wheel (i.e. survive) in the face of the post-Roman instabilities of medieval Europe as a whole:

> Thys warlde ys varyabyll,
> No-thyng þer-in ys stable,
> A-say now, ho-so wyll.
> Syn yt is so mutable,
> how shuld men be stable?
> yt may not be thorow skyll![17]

Though still more stable than in the early Middle Ages, this is a far cry from the organised 'body' of society so often talked of for the high medieval period, with the monarch at its head and everyone knowing their place beneath him – rather it now begins to feel like this and similar poems should instead break into a sub-Yeatsian 'things fall apart'. Thus, perhaps a 'tree' of fortune is symbolic of the new attitude towards the fate of princes, not so much a wheel to hold onto, even in decline, as a branch to fall off of, often from a great height, and with great speed. Figure 13, from Honore de Bonnet's *Tree of Battles*, shows fortune and her wheel securely at the top of the tree, and all the many potentates beneath her. The downward fall from such heights is now much more serious and dangerous than it would have been simply off fortune's wheel, where the individual is often still shown – though not always (see below) – as clinging on, even in the downward swing.

13 BL Royal 20 C. VIII, f. 2v: Honore de Bonnet, *L'Arbre des Batailles*, a tree surmounted by fortune with her wheel; France, early fifteenth century.

In other words, by the later Middle Ages some artists at least realised that the fate of nobles, as of many men, lay not on a rotating wheel so much as on a branch of life, from which the fall could be more deadly. And if the prevalent illumination in manuscripts, the tree of fortune aside, was still a fortune's wheel, which could go up as well as down (see Fig. 14), the text also often as not told of more dramatic and permanent falls. The quote which starts this section from Lydgate's *Fall of Princes* indicates as such, as does the late

14 BL Harley 7353, second picture: *Life of Edward IV*, King Edward IV
on fortune's wheel; England, 1461.

medieval poem *Musing upon Mutability*, with its allusions to the falls of the
duke and duchess of Gloucester and the duke of Somerset – indeed, the poet
in this case felt that one did not need to look much further than the recent
past when searching for material for moralising:

Wee nede not nowe to Seke the cronicles old
off the Romans nor bockas tragedye
to Rede the Ruyen and Fallys manyffolde
off prynces grett put to dethe and misereye
In Sondrye landes For wee haue hardelye
here In thys lande with In thes xx yere
As wonders changes Seen before our eye
As euer I trowe before thys any were.[18]

Moreover, though there is still the idea of a stable wheel here, and even a lack of permanence to falls at times, underneath there also now rumbles the later medieval poet's sense, at least, of the ultimate despair and futility in all human endeavour, in which man must in the end, and despite more secular trends, reject the wheel and trust in the will of God, work hard and hope for the best:

Musyng vppon the mutabilite
off worldlye changes and grett vnstablenes
and me remembering howe grett aduersite
I haue Seen Falle to men off highe noblenes
Furst welthe and then ageyn distres
nowe vppe nowe downe as Fortune turnethe h[ur] whele
Best is me thinke For mannys Sikernes
to trust In god and labour to doo well.[19]

Thomas Hoccleve's *Regiment of Princes* has a similarly defeatist attitude towards all the endeavours of men:

Me fil to mynde how that nat longe agoo
Fortunes strook doun thraste estat rial
Into mescheef, and I took heede also
Of many anothir lord that hadde a fal.
In mene estat eek sikirnesse at al
Ne saw I noon, but I sy atte laste
Wher seuretee for to abyde hir caste.[20]

Part of this more sombre hue may be to do with the more generally negative and defeatist tone of an increasingly politicised and jaded society after the Black Death, but part may be recognition by the writers and illustrators themselves that when the higher echelons now fell from favour, it was far more serious than it had ever been before. Even Camelot now fell more pronouncedly than previously, as a fifteenth-century reorganisation of the Arthur legend shows: according to Blake, when Malory, concerned to emphasise the rise and fall of the court, 'turned the alliterative *Morte Arthure* into prose, he did not include Mordred's treason and Arthur's death in their rightful place,

15 University of Glasgow, Special Collections MS Hunter 371–371(V.1.8–9)
f. 1r: Boccaccio, *Fall of Princes*; France, 1467. Also see the wheel of fortune
in Fig. 1 (from Lydgate's *Troy Book*), as well as the figure in the foreground
of the 1554 print of *The Fall of Princes* – two more individuals who had now
visibly let go of the wheel. For the latter, see Barry, *Art, Culture and the
Semiotics of Meaning*, Plate 4.

but he delayed them until the eighth tale, where they form a suitable
conclusion to the whole cycle'.[21] Whatever the case, in our last image (see
Fig. 15), from a 1467 manuscript of Boccaccio's *Fall of Princes* held in Glasgow
University Library, we see not only that women are now on the wheel
(unsurprising considering both their increasingly important role in the
revival of family fortunes, and the fact that they could now be tried by their

peers and face the impact of attainder),[22] there are more people looking on and the landscape is more real (as befits the more public and well-documented nature of falls), but also that not all individuals are managing to hold onto the wheel, however tenuously, throughout the downward swing. Instead, they are now sometimes being spun off and falling to the ground, far from the wheel. Artistic expression, it would seem, had begun to assimilate the harsher realities of late medieval life, and taken them to their logical, metaphorical conclusions, conclusions which would influence all later talk of wheels and falls. Just as the use of real dismembered bodies had become 'textual' during the course of our period, so had allegory in art and literature become more clearly reconnected with actual events, completing the cyclical weaving of reality and image of the later Middle Ages.[23]

Notes

1   'I shall rule, I rule, I have ruled, I am without a realm': a phrase on or connected with some depictions of wheels of fortune of the period. See Barry, *Art, Culture and the Semiotics of Meaning*, pp. 32–3.

2   Henry of Huntingdon, *History of the English People*, p. 74.

3   See p. 211.

4   Kail, ed. *Twenty-Six Political Poems*, p. 61.

5   On the importance of the public more generally in the later Middle Ages, see J.L. Watts, 'The Pressure of the Public on Later Medieval Politics', in L. Clark and C. Carpenter, eds. *Political Culture in Late Medieval Britain* (Woodbridge, 2004), 159–80.

6   Especially if one also takes into account the attempts in the later Middle Ages by the upper echelons to keep the rest of society in its place, for instance through wage and sumptuary legislation.

7   The *Brut*, as in Keen, 'Treason Trials', 89.

8   *The Book of Chivalry of Geoffroi de Charny* R.W. Kaeuper and E. Kennedy, ed. and trans. (Philadelphia, 1996), p. 137.

9   From G.R. Owst, *Literature and Pulpit in Medieval England* (Oxford, 1933), pp. 312ff.

10 A similar point is made by Valente in justifying the starting point of her study. Valente, *Revolt*, p. 10.

11 *Lydgate's Fall of Princes* H. Bergen, ed. (London, 1924), i, 22.

12 *Book of Chivalry*, p. 135.

13 As it had in the classical period. See H.R. Patch, *The Goddess Fortuna in Medieval Literature* (Cambridge, Mass., 1927), p. 150.

14 For the increasingly active role of the individual on the wheel, especially in the late Middle Ages and the Renaissance, see Barry, *Art, Culture and the Semiotics of Meaning*, pp. 34–8 and Chapter 4.

15 For a collection of verses on this theme, see D. Gray, ed. *The Oxford Book of Late Medieval Verse and Prose* (Oxford, 1985), Chapter 1 ('The Mutability of Worldly

Changes'); for the popularity of the 'de casibus' tradition of the later fifteenth century and the way it was received, see N. Mortimer, *John Lydgate's Fall of Princes: Narrative Tragedy in its Literary and Political Contexts* (Oxford, 2005), pp. 220–4.

16 Radding, 'Fortune and her Wheel', 127.

17 Robbins, ed. *Historical Poems*, p. 148.

18 *The Welles Anthology Ms. Rawlinson C. 813: A Critical Edition* S.L. and K.H. Jordan, eds. (Binghamton, NY, 1991), pp. 111–12; for a discussion of this poem and the *Regiment of Princes*, see N. Perkins, 'Musing on Mutability: A Poem in the Welles Anthology and Hoccleve's *The Regement of Princes*', *Review of English Studies* 50 (1999), 493–8.

19 *Welles Anthology Ms. Rawlinson*, p. 111.

20 Thomas Hoccleve, *The Regiment of Princes* C.R. Blyth, ed. (Kalamazoo, 1999), ll. 22–8.

21 N.F. Blake, 'Late Medieval Prose', in W.F. Bolton, ed. *The Penguin History of Literature: The Middle Ages* (Harmondsworth, 1993), 394.

22 And as we also see earlier in Boccaccio's original title of his work, *De Casibus Virorum et Feminarum Illustrium*.

23 For more on the relationship between the development of literature and the course of historical events in the fifteenth century, see M. Nolan, *John Lydate and the Making of Public Culture* (Cambridge, 2005), Introduction.

Bibliography

Unpublished primary sources

Bibliothèque Nationale de France

FR 2643

British Library

Additional 10294
Additional 42130
Additional 47682
Additional Charter 75476
Additional Charter 75748
Harley 4380
Harley 7353
Royal 14 C. VII
Royal 14 E. IV
Royal 18 D. II
Royal 18 E. II
Royal 20 C. VIII

The National Archives: Public Record Office

Chancery
C44 Court of Chancery: Common Law Pleadings, Tower Series
C47 Miscellanea
C49 Parliamentary and Council Proceedings
C81 Warrants for the Great Seal, Series I
C143 Inquisitions Ad Quod Damnum, Henry III to Richard III
C245 Tower and Rolls Chapel Series, Scire Facias, Series I
C255 Tower and Rolls Chapel Series, Miscellaneous Files and Writs
C257 Tower and Rolls Chapel Series, Certiorari Super Causa Captionis

Court of Common Pleas
CP40 Plea Rolls

Court of King's Bench
KB26 Court of Common Pleas and King's Bench, and Justices Itinerant: Early Plea
   and Essoin Rolls
KB27 Placita Coram Rege
KB138 Court of King's Bench and Other Courts: Various Writs and Returns

Exchequer
E28 Treasury of Receipt: Council and Privy Seal Records
E40 Treasury of Receipt: Ancient Deeds Series A
E142 King's Remembrancer: Extents, Inquisitions and Valors of Forfeited Lands
E154 King's Remembrancer & Treasury of Receipt: Inventories of Goods & Chattels
E159 King's Remembrancer: Memoranda Rolls
E163 King's Remembrancer: Miscellanea
E175 King's Remembrancer & Treasury of Receipt: Parliament & Council Proceed-
   ings, Series II
E208 King's Remembrancer, Brevia Baronibus
E368 Lord Treasurer's Remembrancer: Memoranda Rolls
E403 Issue Rolls

Special collections
SC1 Ancient Correspondence
SC7 Papal Bulls
SC8 Ancient Petitions

Other British archives

Birmingham City Archives
   Papers of Zachary Lloyd family of Areley Hall: MS 3688/259
Bodleian Library
   MS Douce 180 (*Douce Apocalypse*)
British Museum
   MLA 1984, 5–5, 2 (Pilgrim badge)
Rochester Cathedral Library
   Wheel of fortune wall painting
University of Glasgow, Special Collections
   MS Hunter 371–371

Published primary sources

*Adae Murimuth Continuatio Chronicarum: Robertus de Avesbury De Gestis Mirabilibus
   Regis Edwardi Tertii Avesbury* E.M. Thompson, ed. (London, 1889).
Alcuin of York: His Life and Letters S. Allot, ed. and trans. (York, 1987).

The Alliterative Morte Arthur: The Owl and the Nightingale and Five Other Middle English Poems J. Gardner, ed. (London, 1973).

Anglo-Saxon Chronicle M.J. Swanton, ed. and trans. (London, 1996).

Annales Cambriae J. Williams, ed. (London, 1860).

Annales Monastici H.R. Luard, ed. 5 vols. (London, 1864–9).

The Annals of Roger de Hoveden H.T. Riley, ed. and trans. 2 vols. (London, 1853).

The Anonimalle Chronicle 1307–1334 W.R. Childs and J. Taylor, ed. and trans. (Leeds, 1991).

Augustine, *Confessions* R.S. Pine-Coffin, ed. and trans. (Harmondsworth, 1979).

Bartholomew Cotton's Historia Anglicana H.R. Luard, ed. (London, 1859).

The Battle of Malden AD 991 D. Scragg, ed. and trans. (Oxford, 1991).

Bede, *The Ecclesiastical History of the English People* L. Sherley-Price, ed. and trans. (Harmondsworth, 1990).

Beowulf K. Crossley-Holland, ed. and trans. (Oxford, 1999).

Boethius, *The Consolation of Philosophy* V.E. Watts, trans. (Harmondsworth, 1978).

The Book of Chivalry of Geoffroi de Charny R.W. Kaeuper and E. Kennedy, ed. and trans. (Philadelphia, 1996).

Bracton, H. *On the Laws and Customs of England* S.E. Thorne, ed. and trans. 4 vols. (Cambridge, Mass., 1968).

Bradley, S.A.J., ed. and trans. *Anglo-Saxon Poetry* (London, 1995).

Britton F.M. Nichols, ed. and trans. (Washington, 1901).

Brut Y Tywysogion, or Chronicle of the Princes J. Williams, ed. (London, 1860).

Calendar of Ancient Correspondence Concerning Wales J.G. Edwards, ed. (Board of Celtic Studies, Cardiff, 1935).

Calendar of Ancient Petitions Relating to Wales W. Rees, ed. and trans. (Cardiff, 1975).

Calendar of Charter Rolls (1226–1516), 6 vols. (London, 1916–27).

Calendar of Close Rolls (1272–1485), 45 vols. (London, 1892–1954).

Calendar of Fine Rolls (1272–1509), 22 vols. (London, 1911–62).

Calendar of Inquisitions Miscellaneous (1219–1422), 7 vols. (London, 1916–68).

Calendar of Inquisitions Post Mortem (Henry III to 6 Henry IV), 18 vols. (London, 1904–88).

Calendar of Patent Rolls (1232–1509), 52 vols. (London, 1891–1916).

Capgrave, J. *The Chronicle of England* F.C. Hingeston, ed. (London, 1858).

Capgrave, J. *Liber de Illustribus Henricis* F.C. Hingeston, ed. 2 vols. (London, 1858).

A Catalogue of the Medieval Muniments at Berkeley Castle B. Wells-Furby, ed. and trans. 2 vols. (Bristol, 2004).

Chaplais, P., ed. *Diplomatic Documents 1101–1272* (London, 1964).

Chaplais, P., ed. *The War of Saint Sardos (1323–5)* (London, 1957).

Chronica Buriensis 1212–1301 A. Gransden, ed. and trans. (London, 1964).

Chronica Johannis de Oxenedes H. Ellis ed. (London, 1859).

Chronica Magistri Rogeri de Houedene W. Stubbs, ed. 4 vols. (New York, 1964).

The Chronica Maiora of Thomas Walsingham 1376–1422 D. Preest and J.G. Clark, ed. and trans. (Woodbridge, 2005).

Chronica Monastario de Melsa E.A. Bond, ed. 3 vols. (London, 1866–8).

The Chronicle of Adam of Usk 1377–1421 C. Given-Wilson, ed. and trans. (Oxford, 1997).

The Chronicle of Lanercost 1272–1346 H.E. Maxwell, ed. and trans. (Glasgow, 1913).

The Chronicle of Melrose J. Stevenson, ed. and trans. (Lampeter reprint, 1991).

The Chronicle of William de Rishanger J. Halliwell, ed. (London, 1840).

Chronicles of the Reigns of Edward I and Edward II W. Stubbs, ed. 2 vols. (London, 1882–3).

Chronicon Galfridi le Baker de Swynbroke E.M. Thompson, ed. (Oxford, 1889).

Chronique de Jean le Bel J. Viard and E. Déprez, ed. 2 vols. (Paris, 1904–5).

Chroniques de London G.J. Aungier, ed. (London, 1844).

Cicero: Back from Exile: Six Speeches upon His Return D.R. Shackleton Bailey, ed. (Chicago, 1991).

Commynes, P. de *Memoirs: The Reign of Louis XI 1461–83* M. Jones, ed. and trans. (Harmondsworth, 1972).

Coulton, G.G., ed. and trans. *Life in the Middle Ages* 4 vols. (Cambridge, 1967).

Crossley-Holland, K., ed. and trans. *The Anglo-Saxon World: An Anthology* (Oxford, 1984).

Dante, *The Divine Comedy: Inferno*, ed. and trans. C.S. Singleton (London, 1971).

Dialogus de Scaccario C. Johnson, ed. and trans. (London, 1950).

Dobson, R.B., ed. *The Peasants' Revolt of 1381* 2nd edn (London, 1983).

Eadmer, *Vita Anselmi* R.W. Southern, ed. and trans. (London, 1962).

The Ecclesiastical History of Orderic Vitalis M. Chibnall, ed. and trans. 6 vols. (Oxford, 1968–80).

An English Chronicle of the Reigns of Richard II, Henry IV, Henry V, and Henry VI, Written before the Year 1471 J.S. Davies, ed. (London, 1856).

English Historical Documents c. 500–1042 D. Whitelock, ed. and trans. (London, 1996).

English Historical Documents 1042–1189 D.C. Douglas and G.W. Greenaway, ed. and trans. (Oxford, 1953).

English Historical Documents 1189–1327 H. Rothwell, ed. and trans. (London, 1975).

Eulogium Historiarum sive Temporis F.S. Haydon, ed. 3 vols. (London, 1858–63).

Fantosme, J. *Chronicle* R.C. Johnston, ed. and trans. (Oxford, 1981).

Florence of Worcester, *Monachi Chronicon ex Chronicis* B. Thorpe, ed. 2 vols. (New York, 1964).

Flores Historiarum H.R. Luard, ed. 3 vols. (London, 1890).

Fortescue, J. *On the Laws and Governance of England* S. Lockwood, ed. and trans. (Cambridge, 2002).

Fouke le Fitz Waryn S. Knight and T.H. Ohlgren, eds. (TEAMS On-line).

The French Chronicle of London A.D. 1259–A.D. 1343 H.T. Riley, ed. and trans. (London, 1863).

Froissart, J. *Chronicles* G. Brereton, ed. and trans. (Harmondsworth, 1978).

Geoffrey of Monmouth, *The History of the Kings of Britain* L. Thorpe, ed. and trans. (Harmondsworth, 1966).

Gesta Henrici Quinci F. Taylor and J.S. Roskell, ed. and trans. (Oxford, 1975).

The Gesta Normannorum Ducum of William of Jumièges, Orderic Vitalis, and Robert of Torigni E.M.C. van Houts, ed. and trans. 2 vols. (Oxford, 1992–2001).

Gesta Regis Henrici Secundi Benedicti Abbatis W. Stubbs, ed. 2 vols. (London, 1965).

Gesta Stephani K.R. Potter, ed. and trans. (London, 1955).

Gesta Stephani K.R. Potter, ed. and trans. (Oxford, 1976).

Gildas, *The Ruin of Britain and Other Works* M. Winterbottom, ed. and trans. (London, 1978).

Given-Wilson, C., ed. and trans. *Chronicles of the Revolution* (Manchester, 1993).

Gray, D., ed. *The Oxford Book of Late Medieval Verse and Prose* (Oxford, 1985).

Gray, T. *Scalacronica 1272–1363*, A. King, ed. and trans. (Woodbridge, 2005).

The Great Red Book of Bristol E.W.W. Veale, ed. Part IV (Bristol, 1953).

Henry of Huntingdon, *The History of the English People: 1000–1154* D. Greenway, ed. and trans. (Oxford, 2002).

Historical Works of Giraldus Cambrensis T. Forester, ed. and trans.; revised by T. Wright (London, 1887).

Hoccleve, T. *The Regiment of Princes* C.R. Blyth, ed. (Kalamazoo, 1999).

Horrox, R., ed. and trans. *The Black Death* (Manchester, 1994).

Ingulph's Chronicle of the Abbey of Croyland (London, 1854).

Kail, J., ed. *Twenty-Six Political and Other Poems from the Oxford MSS. Digby 102 and Douce 322* (London, 1904).

Knighton's Chronicle 1337–1396 G.H. Martin, ed. and trans. (Oxford, 1995).

Leges Henrici Primi L.J. Downer, ed. and trans. (Oxford, 1972).

The Letters of Lanfranc, Archbishop of Canterbury H. Clover and M. Gibson, ed. and trans. (Oxford, 1979).

Literae Cantuarienses J. Brigstocke Sheppard, ed. 3 vols. (London, 1887–9).

Lodge, E.C. and G.A. Thornton, eds. *English Constitutional Documents 1307–1485* (Cambridge, 1935).

Lydgate's Fall of Princes H. Bergen, ed. 4 vols. (London, 1924–7).

Malory, T. *Le Morte D'Arthur* J. Cowen ed. 2 vols. (Harmondsworth, 1986).

Map, W. *De Nugis Curialium* M.R. James, ed. and trans. (Oxford, 1983).

Memoriale Fratris Walteri de Coventria W. Stubbs, ed. 2 vols. (London, 1872–3).

The Old English Rune Poem: A Critical Edition M. Halsall, ed. (Toronto, 1981).

Paris, M. *Chronica Majora* H.R. Luard, ed. 7 vols. (London, 1964).

Paris, M. *Historia Anglorum* F. Madden, ed. 3 vols. (London, 1866–9).

The Parliament Rolls of Medieval England, 1275–1504 C. Given-Wilson, gen. ed. (Woodbridge, 2005).

The Paston Letters J. Gairdner, ed. (Gloucester, 1986).

Pisan, C. de *The Book of the Body Politic* K. Langdon Forhan, ed. and trans. (Cambridge, 1994).

Prerogativa Regis S.E. Thorne, ed. (New Haven, 1949).

Pronay, N. and J. Taylor, eds. and trans. *Parliamentary Texts of the Later Middle Ages* (Oxford, 1980).

Ranulfi de Diceto Decani Lundoniensis Opera Historica W. Stubbs, ed. 2 vols. (London, 1876).

Registrum Epistolarum Fratris Johannis Peckham C.T. Martin, ed. 3 vols. (London, 1882–5).

Rishanger, W. *Chronica et Annales* H.T. Riley ed. (London, 1865).

The Riverside Chaucer L.D. Benson, ed. 3rd edn (Oxford, 1988).

Robbins, R.H., ed. *Historical Poems of the XIVth and XVth Centuries* (New York, 1959).

Roger de Wendover Liber Qui Dicitur Flores Historiarum H.G. Hewlett, ed. 3 vols. (London, 1886–9).

Roger of Wendover, *Flores Historiarum* H.O. Cox, ed. 4 vols. (London, 1841–4).

Rotuli Litterarum Clausarum T. Duffus Hardy, ed. 2 vols. (London, 1833).

Rotuli Parliamentorum, ed. J. Strachey et al., 6 vols. (London, 1787).

Royal and Other Historical Letters Illustrative of the Reign of Henry III W.W. Shirley, ed. 2 vols. (London, 1862–6).

Select Cases in the Court of King's Bench under Edward I G.O. Sayles, ed. and trans. (London, 1936).

Sir Gawain and the Green Knight B. Stone, ed. and trans. (Harmondsworth, 1962).

Statutes of the Realm 11 vols. (London, 1810–28).

The Treatise on the Laws and Customs of the Realm of England Commonly called Glanvill G.D.G. Hall, ed. and trans. (Edinburgh, 1965).

Trokelowe, Johannis de and Henrici de Blaneforde, *Chronica et Annales* H.T. Riley, ed. (London, 1866).

Vita Edwardi Secundi N. Denholm-Young, ed. and trans. (London, 1957).

Walsingham, T. *Gesta Abbatum Monasterii S. Albani* H.T. Riley, ed. 3 vols. (London, 1867–9).

Walsingham, T. *Historia Anglicana* H.T. Riley, ed. 2 vols. (London, 1863–4).

Walsingham, T. *The St Albans Chronicle: The Chronica Maiora of Thomas Walsingham*, Volume I: *1376–1394* J. Taylor, W.R. Childs and L. Watkiss, ed. and trans. (Oxford, 2003).

Walsingham, T. *Ypodiigma Neustiae* H.T. Riley, ed. (London, 1876).

Ward, J., ed. and trans. *Women of the English Nobility and Gentry 1066–1500* (Manchester, 1995).

The Welles Anthology Ms. Rawlinson C. 813: A Critical Edition S.L. and K.H. Jordan, eds. (Binghamton, NY, 1991).

The Westminster Chronicle L.C. Hector and B.F. Harvey, ed. and trans. (Oxford, 1982).

William of Malmesbury, *Gesta Regum Anglorum* R.A.B. Mynors, ed. and trans. 2 vols. (Oxford, 1998–9).

Wright, T. *Political Songs of England* P. Coss, ed. and trans. (Cambridge, 1996).

Secondary sources

Books and articles

Alexander, M. *Old English Literature* (London, 1983).

Allmand, C.T. *Henry V* (Berkeley, 1992).

Anderson, M. 'Alice Chaucer and her Husbands', *Publications of the Modern Language Association of America* 60 (1945), 24–47.

Archer, R.E. 'Parliamentary Restoration: John Mowbray and the Dukedom of Norfolk in 1425', in R.E. Archer and S. Walker, eds. *Rulers and Ruled in Late Medieval England* (London and Rio Grande, 1995), 99–116.

Archer, R.E. 'Rich Old Ladies: The Problem of Late Medieval Dowagers', in A. Pollard, ed. *Property and Politics* (Gloucester, 1984), 15–35.

Arman, M. *A Short History of Thaxted Church* (Thaxted, 1982).

Ayton, A. *Knights and Warhorses: Military Service and the English Aristocracy under Edward III* (Woodbridge, 1994).

Bachrach, D.S. *Religion and the Conduct of War c. 300–c. 1215* (Woodbridge, 2003).

Baker, J.H. *An Introduction to English Legal History* 4th edn (London, 2002).

Baldwin, J.F. *The King's Council in England during the Middle Ages* (London, 1969).

Barlow, F. *William Rufus* (Berkeley, 1983).

Barron, C.M. 'Centres of Conspicuous Consumption: The Aristocratic Town House in London, 1200–1550', *London Journal* 20 (1995), 1–16.

Barron, W.R.J. 'The Penalties for Treason in Medieval Life and Literature', *JMH* 7 (1981), 187–202.

Barry, J. *Art, Culture and the Semiotics of Meaning: Culture's Changing Signs of Life in Poetry, Drama, Painting and Sculpture* (New York, 1999).

Bartlett, R. *England under the Norman and Angevin Kings 1075–1225* (Oxford, 2000).

Bartlett, R. *Trial by Fire and Water: The Medieval Judicial Ordeal* (Oxford, 1986).

Bates, D.R. 'The Character and Career of Odo, Bishop of Bayeux 1049/50–1097', *Speculum* 50 (1975), 1–20.

Bateson, H. 'The Ancient Penalty of High Treason', *Notes and Queries* 167 (1934), 442–3.

Bateson, M. and J. Denton, 'Usury and Comital Disinheritance: The Case of Ferrers versus Lancaster, St Paul's, London, 1301', *Journal of Ecclesiastical History* 43 (1992), 60–96.

Bean, J.M.W. *The Decline of English Feudalism 1215–1540* (Manchester, 1968).

Bean, J.M.W. *The Estates of the Percy Family 1416–1537* (Oxford, 1958).

Bean, J.M.W. 'Henry IV and the Percies', *History* 44 (1959), 212–27.

Bell, A.E. 'The Revolving Fortunes of the Knights of Rochester', *MP* 16 (1995), 69–109.

Bellamy, J.G. 'Appeal and Impeachment in the Good Parliament', *BIHR* 39 (1966), 35–46.

Bellamy, J.G. *Bastard Feudalism and the Law* (Portland, 1989).

Bellamy, J.G. *Crime and Public Order in the Later Middle Ages* (London, 1973).

Bellamy, J.G. *The Criminal Trial in Later Medieval England* (Stroud, 1998).

Bellamy, J.G. *The Law of Treason in the Later Middle Ages* (Cambridge, 1970).

Bellamy, J.G. 'The Northern Rebellions in the Later Years of Richard II', *BJRL* 47 (1964–5), 254–74.

Bennett, M. *Community, Class and Careerism: Cheshire and Lancashire in the Age of Sir Gawain and the Green Knight* (Cambridge, 2002).

Bennett, M. 'Military Masculinity in England and Northern France c. 1050–c. 1225', in D.M. Hadley, ed. *Masculinity in Medieval Europe* (London, 1999), 71–88.

Bennett, M. *Richard II and the Revolution of 1399* (Stroud, 1999).

Binski, P. *Medieval Death: Ritual and Representation* (Ithaca, 1996).

Binski, P. *Westminster Abbey and the Plantagenets* (New Haven and London, 1995).

Blake, N.F. 'Late Medieval Prose', in W.F. Bolton, ed. *The Penguin History of Literature: The Middle Ages* (Harmondsworth, 1993), 369–400.

Bothwell, J.S. 'Agnes Maltravers (d. 1375) and Her Husband, John (d. 1364): Rebel Wives, Separate Lives and Conjugal Visits in Later Medieval England', in J.S. Hamilton, ed. *Fourteenth Century England IV* (Woodbridge, 2006), 80–93.

Bothwell, J.S. *Edward III and the English Peerage: Royal Patronage, Social Mobility and Political Control in Fourteenth Century England* (Woodbridge, 2004).

Bothwell, J.S. 'Edward III and the "New Nobility": Largesse and Limitation in Fourteenth Century England', *EHR* 112 (1997), 1111–40.

Bothwell, J.S. 'Edward III, the English Peerage and the 1337 Earls', in J.S. Bothwell, ed. *The Age of Edward III* (Woodbridge, 2001), 35–52.

Boyle, L.E. '*E Cathena et Carcere*: The Imprisonment of Amaury de Montfort, 1276', in J.J.G. Alexander and M.T. Gibson, eds. *Medieval Learning and Literature* (Oxford, 1976), 379–97.

Brown, A.L. 'The Commons and the Council in the Reign of Henry IV', *EHR* 79 (1964), 1–30.

Brown, A.L. *The Governance of Late Medieval England 1272–1461* (London, 1989).

Brown, E.A.R. 'Death and the Human Body in the Later Middle Ages: The Legislation of Boniface VIII on the Division of the Corpse', *Viator* 12 (1981), 221–70.

Brown, R.A. 'Framlingham Castle and Bigod 1154–1216', *Proceedings of the Suffolk Institute of Archaeology (& History)* 25 (1951 for 1950), 128–48.

Buck, M.C. 'The Reform of the Exchequer', *EHR* 98 (1983), 241–60.

Burton, D.W. 'Requests for Prayers and Royal Propaganda under Edward I', in P.R. Coss and S.D. Lloyd, eds. *Thirteenth Century England III* (Woodbridge, 1991), 25–35.

Butler, R.F. 'Last of the Brimpsfield Giffards and the Rising of 1321–2', *Transactions of the Bristol and Gloucestershire Archaeological Society* 76 (1958 for 1957), 75–97.

Bynum, C.W. *The Resurrection of the Body in Western Christianity 200–1336* (New York, 1995).

Campbell, M. 'Gold, Silver and Precious Stones', in J. Blair and N. Ramsey, eds. *English Medieval Industries: Craftsmen, Techniques, Products* (London, 1991), 107–66.

Carpenter, C. 'Political and Constitutional History: Before and After McFarlane', in R.H. Britnell and A.J. Pollard, eds. *The McFarlane Legacy: Studies in Late Medieval Politics and Society* (Stroud, 1995), 175–206.

Carpenter, D. 'The Fall of Hubert de Burgh', *JBS* 19 (1980), 1–17.

Carpenter, D. 'From King John to the First English Duke: 1215–1337', in R. Smith and J.S. Moore, eds. *The House of Lords: A Thousand Years of British Tradition* (London, 1994), 28–43.

Carpenter, D. *The Minority of Henry III* (London, 1990).

Carpenter, D. *The Reign of Henry III* (London, 1996).

Carr, A.D. ' "The Last and Weakest of His Line": Dafydd ap Gruffydd, the Last Prince of Wales', *Welsh History Review* 19 (1999), 375–99.

Cazel, F.A. 'Intertwined Careers: Hubert de Burgh and Peter des Roches', *HSJ* 1 (1989), 173–81.

Chandler, V. 'The Last of the Montgomerys: Roger the Poitevin and Arnulf', *HR* 62 (1989), 1–14.

Chaney, W.A. *The Cult of Kingship in Anglo-Saxon England* (Manchester, 1970).

Chaplais, P. *Piers Gaveston: Edward II's Adoptive Brother* (Oxford, 1994).

Cherry, M. 'The Courtenay Earls of Devon: The Formation and Disintegration of a Late Medieval Aristocratic Affinity', *Southern History* 1 (1979), 71–97.

Childs, W. 'Resistance and Treason in the *Vita Edwardi Secundi*', in M. Prestwich, R.H. Britnell and R. Frame, eds. *Thirteenth Century England VI* (Woodbridge, 1997), 177–91.

Church, S.D. *The Household Knights of King John* (Cambridge, 1999).

Clanchy, M.T. *From Memory to Written Record* 2nd edn (Oxford, 1993).

Clarke, M.V. 'Forfeitures and Treason in 1388', in M.V. Clarke, *Fourteenth Century Studies* L.S. Sutherland et al., eds. (Oxford, 1968).

Cohen, E. 'The Expression of Pain in the Later Middle Ages: Deliverance, Acceptance and Infamy', in F. Egmond and R. Zwijnenberg, eds. *Bodily Extremities: Preoccupations with the Human Body in Early Modern European Culture* (Aldershot, 2003), 195–220.

Cohen, E. 'Symbols of Culpability and the Universal Language of Justice: The Ritual of Public Executions in Late Medieval Europe', *History of European Ideas* 11 (1989), 407–16.

Coote, L.A. *Prophecy and Public Affairs in Later Medieval England* (Woodbridge, 2000).

Cosgrove, A. 'Anglo-Ireland and the Yorkist Cause', in A. Cosgrove, ed. *A New History of Ireland*, Volume II: *Medieval Ireland 1169–1534* (Oxford, 1987), 557–68.

Crawford, A. 'Victims of Attainder: The Howard and de Vere Women in the Late Fifteenth Century', *Reading Medieval Studies* 16 (1990), 59–74.

Crook, D.A. 'Central England and the Revolt of the Earls, January 1400', *HR* 64 (1991), 403–10.

Crouch, D. *The Image of Aristocracy 1000–1300* (London, 1992).

Cuttler, S.H. *The Law of Treason and Treason Trials in Later Medieval France* (Cambridge, 2003).

Daniell, C. *Death and Burial in Medieval England 1066–1550* (London, 1997).

David, C.W. *Robert Curthose, Duke of Normandy* (Cambridge, Mass., 1920).

Davies, J.C. 'The Despenser War in Glamorgan', *TRHS* 3rd Ser. 9 (1915), 21–64.

Davies, R.R. *The Age of Conquest: Wales 1063–1415* (Oxford, 1987).

Davis, R.H.C. *King Stephen* 3rd edn (London, 1990).

D'Avray, D.L. 'Magna Carta: Its Background in Stephen Langton's Academic Biblical Exegesis and its Episcopal Reception', *Studi Medievali* 38 (1997), 423–38.

De Aragon, R. 'The Growth of Secure Inheritance in Anglo-Norman England', *JMH* 8 (1982), 381–91.

De Ville, O. 'John de Ville: A Neglected Rebel', *NH* 35 (1998), 17–40.

Dillon, H.A.L. and W.H. St John Hope, eds. 'Inventory of Goods Belonging to Thomas, Duke of Gloucester, and Seized in his Castle at Pleshy, Co. Essex, 21 Richard II (1397)', *Archaeological Journal* 54 (1897), 275–308.

Douglas, D.C. *William the Conqueror* (London, 1964).

Douie, D.L. *Archbishop John Pecham* (Oxford, 1952).

Du Boulay, F.R. *An Age of Ambition: English Society in the Late Middle Ages* (London, 1970).

Dunbabin, J. *Captivity and Imprisonment in Medieval Europe 1000–1300* (London, 2002).

Dunbabin, J. 'Government', in J.H. Burns, ed. *The Cambridge History of Medieval Political Thought c. 350–c. 1450* (Cambridge, 1997), 477–517.

Dunham, W.H. and C.T. Wood, 'The Right to Rule in England: Depositions and the Kingdom's Authority, 1327–1488', *AHR* 81 (1976), 738–61.

Dunn, A. 'Exploitation and Control: The Royal Administration of Magnate Estates, 1397–1405', in M. Hicks, ed. *Revolution and Consumption in Late Medieval England* (Woodbridge, 2001), 27–44.

Dunn, A. 'Henry IV and the Politics of Resistance in Early Lancastrian England, 1399–1413', in L. Clark, ed. *The Fifteenth Century III: Authority and Subversion* (Woodbridge, 2003), 5–23.

Dunn, A. *The Politics of Magnate Power in England and Wales 1389–1413* (Oxford, 2003).

Dunn, A. 'Richard II and the Mortimer Inheritance', in C. Given-Wilson, ed. *Fourteenth Century England II* (Woodbridge, 2002), 159–70.

Edwards, J. 'The Cult of "St" Thomas of Lancaster and its Iconography', *YAJ* 64 (1992), 103–22.

Edwards, J. 'The Cult of "St" Thomas of Lancaster and its Iconography: A Supplementary Note', *YAJ* 67 (1995), 187–91.

Edwards, J.G. 'The Treason of Thomas Turberville', in R.W. Hunt, W.A. Paintin and R.W. Southern, eds. *Studies in Medieval History* (Oxford, 1948), 296–309.

Egmond, F. 'Execution, Dissection, Pain and Infamy – A Morphological Investigation', in F. Egmond and R. Zwijnenberg, eds. *Bodily Extremities: Preoccupations with the Human Body in Early Modern European Culture* (Aldershot, 2003), 92–128.

Ellis, G. *Earldoms in Fee: A Study in Peerage Law and History* (London, 1963).

Epstein, R. 'Prisoners of Reflection: The Fifteenth-Century Poetry of Exile and Imprisonment', *Exemplaria* 15 (2003), 159–98.

Evans, M.R. 'The Ferrers Earls of Derby and the Crusades', *NMS* 44 (2000), 69–81.

Finucane, R.C. 'Sacred Corpse, Profane Carrion: Social Ideals and Death Rituals in the Later Middle Ages', in J. Whaley, ed. *Mirrors of Mortality: Studies in the Social History of Death* (London, 1981), 40–60.

Fleming, R. *Kings and Lords in Conquest England* (Cambridge, 1991).

Forbes, A.H. '*Laesa Majestas* and the Security Legislation of Edward III: The Statutes of Treasons, Provisors and Praemunire', *Studies in Medieval Culture* 4 (1974), 359–67.

Fowler, R.C. 'Secular Aid for Excommunication', *TRHS* 3rd Ser. 8 (1914), 113–17.

Friar, S. *A Companion to the English Parish Church* (Stroud, 1996).

Fryde, E.B. 'The Deposits of Hugh Despenser the Younger with Italian Bankers', *EcHR* 2nd Ser. 3 (1951), 344–62.

Fryde, N. *The Tyranny and Fall of Edward II 1321–1326* (Cambridge, 1979).

Gee, L.L. *Women, Art and Patronage from Henry III to Edward III 1216–1377* (Woodbridge, 2002).

Gillingham, J. '1066 and the Introduction of Chivalry into England', in G. Garnett and J. Hudson, eds. *Law and Government in Medieval England and Normandy* (Cambridge, 1994), 31–55.

Gillingham, J. 'Killing and Mutilating Political Enemies in the British Isles from the Late Twelfth to the Early Fourteenth Century: A Comparative Study', in

B. Smith, ed. *Britain and Ireland 900–1300: Insular Responses to Medieval European Change* (Cambridge, 1999), 114–34.

Given-Wilson, C. 'Adam of Usk, the Monk of Evesham and the Parliament of 1397–8', *HR* 66 (1993), 329–35.

Given-Wilson, C. *Chronicles: The Writing of History in Medieval England* (London and New York, 2003).

Given-Wilson, C. *The English Nobility in the Late Middle Ages: The Fourteenth Century Political Community* (London, 1987).

Given-Wilson, C. 'Royal Charter Witness Lists, 1327–99', *MP* 12 (1991), 35–93.

Given-Wilson, C. *The Royal Household and the King's Affinity: Service, Politics and Finance in England 1360–1413* (New Haven and London, 1986).

Given-Wilson, C. 'Wealth and Credit, Public and Private: The Earls of Arundel 1306–97', *EHR* 106 (1991), 1–26.

Goebel, J. *Felony and Misdemeanour: A Study in the History of Criminal Law* (Philadelphia, 1976).

Golding, B. 'Simon of Kyme: The Making of a 1214 Rebel', *NMS* 27 (1983), 23–36.

Goulding, B. 'The Religious Patronage of Robert and William of Mortain', in R. Gameson and H. Leyser, eds. *Belief and Culture in the Early Middle Ages* (Oxford, 2001), 211–30.

Goodman, A. *John of Gaunt: The Exercise of Princely Power in Fourteenth-Century Europe* (Harlow, 1992).

Goodman, A. *The Loyal Conspiracy: The Lords Appellant Under Richard II* (London, 1971).

Gransden, A. *Historical Writing in England* 2 vols. (New York and London, 1974–82).

Green, J.A. *The Aristocracy of Norman England* (Cambridge, 1997).

Green, J.A. *The Government of England under Henry I* (Cambridge, 1986).

Griffiths, R.A. *The Reign of King Henry VI* (Stroud, 1998).

Grupp, S. 'Some Historical Aspects of the Pardon in England', *American Journal of Legal History* 7 (1963), 51–62.

Gundy, A. 'The Earl of Warwick and the Royal Affinity in the Politics of the West Midlands, 1389–1399', in M. Hicks, ed. *Revolution and Consumption in Late Medieval England* (Woodbridge, 2001), 57–70.

Gunn, S.J. 'The Act of Resumption of 1515', in D. Williams, ed. *Early Tudor England* (Woodbridge, 1989), 87–106.

Haines, R.M. 'An Innocent Abroad: The Career of Simon Mepham, Archbishop of Canterbury', *EHR* 112 (1997), 555–96.

Hamilton, J.S. 'Charter Witness Lists for the Reign of Edward II', in N. Saul, ed. *Fourteenth Century England I* (Woodbridge, 2000), 1–20.

Hamilton, J.S. *Piers Gaveston, Earl of Cornwall 1307–1312* (Detroit, 1988).

Harding, A. *The Law Courts of Medieval England* (London, 1973).

Harding, A. *A Social History of English Law* (Harmondsworth, 1966).

Hares-Stryker, C. 'Adrift on the Seven Seas: The Medieval Topos of Exile at Sea', *Florilegium* 12 (1993), 79–98.

Harris, E.K. 'Censoring Disobedient Subjects: Narratives of Treason and Royal Authority in Fifteenth-Century England', in D. Biggs, S.D. Michalove and C. Reeves, eds. *Reputation and Representation in Fifteenth-Century Europe* (Leiden, 2004), 211–33.

Harriss, G.L. 'The Formation of Parliament, 1272–1377', in R.G. Davies and J.H. Denton, eds. *The English Parliament in the Middle Ages* (Manchester, 1981, 1999), 29–60.

Harriss, G.L. *King, Parliament and Public Finance in Medieval England to 1369* (Oxford, 1975).

Harriss, G.L. *Shaping the Realm: England 1360–1461* (Oxford, 2005).

Haskins, G.L. 'The Doncaster Petition, 1321', *EHR* 53 (1938), 478–85.

Hayward, J. 'Hereward the Outlaw', *JMH* 14 (1988), 293–304.

Heath, P. *Church and Realm 1272–1461* (London, 1988).

Heiser, R. 'The Royal *Familiares* of King Richard I', *MP* 10 (1989), 25–50.

Hicks, M. 'Attainder, Resumption and Coercion, 1461–1529', *Parliamentary History* 3 (1984), 15–31.

Hicks, M. 'Chantries, Obits and Almshouses: The Hungerford Foundations, 1325–1478', in C.M. Barron and C. Harper-Bill, eds. *The Church in Pre-Reformation Society* (Woodbridge, 1985), 123–42.

Hicks, M. 'An Escheat Concealed: The Despenser Forfeitures 1400–1461', *Proceedings of the Hampshire Field Club Archaeological Society* 53 (1998), 183–9.

Hill, R.T. 'The Theory and Practice of Excommunication in Medieval England', *History* 42 (1957), 1–11.

Holden, B.W. 'The Balance of Patronage: King John and the Earl of Salisbury', *HSJ* 8 (1996), 79–89.

Hole, C. *English Shrines and Sanctuaries* (London, 1954).

Hollister, C.W. 'The Campaign of 1102 against Robert of Bellême', in C. Harper-Bill, C.J. Holdsworth and J.L. Nelson, eds. *Studies in Medieval History Presented to R. Allen Brown* (Woodbridge, 1989), 193–202.

Hollister, C.W. *Henry I* (New Haven and London, 2001).

Hollister, C.W. 'Henry I and the Anglo-Norman Magnates', in R.A. Brown, ed. *Battle Conference II* (Woodbridge, 1980), 93–107.

Hollister, C.W. 'Henry I and Robert Malet', *Viator* 4 (1973), 115–22.

Hollister, C.W. 'Royal Acts of Mutilation: The Case Against Henry I', *Albion* 10 (1978), 330–40.

Holmes, G.A. *The Estates of the Higher Nobility in Fourteenth-Century England* (Cambridge, 1957).

Holmes, G.A. *The Good Parliament* (Oxford, 1975).

Holmes, G.A. 'Judgement on the Younger Despenser, 1326', *EHR* 70 (1955), 261–7.

Holmes, G.A. 'A Protest Against the Despensers', *Speculum* 30 (1955), 207–12.

Holmes, G.A. 'The Rebellion of the Earl of Lancaster', *BIHR* 28 (1955), 84–9.

Holt, J.C. *The Northerners: A Study in the Reign of King John* (Oxford, 1961).

Horrox, R. 'Caterpillars of the Commonwealth? Courtiers in Late Medieval England', in R.E. Archer and S. Walker, eds. *Rulers and Ruled in Late Medieval England* (London, 1995), 1–15.

Hudson, J. *The Formation of the English Common Law* (Harlow, 1996).

Hudson, J. *Land, Law, and Lordship in Anglo-Norman England* (Oxford, 1997).

Jacob, E.F. *The Fifteenth Century* (Oxford, 1993).

Johns, S.M. *Noblewomen, Aristocracy and Power in the Twelfth-Century Anglo-Norman Realm* (Manchester, 2003).

Johnson, S.F.H. 'The Lands of Hubert de Burgh', *EHR* 50 (1935), 418–32.

Jones, W.R. 'Sanctuary, Exile and Law: The Fugitive and Public Authority in Medieval England and Modern America', in W.R. Jones et al., *Essays on English Law and the American Experience* (Arlington, 1994), 19–41.

Kaeuper, R. *War, Justice and Public Order: England and France in the Later Middle Ages* (Oxford, 1988).

Keefe, T.K. *Feudal Assessments and the Political Community under Henry II and His Sons* (Berkeley, 1983).

Keen, M.H. *The Outlaws of Medieval Legend* (London, 1987).

Keen, M.H. 'Treason Trials Under the Law of Arms', *TRHS* 5th Ser. 12 (1962), 85–103.

Kelemen, E. '*Clyppan* and *Cyssan*: The Formulaic Expression of Return from Exile in Old English Literature', *English Language Notes* 38 (2001), 1–19.

Kennett, D.H. 'Falke de Bréauté: Henchman of King John', *Bedfordshire Magazine* 14 (1974), 278–82.

Keynes, S.D. 'Crime and Punishment in the Reign of King Æthelred the Unready', in I.N. Wood and N. Lund, eds. *People and Places in Northern Europe 500–1600* (Woodbridge, 1991), 67–81.

King, A. ' "They have the Hertes of the People by North": Northumberland, the Percies and Henry IV, 1399–1408', in G. Dodd and D. Biggs, eds. *Henry IV: The Establishment of the Regime, 1399–1406* (Woodbridge, 2003), 139–60.

Kingsford, C.L. 'Two Forfeitures in the Year of Agincourt', *Archaeologia* 20 (1920), 71–100.

Knight, J.K. 'Usk Castle and its Affinities', in M.R. Apted, R. Gilyard-Beer and A.D. Saunders, eds. *Ancient Monuments and their Interpretation* (London, 1977), 139–54.

Knowles, C.H. 'Provision for the Families of the Montfortians Disinherited after the Battle of Evesham', in P.R. Coss and S.D. Lloyd, eds. *Thirteenth Century England I* (Woodbridge, 1986), 124–7.

Knowles, C.H. 'The Resettlement of England after the Barons' War, 1264–7', *TRHS* 5th Ser. 32 (1982), 25–41.

Lacey, H. ' "Mercy and Truth Preserve the King": Richard II's Use of the Royal Pardon in 1397 and 1398', in J.S. Hamilton, ed. *Fourteenth Century England IV* (Woodbridge, 2006), 123–35.

Lachaud, F. 'Liveries of Robes in England, c. 1200–1330', *EHR* 111 (1996), 279–98.

Lally, J.E. 'Secular Patronage at the Court of Henry II', *BIHR* 49 (1976), 159–84.

Lander, J.R. 'Attainder and Forfeiture, 1453 to 1509', *HJ* 4 (1961), 119–51.

Lander, J.R. *Crown and Nobility 1450–1509* (Montreal, 1976).

Langbein, J.H. *Torture and the Law of Proof* (Chicago, 1977).

Langston, J.N. 'The Giffards of Brimpsfield', *Transactions of the Bristol and Gloucestershire Archaeological Society* 65 (1946–7), 105–28.

Lawrence, M. ' "Too Flattering Sweet to be Substantial"? The Last Months of Thomas, Lord Despenser', in J.S. Hamilton, ed. *Fourteenth Century England IV* (Woodbridge, 2006), 146–58.

Lawson, M.K. *Cnut: The Danes in England in the Early Eleventh Century* (Harlow, 1993).

Leedom, J.W. 'Lady Matilda Holland, Henry of Lancaster and the Manor of Melbourne', *American Journal of Legal History* 118 (1987), 118–25.

Leland, J.L. 'The Abjuration of 1388', *MP* 15 (1994), 115–38.

Leland, J.L. 'Unpardonable Sinners? Exclusions from the General Pardon of 1388', *MP* 17 (1996), 181–95.

Lindley, P.G. 'The Black Death and English Art: A Debate and Some Assumptions', in W.M. Ormrod and P.G. Lindley, eds. *The Black Death in England* (Stamford, 1996), 125–46.

Lloyd, S. 'Gilbert de Clare, Richard of Cornwall and the Lord Edward's Crusade', *NMS* 30 (1986), 46–66.

Logan, F.D. *Excommunication and the Secular Arm in Medieval England* (Toronto, 1968).

Lovell, C.R. 'The Trial of Peers in Great Britain', *AHR* 55 (1949–50), 69–81.

Loyn, H.R. *The Governance of Anglo-Saxon England 500–1087* (London, 1984).

McFarlane, K.B. *The Nobility of Later Medieval England* (Oxford, 1973).

MacGregor, P. *Odiham Castle 1200–1500: Castle and Community* (Stroud, 1983).

McHardy, A.K. 'Some Reflections on Edward III's Use of Propaganda', in J.S. Bothwell, ed. *The Age of Edward III* (Woodbridge, 2001), 171–89.

Maddicott, J.R. 'Follower, Leader, Pilgrim, Saint: Robert de Vere, Earl of Oxford, at the Shrine of Simon de Montfort, 1273', *EHR* 109 (1994), 641–53.

Maddicott, J.R. *Simon de Montfort* (Cambridge, 1997).

Maddicott, J.R. *Thomas of Lancaster* (Oxford, 1970).

Maitland, F.W. 'The Praerogativa Regis', *EHR* 6 (1891), 67–72.

Makinson, A. 'Thomas of Lancaster: The Turbulent Earl', *History Today* 10 (1960), 702–12.

Manning, R.B. 'The Origins of the Doctrine of Sedition', *Albion* 12 (1980), 99–121.

Mason, E. 'Magnates, Curiales and the Wheel of Fortune', *Battle Conference II* (Woodbridge, 1980), 118–40.

Mertes, K. *The English Noble Household 1250–1600: Good Governance and Political Rule* (Oxford, 1988).

Milsom, S.F.C. *Historical Foundations of the Common Law* 2nd edn (London, 1981).

Morgan, P. 'Henry IV and the Shadow of Richard II', in R.E. Archer, ed. *Crown, Government and People in the Fifteenth Century* (Stroud, 1995), 1–31.

Morris, R. 'Tewkesbury Abbey: The Despenser Mausoleum', *Transactions of the Bristol and Gloucestershire Archaeological Society* 93 (1975 for 1974), 142–55.

Mortimer, N. *John Lydgate's Fall of Princes: Narrative Tragedy in its Literary and Political Contexts* (Oxford, 2005).

Mott, R.A.K. 'Richard II and the Crisis of July, 1397', in I. Wood and G.A. Loud, eds. *Church and Chronicle in the Middle Ages* (London, 1991), 165–77.

Murdoch, B. *Adam's Grace: Fall and Redemption in Medieval Literature* (Woodbridge, 2000).

Murray, A. *Reason and Society in the Middle Ages* (Oxford, 1978).

Musson, A. *Medieval Law in Context: The Growth of Legal Consciousness from Magna Carta to the Peasants' Revolt* (Manchester, 2001).

Musson, A. and W.M. Ormrod, *The Evolution of English Justice: Law, Politics and Society in the Fourteenth Century* (Basingstoke, 1999).

Neville, C.J. 'The Law of Treason in the English Border Counties in the Later Middle Ages', *Law and History Review* 9 (1991), 1–30.

Newton, K.C. *Thaxted in the Fourteenth Century* (Chelmsford, 1960).

Nolan, M. *John Lydgate and the Making of Public Culture* (Cambridge, 2005).

Orme, N. *From Childhood to Chivalry: The Education of the English Kings and Aristocracy 1066–1536* (London, 1984).

Orme, N. *English Schools in the Middle Ages* (London, 1973).

Ormrod, W.M. 'Edward III and his Family', *JBS* 26 (1987), 398–442.

Ormrod, W.M. *Political Life in Medieval England 1300–1450* (Basingstoke, 1995).

Ormrod, W.M. *The Reign of Edward III: Crown and Political Society in England 1327–1377* (New Haven and London, 1990).

Owst, G.R. *Literature and Pulpit in Medieval England* (Oxford, 1933).

Park, K. 'The Life of the Corpse: Division and Dissection in Late Medieval Europe', *Journal of the History of Medicine and the Allied Sciences* 50 (1995), 111–32.

Patch, H.R. *The Goddess Fortuna in Medieval Literature* (Cambridge, Mass., 1927).

Perkins, N. 'Musing on Mutability: A Poem in the Welles Anthology and Hoccleve's *The Regement of Princes*', *Review of English Studies* 50 (1999), 493–8.

Peters, E. *Torture* (Oxford, 1985).

Phillips, J.R.S. 'Simon de Montfort (1265), the Earl of Manchester (1644), and Other Stories: Violence and Politics in Thirteenth and Early Fourteenth Century England', in R.W. Kaeuper, ed. *Violence in Medieval Society* (Woodbridge, 2000), 79–90.

Pimlott, J.A.R. *The Englishman's Christmas: A Social History* (Hassocks, Sussex, 1978).

Piponnier, F. and P. Mane, *Dress in the Middle Ages* (New Haven and London, 1997).

Platt, C. *King Death* (London, 1996).

Plucknett, T.F.T. *A Concise History of the Common Law* 5th edn (Boston, 1956).

Plucknett, T.F.T. *Studies in English Legal History* (London, 1983).

Pollock, F. and F.W. Maitland, *The History of English Law before the Time of Edward I* 2nd edn. 2 vols. (Cambridge, 1968).

Potter, H. *Potter's Historical Introduction to English Law and its Institutions* 4th edn (London, 1958).

Powell, E. 'After "After McFarlane": The Poverty of Patronage and the Case for Constitutional History', in D.J. Clayton, R.G. Davies and P. McNiven, eds. *Trade, Devotion and Governance* (Stroud, 1994), 1–16.

Powell, E. *Kingship, Law and Society: Criminal Justice in the Reign of Henry V* (Oxford, 1989).

Powell, J.E. and K. Wallis, *The House of Lords in the Middle Ages* (London, 1968).

Powicke, F.M. 'Guy de Montfort (1265–71)', *TRHS* 4th Ser. 18 (1935), 1–23.

Powicke, F.M. *King Henry III and the Lord Edward: The Community of the Realm in the Thirteenth Century* (Oxford, 1947).

Powicke, F.M. *The Loss of Normandy 1189–1204* (Manchester, 1960).

Pratt, D. 'The Marcher Lordship of Chirk, 1329–1330', *Transactions of the Denbighshire Historical Society* 39 (1990), 5–41.

Prestwich, M. 'The Charges Against the Despensers, 1321', *BIHR* 58 (1985), 95–100.

Prestwich, M. *Edward I* (New Haven and London, 1997).

Prestwich, M. 'The Ordinances of 1311 and the Politics of the Early Fourteenth Century', in J. Taylor and W.R. Childs, eds. *Politics and Crisis in Fourteenth-Century England* (Gloucester, 1990), 1–18.

Prestwich, M. *Plantagenet England 1225–1360* (Oxford, 2005).

Pugh, R.B. 'Early Register of English Outlaws', *American Journal of Legal History* 27 (1983), 319–29.

Pugh, R.B. *Imprisonment in Medieval England* (Cambridge, 1968).

Pugh, R.B. 'The King's Prisons before 1250', *TRHS* 5th Ser. 5 (1955), 1–22.

Pugh, T.B. *Henry V and the Southampton Plot of 1415* (Southampton, 1988).

Pugh, T.B. 'Henry VII and the English Nobility', in G.W. Bernard, ed. *The Tudor Nobility* (Manchester, 1992), 49–110.

Radding, C. 'Fortune and her Wheel: The Meaning of a Medieval Symbol', *Mediaevistik* 5 (1992), 127–38.

Reynolds, A. *Later Anglo-Saxon England: Life and Landscape* (Stroud, 1999).

Rezneck, S. 'Constructive Treason by Words in the Fifteenth Century', *AHR* 33 (1928), 544–52.

Richardson, H.G. 'John Oldcastle in Hiding, August–October, 1417', *EHR* 55 (1940), 432–8.

Ridgeway, H.W. 'William de Valence and His *Familiares*, 1247–1272', *HR* 65 (1992), 239–57.

Roberts, R.A. 'Edward II, the Lords Ordainers, and Piers Gaveston's Jewels and Horses, 1312–1313', *Camden Miscellany* 15 (3rd Ser. 41) (1929).

Rogers, A. 'Parliamentary Appeals of Treason in the Reign of Richard II', *American Journal of Legal History* 8 (1964), 95–124.

Rosenthal, J.T. *Patriarchy and Families of Privilege in Fifteenth-Century England* (Philadelphia, 1991).

Roskell, J.S. *The Impeachment of Michael de la Pole, Earl of Suffolk* (Manchester, 1984).

Ross, C. *Edward IV* (New Haven and London, 1997).

Ross, C. 'Forfeiture for Treason in the Reign of Richard II', *EHR* 71 (1956), 560–75.

Ross, J. 'Seditious Activities: The Conspiracy of Maud de Vere, Countess of Oxford, 1403–4', in L. Clark, ed. *The Fifteenth Century III: Authority and Subversion* (Woodbridge, 2003), 25–42.

Royer, K. 'The Body in Parts: Reading the Execution Ritual in Late Medieval England', *Historical Reflections* 29 (2003), 319–39.

Ruddock, J.G. *Boothby Graffoe and Somerton Castle* (Lincoln, 1980).

Russell, J.C. *Twelfth Century Studies* (New York, 1978).

Salzman, L.F. 'The Property of the Earl of Arundel, 1397', *Sussex Archaeological Collections* 91 (1953), 32–52.

Saul, N. 'The Despensers and the Downfall of Edward II', *EHR* 99 (1984), 1–33.

Saul, N. *Richard II* (New Haven and London, 1997).

Scattergood, J. *Politics and Poetry in the Fifteenth Century* (London, 1971).

Scattergood, J. '*Sir Gawain and the Green Knight* and the Sins of the Flesh', *Traditio* 37 (1981), 347–71.

Scattergood, J. 'Social and Political Issues in Chaucer: An Approach to *Lak of Stedfastnesse*', in J. Scattergood, *Reading the Past: Essays on Medieval and Renaissance Literature* (Dublin, 1996), 192–8.

Scattergood, J. '*The Tale of Gamelyn*: The Noble Robber as Provincial Hero', in J. Scattergood, *Reading the Past: Essays on Medieval and Renaissance Literature* (Dublin, 1996), 81–113.

Scott, F.S. 'Earl Waltheof of Northumbria', *Archaeologia Aeliana* 4th Ser. 30 (1952), 149–215.

Scott, F.S. 'Valdjofr Jarl: An English Earl in the Icelandic Sources', *Saga Book of the Viking Society of Northern Research* 14 (1955 for 1953), 78–94.

Seal, G. *The Outlaw Legend: A Cultural Tradition in Britain, America and Australia* (Cambridge, 1996).

Senderowitz Loengard, J. '"Plate, Good Stuff, and Household Things": Husbands, Wives and Chattels in England at the End of the Middle Ages', *The Ricardian* 13 (2003), 328–40.

Shenton, C. 'Edward III and the Coup of 1330', in J.S. Bothwell, ed. *The Age of Edward III* (Woodbridge, 2001), 13–35.

Simcoe, E. *Short History of the Parish and Ancient Borough of Thaxted* (Saffron Walden, 1934).

Smith, W.J. 'The Rise of the Berkeleys: An Account of the Berkeleys of Berkeley Castle 1243–1361', *Transactions of the Bristol and Gloucestershire Archaeological Society* 70 (1952 for 1951), 64–80.

Somerville, R. *History of the Duchy of Lancaster*, Volume I: 1265–1603 (London, 1953).

Southern, R.W. 'The Place of Henry I in English History', *Proceedings of the British Academy* 48 (1962), 127–69.

Squibb, G.D. *The High Court of Chivalry: A Study of the Civil Law in England* (Oxford, 1997).

Stafford, P. *Unification and Conquest: A Political and Social History of England in the Tenth and Eleventh Centuries* (London, 1989).

Staley, L. *Languages of Power in the Age of Richard II* (Philadelphia, 2005).

Stones, E.L.G. 'The Date of Roger Mortimer's Escape from the Tower of London', *EHR* 66 (1951), 97–8.

Strickland, M. *War and Chivalry: The Conduct and Perception of War in England and Normandy 1066–1217* (Cambridge, 1996).

Summerson, H.R.T. 'Attitudes to Capital Punishment in England, 1200–1350', in M. Prestwich, R. Britnell and R. Frame, eds. *Thirteenth Century England VIII* (Woodbridge, 2001), 123–33.

Summerson, H.R.T. *Medieval Carlisle: The City and the Borders from the Late Eleventh to the Mid Sixteenth Century* Volume I (Kendal, 1993).

Swanson, R.N. *Church and Society in Late Medieval England* (Oxford, 1989).

Swanson, R.N. *The Twelfth Century Renaissance* (Manchester, 1999).

Taylor, J. 'The Judgment on Hugh Despenser, the Younger', *Medievalia et Humanistica* 12 (1958), 70–7.

Taylor, R. *The Political Prophecy in England* (New York, 1911).

Thacker, A.T. 'Introduction: The Earls and Their Earldom', *Journal of the Chester Archaeological Society* 71 (1991), 7–21.

Theilmann, J.M. 'Political Canonisation and Political Symbolism in Medieval England', *JBS* 29 (1990), 241–66.

Tout, T.F. *Chapters in the Administrative History of Mediaeval England: the Wardrobe, the Chamber and the Small Seals* 6 vols. (Manchester, 1928).

Tuck, A. *Crown and Nobility 1272–1461* (London, 1985).

Turner, R.V. *King John* (London, 1994).

Turner, R.V. *Men Raised from the Dust: Administrative Service and Upward Mobility in Angevin England* (Philadelphia, 1988).

Tyerman, C. *England and the Crusades 1095–1588* (Chicago, 1996).

Ullmann, W. *A History of Political Thought: The Middle Ages* (Harmondsworth, 1965).

Underhill, F.A. *For Her Good Estate: The Life of Elizabeth de Burgh* (Basingstoke, 1999).

Vale, M. *The Princely Court: Medieval Courts and Culture in Northwest Europe* (Oxford, 2003).

Valente, C. 'The Deposition and Abdication of Edward II', *EHR* 113 (1998), 852–81.

Valente, C. 'Simon de Montfort, Earl of Leicester, and the Utility of Sanctity in Thirteenth-Century England', *JMH* 21 (1995), 27–49.

Valente, C. *The Theory and Practice of Revolt in Medieval England* (Aldershot, 2003).

Van Eickels, L. 'Gendered Violence: Castration and Blinding as Punishment for Treason in Normandy and Anglo-Norman England', *Gender and History* 16 (2004), 588–602.

Van Houts, E. 'Hereward and Flanders', *Anglo-Saxon England* 28 (1999), 201–23.

Vernon Harcourt, L.W. *His Grace the Steward and Trial of Peers* (London, 1907).

Vincent, N. *Peter Des Roches: An Alien in English Politics 1205–1238* (Cambridge, 1996).

Virgoe, R. 'The Death of William de la Pole, Duke of Suffolk', *BJRL* 47 (1965), 489–502.

Vodola, E. *Excommunication in the Middle Ages* (Berkeley, 1986).

Walker, S. 'Political Saints in Later Medieval England', in R.H. Britnell and A.J. Pollard, eds. *The McFarlane Legacy: Studies in Late Medieval Politics and Society* (Stroud, 1995), 77–106.

Walker, S. 'Richard II's Views on Kingship', in R.E. Archer and S. Walker, eds. *Rulers and Ruled in Late Medieval England* (London, 1995), 49–64.

Ward, J. 'Elizabeth de Burgh, Lady of Clare (d. 1360)', in C.M. Barron and A.F. Sutton, eds. *Medieval London Widows, 1300–1500* (London, 1994), 29–46.

Ward, J. *English Noblewomen in the Later Middle Ages* (London, 1992).

Wareham, A. 'The Motives and Politics of the Bigod Family, c. 1066–1177', *ANS* 17 (1994), 223–42.

Warner, M. 'Chivalry in Action: Thomas Montagu and the War in France, 1417–1428', *NMS* 42 (1998), 146–73.

Warren, W.L. *Henry II* (London, 1973).

Warren, W.L. *King John* (London, 1961).

Watkins, C. 'The Cult of Earl Waltheof at Crowland', *Hagiographica* 3 (1996), 95–111.

Watts, J.L. 'The Pressure of the Public on Later Medieval Politics', in L. Clark and C. Carpenter, eds. *Political Culture in Late Medieval Britain* (Woodbridge, 2004), 159–80.

Waugh, S.L. *The Lordship of England: Royal Wardships and Marriages in English Society and Politics* (Princeton, 1988).

Waugh, S.L. 'The Profits of Violence: The Minor Gentry in the Rebellion of 1321–1322 in Gloucestershire and Herefordshire', *Speculum* 52 (1977), 843–69.

Weinberg, C. 'Victor and Victim: A View of the Anglo-Saxon Past in Layamon's *Brut*', in D. Scragg and C. Weinberg, eds. *Literary Appropriations of the Anglo-Saxons from the Thirteenth to the Twentieth Century* (Cambridge, 2000), 22–38.

Wilkinson, B. 'The Sherburn Indenture and the Attack on the Despensers, 1321', EHR 63 (1948), 1–28.

Williams, A. *The English and the Norman Conquest* (Woodbridge, 1997).

Wolffe, B.P. 'Acts of Resumption in the Lancastrian Parliaments, 1399–1456', EHR 73 (1958), 583–613.

Wolffe, B.P. *The Royal Demesne in English History: The Crown Estate in the Governance of the Realm from the Conquest to 1509* (Athens, OH, 1971).

Woolgar, C.M. *The Great Household in Late Medieval England* (New Haven and London, 1999).

Wormald, P. *The Making of English Law: King Alfred to the Twelfth Century* Vol. I (Oxford, 1999).

Reference works

Cokayne, G.E. et al. *The Complete Peerage* 12 vols. (London, 1910–59).

Oxford Dictionary of National Biography (online) (Oxford, 2004).

Pevsner, N. *The Buildings of England: Cumberland and Westmorland* (Harmondsworth, 1973).

Tyerman, C. *Who's Who in Early Medieval England* (London, 1996).

Victoria County Histories (for Gloucestershire, Hampshire, Wiltshire and Worcestershire) (London and Oxford, 1901–present).

Dissertations

Bothwell, J.S. 'Royal Endowment of Peerage Creations in the Reign of Edward III', University of St Andrews PhD (1996).

Meredith, K.F. 'The Penalty of Banishment in Medieval France and England', University of Virginia PhD (1979).

Waugh, S.L. 'The Confiscated Lands of the "Contrariants" in Gloucestershire and Herefordshire in 1322: An Economic and Social Study', University of London PhD (1975).

Index